The President and American Capitalism since 1945

The Alan B. Larkin Series on the American Presidency

UNIVERSITY PRESS OF FLORIDA

Florida A&M University, Tallahassee
Florida Atlantic University, Boca Raton
Florida Gulf Coast University, Ft. Myers
Florida International University, Miami
Florida State University, Tallahassee
New College of Florida, Sarasota
University of Central Florida, Orlando
University of Florida, Gainesville
University of North Florida, Jacksonville
University of South Florida, Tampa
University of West Florida, Pensacola

THE PRESIDENT AND AMERICAN CAPITALISM SINCE 1945

EDITED BY

Mark H. Rose and Roger Biles

University Press of Florida

Gainesville · Tallahassee · Tampa · Boca Raton

Pensacola · Orlando · Miami · Jacksonville · Ft. Myers · Sarasota

Printed in the United States of America on acid-free paper

This book may be available in an electronic edition.

22 21 20 19 18 17 6 5 4 3 2 1

Library of Congress Cataloging-in-Publication Data
Names: Rose, Mark H., 1942– editor. | Biles, Roger, 1950– editor.
Title: The president and American capitalism since 1945 / edited by Mark H. Rose and Roger Biles.
Other titles: Alan B. Larkin series on the American presidency.
Description: Gainesville : University Press of Florida, 2017. | Series: The Alan B. Larkin series on the American presidency | Includes index.
Identifiers: LCCN 2017030454 | ISBN 9780813056524 (cloth : alk. paper)
Subjects: LCSH: Presidents—Economic aspects—United States. | United States—Economic conditions—History. | United States—Economic policy—History. | Presidents—United States—History—20th century. | Economic development—Political aspects—United States.
Classification: LCC HC103 .P845 2018 | DDC 330.973—dc23
LC record available at https://lccn.loc.gov/2017030454

The University Press of Florida is the scholarly publishing agency for the State University System of Florida, comprising Florida A&M University, Florida Atlantic University, Florida Gulf Coast University, Florida International University, Florida State University, New College of Florida, University of Central Florida, University of Florida, University of North Florida, University of South Florida, and University of West Florida.

University Press of Florida
15 Northwest 15th Street
Gainesville, FL 32611-2079
http://upress.ufl.edu

In Memory of Alan B. Larkin (1922–2002)

Contents

Figures

Acknowledgments

The chapters of this book are revised versions of solicited papers originally presented in February 2016 at the Alan B. and Charna Larkin Symposium on the American Presidency. Hosted by the history department at Florida Atlantic University, the symposium and the series that shares its name are testaments to the vision and generosity of the Larkin family. Their gift to the university has been a gift to history itself and is a fitting tribute to the late Alan Larkin's personal fascination with America's past.

Stephen D. Engle converted Charna Larkin's generosity into the presidential symposia. Steve, a distinguished scholar of nineteenth-century America, invited us to take the lead in creating the 2016 symposium. Steve supported our thematic choice of presidents and American capitalism—and, from the early planning period to the last days before publication, he supervised the logistical and financial arrangements that led to a successful conference and to the publication of a top-notch volume. As always, Zella Linn, Steve's program assistant, anticipated obstacles, made every arrangement, and ran the symposium on the ground. Sian Hunter, our editor at the University Press of Florida, told us about her conviction that "publishing is made up of 100 thousand million details." Sian noticed those details in our proposal and again in what we thought were final drafts. Sian also sharpened and improved our focus on the larger thematic picture. Her guidance proved invaluable. Ali Sundook, who works with Sian, took us by the hand as our volume entered production. Eleanor Deumens guided the volume through production. Still others at the University Press of Florida proved helpful and wise. Altogether, Steve, Zella, Sian, Ali, Eleanor, and others are among the invisible actors who make scholarly publishing take place. We hope these few sentences confer recognition that is richly deserved. Raymond A. Mohl, our friend, collegue, and coeditor, passed in 2015. We miss his warmth, intelligence, and wise counsel.

Our authors were a treat to work with. In our introductory chapter, we set the rest of the contributions in the contexts of Americanist scholarship and American history since 1945. Here's what we can tell you about them with absolute confidence. Most earned the PhD during the past few years—and all are on the cusp of turning manuscripts into books and articles that will guide us toward enhanced understandings of presidents and the ways they helped frame shopping, politics, corporations, universities, computers, gendered employment, credit, retirement, cities, poverty, energy, and genetically modified organisms. Their well-crafted chapters in this volume and their publications soon to follow will inform key directions of study in recent American history for some time to come.

Roger Biles and Mark H. Rose

1

The President and American Capitalism since 1945

MARK H. ROSE AND ROGER BILES

On September 11, 2001, Al-Qaeda terrorists flew hijacked commercial jets into the Pentagon and World Trade Center towers. Approximately 3,000 Americans perished in that day's attacks. That death toll included 72 law enforcement officers and 343 firefighters who braved the infernos to rescue people trapped inside the crumbling structures. 9/11 was also a live television event. The flaming collapse of hundred-story buildings (in real time) and word of the soaring death count reminded U.S. citizens that they, too—even the most prosperous and seemingly well protected—would have to reside in cities, work in buildings, and eat in restaurants that might come under attack at any moment. A few days later, Americans learned that President George W. Bush had not returned immediately to the White House on 9/11. Members of the president's Secret Service team judged the situation too uncertain.[1]

On September 14, Bush addressed his fellow citizens from the World Trade Center site. Smoke and debris could be seen in the background, a standing notice that the nation was about to go to war. Bush, speaking through a bullhorn, mixed compassion for 9/11 victims with a stern promise to kill those who had planned the attack. No one could have doubted that the president had taken up his responsibility to protect and defend as the Constitution mandated. Bush was the commander in chief. On October 7, less than one month after the terrorist attacks, U.S. armed forces headed to Afghanistan and to other distant lands as part of Operation Enduring Freedom.[2]

In this volume, Brian Balogh alerts us to another presidential responsibility that emerged after the 9/11 attacks. Airline executives had already laid off more than one hundred thousand employees. On September 27, Bush spoke to airline workers and to his fellow citizens at Chicago's O'Hare International Airport. Rather than extend his commander-in-chief role, Balogh points out, Bush struck a cheery, upbeat message in support of both American morale and the beleaguered airline and travel business. Bush exhorted Americans still in shock from the recent horrors not to hunker down in fear but instead to keep their business commitments and make time for leisure. Bush urged parents to take their families to one of the nation's many inviting vacation spots such as the Disney parks in Orlando, Florida. The president, Balogh contends, had shifted into an altogether different role: that of consumer in chief.[3]

Bush's remarks about travel and holidays marked a striking shift in presidential rhetoric that reflected the growing importance of consumerism in twentieth-century America. The Constitution's authors were silent on this part of the president's responsibilities to the nation. No court decision or legislative enactment directed presidents to advise Americans regarding their vacation plans. Just as surely, the Constitution's authors offered no prescriptions regarding where tourists ought to visit.

In 2001, Americans perhaps judged the idea of the president of the United States as a cheerleader for air travel and shopping sprees as unfamiliar, undignified, and maybe even inappropriate. Older Americans in particular took as a guiding principle that life revolved around their responsibilities as producers—as farmers who grew crops, as truckers who delivered those crops, as factory employees who turned the raw materials into useful products, and as corporate executives who financed and organized manufacturing. Railroads, trucks, skyscrapers, machine tools, clicking keyboards, noise, and smoke served as widely acknowledged symbols of production, jobs, overtime pay, and prosperity. Among adults listening to President Bush that day, few had reason to doubt the simple tenets taught by most parents and in every grade school. The combination of religious and patriotic devotion, hard work, and the avoidance of debt, these trusted authority figures had urged, represented the one true path toward job security, home ownership, acceptance among neighbors, and preparation for a modest retirement.[4]

President Bush's admonition to take a holiday flipped those traditional virtues on their heads. Bush would not ask civilians to sacrifice time or money for wars in Afghanistan and Iraq. That responsibility fell on members of a volunteer military and their families. Everyone else, Bush seemed to say, remained at liberty to shop and travel, buy a larger house, max out credit cards, and look for ways to secure a quick income boost. The president was the nation's most visible and influential lawmaker. And, at his urging, self-indulgence in the form of travel, shopping, and leisure officially replaced self-sacrifice as Americans' major wartime responsibility and highest patriotic duty.

Bush's first steps in response to the 9/11 attacks also direct our attention to one of the president's most venerable responsibilities: to foster prosperity. Congressional legislation immediately after World War II greatly expanded presidential power and responsibility in that regard. Members of Congress approved the Employment Act of 1946, which assigned the president official responsibility to bring about a growing economy. At the conclusion of World War II, lawmakers had feared a return to recession and high unemployment, which had occurred after World War I. In the Full Employment Act, congressional authors made the president's budget—and his decisions whether to recommend increased or decreased spending on everything from farm aid to highway construction—the key federal tool to sustain business profits and employment on an upward trend line. The president's guiding hand in the form of the federal budget replaced the market's invisible one. Three decades later, with unemployment and inflation soaring, President Jimmy Carter worked with congressional leaders to eliminate federal supervision of air, truck, and railroad rates. Lower travel and freight rates were supposed to knock the legs out from under fast rising consumer prices. By the 1970s, then, the president's decisions about such disparate matters as war and peace, freight rates, and employment reached into every workplace and household in the land.

After 1945, presidents were quick to claim credit for a thriving economy. And every four years, Americans enjoyed an opportunity to hold the president responsible for whether the economy worked for them and for family and neighbors. Presidents also routinely shouldered the blame when the economy sputtered. In truth, however, voters possessed no more than a vague impression about how decisions in the White House actually enhanced or limited economic growth. Rare was the citizen who possessed the time and knowledge to grasp the massive and specialized projects that emanated from the president's budget. Federal programs to support space exploration, aid farmers, underwrite cancer research, construct highways and runways, purchase military weapons, and regulate freight rates remained mostly out of popular view. In what posed yet a final barrier to understanding the president's role in the economy, federal officials wrote contracts to private firms and universities to fight the nation's wars and seek cures for diseases such as cancer. Every newspaper and TV station mentioned the president's blueprint for spending in general, but the budget's details and its multiple consequences for travel, health, employment, or medical knowledge remained, in historian Balogh's excellent phrase, "hidden in plain sight."[5]

Nor were many Americans aware that after 1946 the process of shaping the federal budget started with personnel in the president's Bureau of the Budget (after 1970, the Office of Management and Budget). The Budget Bureau staff consisted of a mix of presidential appointees and career employees. They labored in obscurity. Journalists rarely wrote stories detailing how the Budget Bureau worked, and TV producers never stationed camera crews outside the bureau's doors in anticipation of a "breaking" story. As a result of the budget's size, complexity, and obscure origins, Americans might still believe that the president and the federal budget were largely irrelevant, and that only they—and they alone—were and remained masters of their own fates.[6]

Curiously, historians and even political scientists also contributed to this lack of understanding about the president's strong hand in so many facets of American life. That lack of understanding had a history. Many leading scholars, influenced by social movements such as the decades-long struggles for racial and gender equality, distrusted histories focused on the White House. With social history and social historians in the professional ascendance, political historians and presidential studies fell into some disfavor. Biographies and White House narratives written by "presidential historians" such as Doris Kearns Goodwin and Michael Beschloss often appealed to wide audiences, but academic historians continued to analyze the powerful effects of gender, class, and race.[7]

Scholars advanced still other reasons to dismiss presidential action and rhetoric. From around 1980 through the early 2000s, popular conversations as well as presidential speeches were often stuck in an unceasing rhetoric that assigned political and social change to the work of markets and personal choices. Most basically, the conversations in which presidents and ordinary Americans engaged each day added to the illusion that markets mattered and that presidents did not. "You can't fight the market" emerged as a popular expression on CNBC and in other business-oriented programming to reinforce the idea that markets rather than lawmakers set the outlines of daily life. And where indeed was precise and concrete evidence of the president and government action in reducing poverty, fostering a higher level of literacy, inventing the Internet, boosting farm production, making highways safer, finding a cure for incurable diseases, or shaping sovereign markets? That evidence existed in the form of countless general and sometimes confusing news reports, but it was an exhausting task for busy and sometimes unengaged Americans to assemble that evidence in one place. Instead, market talk prevailed. Thus, when President Barack Obama sought to limit banks' speculative activities after the financial crisis of 2008, congressional and media critics described his actions as an unwarranted and unwise intrusion in self-governing markets. In the plainest terms, the slant of popular rhetoric further shuttered the president from the view of ordinary citizens and professional historians. Overall, it is perhaps no wonder that historians largely shied away from the president.[8]

In 2015, however, the distinguished historian Bruce J. Schulman redirected our attention to the presidents' importance in American life. Schulman rejected the idea of treating the presidency or any one president in isolated fashion, as if he were the sole author of regulations and legislation. Rather, Schulman recommended that historians, and all of us, think in terms of the multiple connections among lawmakers, concerned voters, and leaders of broad popular movements seeking gender and racial equality. In other words, Schulman advised that historians bring generations of sophisticated social history to bear on presidents and on the presidential office. Who could deny such an important call to scholarship?[9]

We asked fifteen historians to prepare original chapters linking presidents and their administrations to major changes in capitalism. We conceived capitalism broadly to include the president's changing responsibilities for the economy as a whole and in distinct areas such as promoting computer use, women's climb up corporate ladders, the war on poverty, and encouraging the consumption of genetically modified foods. What started as a quest to understand presidents and the presidency in American life since 1945 turned into a wide-ranging production of articles that are remarkable for their exploration of new topics and extraordinary in their scholarly depth.

Few of the talented authors of chapters in this volume would describe themselves as presidential or even political historians. Brian Balogh and Iwan Morgan, the two authors whose books and articles have often traced important changes in American life to the White House, are not presidential historians. But like Morgan and Balogh, the remaining thirteen authors possess no doubt about the importance of re-centering presidents in American history. They seek to excavate and illuminate the presidential hand in topics formerly treated solely as economic or social history, as for instance credit card use and retirement accounts.

Many of our authors also seek to align their work with publications in the history of capitalism, a vibrant new field of study that has emerged in only the past few years. In September 2014, editors of the *Journal of American History* published an "Interchange" among ten prominent historians whose publications are helping to determine this field's themes and borders. Elizabeth Tandy Shermer launched that interchange by asking rhetorically, "I wonder why there has been a surge in this scholarship." Shermer reports arriving at capitalist studies as a result of the apparent disjuncture between popular and scholarly accounts of postwar American prosperity and daily reports of declining wages, shuttered factories, busted unions, and triumphant conservatism.[10]

Perhaps a generation earlier, Shermer and her colleagues would have described their work with an older term, that of political economy. But authors of capitalist studies now aspire to include detailed accounts of gender and race alongside studies of the wealthiest, poorest, and middle layers of American society. Black, Latino, Asian, and white Americans, including women as well as men, need to be pulled into the history of capitalism and into the history of presidents and their administrations. Authors in this volume certainly lead us along these multiple paths.

So, too, we asked authors to situate the president in the history of capitalism after World War II. And indeed, because the history of capitalism is such a new field, and because presidents and the presidency have remained understudied in recent decades, our authors took on a tall order. They succeeded magnificently.[11]

Before we turn to their articles, however, a word of caution is in order. Capitalism is an immense and complex topic. As well, capitalism is not static. American lawmakers, jurists, presidents, and common people have altered capitalism in large and small ways during the nation's more than two hundred years of history. As an example, we cannot read the eighteenth-century Scottish philosopher Adam Smith and come away with an understanding of how capitalism has worked or should have worked. At the time of the Declaration of Independence in 1776 or when the Constitution was adopted in 1787, America was not a free enterprise nation. As late as 1846, founders of corporations such as the Pennsylvania Railroad still had to secure a charter to operate from notoriously venal state legislators meeting in Harrisburg. Not until the 1840s did lawmakers in Pennsylvania and other states take the first steps to make it possible for ordinary citizens to create corporations without the legislature's direct approval.[12]

Later generations of lawmakers, jurists, presidents, and citizens reshaped capitalism further. Slavery was a capitalist institution, and the president and members of Congress abolished it. After the civil war and up to the present day, it is not possible to appreciate capitalism's rich institutional history simply by reading news accounts of lawmakers who have railed against bank regulations or insisted on greater oversight of the Federal Reserve System. Capitalism, it is clear, is not just one big, unchanging idea or simply a heralded, one best way to accomplish personal and societal goals. Capitalism, we can be certain, has revolved around far more than private persons or top corporate leaders who sought to drum up business, reduce expenses, and increase monetary gain. In American history, profit maximization, slave labor, and shared profit and loss among owners and workers have existed inside capitalism's wide and shifting boundaries. And just as surely, women and African Americans have been both shabbily and positively treated inside capitalist firms at different times. Again, capitalism includes such seemingly dissimilar topics as outlooks on gender and race, ways of hiring and organizing workers in tiny factories and offices, and of course the management of vast financial and manufacturing corporations such as Bank of America, Lehman Brothers Holdings, Microsoft, and ExxonMobil. And as historians, we must reaffirm the importance of historical context—capitalist enterprises and ways of working and living in the twenty-first century are not extensions of our grandmother's capitalism cloaked in modern garb. With these caveats in mind, here are the themes our authors uncovered in their search for the president and capitalism since 1945.[13]

We title our first section "Patterns and Politics." Every president, we learn, has inherited obligations, including the responsibility to nurture capitalist institutions. But those responsibilities and each president's interpretation of them never remained static. To develop this idea of politically constituted institutions, the subject of our first batch of chapters, let's return for a moment to chapter 1 and Balogh's concept of the president as shopper in chief. In 1959, Balogh also reports, President Richard M. Nixon debated with Soviet Premier Nikita Khrushchev in front of a mock kitchen display at the American National Exhibit in Moscow. Nixon stressed the superiority of American-built refrigerators and new color TV sets, just then becoming available. Nixon surely overlooked the uneven distribution of refrigerators and black and white TVs across the American landscape. His celebration of domestic material comfort probably won widespread recognition among employed Euro-Americans residing in recently opened suburbs. Indeed, Nixon was directing his paean to American capitalism more to the new homeowner in Levittown than to the Russian leader in Moscow. And not coincidentally, Nixon won publicity in the Moscow Kitchen Debate for his 1960 presidential bid.[14]

The president's institutional responsibilities were thus not only about economic growth but also about the triumph of capitalism as an idea and as the nation's most important institution. Preaching the gospel of free enterprise from the White House—making effective use of what Theodore Roosevelt called the "bully pulpit"—the American president consistently proselytized to a worldwide audience on behalf of American capitalism.

As Margaret O'Mara reminds us in "Capitalism on the Campaign Trail," the capitalism-government dynamic has shaped presidential candidacies as well as presidential administrations. Her chapter considers two important elections, the Jimmy Carter–Gerald R. Ford contest of 1976 and the George H. W. Bush–Bill Clinton–H. Ross Perot election of 1992. In both cases, Republican incumbents lost to moderate southern Democrats at times of economic uncertainty in the U.S. Portraying himself as an outsider to big government with an aversion to big business, capitalizing on his image as a simple peanut farmer from Georgia, Carter became an avatar for small business centrism. In turn, Clinton advocated a "third way" between state-centered liberalism and private enterprise, touting a kind of "grassroots capitalism" well suited to the changing economy of the late twentieth century. In her careful examination, O'Mara finds no monolithic business community or "party of business" at work in the two elections. Rather, she concludes, "the new attitude toward big government on both left and right comported with the ways the economy itself was changing." The increasing desire for more limited government went hand-in-hand with more entrepreneurial forms of capitalism.

Once in office, presidents have relied on their substantial control of the federal budget to hasten the growth of capitalist institutions. Presidents since 1945, as Iwan Morgan notes, have served as the economy's chief stewards, principal architects of long-term economic planning, and discerning arbiters of spending priorities. Aided by a vast army of economists and aides in the Office of Management and Budget and the White House, the presidents exercised considerable influence over the pace of economic growth, the rate of inflation, and other consequential matters not normally thought to have originated in the Oval Office. Morgan also reminds us, as when Jimmy Carter appointed Paul A. Volcker Jr. as chairman of the Federal Reserve Board of Governors, that the president has at times ceded economic authority to other powerful actors in the federal bureaucracy.

Many of the presidents' institutional behaviors revolved around economic development. In past decades, every president sought to accelerate economic growth, boost computer usage, and promote the sale of American TVs, refrigerators, and genetically engineered seeds. Indeed, we might begin to imagine postwar presidents standing in the aisles of prominent chain stores like Nordstrom's, Best Buy, and Home Depot and making a sales pitch to each passing customer. That pitch traditionally included a quick explanation of why this year's seeds, flat-screened TVs, and new Disney attractions were the best ever.

But the products were almost beside the point. The sales pitch also contained a hard sell regarding the advantages of American-style capitalism for the nation's residents. The high-powered salesmanship, of course, presumed benefits for American citizens. The presidential sales talk regarding American-style capitalism was fundamentally political, underscoring the wealth and well-being of Americans in comparison with the unfortunate residents of state-controlled economies.[15]

Presidents also helped promote ideas about the federal government's size and reach. Brent Cebul, in "The Antigovernment Impulse," describes the ways in which presidential candidates since the 1960s have invariably criticized the federal government's excessive influence. The recurring censure of the Washington, DC, leviathan by presidential aspirants has thus become both a cause and a consequence of the rising antigovernment impulse. Yet, Cebul reminds us, each president left behind a larger and more powerful bureaucracy. At the same time, the popular belief in "the market" as the most influential determinant of economic change and even social relationships has likewise contributed to a declining faith in government. The net result of this antigovernment rhetoric, Cebul finds, has been to "narrow . . . the political basis for critically important policies meant to benefit the entire polity." Cebul's ideas about the importance of presidents and their rhetorical invocation of "the market" as an explanation for virtually every American development further connect themes developed by most of the authors in this volume.

Our second theme is "Sectors: The Way Politics Organizes the Economy." Presidents, as our authors show so well, have often taken a decisive hand in shaping closely related parts of the American economy. Transportation, health care, financial services, entertainment, and defense are among the economy's largest sectors. But there is more to an economic sector than firms engaged in similar lines of work, such as transportation and banking. In these sector firms, employees have shared similar experiences and employed a specialized jargon. Often, presidents and members of Congress have created specific regulations for transportation (safety rules, for instance) and banking firms (reserve requirements, as an example), adding to their distinctive characteristics.

Few sectors have attracted more attention in recent decades than personal computers. Andrew Meade McGee explores the efforts of American presidents to develop the nation's computer industry. Cold War presidents initially gave a green light to hardware and software research because of the potential applications for national defense. Recent presidents, McGee finds, "embraced the computer" to advance their policy goals and to improve their campaigns, and as a recognizable metaphor for the progress certain to flow from science and technology. As surely as Microsoft's Bill Gates and Apple's Steve Jobs played essential roles in ushering the nation into the digital age, presidents did so as well behind the scenes through their generous support of research and development.

Presidents, in their role as commander in chief, also exercised considerable influence over preparations for war in the form of weapons acquisition. In the post–World War II era, as Mark R. Wilson describes, Democratic and Republican presidents alike became active participants in reconfiguring the U.S. military. Starting as early as the 1950s, in fact, former President Herbert C. Hoover and a host of influential businessmen sought to privatize the U.S. armed forces. Wilson describes this change as the "Hoovering" of the American military. As a result of this transformation, the U.S. government increasingly took a backseat to private contractors and commercial vendors in the provision of weapons, transportation, and logistics expertise. Pentagon officials began to order the closing of production plants and shipyards in the 1960s, accelerating the shift to private enterprise in later decades. Reacting to defense procurement scandals in the 1980s and 1990s, presidents yielded to the argument that private enterprise was best suited to conduct the business of war. The replacement of U.S. soldiers with mercenary forces in the employ of private firms such as Blackwater brought the "Hoovering" of the American military full circle.

National defense also figured in presidential involvement with another important sector of the American economy: the university. In the Cold War years, political leaders judged mass higher education prerequisite to a sturdy defense. International business competition, those same leaders concluded, provided another reason to underwrite university expansion, which occurred at an unprecedented rate from the 1950s to the 1980s. With this new funding in hand, university officials constructed buildings and admitted additional students. Generous federal funding also fed the development of the modern research university, which served as an increasingly important site for government-sponsored scientific, medical, and military investigation. Originally hesitant to inject the federal government into university affairs, notes Elizabeth Tandy Shermer, presidents beginning with Franklin D. Roosevelt indirectly nurtured the growth of higher education. Constitutional limits, past policies, and thorny politics limited their ability to aid universities directly. But presidents did collaborate with their advisors to offer a range of financial assistance to students, and that tuition money in turn became the only real federal guarantee that colleges had from the government. This presidential approach unintentionally created the massive student loan industry.

Postwar presidents also helped push the growth of another sector of the American economy: credit purchasing. When George W. Bush urged Americans to spend freely in the wake of the 9/11 attacks, he stood in a long line of presidents who encouraged the widespread use of consumer credit—particularly credit cards. Jimmy Carter proved to be the notable exception, as Sean H. Vanatta recounts in his chapter on the embattled president's unsuccessful efforts to stem runaway inflation and slow down an overheated economy in the late 1970s. Personally skeptical of an intemperate reliance on credit, which he deemed immoral as well as unwise, Carter persuaded enough Americans to curtail use of their credit cards that such purchasing declined during the few months of the policy's implementation. Diminished credit card spending, however, produced disastrous results for the U.S. economy, which had come to rely heavily on credit-driven consumption, and for Carter, who lost decisively to Ronald W. Reagan in the 1980 election. Reagan and George H. W. Bush dismissed Carter's concerns about personal debt, and subsequent presidents tacitly accepted—and even encouraged—the centrality of consumer credit to the nation's economic health.

In another significant exercise of presidential initiative that remained largely invisible to the general public, Nixon's revision of landmark legislation altered the private retirement practices of the American worker. With little fanfare, in 1971 Nixon insisted on a small change to the Employee Retirement Income Security Act (ERISA) that allowed individuals to fashion their own Individual Retirement Accounts (IRAs). After President Gerald R. Ford signed ERISA into law in 1974, the IRA quickly became the cornerstone of retirement planning for millions of Americans. Paula K. Gajewski's chapter relates how the proliferation of IRAs created billions of dollars of investment capital, thereby augmenting and reshaping financial markets. As Gajewski makes clear, moreover, ordinary Americans understood ERISA's consequences in terms of a new way of saving for retirement. Prior to ERISA, corporate pension plans promised a guaranteed payout each month. After 1974, however, employees exercised greater control of their retirements—for better or worse. In truth, the amount of money available to them in retirement now rested on stock market fluctuations. Perhaps the market would boom or take a dive. But employees exercised no control of the stock market, and, in fact, they were often confused and uncertain about its unpredictable (and sometimes scary) fluctuations.

Corporate sectors are also gendered. Men and women have occupied different rungs and ladders in the workplace, even after changes in labor law during the twentieth century ostensibly removed many invidious obstacles to hiring and promotion. Pamela Walker Laird examines the chances of women rising above glass ceilings that have traditionally formed barriers. Laird's method is straightforward. She compares female appointees to presidential cabinets with their CEO counterparts in the corporate executive realm. "Pull" is Laird's apt term to describe the process by which people with influence—gatekeepers such as presidents and corporate leaders—have helped women to ascend political and corporate ladders. These comparisons show that gatekeepers' incentives for pulling women into powerful positions differ between democratic and capitalist arenas. She also contrasts capitalism's lofty rhetoric with the uneven way in which promotions take place. "The constraints affecting women on these . . . ladders," Laird contends, "show that the meritocratic pretensions so vigorously proclaimed to justify both American capitalism and politics collide with glass ceilings in almost every professional arena."[16]

Complementing Laird's examination of women in the upper echelons of government and corporate sectors, Allison Elias's chapter assesses the role played by presidents in the shift from "fair employment" to "affirmative action" for "pink collar" workers. What role, in other words, have presidents played in the eradication of occupational segregation for female office workers? Elias's discerning case study looks at Karen Nussbaum and 9to5, the National Association of Working Women, and finds that presidential indifference in some instances and outright hostility in others created a battleground over affirmative action. Repeatedly establishing broad goals, flexible timetables, and other nonbinding guidelines, presidents evinced a willingness to condemn sex-based discrimination in principle but stopped well short of institutionalizing effective measures to end the practice. From the 1970s to the present, corporate leaders remained largely free to circumvent affirmative action for female clerical workers.

"Environments: The Larger Setting" is our third and final theme. The environment, for our authors, signifies both the constructed and natural realms. Used this way, capitalist institutions emerge as creatures of presidential handiwork and local political environments. Tracy Neumann finds that policies made in the Oval Office hastened the decline of Rust Belt cities from thriving manufacturing centers to ailing postindustrial metropolises. In that regard, she demonstrates, Presidents Nixon, Carter, and Reagan sought to relocate central city residents to the suburbs while at the same time eliminating or failing to enforce protective tariffs that had helped maintain vital local industries such as steel, automobiles, and textiles. Round after round of massive flight to the metropolitan periphery—and to booming Sunbelt communities—ensued. During the next three decades, lacking the necessary resources to keep their cities afloat financially, mayors sought to remake central cities as entertainment zones where middle-class suburbanites and tourists attended ball games, concerts, and conventions, gambled at glitzy casinos, and ate at trendy, four-star restaurants. Changes in urban America reflected the transformation of the nation's economy from industrial production to service, real estate, and finance; under presidential leadership, the federal government reduced spending on the liberal programs of the 1960s and turned to individualistic, market-oriented solutions for recurring social problems.

Daniel Amsterdam, however, determines that presidents in the 1970s did not reflexively dismiss the liberal social welfare programs of the 1960s in a headlong rush to embrace market-based solutions to societal problems. Presidents Nixon, Ford, and Carter signed federal legislation creating Community Development Block Grants, Section 8 housing vouchers, Supplemental Security Income, and Earned Income Tax Credits, among other important programs. As one particularly noteworthy example, the Carter administration significantly increased the federal government's support of public service employment, providing 750,000 jobs for the chronically unemployed in state and local governments, as well as in nongovernmental organizations (NGOs). Whereas President Lyndon B. Johnson's War on Poverty principally offered job training programs and vocational education to the inner-city poor, Carter patterned his antipoverty efforts after earlier New Deal experiments and sponsored public service employment for the nation's indigent population. Amsterdam's discussion of Carter's overlooked initiative complicates the story of the War on Poverty's demise. Amsterdam also reminds us that in the 1970s, recently characterized by historians as a "pivotal decade," occupants of the White House continued to struggle with the intractable problem of poverty.[17]

Presidents were equally avid supporters of capitalism in the energy sector. Like many of the developments discussed above such as computers and defense, energy production contained important implications for national security, trade policy, and environmental concerns—as well as for consumer prices. But, as Gavin Benke illustrates, the relationship between Presidents George H. W. Bush, Bill Clinton, and George W. Bush on the one hand and powerful energy conglomerates such as Enron on the other proved to be complex. Enron chairman Kenneth L. "Ken" Lay sought to cultivate close relationships with the White House, all the while advocating policies designed to benefit his company. Each of those three presidents, however, carefully calibrated their dealings with energy executives to advance their own political goals, sometimes seeking to foster energy independence and at other times encouraging a shift toward renewable resources in deference to the growing environmental movement.

This dynamic, and Ken Lay's relationship with these different presidents, provided a point of contention and continuity between administrations when it came to the emerging politics of climate change.

Bartow "Bart" Elmore returns the idea of "environment" to its standard meaning, that of the air, seas, and earth in consideration of human influences on them. Elmore, however, brings a strong political twist to his environmental history of executive branch policy, examining how presidents from Ronald Reagan to Barack Obama lobbied for international expansion of genetically engineered (GE) crops. Even as members of the scientific community debated the safety of GE crops, Republican and Democratic presidents alike helped construct an international regulatory framework for agricultural biotechnology that facilitated the worldwide dispersal of GE seeds created and proprietarily claimed by American firms. Elmore discards the standard trope of a presidential payback for corporate campaign contributions and explains these presidents' actions in terms of diplomatic concerns and trade patterns. From the 1980s to the 2010s, presidents pitched GE technology as a means to feed the world, but behind the rhetoric, Elmore contends, there existed a more fundamental desire to keep American biotechnology businesses competitive in a world filled with hungry capitalist competitors. Elmore concludes that while speaking words of liberation, the White House helped to create a new system of agricultural dependency in the developing world.

Our talented authors force us toward a broad and deep reappraisal of American presidents and capitalism since 1945. Their chapters remind us that the presidents, both Democrats and Republicans, inherited the office's institutionalized requirements. The occupants of the nation's highest office have shouldered two discrete yet closely related obligations: promoting the economic good and praising the virtues of capitalism to a global audience. To be sure, a thriving economy helped immeasurably to make the case for American-style capitalism. Held accountable by voters who looked to the White House for action to limit unemployment, control interest rates, and curtail inflation, presidents utilized the budget, national legislation, persuasion, exhortation, and a host of other tools to stimulate high levels of production and consumption. The grumblings about the concentration of too much power in the federal government notwithstanding, Americans expected the exercise of sound economic growth management in the Oval Office. In times of prosperity and recession alike, the president remained the face of the U.S. economy. Whether Nixon extolled refrigerators in 1959 or Bush urged more trips to Disney in 2001, no obligation embedded in the presidential office loomed larger than that of advancing that day's version of capitalist practices at home and around the world.[18]

Our authors also offer several examples of how presidents have nurtured capitalist institutions, shaped the various sectors of the U.S. economy, and altered natural and constructed environments—sometimes in plain view of the public and at other times behind the scenes in largely unappreciated ways. Presidents took a decisive hand in writing the rules for retirement and in framing other strictures for company officials who sought to provide consumers with such varied products as energy, personal computers, and genetically modified organisms. Just as much, postwar presidents helped determine the vitality of city government, the competitive environment for steel and auto companies, and the employment opportunities that would be offered to women and central city residents. To be clear, however, no president simply hustled on behalf of corporate sales.

Presidents of the United States, our authors so clearly show, have exercised a powerful if often unseen hand in fashioning American capitalism. If that is so, we might do well to banish the concept of government "intervention" in favor of a more nuanced approach that treats presidents and capitalist institutions as being of one piece. The president's ubiquity in the American economy since World War II reveals the existence of a symbiotic relationship of unsurpassed importance for policymaking. This volume, far from exhaustive in its consideration of a few instructive examples, suggests that much more remains to be learned about such an important topic. The task for future generations of scholars, social and economic historians as well as political historians and political scientists, will be to analyze in greater detail how the intersection of the presidency and capitalism has shaped American life in the late twentieth and early twenty-first centuries.

The 2016 election, in which virtually no political pundits or pollsters predicted Republican Donald J. Trump's triumph over Democrat Hillary Rodham Clinton, proved confounding in many respects but also affirmed the salience of economic management in presidential politics. Historians and political scientists will doubtless spend decades sorting out the relative importance of racism, misogyny, nativism, class antagonism, and a stark aversion to the Democratic candidate in Trump's stunning victory.

Still, deep concern among less-well-educated voters about economic changes that left them behind prospering business and professional Americans clearly fueled much of the Republican's "populist" appeal. Persuaded by the billionaire Trump's claims of financial wizardry, many of his supporters believed that his self-proclaimed business acumen would translate into more effective management of the national economy. His tough talk on trade and promise to bring manufacturing back to desiccated cities in places like Central Michigan, vast swaths of Ohio, and coal country West Virginia resonated with an anxious blue-collar electorate faced with uncertain employment, low wages, and the loss of prestige long associated with hard work in the nation's manufacturing plants. In many quarters, smoke and noise still meant prosperity.[19] To make it all work, it seems, Trump would have to reconsider parts of the free trade, small government, and deregulatory agendas that had captured the attention of America's leaders since the 1970s. Trump's ability to shape such a program and deliver on his bold promises would go far in determining his presidency's success. As Trump had observed in 1987, he would be "measured not by how much . . . [he undertook] but by what . . . [he] finally [accomplished]."[20]

Notes

1. R. W. Apple Jr., "After the Attacks, The Trip Back; Aides Say Bush Was One Target of Hijacked Jet," *New York Times,* accessed March 17, 2016, http://www.nytimes.com/2001/09/13/us/after-the-attacks-the-trip-back-aides-say-bush-was-one-target-of-hijacked-jet.html.

2. George W. Bush, "Remarks to Police, Firemen, and Rescue Workers at the World Trade Center Site in New York City," September 14, 2001, http://www.presidency.ucsb.edu/ws/index.php?pid=65078&st=&st1=.

3. Richard W. Stevenson and Joseph Kahn, "A Nation Challenged: The Economy; Bush Tries to Steady Economy Jolted by Attack," *New York Times,* September 23, 2001, accessed March 15, 2016, http://www.nytimes.com/2001/09/23/a-nation-challenged-the-economy-bush-tries-to-steady-economy-jolted-by-attack.html; George W. Bush, "Remarks to Airline Employees in Chicago, Illinois," September 27, 2001, http://www.presidency.ucsb.edu/ws/index.php?pid=65084&st=disney&st1=. Also see Nicholas Dagen Bloom, *The Metropolitan Airport: JFK International and Modern New York* (Philadelphia: University of Pennsylvania Press, 2015), for the importance of passenger and air cargo to New York's economy.

4. On the relevance of these traditional virtues up to the present day, see Ashley Parker, "Covering Donald Trump and Witnessing the Danger Up Close," *New York*

Times, March 12, 2016, accessed March 15, 2016, http://www.nytimes.com/2016/03/13/us/politics/covering-donald-trump-and-witnessing-the-danger-up-close.html?smprod=nytcore-iphone&smid=nytcore-iphone-share.

5. Brian Balogh, *A Government Out of Sight: The Mystery of National Authority in Nineteenth-Century America* (Cambridge, UK: Cambridge University Press, 2009), 395.

6. Balogh, *Government Out of Sight*, 382–83.

7. Brian Balogh, "Introduction: Confessions of a Presidential Assassin," 2–3, and Bruce J. Schulman, "Conclusion: The Perils and Prospects of Presidential History," 252–53, both in *Recapturing the Oval Office: New Historical Approaches to the American Presidency*, ed. Balogh and Schulman (Ithaca: Cornell University Press, 2015).

8. Edward Wyatt, "Dodd-Frank Act a Favorite Target for Republicans Laying Blame," *New York Times*, September 20, 2011, accessed March 16, 2011, http://www.nytimes.com/2011/09/21/business/dodd-frank-act-is-a-target-on-gop-campaign-trail.html.

9. Schulman, "Conclusion," 256.

10. "Interchange: The History of Capitalism," *Journal of American History* 30 (September 2014): 505–6. On the history of capitalism, see Sven Beckert, "History of Capitalism," in *American History Now*, ed. Eric Foner and Lisa McGirr (Philadelphia: Temple University Press, 2011); Louis Hyman, *Debtor Nation: The History of America in Red Ink* (Princeton: Princeton University Press, 2011); and Julia Ott, *When Wall Street Met Main Street: The Quest for an Investors' Democracy* (Cambridge, MA: Harvard University Press, 2011). Also see books published in the University of Pennsylvania Press series "American Business, Politics, and Society," http://www.upenn.edu/pennpress/series/BPS.html.

11. The president and American capitalism is a new field of study. See, for example, the excellent introductions prepared by Edward J. Balleisen and David A. Moss, eds., *Government and Markets: Toward a New Theory of Regulation* (Cambridge, UK: Cambridge University Press, 2010), 1–9; and Kim Phillips-Fein and Julian E. Zelizer, eds., *What's Good for Business: Business and American Politics since World War II* (New York: Oxford University Press, 2012), 3–15. Thomas Piketty, *Capital in the Twenty-first Century* (Cambridge, MA: Belknap Press of Harvard University, 2014), enjoyed remarkable scholarly and journalistic attention at the time of its publication. Piketty devotes part of only 3 pages (out of 577) to U.S. presidents, and he advances the remarkable claim that federal policies "have had little effect" on economic growth (99). Balogh and Schulman, eds., *Recapturing the Oval Office* is the first volume focused on a social, economic, and political history of the presidency and serves as the immediate antecedent to our book.

12. Albert J. Churella, *The Pennsylvania Railroad*, vol. 1, *Building an Empire, 1846–1917* (Philadelphia: University of Pennsylvania Press, 2012), xiv, 8, 84–90; Richard R. John, *Network Nation: Inventing American Telecommunications* (Cambridge, MA: Belknap Press of Harvard University, 2010), 90–91.

13. We are indebted to Pamela Walker Laird for sharing her nuanced understanding of capitalism with us. See also Neil Fligstein, *The Architecture of Markets: An Economic Sociology of Twenty-First-Century Capitalist Societies* (Princeton: Princeton University Press, 2001) and the classic Karl Polanyi, *The Great Transformation* (New York: Rinehart, 1944).

14. As part of our development of the concept of inherited elements in the institutional office of the president, we adopted the arguments put forth by economic sociologists such as Victor Nee, "The New Institutionalism in Economics and Sociology" in *The Handbook of Economic Sociology*, 2nd ed., ed. Neil J. Smelser and Richard Swedberg, 55 (Princeton: Princeton University Press, 2005). Nee understands an institution as "*a dominant system of interrelated informal and formal elements.*" To change that system, Nee adds, requires the realignment of interests, norms, and power. In other words, not even the president possesses the capital and skill to overthrow inherited ideas and tried and true ways of achieving goals. To be elected president, candidates had to genuflect toward history, and they could not escape it once in office. For first ladies and the promotion of American fashion designers, see Vanessa Friedman, "State Dinner Becomes a Catwalk for Canadian Style," *New York Times*, March 11, 2016, accessed March 15, 2016, http://www.nytimes.com/2016/03/11/fashion/state-dinner-canada-sophie-trudeau.html?smprod=nytcore-iphone&smid=nytcore-iphone-share#. Jacqueline Bouvier Kennedy first brought sustained attention to American fashion and the arts. See for example, "Jacqueline Kennedy: The White House Years," The Metropolitan Museum, May 1–July 29, 2001, accessed March 16, 2016, http://metmuseum.org/press/exhibitions/2000/jacqueline-kennedy-the-white-house-years.

15. Nobel Prize–winning economist Paul Krugman finds that "global trade agreements from the 1940s to the 1980s were used to bind democratic nations together during the Cold War" ("Trade and Tribulation," *New York Times*, March 11, 2016, http://www.nytimes.com/2016/03/11/opinion/trade-and-tribulation.html). Judith Stein, *Pivotal Decade: How the United States Traded Factories for Finance in the Seventies* (New Haven, CT: Yale University Press, 2010), is the starting point for the study of the way in which lawmakers sought to tie overseas firms to the U.S. economy. The American style of capitalism after World War II is not easily captured in one sentence or in a single paragraph. Starting in the 1970s, however, that style included a strong preference for private ownership of business firms, reduced regulation of rates in industries such as banking and transportation, and a relaxation of antitrust rules. See for example, Mark H. Rose, *The Best Transportation System in the World: Railroads, Trucks, Airlines and American Public Policy in the Twentieth Century* (Philadelphia: University of Pennsylvania Press, 2010).

16. See also Pamela Walker Laird, *Pull: Networking and Success since Benjamin Franklin* (Cambridge, MA: Harvard University Press, 2006). For the relevance of Laird's findings up to the present, see Carol Hymowitz, Brandon Kochkodin, and Stephanie Ruhle, "Icahn, Loeb and Other Activists Overlook Women for Board Seats," *Bloomberg-Business*, March 8, 2016, accessed March 16, 2016, http://www.bloomberg.com/news/articles/2016-03-08/activists-from-icahn-to-loeb-overlook-women-for-board-positions.

17. In addition to Judith Stein's *Pivotal Decade*, recent historical assessments of the 1970s include Bruce J. Schulman, *The Seventies: The Great Shift in American Culture, Society, and Politics* (New York: Free Press, 2001); Edward Berkowitz, *Something Happened: A Political and Cultural Overview of the Seventies* (New York: Columbia University Press, 2005); Philip Jenkins, *Decade of Nightmares: The End of the Sixties and the Making of Eighties America* (New York: Oxford University Press, 2006); Beth Bailey and David Far-

ber, eds., *America in the 1970s* (Lawrence: University Press of Kansas, 2004); and Bruce J. Schulman and Julian E. Zelizer, eds., *Rightward Bound: Making America Conservative in the 1970s* (Cambridge, MA: Harvard University Press, 2008).

18. See for yet another example of the president's responsibility to promote capitalism "Remarks by President Obama at an Entrepreneurship and Opportunity Event—Havana, Cuba," White House website, March 21, 2016, accessed March 22, 2016, https://www.whitehouse.gov/the-press-office/2016/03/21/remarks-president-obama-entrepreneurship-and-opportunity-event-havana.

19. Amanda Taub, "Behind 2016's Turmoil, a Crisis of White Identity," *New York Times* November 1, 2016, accessed November 27, 2016, http://www.nytimes.com/2016/11/02/world/americas/brexit-donald-trump-whites.html; Declan Walsh, "Alienated and Angry, Coal Miners See Donald Trump as Their Only Choice," *New York Times*, August 19, 2016, accessed November 27, 2016, http://www.nytimes.com/2016/08/20/world/americas/alienated-and-angry-coal-miners-see-donald-trump-as-their-only-choice.html; Mark Muro and Sifan Liu, "Another Clinton-Trump Divide: High Output America vs. Low-Output America," *Brookings*, November 29, 2016, accessed December 1, 2016, https://www.brookings.edu/blog/the-avenue/2016/11/29/another-clinton-trump-divide-high-output-america-vs-low-output-america/?utm_campaign=Metropolitan+Policy+Program&utm_source=hs_email&utm_medium=email&utm_content=38550371.

20. Donald J. Trump with Tony Schwartz, *Trump: The Art of the Deal* (New York: Ballantine Books, 2015), 355.

2

Consumer in Chief

Presidential Leadership in America's "Consumer Republic"

BRIAN BALOGH

On September 16, 1920, a bomb that had been hidden in a horse-drawn carriage ripped through the lunchtime crowd in the heart of New York's financial district. The blast killed thirty-eight people and wounded hundreds more.[1] Despite years of investigations, the crime was never solved, but it is likely that the bombing was carried out by radical anarchists protesting the power of Wall Street's corporate institutions.

Even more remarkable than the bombing is what ensued the following day: business as usual. The *New York Tribune* described the scene at Morgan Bank—the likely target of the attack—on September 17: "It was a novel sight . . . to see dignified executives at work with heads bandaged, to see clerks operating typewriters and adding machines with one disabled hand."[2] In less than twenty-four hours, as the *New York Tribune* put it, Wall Street had "returned to routine work."[3]

Eighty-one years later, another New York City symbol of finance was struck by terrorists. The attacks of September 11, 2001, were grander in scale, killing and wounding many more than the Wall Street bombing. But in remarks following the attacks, President George W. Bush echoed his twentieth-century forbearers by calling on Americans to get back to business. Speaking to workers at O'Hare International Airport, Bush told the crowd that "one of the great goals of this nation's war is . . . to tell the traveling public: Get on board; do your business around the country; fly and enjoy America's great destination spots; get down to Disney World in Florida; take your families and enjoy life the way we want it to be enjoyed."[4] In short, don't let the terrorists deter you from spending—the economy needs you.

In spite of their similarities, it was the differences in the responses to terrorism in 1920 and 2001 that captured just how much the American economy had changed in less than a century. More specifically, Bush's remarks demonstrated the importance that consumption had come to play for the economy by the twenty-first century. When workers limped back to financial institutions the day after the Wall Street bombing, a large part of their waking lives were devoted to work. An even greater part of their identities were defined by work.

Americans in 2001 still worked, of course—President Bush did not neglect "business" in his call to arms. But citizens in Bush's America also spent a lot of time and money consuming. They consumed lots of stuff. But they also spent an increasing amount of their income on services like travel, health care, and financing all of this spending. That's because they had far more time for leisure than their early twentieth-century counterparts. Most significantly, for many of these Americans, what they bought, the car they drove, the cell phone they used, the neighborhood they lived in, and the places where they traveled defined who they were.

Some people made fun of President Bush when he blithely told Americans to "get down to Disney World in Florida; take your families and enjoy life." But in fact, President Bush was carrying out what had become an essential responsibility of the twenty-first-century president. In his response to the 9/11 attacks, even as Bush modeled what it meant to be a strong commander in chief, he juggled another role that had become almost as important: *consumer in chief.*

Apropos of my theme, this chapter will serve as something of a historical shopping trip. In it, I survey the history of the presidency in the twentieth century, perusing and collecting some of the key moments in the evolution of the office of the presidency, particularly after World War II. Over that period, two features of the White House's role in national life have contributed to the emergence of a full blown consumer-oriented economy and to creating a culture in which consumption is as natural as the air we breathe. (Or the bottled water we drink?) One of these features is the growing power of the modern president to shape public policy. The other is symbolic: the president as the nation's first and leading consumer. At times, these dual roles add up to a responsibility that rivals the president's obligation as commander in chief.[5]

How did the president emerge as consumer in chief? The presidential part of the answer is easy. From relative nonentities in the nineteenth century, presidents evolved into the acknowledged leaders of the free world in the twentieth. This transformation was the product of many factors: American economic growth, the development of national—and then international—communications networks, and, finally, America's military might. With the emergence of a mixed economy in which the federal government was responsible for priming the economic pump directly, by increasing government spending when the economy faltered, and indirectly subsidizing major sectors of the economy—from the military industrial complex to millions of mortgages and student loans—presidents ignored economic conditions at their peril. If they broke the economy, they owned it.

The consumer part of the answer is a little more complicated. But if one were to simplify and reduce it to a bumper sticker, it too would read, "It's the economy, stupid." The emergence of the modern presidency coincided with a major transformation in American economic culture and political economy. In the nineteenth century, the economy was powered by a producer ethic. But by the middle of the twentieth, a powerful consumer ethic shaped the economy.

The producer ethic in American culture was epitomized by the Protestant work ethic, in which religion was a cornerstone that also sanctioned work in the material world. Nineteenth-century Americans valued things like labor, sacrifice, and saving. Capitalism and good citizenship, they believed, required hard work and self-denial. These were values that served both God *and* the republic.

By the end of the nineteenth century, however, the political economy was changing dramatically. Charles Darwin's ideas about evolution had penetrated deeply into elite circles, replacing religious motivation with secular goals. A truly national market had emerged, overshadowing regional economies. By the 1920s, industrialization churned out mountains of mass-produced goods, from Uneeda Biscuits to automobiles. Waves of immigration from abroad, and internal migration from the country to cities, transformed what had been a rural and provincial nation into an urban and international leader. Together with industrialization, the emergence of white-collar professions like medicine, law, and management meant that the United States was no longer a nation of individual producers.

It was against this backdrop in the early twentieth century that the consumer ethic appeared. This ethic was characterized by an emphasis on the individual fulfillment through the purchase of commodities and the quest for the "good life." That good life included plenty of "stuff," but, increasingly, it also included services, often delivered by professionals. It also embraced leisure, travel, education, teaching, and mass-produced entertainment.

The consumer ethic and the political economy that emerged in the twentieth century pushed aside notions of thrift. Spending, not saving, now fueled the economy. Not only was this consumer ethos crucial to personal success but it also became central to a new ideal of citizenship. Buying, rather than saving, would sustain the health of the national economy. Many Americans believed that they had left a world of scarcity behind and that the nation had entered a world of abundance. And it was the role of the government to ensure that purchasing power remained strong. This idea led to the birth of what one scholar has called "pocketbook politics"—citizens' efforts to lobby the federal government to keep access to consumer goods affordable and policymakers' commitment to intervene in the marketplace to that end.[6]

Work, of course, still mattered. But increasingly, Americans were working in order to afford the leisure that wages could buy. Corporations as well reoriented their strategies to promote growth through "new competition." Prosperity—not thrift—was the order of the day, and corporations went to great lengths to ensure that manufacturers, laborers, and retailers worked together to that end. "The basis of American prosperity," New York attorney and banker Orion Howard Cheney put it in 1928,

> is high efficiency, high buying power and a high standard of living. The prosperity of the manufacturer and merchant depends on the prosperity of the wage-earner and the prosperity of the wage-earner depends on that of the manufacturer and merchant. The wheels of American prosperity keep on going at a good speed as long as there is nothing seriously affecting efficiency, buying power or standard of living. . . . The new competition has become an overwhelming influence towards higher efficiency, higher buying power and higher standards of living. In fact, it is probably the most important influence on these factors today.[7]

Not surprisingly, the Great Crash of 1929 and ensuing Depression punctured these notions of security, abundance, and self-fulfillment through leisure and corporate efficiency.

It was the New Deal and World War II that turned the Great Depression from potential death bed to seed bed of the emerging consumer ethic. The most famous New Deal programs—programs like the Public Works Administration (PWA) and the Federal Emergency Relief Administration (FERA)—put government dollars in the pockets of the unemployed. But it was programs like the Federal Housing Administration (FHA), created in 1934, that permanently altered American's relationship to consumption. The FHA and the Federal National Mortgage Association (Fannie Mae) never lent directly to homeowners, but they *did* create a standardized mortgage market. That market tapped private capital for private profit and, in short, turned the home mortgage into a commodity and consumer good all-in-one. The FHA financed more than ten times as many housing units as the PWA. Further, the FHA created a template that expanded tremendously after the New Deal. A standardized housing market encouraged a rush to the suburbs, and with suburban life came consumption.

The architects of the New Deal recognized that workers were also consumers. Like the FHA, the National Labor Relations Act of 1935 organized a new market—the labor market—by providing regulatory protection for industrial and craft unions. And like the FHA, it did so without government expenditures. Labor thus became a crucial part of the New Deal coalition. The spending power of workers was seen as an essential tool in the fight against deflation. FDR was able to broaden his appeal beyond organized labor by framing higher wages as increased purchasing power.

Ironically, there was little purchasing during WWII. Rationing and planned production ensured that steel went into planes and tanks, not automobiles. But after the war, citizens with money would propel a surge in demand for consumer goods once they were produced again. That is because the "Arsenal of Democracy" pumped out arms and materiel at a record pace, fueled by massive deficit spending. It was this government-stimulated demand that finally lifted the nation out of the Great Depression and put money in citizens' pockets.

It wasn't until after WWII that the economic importance of purchasing power was cemented. The centrality of purchasing power was written into law in the Employment Act of 1946, Truman's legislation that set up the Council of Economic Advisors. Although watered down by conservatives, the legislation boldly proclaimed that it was now the federal government's responsibility to promote "maximum employment, production, and purchasing power."[8] While some traditional conservatives continued to warn of the dangers of deficit spending, a large number of corporate executives, and an even larger segment of the American people, embraced Keynesian economics after World War II. More often than not, government stimulus was designed to bolster consumer purchasing power.

With the growing tension between the United States and the Soviet Union after World War II, military leaders added the final element of a full-fledged consumer republic. In NSC-68, the document that outlined an American strategy for confronting and containing Soviet power, the National Security Council endorsed the proposition that the nation had to spend whatever it took to win the Cold War. As the 1950 report put it, "budgetary considerations will need to be subordinated to the stark fact that our independence as a nation may be at stake." What's more, the deficit spending that this would require would be good for the economy. The report proclaimed,

> One of the most significant lessons of our World War II experience was that the American economy, when it operates at a level approaching full efficiency, can provide enormous resources for purposes other than civilian consumption while simultaneously providing a high standard of living.[9]

World War II had shown that the American economy could actually provide *more* butter when it was churning out more guns—whatever the "budgetary considerations." In the Cold War, this would become an even firmer article of faith as the military expanded practices of contracting and using commercial vendors to meet U.S. defense needs—the "Hooverization" of the military that Mark R. Wilson describes in his chapter in this volume.[10]

The experiences of the first half of the twentieth century had created a broad political consensus around using military expenditures to stimulate the overall economy. American presidents soon emerged as key champions and symbols of the consumer ideal. Both Democratic and Republican presidents applauded a "mixed economy" that embraced federal fiscal stimulus for consumption. And all presidents "sold" this

Figure 2.1. Soviet premier Nikita Khrushchev (*center left*) talks with U.S. vice president Richard Nixon during their famous "Kitchen Debate," July 24, 1959. Courtesy of AP Images.

approach to the public. Here is what President Harry S. Truman had to say about the government's role in fostering stimulus in 1950: "The uses of the powers of Government to achieve a higher living standard and a fair deal for all of the people is not statism and it is not socialism. It is part of the American tradition."[11] Eight years later, facing a recession, Dwight D. Eisenhower assured Americans that "millions of citizens making their purchases" could be confident that the federal government would do its part by easing credit, building highways, and accelerating federal spending.[12]

Consumers in chief did not just press for public policies that would stoke consumer demand; they frequently were salesmen for American abundance. And what better way to pitch it than in a model kitchen in the Soviet Union? That was the scene of Richard M. Nixon's (okay, *vice* consumer in chief) famous exchange with Soviet premier Nikita Khrushchev in July 1959. When Khrushchev boasted to Nixon that the Soviet Union would soon surpass U.S. achievements, Nixon noted, "There are some instances where you may be ahead of us—for example in the development of the thrust of your rockets for the investigation of outer space. There may be some instances, for example, color television, where we're ahead of you."[13]

For Nixon, the kitchen debate was about using the friendly competition over consumer goods to open up a free exchange. But make no mistake about it: ultimately, selling color TVs and all-electric kitchens was an even higher-stakes game than that. As Khrushchev well understood, consumption was key to winning the hearts and minds of the Third World. Nixon's reference to "booster rockets" was really a reference to Sputnik. The Soviet launch of a satellite in 1957 had captured the world's attention. In the all-out race between two competing ideologies, Nixon was banking on the American way of life. Built around consumer goods and the comfortable life these products created, winning the war to demonstrate superiority in the quality of life race with the Soviet Union would capture the loyalties of neutral nations around the world. Cold War presidents of both parties would take an active role in ensuring that the American model of capitalism succeeded abroad by making sure that companies could grow globally, as Gavin Benke's and Bartow Elmore's chapters in this collection demonstrate.[14]

In 1964, President Lyndon Johnson called for Americans to embrace the "Great Society." The phrase Great Society is usually associated with another iconic phrase, "the War on Poverty," which Johnson launched a few months earlier. What is often forgotten is that Johnson's Great Society focused first on improving the quality of life for those who were already in the middle class. Johnson was no historian, but he too put his finger on one of the great pivots within the century of consumption.

Johnson divided the century into two halves. Speaking in 1964, Johnson stated that the past fifty years had created "an order of plenty." The next half a century demanded that U.S. citizens move beyond this stage, to "enrich and elevate our national life" and to "advance the quality of American Civilization." Without attaching a name to it, Johnson had just categorized the shift from an era of ever-expanding consumer goods to a greater emphasis on services. The Great Society that Johnson envisioned was one that fulfilled man's desire for beauty and his "hunger for community." It would be a place where he could "renew contact with nature." The Great Society would even address loneliness, boredom, and indifference. In short, the Great Society would ease the shift from consuming goods to consuming services, like education and travel. For instance, schools would prepare students to "enjoy their hours of leisure as well as their hours of labor."[15]

Consumers in chief were not just dreamers; they were also enforcers. Their key role in this regard was to ensure that prices did not get out of control. On August 15, 1971, Richard Nixon took to the airwaves in a presidential address to announce a ninety-day freeze on prices and wages designed "break the vicious circle of spiraling prices and costs."[16] Nixon stressed that the freeze was necessary medicine to keep inflation from sapping the consumer economy. "To put the strong, vigorous American economy into a permanent straitjacket would . . . stifle the expansion of our free enterprise system," he reasoned. More importantly, the price controls would not be accompanied by a government bureaucracy that could dampen capitalism's energy. Instead, the United States would rely upon "workers, employers, consumers" to make sure the freeze achieved its goal of boosting consumerism in the long run. Nixon's address confirmed that by the 1970s, consumers had become part of the trinity of American growth. Three years later, Gerald Ford echoed Nixon when he called on the congress to "whip inflation now."[17] The arc created by presidents as price enforcers bent strongly toward using the president's rhetorical powers and media coverage of the presidency to dampen inflation, and away from legislative and bureaucratic control. Presidents after the 1960s were at pains to demonstrate that they could advance consumerism in ways that did not impede the alluring power of the market—even as, as Brent Cebul argues in his chapter in this volume, they worked behind the scenes to sustain and protect those markets.[18]

In the epoch of mass consumption, it was rare to see a president challenge the notion that the nation's objective should be ever-expanding growth, usually expressed by the consumption of goods and services. But then again, Jimmy Carter was nothing if not rare. Carter is perhaps the only post-WWII president to refuse to play the role of consumer in chief. Jimmy Carter rose to power in the post-Vietnam and post-Watergate era, and his presidential campaign challenged the establishment. He even carried his own coat bag while campaigning. Though Carter was governor of Georgia, he pitched himself as an unknown. Nothing encapsulated his outsider status better than his appearance on *What's My Line?* in 1973, when contestants guessed futilely for seven rounds before finally identifying Carter as a sitting governor.

Carter imbibed a part of the counterculture that questioned the fundamental elements of materialism. In the early 1970s, even large corporations worked hard to wrap the consumer products they produced in a zeitgeist that embraced countercultural symbols, including those that questioned unbridled materialism. Jimmy Carter was the 7 Up of consumers in chief—an "un-cola" who tried to stay hip while simultaneously increasing his market share. But Carter went well past this superficial adaptation to the counterculture. In what became known as the "malaise" speech, a televised address to the nation on July 15, 1979, the president grappled with the question of what was wrong with America. One of the answers he offered was an obsession with material goods. Too many Americans, Carter preached,

> now tend to worship self-indulgence and consumption. Human identity is no longer defined by what one does, but by what one owns. But we've discovered that owning things and consuming things does not satisfy our longing for meaning. We've learned that piling up material goods cannot fill the emptiness of lives which have no confidence or purpose.[19]

President Carter was calling for a return to a modern-day version of the nineteenth-century producer ethos. In his chapter for this collection, Sean H. Vanatta highlights Carter's attempts to rein in American's rising proclivity for spending on credit, fearing that its negative effects on the economy and the nation's moral character.[20]

The American people rejected Carter's appeal, and in the 1980s they doubled down on consumption. And what better consumer in chief to sell that idea to the American people than Ronald W. Reagan, who had made the conversion from movie actor to politics by serving as a spokesperson for General Electric in the 1950s. As a GE shill, Reagan traveled across the country to meet and speak to thousands of the company's employees. Drawing on the model of labor relations developed at GE, Reagan portrayed the company as fulfilling a responsibility to satisfy a broader set of employee needs beyond simple labor—indeed, including their role as consumers in a commercial economy.[21] But Reagan was also a public spokesperson, appearing in GE advertisements and infomercials to sell the superiority of GE consumer products to the buying public. One such TV spot looked in on a meal with the Reagan family, which marveled at

Figure 2.2. Television image of President Jimmy Carter delivering his "Crisis of Confidence" speech, July 15, 1979. The speech was quickly dubbed the "malaise" speech. Courtesy of AP Images/Dale G. Young.

how their GE toaster, percolator, and appliances were helping them to "live better electrically."[22]

In the 1950s, Reagan was selling the consumer side of GE's products—not their military R&D. As president, however, Reagan was determined to restore the strength of the military through increased defense spending. "Isn't it smart to be as strong as the bear?" Reagan's famous 1984 campaign ad asked, alluding to the Soviet Union. This wasn't just beltway politics. Reagan's rhetoric about increasing the defense budget was successful in part because it tapped into a consumer culture that reflected themes of patriotism and American power. The 1984 Olympics, in particular, became a time for advertisers to embed red, white, and blue in every purchase—and every sip of beer. In a 1984 commercial that seemed to perfectly capture Reagan's America, a factory worker—"Mike Prescott"—gets off work and heads to the local bar to watch the Olympics with his fellow laborers. These guys are the working-class Democrats who voted for Reagan,

Figure 2.3. Ronald Reagan as poster child for living better electronically, October 18, 1958. Courtesy of the Museum of Innovation and Science.

though, notably, in spite of the hard hats (yes, they wear them at the bar), we only see them on the job for about four seconds of the ad. "I've never been much of a flag waver," Prescott narrates, "maybe 'cause I never grew up in a depression or went to war, like my dad." But at the bar, surrounded by fellow workers, he muses wistfully as he watches U.S. Olympic runners going for the gold, Budweiser in hand: "There's something about seeing the Olympics; gets you thinkin' those guys out there: that's America." The message was clear: it was consuming, patriotic-style, that would make America strong again. In the Reagan years, this Bud was for consumers.

If Reagan reflected the culture's peak consumption in the 1980s, his successors demonstrated that the president's personal prowess at consumption—or lack of it—mattered too. President George H. W. Bush led the strongly pro-growth, consumption-oriented Republican coalition. But when it came to modeling consumption, Bush dropped the ball. In a now infamous—and contested—episode, Bush looked mystified by the working of a common grocery store scanner showcased at the at the National Grocers Association convention. Whether or not he was actually stupefied or just the victim of an unfortunate photo, the image of Bush looking out of place in the supermarket resonated with many Americans for whom shopping for groceries was a pillar of life.

Bill Clinton led a coalition of Democrats that was more ambivalent about unbridled growth and consumption. But that did not prevent Clinton from going further than any president before him when it came to revealing personal consumption preferences. In April 1994, appearing before an MTV town hall meeting called "Enough is Enough," the president was asked, "Boxers or briefs?" His sheepish answer—"usually briefs"—was more than a scandalous politics-meets-pop culture moment.[23] It lays bare the pretense that a new generation of voters saw the president not just as a leader of the free world but also as a consumer in presidential clothing.

Presidents and presidential candidates now frequently appear on late-night television programs, Internet shows, podcasts—and even Reddit discussions. With the rise of a service economy, and with entertainment a crucial part of the service economy, we may be entering an era in which the consumer in chief must also be an entertainer in chief. Donald Trump certainly hopes so.

It is easy to scoff at this. But for much of the nineteenth century, when the producer ethic reigned, people were defined by what they produced, where they worshiped, and their race and ethnicity. Simultaneously, politics was a major form of entertainment. Of course, presidents did not even actively campaign then; it was the political parties that were in charge of entertainment. Although we are not about to accept Jimmy Carter's plea to reject material goods and services in favor of thrift and moderation, I do think that we may be returning to an era when one of the key tasks of the president is entertaining the masses. It is worth noting that when politics was the major form of mass entertainment in the nineteenth century, voter participation was sky high. Most historians would agree that attracting more voters to the election store would be a good thing. To find out whether such voters have selected wisely or simply opted for the most attractive packaging remains to be seen. We can be certain, however, that presidents were powerful agents in connecting capitalism and consumption.

Notes

Author's note: This chapter was adapted from a lecture given at a symposium, "The President and American Capitalism since 1945," sponsored by Florida Atlantic University. I would like to thank Evan D. McCormick for his research assistance and video expertise in preparing that lecture and for his editorial work in converting the lecture into this chapter. I would also like to thank Saladin Ambar, Katie Brownell, Brent Cebul, Christy Chapin, Bart Elmore, David Freund, Beverly Gage, David Greenberg, Louis Hyman, Margaret O'Mara, Julia Ott, Laura Phillips, Louis Hyman, and Bruce Schulman for their suggestions that I have drawn upon for both the lecture and the chapter. Miller Center Scrips librarian Sheila Blackford was extraordinarily helpful in procuring permission for the images used in this chapter. Roger Biles was a generous and skillful editor. Stephen Engel and Mark H. Rose were the intellectual and logistical forces behind the entire endeavor. I am grateful for their wise counsel throughout.

1. Beverly Gage, *The Day Wall Street Exploded: A Story of America in Its First Age of Terror* (New York: Oxford University Press, 2009), 1–2.

2. As quoted in Gage, *Day Wall Street Exploded*, 164.

3. "Market Strong as Wall St. Returns to Routine Work," *New York Tribune*, September 18, 1920. Beverly Gage generously shared her copy of this article with me.

4. "At O'Hare, President Says 'Get On Board': Remarks by the President to Airline Employees O'Hare International Airport, September 27, 2001," White House Archive website, http://georgewbush-whitehouse.archives.gov/news/releases/2001/09/20010927-1.html.

5. I am indebted to Liz Cohen's conception of a "consumer republic" in coining this term.

6. See Meg Jacobs, *Pocketbook Politics: Economic Citizenship in Twentieth-Century America* (Princeton, NJ: Princeton University Press, 2005), 1–2, 6; Lizabeth Cohen, *A Consumers' Republic: The Politics of Mass Consumption in Postwar America* (New York: Vintage, 2003); William Leach, *Land of Desire: Merchants, Power and the Rise of a New American Culture* (New York: Pantheon Books, 1993); Louis Hyman, *Debtor Nation: The History of America in Red Ink* (Princeton, NJ: Princeton University Press, 2011); Roland Marchand, *Advertising the American Dream: Making Way for Modernity, 1920–1940* (Berkeley: University of California Press, 1985); and Warren Susman, *Culture As History: The Transformation of American Society in the Twentieth Century* (New York: Pantheon Books, 1984).

7. Orion H. Cheney, "Keeping Up with the New Competition," *Chamber Records*, box 12, May 7, 1928, 195–96, as cited in Laura Dickson Phillips, "The American Fair Trade Controversy: Law and Economics in Transition, 1890–1940" (PhD diss., University of Virginia, 2011), 123.

8. Employment Act of 1946, Pub. L. 79–304, Ch. 33, 60 Stat. 23 (1946).

9. "A Report to the National Security Council—NSC 68," April 12, 1950, President's Secretary's File, Truman Papers, Truman Library website, https://www.trumanlibrary.org/whistlestop/study_collections/coldwar/documents/pdf/10-1.pdf.

10. See Mark R. Wilson, "Presidents, the Military-Industrial Complex, and the Ascendant Politics of 'Free Enterprise,'" in this volume. On butter and guns after World War II, see Robert M. Collins, *More: The Politics of Economic Growth in Postwar America* (New York: Oxford University Press, 2000).

11. Truman, as quoted in Cohen, *Consumers' Republic*, 119.

12. Eisenhower, as quoted in Cohen, *Consumers' Republic*, 119.

13. "The Kitchen Debate—Transcript," July 24, 1959, Central Intelligence Agency FOIA website, http://www.foia.cia.gov/sites/default/files/document_conversions/16/1959-07-24.pdf.

14. See Gavin Benke, "'The Follow-Through is the Key,'" and Bartow Elmore, "Ecological Imperialism Revisited," both in this volume.

15. Lyndon B. Johnson, commencement address, University of Michigan, May 22, 1964, PBS.com, http://www.pbs.org/wgbh/americanexperience/features/primary-resources/lbj-michigan/.

16. Richard Nixon, "Address to the Nation Outlining a New Economic Policy: 'The Challenge of Peace,'" August 15, 1971, American Presidency Project, http://www.presidency.ucsb.edu/ws/?pid=3115.

17. Gerald R. Ford: "Address to a Joint Session of the Congress on the Economy," October 8, 1974, American Presidency Project, http://www.presidency.ucsb.edu/ws/?pid=4434.

18. See Brent Cebul, "The Antigovernment Impulse," in this volume.

19. Jimmy Carter, "Address to the Nation on Energy and National Goals: 'The Malaise Speech,'" July 15, 1979, American Presidency Project, http://www.presidency.ucsb.edu/ws/?pid=32596.

20. See Sean H. Vanatta, "Executive Stewardship of America's Credit Card Economy," in this volume.

21. Thomas W. Evans, *The Education of Ronald Reagan: The General Electric Years and the Untold Story of His Conversion to Conservatism* (New York: Columbia University Press, 2006), 48–53.

22. "Live Better Electrically," General Electric Advertisement, 1957, https://www.youtube.com/watch?v=Z5KEu5WvdnE, accessed May 2, 2017.

23. William J. Clinton, "Interview on MTV's 'Enough is Enough' Forum," April 19, 1994, American Presidency Project, http://www.presidency.ucsb.edu/ws/?pid=49995.

PART I

PATTERNS AND POLITICS

3

Capitalism on the Campaign Trail

MARGARET O'MARA

Bashing the capitalist class has been an enduringly popular sport in modern American presidential campaigning. Dislike of bigness—big monarchies, big manufacturing, big government—has been a theme in national politics ever since the days of Jeffersonian agrarians and Hamiltonian federalists, but the rise of industrial capitalism in the late nineteenth century took the rhetoric into overdrive. Republican Teddy Roosevelt staked his claim as the progressive standard-bearer of 1912 by calling out "a small class of enormously wealthy and economically powerful men, whose chief object is to hold and increase their power." His Democratic cousin Franklin sounded a similar theme as he fought for reelection in 1936, declaring, "Government by organized money is just as dangerous as Government by organized mob." Amid the cornfields of Iowa in 1948, another embattled incumbent, Harry S. Truman, derided the "gluttons of privilege" on Wall Street.[1]

Even more ostensibly business-friendly leaders joined in the game. "I am no millionaire," Dwight D. Eisenhower impishly remarked to the moderator of a 1956 campaign broadcast, "so we are trying to keep on the side of keeping those boys from bossing us." The throwaway line won warm applause from the studio audience. And it retained its potency four decades later. "For more than a decade our government has been rigged in favor of the rich and special interests," Bill Clinton declared in 1992. It was time, he said, to make "the rich pay their fair share." As America rounded the corner into the twenty-first century, both the lifelong politician Al Gore in 2000 and the millionaire trial lawyer John Edwards in 2004 thundered about "the people versus the powerful."[2]

Yet at the same time, American presidential candidates have made it a point to show off their *own* business bona fides whenever they could.

When "the Great Engineer" Herbert Hoover first ran for president in 1928, his campaign literature made much of his huge success in the mining industry, as well as how he put that managerial sensibility to work in running giant government operations like the U.S. Food Administration and the Commerce Department. Truman distinguished himself as the first small businessman to occupy the Oval Office, and he and his supporters invoked these modest entrepreneurial beginnings throughout the tough reelection fight of 1948. Eisenhower was a soldier, but many of his closest friends were CEOs, notably IBM's Tom Watson Sr., who finagled Eisenhower a postwar gig as president of Columbia University to give him a platform from which to run for office. It wasn't the executive suite, but it was close.[3]

In the post-Watergate, post–oil shock era of the late 1970s and beyond, both strains of rhetoric endured, but with a twist. The greedy oligarchs now had a villainous companion: the federal government, which had now grown to a size of remorseless bigness, collecting taxes and imposing devilish regulations that unfairly burdened virtuous businesspeople and hard-working families. "You are the forgotten Americans," Jimmy Carter told a group of small businessmen as he stumped in 1976, lamenting "the red tape and paperwork imposed on [their] time and overhead by this Republican Administration." Although he had spent the better part of two decades either holding elected office or running for it, Carter ran aggressively as a small businessman—a farmer and a manager—and promised "tight businesslike management" of government if he were elected. Ronald Reagan hadn't been a businessman either, yet he didn't hesitate to wax poetic about entrepreneurs as "the forgotten heroes of America" and promised to "set you free to do what you do best." Government contracts had made presidential candidate Ross Perot a billionaire, but they didn't keep him from railing against bureaucratic excess and assuring voters that he could "make government run like a business" in 1992. The next business type to run as a major-party nominee, Mitt Romney, made a nearly identical promise in 2012.[4]

Yet as would-be presidential candidate New York governor Mario Cuomo once said, "you campaign in poetry; you govern in prose." After Inauguration Day, it became harder to push out the plutocrats and to shift the governmental scales to favor the small over the big, and the entrepreneurial over the corporate. Government isn't a business, and it balks at attempts to run it like one. And because every president has a

Congress, stories of governance are, by necessity, ones of compromise and contingency. No matter how large a president's electoral mandate, the high-flying rhetoric of the campaign trail quickly and reliably comes down to earth, morphing and muting as it translates into actual policy.

A large and dynamic body of academic and popular work on the role of capitalist interests and issues in American politics focuses chiefly on governance and actual policymaking—the laws politicians make once they get to office, rather than the promises they make while running for it. Separately, there is the robust and rollicking literature on the elections themselves, often focused on the horserace of tactics and tacticians, media and spin, money flowing into coffers and money spent on ads, pollsters, and getting out the vote. But what if we unite the two? What if we ask: does rhetoric about capitalism, and relationships to capital and capitalists on the campaign trail, bear on who wins, who loses, and the possibilities of governance? Does this change over time? What can it reveal about broader patterns of partisan alignment, political communication, and voter sentiment? What can it tell us about the changing relationship of American business to the American presidency since 1945?[5]

With these questions in mind, this chapter examines two elections, both occurring in moments of economic crisis, both won by centrist Southern Democrats: the Carter-Ford race of 1976 and the Bush-Clinton-Perot election of 1992. To distinguish how the business-government dynamic shapes *campaigning* (rather than governing), my focus here is on the challengers—Carter, Clinton, and Perot—and the way they articulated capitalist alternatives to the status quo. Both 1976 and 1992 were "change" elections, in which voters chose self-styled Washington outsiders over embattled incumbents. Both contained an abundance of anticapitalist, antigovernment rhetoric. Business interests nonetheless provided key support, advice, and public endorsement to the populist-leaning outsiders in the race. The stories reveal that there is neither a single "party of business" nor a monolithic "business community" and show the electoral dynamics at work in America's post-1980 turn toward more limited government and more unbounded and entrepreneurial forms of capitalism.

1976: "I owe the people everything."

On December 12, 1974, the day that a little-known southern governor named Jimmy Carter announced he was running for president, the morning papers heaved with glum economic news. The inflation rate stood at over 12 percent, propelled upward by rising food prices, rising oil prices, and the end of the federal wage-price control program. New York City had laid off close to four thousand city employees—teachers, police officers, firefighters, and more—in an effort to hack away at its spiraling budget deficit. The stock market perked up the previous day in the hope that President Gerald R. Ford might reveal some new economic fixes at a meeting of business leaders in Washington that evening. The president dashed those dreams. "The economy is in difficult straits," he told the executives, and "I cannot and will not promise you a sudden change for the better."[6]

Carter said very little about these economic woes in his announcement, however. Instead, he talked about honesty, decency, and the homespun values of rural Georgia. "With the shame of Watergate still with us and our 200th birthday just ahead," Carter declared, "it is time for us to reaffirm and to strengthen our ethical and spiritual and political beliefs." Richard M. Nixon had resigned in disgrace mere months before. Carter's campaign—like those of the many others who jostled for the Democratic Party's nomination that year—put trust, ethics, and political reform front and center. In Campaign '76, as Ben Wattenberg (an advisor to Democratic rival Senator Henry "Scoop" Jackson) observed, "traditional American values" took center stage.[7]

It wasn't only Richard Nixon who had been corrupted by power, Carter argued. The entire federal government had turned into an unresponsive bureaucracy, bound up in red tape, out of touch with the people it served. Both Democrats and Republicans had gotten the country into this mess, and it required an outsider to fix it. Carter's close friend, Georgia banker Bert Lance, put it best: "Jimmy Carter didn't run against Gerry Ford in 1976. He ran against Washington."[8]

The outsider message was particularly effective in setting apart the obscure Georgian from a crowded primary filled with familiar veterans of the Senate and House. These Democrats were similarly fierce in their opposition to Nixon, but could be tone-deaf when it came to Americans' distrust of government altogether. One rival, Birch Bayh of Indiana, placed his political experience front and center, actually running television ads saying, "it takes a good politician to make a good President." Carter played up the contrast. "Of all the speakers here tonight," he often said on the stump, to cheers, "I am the only one who is not a lawyer."[9]

In fact, Carter didn't run as a politician at all but as a peanut farmer and small businessman. Carefully constructed campaign advertising positioned him as "a working man who knows what it is to work with his hands at harvest time." Television spots showed him clad in blue denim, walking through the peanut fields and leaning against a split-rail fence in front of his rustic boyhood home in the tiny town of Plains. The Carter campaign headquarters wasn't in Washington, but in Atlanta, and he played up his southern, rural roots as he traversed the country over the course of his twenty-three-month campaign. In key early states like Iowa, the workingman rhetoric—coupled with Carter's indefatigable campaigning ("no one outworked Jimmy Carter," wrote one biographer)—played especially well. He wrote an outsider's playbook that candidates of both parties have employed ever since.[10]

The press verdict on Jimmy Carter at the time, and that of many historians after, was that his 1976 run was all style and little substance—that he was infuriatingly "fuzzy" and noncommittal on the issues, including economic policy. The improbable victory of this humbly pious southerner seemed to be a proof point that voters cared more about the disgrace of Watergate than the stagflating economy, and a harbinger of the era of social conservatism to come.

However, post-election polls showed that while Watergate certainly was on Carter voters' minds, economic insecurity mattered even more. And in talking about small-town values and the need for a more efficient and friendly federal bureaucracy, Carter was in fact putting forth a distinctly new capitalist worldview on the 1976 campaign trail. Government was necessary and important, argued Carter, but it was beholden to big interests—corporations, labor unions, and its own bureaucratic momentum—and had lost sight of the little guy. Upward mobility had stalled, inflation spiraled, and markets teetered, but in Carter's diagnosis the problems of capitalism stemmed from bureaucratic failure rather than deeper structural imbalances. America needed a president who was the foe of the big and the champion of the small. "I owe the special interests nothing," Carter declared as he launched his fall general-election campaign on the steps of Franklin Roosevelt's vacation retreat in Warm Springs, Georgia. "I owe the people everything."[11]

Such populism showed Carter's political savvy, but it also bore the influence of his experience as a farmer and small-town businessman. He had grown up in a small place where everyone knew one each other; he had governed a southern state where personal connections and family ties had an outsized influence on political life. He had little experience with—or fealty to—the people and places of unionized manufacturing sector whose priorities had propelled Democratic growth liberalism (rising wages, rising government support for the working class and poor, rising purchasing power) since Roosevelt's New Deal. Carter's life experience had been different from that, just as it had been rather different from the peanut-populist mythos put forth in his campaign advertising.

Like so much of the twentieth-century agricultural economy, the Carter farm was more agribusiness than family homestead. Jimmy Carter hadn't labored in the fields since boyhood. In the seventeen years he'd spent actively running the business, he had devoted most of his time to the peanut warehouse that was the hub of the enterprise and the main source of its profits. And like so much of the American business sector overall, the Carter farm and warehouse was not a free-market operation but one intricately bound up in federal programs and Washington politics. Crop subsidies introduced under Franklin Roosevelt continued to make the difference between profit and business failure in the hard and sandy soil of southwest Georgia, as they did in the rest of rural America. While the Carter family did not receive all that many direct subsidies, the peanut farmers who patronized their warehouse certainly did, making the warehouse part of this broader agricultural ecosystem heavily dependent on the farm program for its continued existence.[12]

The farm economy of Carter country was a prime example of how the indirect and privatized nature of U.S. government spending kept Washington, DC's full scope and influence hidden, even to its beneficiaries. In a place like Plains, the only public face of federal agricultural programs was the county extension office, staffed with local personnel who were on a friendly, first-name basis with the men and women they served. Rural people understood that farm subsidies were critical to their regional economy, and they (and their congressional delegations) readily mobilized against any efforts to cut them back. (Gerald Ford earned the eternal outrage of Plains-area folk when his administration proposed trimming peanut subsidies.) But it was hard to connect the taxes they paid to the benefits that were eventually returned back to them through the farm program.[13]

Because of this disconnect, from the subsidy-saturated rural heartland to the defense-contracting capitals of the Sunbelt, voters in 1976 became increasingly responsive to political messages that labeled *other* government programs (many targeted to people and places left out of the New Deal's original bounty) as "welfare." In the 1976 GOP primaries, the hawkish Californian Ronald Reagan tested out this messaging to great success by telling an apocryphal and racially tinged story about a "welfare queen" who was fleecing the system to the tune of one hundred fifty thousand dollars a year. Attacks like this weren't part of Carter's playbook, nor were they compatible with his Christian beliefs, but tax cuts were front and center. The welfare royalty in Carter's book were the wealthy who didn't pay their fair share. "The present tax structure is a disgrace to this country," he asserted in a debate against Ford that fall. "It is a welfare program for the rich."[14]

By that time, Carter's message had propelled him past his many primary rivals and into the Democratic nomination without having to pay much attention to the "special interests" that composed much of the party's base. Such populist independence also became possible because of a changed campaign financing landscape. After the excesses of Watergate, which began as a crime financed by a few deep-pocketed Nixon campaign donors, Congress pushed through the Federal Election Campaign Act in 1975, which transformed the financing of presidential elections. No individual could give more than one thousand dollars to a candidate. No candidate could spend more than ten million dollars during primary season. A federal election fund, raised by ticking off a box on individual tax returns, provided public matching dollars to candidates. Campaigns no longer had the resources for bloated staff, costly direct-mail campaigns, or lavish fundraising dinners. On top of it all, the Democratic National Committee was broke, its resources tapped out by the bruising 1972 campaign and lacking a big-name candidate who could re-energize its traditional donor base. As Morris Dees, Carter's veteran media consultant, sighed, the new reality meant "running a Presidential race on a mayor's race budget."[15]

Campaign finance reform richly rewarded a candidate like Jimmy Carter: frugal by nature, lacking many wealthy friends or connections to traditional donor pools, and willing to do the shoe-leather campaigning necessary to attract many small donors. In the first year of his campaign, he raised seven hundred thousand dollars through donations that averaged about thirty-five dollars apiece, and the small-donor pattern continued into 1976. (In contrast, his rival Scoop Jackson *began* the campaign with a million-dollar war chest.) Even as Carter became the nominee and began to attract the lions of the Democratic financial establishment to his side, money-raising events remained more modest affairs. One New York breakfast fundraiser—whose host committee was a who's who of Democratic power brokers like investment banker and former Treasury secretary Douglas Dillon and super-lawyer and Kennedy/Johnson advisor Cyrus Vance—cost a rather restrained five thousand dollars per person and yielded seventy-five thousand dollars.[16]

New York seances aside, the public mood and reformed campaign finance environments gave the Democrats a nominee with fewer ties to the Dillons, Vances, and their Wall Street kin than the party had seen in several generations. No millionaire patrons lurked in the wings; campaign finance laws had made them obsolete. Carter's closest campaign advisors remained the "Georgia mafia" that had been with him since the start, and this group included fundraisers and financiers as well as strategists. The small cadre of Georgians who had raised the money for Carter to run for governor in 1970 remained around him six years later. Right at the center was a banker from Calhoun, a wide spot in the road on the way from Atlanta to Chattanooga, named Bert Lance.[17]

After winning the White House, Carter placed Lance in the powerful job of federal budget director, also charging him with being the White House's chief liaison to the business community. Having run and won without much counsel from the titans of the Fortune 500, Carter felt that there was little need to build these relationships now; he could simply delegate to a trusted subordinate. While executives initially balked at their lack of access to the Oval Office, Lance proved to be an excellent advocate. He had the president's ear, and his pragmatic sensibility comported well with the president's views. "Jimmy may campaign liberal," Lance remarked at the time, "but he governs conservative."[18]

Barely six weeks had passed since Lance's confirmation to the post, however, when disturbing questions started to swirl about ethical and legal lines he might have crossed as a banker in Georgia. A hungry and skeptical post-Watergate White House press corps was not going to let any potentially shady dealings go on under their noses, especially in an administration of a man who had campaigned on promises of honesty and faith. By the summer, Lance was officially under investigation, and by the fall he had resigned and returned home to Georgia. An official indictment—for making illegal personal loans out of bank assets—came down the following May.[19]

Carter was not the first, or the last, presidential candidate to be embarrassed by crony capitalists in his orbit, and his dilemma underscored the danger of running as an outsider surrounded by lightly vetted, untested confidants from home. The national spotlight could be harsh and unforgiving to those experiencing it for the very first time. And Carter also was not the first or last to realize that a commander in chief eventually needed capitalists in chief on his side, even at the most populist of political moments.

After Lance's exit, at the encouragement of his Treasury secretary, Michael Blumenthal, and longtime Democratic *consigliere* Robert Strauss, Carter started to forge direct relationships with key business leaders. By early 1978, limousines regularly rolled up the White House drive to disgorge their CEO passengers for private meetings with the president. Left out of Carter's newly warm embrace: the small business community that had such high hopes about having one of their own in the White House. "He started off good," bitterly observed James McKevitt of the National Federation of Independent Business, the nation's most influential small-business lobby. "Now things are different with all those big shooters in the Oval Office."[20]

The Carter victory showed that—under certain political conditions—a bad economy didn't necessarily require a candidate to place economic policy front and center, nor propose specific fixes on the campaign trail. The campaign also was able to leverage a reformed campaign finance system to win without the early money and Eastern Establishment support that had propelled candidates to victory in past elections. While a skeptical press corps derided Carter as being "fuzzy" on the issues, his campaign rhetoric influenced elections for many cycles afterward, reframing America's economic problems as something related to dysfunction in government, rather than a manifestation of basic structural and social inequalities. Unlike his Republican successors, however, Carter believed that government could be the solution as well, and that sound, fair, "businesslike management" would stack the deck back in favor of working people and small-scale entrepreneurs.

The peanut capitalism of Jimmy Carter wasn't enough to assuage core Democratic constituencies—African Americans, labor unions, and women—who by 1979 were flocking to a new liberal standard-bearer, Senator Edward M. Kennedy. Kennedy's strong challenge to Carter for the Democratic nomination further weakened a leader already besieged by terrorism abroad and economic crisis at home. The 1980 election wasn't just about values anymore; it was about a financial breakdown that made the core groups of the New Deal coalition less willing to go along with the most economically conservative Democratic president since Woodrow Wilson. It would take another twelve years for a candidate to emerge who could fuse Carter's small-business centrism with a compelling appeal to the men and women at the core of Democratic Party liberalism.

1992: "It's the economy, stupid."

"Who is this guy?" asked *New York Magazine* about Bill Clinton at the start of 1992, three months after the Arkansas governor announced that he would be joining the pack of Democrats vying to unseat President George H. W. Bush. Just like the little-known "Jimmy Who?" of 1976, Clinton hailed from the agricultural South, billed himself as a Washington outsider, and propounded centrist positions that challenged traditional liberal orthodoxy on social welfare, military spending, and taxes and budgeting. Like Carter, he was a shrewd and occasionally ruthless political strategist, possessed an explosive temper, and had a superhuman tolerance for the grind of one-on-one campaigning. Powerfully charismatic and able to remember names and personal details of nearly every person he encountered, Bill Clinton spent every waking moment and human interaction trying to win votes. To get to the White House, Clinton had to first overcome a crowded Democratic field and then successfully challenge a patrician incumbent whose approval ratings had plummeted along with a sinking economy.[21]

The similarities ended there. The political landscape of 1992 was profoundly different from that of 1976, transformed by twelve years of small-government Republicanism in the White House, the end of the Cold War, and the emergence of a relentless round-the-clock cable news cycle. The Arkansan also was a different kind of candidate—where Carter had been fuzzy, Clinton was a policy wonk, eager to deliver what one bemused editor called "a torrent of information" to anyone who'd listen.[22]

The young governor and the advisors who surrounded him also were painfully aware of the mistakes that Carter—and the two other defeated

Democratic candidates of the 1980s, Walter Mondale and Michael Dukakis—had made in failing to assure voters that they had the right economic answers for a postindustrial era of flat wages, outsourced jobs, and diminished opportunity. Many on Clinton's campaign staff had in fact worked on Dukakis's failed 1988 bid, when aggressive Republican attacks had managed to transform a centrist and generally business-friendly governor into a figure that voters perceived as a dangerously inept, soft-on-crime left-winger. They thus understood how important it was that their candidate not be seen as a "liberal."[23]

The Democrats' financial environment was also quite different from how it was in 1976—both in the nature of the fundraising machine and the people and interests who surrounded the party machinery and in candidates like Clinton. Carter had run without courting the big-business establishment and the Democratic "special interests," a miss that came back to haunt him in 1980. By 1992, however, the Democratic National Committee was under the leadership of Ron Brown. An African American who had worked both on Ted Kennedy's 1980 challenge to Carter and on Jesse Jackson's historic 1984 run for the nomination, but who also had spent two decades as a partner at one of Washington's most prestigious law firms, Brown was uniquely positioned to bring the liberal and centrist interests in the party together. "He instilled the party with a sense of mission . . . that we could elect and would elect a Democratic president in 1992," said Democratic leader David Wilhelm of Brown. "A lot of it was through sheer force of will." No matter the political differences in the party's big tent, everyone had a shared interest in winning this go around, and Brown's machine raised the money to do it.[24]

Although little known outside political circles, Bill Clinton had been a leading voice in the Democratic Leadership Council (DLC), a think tank and policy organization formed in the wake of Mondale's landslide defeat. Composed chiefly of Democrats from suburban and Sunbelt districts who—like Jimmy Carter two decades before—had little loyalty to the old union constituencies or manufacturing industries that had made up the Democrats' New Deal coalition, the DLC put forth a new vision of the government-market relationship that blended liberal ideas about an expansive and energetic federal government with conservative precepts of efficiency, privatization, and state and local autonomy.[25]

Many DLC-ers were of the Baby Boom generation like Clinton or slightly older, "Watergate babies" first elected to Congress in the wake of

Nixon's resignation. Some of them—like Colorado's Gary Hart and Massachusetts's Paul Tsongas—had been such ardent advocates of high-tech industry in the early 1980s that pundits briefly labeled them "Atari Democrats" in a nod to the pioneering Silicon Valley company responsible for the wildly popular game video game *Pong*. They became strong advocates of a national industrial policy akin to the programs that had propelled Japan into the economic stratosphere, encouraging government action that would pour resources and special tax treatment into "sunrise" industries like electronics rather than "sunset" sectors of heavy manufacturing. Some had even come around to supply-side ideas beloved by business-minded Republicans like cuts in the capital gains tax intended, among other things, to encourage investors to put money into high-tech start-ups. "Entrepreneurship is the engine that moves our economy," effused Tsongas in a 1986 tax reform hearing, "and the capital gains differential will help insure that our current and potential entrepreneurs will stay the course."[26]

After Bush's victory over Dukakis in 1988, centrist Democrats had become even more convinced that big-state liberalism would no longer win elections. "Whether the issue is the working poor, racial justice, educational excellence, or national defense," wrote two of the DLC's leading thinkers, William Galston and Elaine Kamarck, in an incendiary electoral postmortem, "the liberal fundamentalist prescription is always the same; pursue the politics of the past. The result, predictably, has been programmatic stagnation and political defeat."[27]

The DLC became the de facto think tank for the Clinton campaign, including supplying its earliest and most senior policy aide, Bruce Reed. A native Idahoan and former Rhodes Scholar (like Clinton), Reed had choirboy looks and a genial manner that belied a whip-smart political mind and a gift for crafting pungent sound bites. Reed's eloquent wordsmithing gave voice to the centrist policy principles of Clinton: an economic program that "put people first," welfare reform that "gave a hand up, not a hand out," and tax policy to reward "working families."[28]

The result was a yet-again-revised Democratic vision of what American capitalism could and should be. Franklin Roosevelt was about ensuring economic security for all, and Jimmy Carter was about cutting red tape in an age of limits. Bill Clinton put forth a mélange of both, designed to appeal to a wide swath of the political spectrum, including the growing bloc of independent voters who professed not to have a preference for either party. Here were expansive government-led initiatives like universal health insurance and job retraining for blue-collar workers thrown out of work by globalization, coupled with promises to move poor people "from welfare rolls to job rolls," to "reinvent" government, boost U.S. business interests with free trade deals, and balance the budget.

The move to the center was not merely a matter of political gamesmanship for either Bill or Hillary Clinton. Although children of the 1960s who had cut their political teeth on the McGovern '72 campaign, they believed in what the DLC crowd called "the third way" between state-centered liberalism and private enterprise. In the mid-1980s in Arkansas, the Clintons had spearheaded the creation of a microfinance bank—designed along the lines of Muhammad Yunus's famed Grameen Bank in Bangladesh—that gave small-business loans to the rural poor (more than half of whom were women and over 80 percent of whom were African American). Both at the state level and nationally, Bill Clinton had pushed for welfare reforms that would bring poor and minority mothers into the paid workforce, and had headed up the National Governors' Association lobbying push for a national welfare reform bill in 1991. He was a champion of "empowerment zones," a brainchild of business-minded Republicans, which used government incentives and tax breaks to encourage private investment in inner cities. Grassroots capitalism was the way out of poverty, argued Clinton as he hit the campaign trail, declaring, "We need to create a small-business entrepreneurial economy in every underclass urban area and rural area in the country."[29]

The budget-balancing, market-attuned Clinton economic platform also reflected his close and mutually admiring relationship with a small group of Wall Street financiers, who became key advisors and donors during the campaign and high-level appointees in his first term. Democrats still were a minority on the Street, and they were gun-shy about backing the wrong candidate. Warned one industry insider, "Wall Street isn't into lost causes." At first, it seemed like the most lost cause of all was Bill Clinton, whose campaign was nearly sunk by various scandals as he slogged through the first primaries of the year. Yet the Arkansas governor drew some ardent and influential fans by early spring. Leading the pack were Roger Altman, a rangy, politically influential investment banker, and Robert Rubin, a quiet power broker who later became Clinton's economic advisor and the architect of a federal stimulus and balanced-budget plan to revive the moribund Bush-era economy. Altman, Rubin, and other Wall Street supporters saw Clinton as someone who was like them: resilient, smart, risk-taking. Said one, "I tell people, if Clinton worked here, he would be a star."[30]

No sooner had Clinton begun to get traction in the Democratic primaries, however, than another challenger emerged: Texas computer-services magnate H. Ross Perot. His independent candidacy would disrupt the 1992 race more than any other third-party run since Teddy Roosevelt's in 1912. Ross Perot had always been a maverick, and nearly everything about his presidential bid went against the rules of modern campaigning. He announced his candidacy on Larry King's CNN talk show. He hired two top strategists—one Republican and one Democrat. The Dem was none other than Jimmy Carter's ultimate Georgia loyalist and right-hand man, Hamilton Jordan. Proclaiming himself free of the influence of special interests, Perot self-financed his campaign and relied on an ardent volunteer grassroots army rather than highly paid campaign consultants. Later in the campaign, instead of glossy thirty-second ads, he bought thirty-minute blocks of network time for infomercials at which he sat behind a desk armed with nothing but some charts on poster board and a wooden pointer.[31]

Although Perot's net worth exceeded that of nearly anyone who'd ever run for the White House, his folksy demeanor appealed mightily to a disconsolate mid-American electorate who saw both major parties as out-of-touch and elitist. "I suppose Mr. Perot may be a good ol' boy," said one voter, "but he went out and made his own money, started from nothing. God bless him. Bush was born into money." Noted a cable-TV talking head, "Everybody thinks that [Perot] agrees with them. Moderates think he's moderate; liberals think he's liberal; conservatives think he's conservative."[32]

By the start of the summer, polls were showing a three-way split between Perot, Clinton, and Bush. The iconoclastic populism of Perot had become such a force in the election that both of the major-party candidates had to respond in some way. The Bush campaign was staffed with people who knew Perot from Texas and from earlier Republican administrations and considered him to be a flash-in-the-pan kook. If anything, they reasoned, H. Ross Perot would take votes away from the other "change" candidate, Bill Clinton, helping Bush keep his job. They were dead wrong.

Perhaps more than any other candidate in modern memory, Perot's campaign showcased the rather schizophrenic way in which voters understood the capitalist system and the relationship of their government and their political leaders to it. Here was a man who one liberal commentator had quite accurately labeled "the world's first welfare billionaire" for building his company through lucrative public Medicare and Medicaid contracts but who had also long been an outspoken foe of big government and self-styled champion of private enterprise. Just like the farmers of peanut country and the defense contractors of Reagan's California, Perot could pretend he was self-made because the public spending that made his fortune was indirect and competitively awarded. Here also was a candidate who, like Jimmy Carter and Ronald Reagan before him, gained credibility in many voters' eyes because he *lacked* Washington experience. Two decades after Vietnam and Watergate shattered Americans' faith in professional politicians, being a corporate CEO had become a fine (even desirable) prerequisite for becoming U.S. president.[33]

Yet Perot's run also showed how ill-suited a maverick businessman could be for the slickly polished business of modern presidential politics. Once he started to surge in the polls, the press corps started to take him seriously, and they started asking much harder questions. The jug-eared Texan wilted under the pressure. As Clinton secured the Democratic nomination and sailed into a glorious, made-for-TV convention, Perot abruptly announced he was dropping out. Although he later reentered in the fall campaign, and managed to gather a larger chunk of popular votes than any other third-party contender in eighty years, Perot had missed his opportunity for victory.

Only one "change" candidate was left, and the Democratic nominee doubled-down on an outsider message that was targeted straight at America's independent voters. While the Bush campaign remained in Washington, Clinton consolidated campaign operations in Little Rock. The beating heart of his headquarters was a room on the third floor that housed all of the campaign's key policy and communications strategists. Clinton's wife, Hillary, gave it a name: "the War Room." A smudgy scrawl on a whiteboard hanging in the middle of the room reminded everyone of the key messages of the campaign. Rule #1: "Change vs. more of the same." Rule #2: "It's the economy, stupid."[34]

While some themes and trends apparent in 1992 were perennial—attacks on big business and big government, defense of the hard-working entrepreneurs and average American taxpayer—others reflected the great changes afoot in the American economy, and presaged bigger shifts to come. The influence of a new generation of Wall Streeters on the Democratic Party was one difference, as was the mainstream influence of people like Ron Brown. Racial minorities, women, and others who had been "interest groups" in 1976 were now quite firmly at the center of the political establishment by 1992. The evangelicals Carter had courted were in the GOP column; the social liberals were nearly all Democrats.

Another sign of change came very late in the campaign, in a moment that didn't have much impact on the Electoral College but that was a harbinger of a new, influential business constituency migrating to the Democratic column. In the years since Jimmy Carter's election, personal computers had wrought an economic, cultural, and communications revolution that ultimately would prove as consequential as the end of the Cold War. Along with it, the computer hardware and software companies in Northern California's Silicon Valley had become billion-dollar enterprises, and the men who ran them became new-style icons of American capitalism. The first generation of Silicon Valley types had generally stayed out of politics; when they did, they generally supported Republicans.[35]

Democrats in the Valley of the early 1990s remained few and far between, but they included some well-connected people. Chief among them was the dapper king of high-tech public relations, Regis McKenna, who had been the wizard behind the curtain of Apple's friendly, countercultural advertising and marketing campaigns of the late 1970s and early 1980s. Apple happened to be home to another leading Democrat, David Barram, the company's vice president for policy and public affairs. Barram had been trying to get the attention of Democratic lawmakers since the 1970s; he had mailed helpful missives into the Carter White House about how the president might engage the tech industry, and never got a reply. McKenna also had tried political matchmaking before, when "Atari Democrat" Gary Hart ran for president in 1984, but the relationship didn't outlast Hart's candidacy.[36]

In Bill Clinton, McKenna and Barram saw a new-style politician to whom Silicon Valley techies could relate. He was a Baby Boomer, a social liberal, and a fiscal conservative. While he didn't know much about technology, he had an eagerness and appreciation for what the Valley was doing that other politicians had lacked. And he'd chosen longtime high-tech advocate Al Gore as his running mate. What's more, George H. W. Bush had been generally uninterested in the tech community and had done little to woo its increasingly wealthy and powerful executives. Silicon Valley believed it was changing the world, and the Bush White House didn't seem to notice.

In the spring of 1992, Barram took a sabbatical from Apple to devote his full-time energies toward electing Bill Clinton, who in turn asked him to take the lead on developing a technology policy for the campaign. By the fall, McKenna had joined Barram in an effort to convince the industry's top CEOs—Democrat, Republican, and independent—to give a collective public endorsement of the Arkansas governor. The result was a headline-making event in late October 1992 with an all-star lineup of technology executives, including lifelong GOP voter John Sculley, the chairman of Apple. "I am still a Republican," said Sculley, "but I am voting for Bill Clinton because I don't believe America's industries can survive four more years of President Bush."[37]

The endorsement event came too late in the campaign season to make a difference, even though it had enough symbolic import to prompt the Bush team to scramble together a similar showcase with the Valley's most stalwart Republican guard. But it created an alliance between the Clinton Democrats and the titans of the new economy that strengthened over the dot-com era and into the twenty-first century. By the time Barack Obama and Hillary Clinton became the party's national standard-bearers, Silicon Valley was reliably Democratic in its voting patterns, a potent source for Democratic fundraising, and home to individuals and groups using high-tech platforms to effect left-leaning political change.

Not coincidentally, this new face of American capitalism presented itself as quite different from the old. Instead of corporate plutocrats, there were plucky entrepreneurs. Instead of family connections and old money launching careers, success came from engineering smarts and hard work. That was the mythos, at least; the reality was far less meritocratic and serendipitous. But for politicians looking for a bright and hopeful symbol of what American capitalism could accomplish, the startup kids and venture-capital cowboys of Silicon Valley were the best kind of political allies you could get.

The Business of Politics, the Politics of Business

In the modern era, the rhetoric and policy of capitalism and capitalist interests on the campaign trail revealed a shifting of blame and responsibility. In the first third of the twentieth century, corporate capitalism was the problem, and government was the solution. The American state became understood as the proper tool to constrain and properly regulate capitalism so that the system could work more fairly, and more predictably. In the middle third, the presence of the state was a given. While fractious rhetoric continued, government and large-corporate actors could have symbiotic and mutually constitutive interests in growing the defense complex, building infrastructure, advancing upward mobility, and more. In the last third of the century, government itself became the problem, an out-of-control octopus that was strangling free enterprise and burdening the noblest kinds of capitalists: small-business owners, entrepreneurs, and ordinary working people. The embrace of this anti-bureaucratic rhetoric on the campaign trail by Democratic presidential candidates as well as their GOP rivals turned it from being a partisan attack to becoming an article of faith. Even the most liberal candidates emerging in the decades since, such as left-populist Vermonters Howard Dean and Bernie Sanders, coupled bold plans for new government programs with a sharp critique of government dysfunction and corruption by special interests.

The new attitude toward big government on both left and right comported with the ways the economy itself was changing. Earlier candidates had railed against industrial bigness, but by the beginning of the twenty-first century many formerly big things had fractured and fragmented dramatically. A mass media dominated by network TV and daily newspapers had shattered into a thousand-headed cacophony of websites and blogs, cable punditry and talk-radio partisanship, and tweets and posts and Ask-Me-Anythings. Corporations scattered offices and manufacturing facilities across the planet, outsourcing and subcontracting in ways that obscured the size and environmental impact of their work, while their snazzy U.S.-based headquarters created playful, amenity-rich environments dotted with climbing walls and Ping-Pong tables. The only big and lumbering thing left seemed to be the federal government itself.

Since the founding days of the republic, American presidential campaigning has been a business of heat and light, right and wrong, us versus them, soaring rhetoric and piercing attacks. There is not much room in a thirty-second campaign ad or stump-speech sound bite to convey the complicated relationship between government and markets that contours and dictates what a president can do once she or he reaches the Oval Office. Likewise, campaign appeals to the mass of voters can convey a populist sensibility starkly at odds with the way campaigns actually operate—with wealthy and influential people who are the counselors, mentors, and financial supporters for campaigns that can cost hundreds of millions of dollars. While the hyperspeed of election season has little in common with the more pedestrian business of governing, it nonetheless is a revealing window into the distinctive way public and private interact with, and depend upon, one another in American life, past and present.

Notes

1. Theodore Roosevelt, Speech at Osowatamie, Kansas; Franklin Roosevelt, Speech at Madison Square Garden, October 31, 1936; Harry S. Truman, "Address at Dexter, Iowa, on the Occasion of the National Plowing Match," September 18, 1948. All presidential speeches cited here are found online at the American Presidency Project, http://presidency.ucsb.edu. As political scientist Mark A. Smith observes, "within American political discourse, one can invoke a jaundiced view of virtually any institution simply by labeling it 'big.'" (Smith, *American Business and Political Power: Public Opinion, Elections, and Democracy* [Chicago: University of Chicago Press, 2000]).

2. Dwight D. Eisenhower, "Television Broadcast: 'The People Ask the President,'" October 12, 1956; Bill Clinton, "Putting People First"; Philip James, "The People versus the Powerful," *Guardian*, February 5, 2004, https://perma.cc/K836-9HUD.

3. On the political rhetoric of business expertise, see Kim McQuaid, *Uneasy Partners: Big Business in American Politics, 1945–1990* (Baltimore: Johns Hopkins University Press, 1994).

4. "Carter Scores Officials' 'Cheap Shots' at Business," *Los Angeles Times*, September 13, 1976; Ronald Reagan, "Remarks at a White House Briefing on the State of Small Business," March 1, 1982; H. Ross Perot, *United We Stand: How We Can Take Back our Country*, quoted in Sean Wilentz, "Pox Populi," *New Republic*, August 8, 1993.

5. Both are large and growing literatures. On the business-government relationship, in addition to the other chapters in this volume see Benjamin C. Waterhouse, *Lobbying America: The Politics of Business from Nixon to NAFTA* (Princeton, NJ: Princeton University Press, 2014); Kim Phillips-Fein and Julian E. Zelizer, eds., *What's Good for Business: Business and American Politics since World War II* (New York: Oxford University Press, 2012); Elizabeth Popp Berman and Nicholas Pagnucco, "Economic Ideas and the Political Process: Debating Tax Cuts in the U.S. House of Representatives, 1962–1981," *Politics & Society* 38, no. 3 (2010): 347–72; Kim Phillips-Fein, *Invisible Hands: The Making of the Conservative Movement from the New Deal to Reagan* (New York: W. W. Norton, 2009); Cathie Jo Martin, *Stuck in Neutral: Business and the Politics of Human Capital Investment Policy* (Princeton, NJ: Princeton University Press, 2000); and Richard L. Hall and Frank W. Wayman, "Buying Time: Moneyed Interests and the Mobilization of Bias in Congressional Committees," *American Political Science Review* 84, no. 3 (September 1990): 797–820. On post-1945 American presidential elections, some recently published examples include Michael Cohen, *American Maelstrom: The 1968 Election and the Politics of Division* (New York: Oxford University Press, 2016); Margaret O'Mara, *Pivotal*

Tuesdays: Four Elections That Shaped the Twentieth Century (Philadelphia: University of Pennsylvania Press, 2015); David Pietrusza, *1948: Harry Truman's Improbable Victory and the Year That Transformed America's Role in the World* (New York: Union Square Press, 2011); William Rorabaugh, *The Real Making of the President: Kennedy, Nixon, and the 1960 Election* (Lawrence: University Press of Kansas, 2009); and Theodore Rosenof, *Realignment: The Theory That Changed the Way We Think about American Politics* (New York: Rowman & Littlefield, 2003). On "spin" and the public image of the president in particular, see David Greenberg, *Republic of Spin: An Inside History of the American Presidency* (New York: Simon & Schuster, 2015).

6. Gerald R. Ford, "Remarks at a Meeting of the Business Council," December 11, 1974; Fred Ferretti, "City, in Dismissing 3,275, Includes 1,100 in Schools, 900 in Uniform," *New York Times*, December 11, 1974; Alan S. Blinder, "The Anatomy of Double-Digit Inflation in the 1970s," in *Inflation: Causes and Effects*, ed. Robert E. Hall (Chicago: University of Chicago Press, 1982), 261–82.

7. Jimmy Carter, Speech at the National Press Club, December 12, 1974, in *Addresses of Jimmy Carter, Governor of Georgia, 1971–1975*, compiled by Frank Daniel (Atlanta: Georgia Department of Archives and History, 1975), 286; Jonathan Moore and Janet Fraser, *Campaign for President: The Managers Look at 1976* (Cambridge, MA: Ballinger, 1977), 154.

8. Bert Lance, *The Truth of the Matter: My Life in and out of Politics* (New York: Summit Books, 1991), 61. Carter was hardly a political neophyte: in addition to having been governor, he had run the Democrats' congressional reelection effort in 1974. Among other things, that position gave him an insider's understanding of how a recently revamped Democratic nomination process, in which primaries and caucuses played a more decisive role than ever before, could work in his favor.

9. Martin Schram, *Running for President, 1976: The Carter Campaign* (New York: Stein and Day, 1977), 21; R. W. Apple, "Carter Appears to Hold a Solid Lead in Iowa as the Campaign's First Test Approaches," *New York Times*, October 27, 1975.

10. Joseph Lelyveld, "The Selling of a President," *New York Times Magazine*, March 28, 1976, 17, 65–71; Randall Ballmer, *Redeemer: The Life of Jimmy Carter* (New York: Basic Books, 2014), 31.

11. Carter quoted in Schram, *Running for President*, 273. Timothy Stanley lays out a compelling case for why 1976 voters were more focused on the economy—and more supportive of liberal approaches—than is commonly understood. As Stanley notes, a Democratic National Committee–commissioned poll of Carter voters found that more than 90 percent voted for him because of economic issues and understood Carter as an economic liberal. See Stanley, *Kennedy vs. Carter: The 1980 Battle for the Democratic Party's Soul* (Lawrence: University Press of Kansas, 2010), 1–31.

12. During the campaign, Ford's blustery and impolitic Agriculture secretary, Earl L. Butz, accused Carter of "growing fat" on peanut subsidies and warned, "I'm going to disturb his little playhouse." Yet voters and reporters mostly shrugged, the fiercely loyal (and subsidy-dependent) people of Plains took it as a personal affront, and Ford administration officials scrambled to clarify Butz's remarks as an "exaggeration." See "Carter Accused on U.S. Subsidies," *New York Times*, March 31, 1976; Roy Reed, "In Plains, Ga.,

Carter Is a Hero and Butz a Villain," *New York Times*, March 31, 1976; "Butz and Carter Both Inaccurate in Peanut Dispute," *Los Angeles Times*, March 30, 1976; and Dan Morgan, "Butz Aides Soften His Jab at Carter Over Peanut Subsides," *Washington Post*, March 30, 1976.

13. Interestingly, but not surprisingly, the southern and western regions that were most dependent on this stealthy federal largesse produced some of the era's most stridently free-enterprise presidential contenders, from Goldwater in 1964 to Reagan in 1976 and 1980. See Bruce J. Schulman, *From Cotton Belt to Sunbelt* (New York: Oxford University Press, 1993); Lisa McGirr, *Suburban Warriors* (Princeton, NJ: Princeton University Press, 2002); and Margaret Pugh O'Mara, *Cities of Knowledge: Cold War Science and the Search for the Next Silicon Valley* (Princeton, NJ: Princeton University Press, 2005).

14. "'Welfare Queen' Becomes Issue in Reagan Campaign," *New York Times*, February 15, 1976; Carter quoted in Schram, *Running for President*, 297. On welfare, race, and stigma, see Michael B. Katz, *The Price of Citizenship: Redefining the American Welfare State* (New York: Metropolitan Books, 2001); and Jill Quadagno, *The Color of Welfare: How Racism Undermined the War on Poverty* (New York: Oxford University Press, 1994).

15. Nicholas M. Horrock, "Experts Say New Election Fund Law Saved Carter from a Blitz by Rivals," *New York Times*, May 28, 1976; Christopher Lydon, "Fund-Raising Image of Strauss Strained by Party's Shortages," *New York Times*, September 15, 1976.

16. Horrock, "Experts Say New Election Fund Law Saved Carter from a Blitz by Rivals"; B. Drummond Ayres Jr., "1976 Surprise: Carter Is Running Well," *New York Times*, December 26, 1975. Public financing also helped the campaign of another insurgent, Ronald Reagan; see "Reagan Is Leading Ford in Donations," *New York Times*, January 7, 1976; and Rick Perlstein, *The Invisible Bridge: The Fall of Nixon and the Rise of Reagan* (New York: Simon & Schuster, 2014).

17. Nicholas M. Horrock, "Carter Campaign Funds Raised by a Group of Georgia Lawyers," *New York Times*, May 27, 1976.

18. Quoted in Hobart Rowen, "Confidante Lance: Rare Carter Naysayer," *Washington Post*, September 6, 1977. Carter's appointments reflected continued loyalty to the Georgians who got him to the White House but also brought in a slew of Washington and Wall Street insiders, including Cyrus Vance as secretary of state.

19. Nicholas M. Horrock, "Variety of Charges Caused Bert Lance's Decline and Fall," *New York Times*, September 2, 1977; L. J. Davis, "The Money Vanishes," *Harper's*, September 1, 1979, 259–77; for more information, see Lance, *The Truth of the Matter*.

20. Louis M. Kohlmeier, "The Big Businessmen Who Have Jimmy Carter's Ear," *New York Times*, February 5, 1978.

21. Joe Klein, "Bill Clinton: Who Is This Guy?" *New York Magazine*, January 20, 1992, https://perma.cc/T558-GRA3. On the 1992 campaign, and the Clinton campaign in particular, see Jack W. Germond and Jules Witcover, *Mad As Hell: Revolt at the Ballot Box, 1992* (New York: Warner Books, 1993); Peter Goldman, Thomas M. DeFrank, Mark Miller, Andrew Murr, and Tom Matthews, *Quest for the Presidency 1992* (College Station: Texas A&M University Press, 1994); Mary Matalin, James Carville, and Peter Knobler, *All's Fair: Love, War, and Running for President* (New York: Random House, 1994); and O'Mara, *Pivotal Tuesdays*, chs. 7 and 8. Details of the 1992 campaign are also informed

by the personal recollections of the author, who worked at the Clinton-Gore Little Rock headquarters from July through October 1992, in the Michigan field office in October 1992, on the transition team from November 1992 until January 1993, and as a political appointee in the Clinton administration until August 1997.

22. Quoted in Klein, "Bill Clinton."

23. One Dukakis veteran who advised Clinton was George Stephanopoulos, who discussed the two campaigns in his memoir, *All Too Human: A Political Education* (Boston: Little, Brown, 2000).

24. Dan Balz and Sharon Walsh, "Brown, a Pioneer at Home in Black and White America," *Washington Post*, April 4, 1996. Brown became Clinton's secretary of commerce and amassed a prolific record of building new trade and commercial initiatives domestically and internationally. Tragically, he and thirty-three others were killed in a plane crash while on a trade mission to Croatia in the spring of 1996.

25. On the DLC, see Kenneth S. Baer, *Reinventing Democrats: The Politics of Liberalism from Reagan to Clinton* (Lawrence: University Press of Kansas, 2000).

26. "Testimony of Honorable Paul Tsongas (Foley, Hoag, and Eliot, Boston MA) before the Senate Small Business Committee on the Elimination of the Capital Gains Differential for Individuals and Its Impact on Small Business Capital Formation," June 2, 1986, box 51, Capital Gains II, Ed Zschau Papers, Hoover Institution Archives, Stanford, CA.

27. William Galston and Elaine Kamarck, "The Politics of Evasion: Democrats and the Presidency," Progressive Policy Institute, September 1989. Also see Paul Starr, "From the Frame-Maker," *Democracy Journal* 33 (Summer 2014).

28. Bill Clinton and Al Gore, *Putting People First: How We Can All Change America* (New York: Times Books, 1992). Reed went on to later serve as chief of staff to Vice President Joe Biden during the Obama administration; see "For Biden Chief of Staff Bruce Reed, Less Is More," *Seattle Times*, March 9, 2013.

29. Clinton quoted in Lily Geismer, "Agents of Change: The Clintons and the Long History of Microfinance in the United States and the World," working paper presented to the Warren Center Seminar, Harvard University, March 2016, p. 46. Geismer's paper makes important interventions in understanding the market-oriented philosophy of the "neoliberal" Clintonites as deeply rooted and more closely adjacent to the liberalism of both New Deal and New Left than is often understood. On the Clintons and welfare reform, see Jason DeParle, *American Dream: Three Women, Ten Kids, and a Nation's Drive to End Welfare* (Viking Books: New York, 2004). On discourses of "empowerment" and "entrepreneurship" more generally, see Luc Boltanski, Eve Chiapello, and Gregory Elliott, *The New Spirit of Capitalism* (London: Verso, 2005).

30. Mary Billard, "The Executive Life: Wall Street Dems Find Little to Like in 1992," *New York Times*, March 1, 1992. On Rubin's first-year influence, see Bob Woodward, *The Agenda: Inside the Clinton White House* (New York: Simon & Schuster, 1994).

31. T. Carroll Morganthau, "The Wild Card," *Newsweek*, April 27, 1992. Also see Gerald Posner, *Citizen Perot: His Life and Times* (New York: Random House, 1996), and the candidate's own campaign biography: H. Ross Perot, *United We Stand: How We Can Take Back Our Country* (New York: Hyperion, 1992).

32. Quoted in O'Mara, *Pivotal Tuesdays*, 181–82.

33. Transcript of "Spectrum" commentary by Nicholas von Hoffman on the CBS Radio network, October 14, 1971, in FF "Ross Perot" 2 of 2, box 147, WHSF: SMOF: H. R. Haldeman, Alpha Subject Files, Richard M. Nixon Presidential Library, Yorba Linda, Calif.

34. The mood and spirit of the campaign war room was captured well by Joel Achenbach, "Little Rock, Where Spin Meets Homespun," *Washington Post*, October 2, 1992.

35. The leader of that group had been David Packard, cofounder of HP, a vocal defender of free enterprise who served as Richard Nixon's deputy secretary of defense.

36. Joseph Kraft, "Atari Democrats," *Washington Post*, October 19, 1982; Haynes Johnson, "Election '84: Silicon Valley's Satisfied Society," *Washington Post*, October 10, 1984.

37. Regis McKenna, interview with the author, April 21, 2015, Stanford, CA: Calvin Sims, "Silicon Valley Takes a Partisan Leap of Faith," *New York Times*, October 29, 1992.

4

Presidents, the Military-Industrial Complex, and the Ascendant Politics of "Free Enterprise"

MARK R. WILSON

Since the 1940s, the military-industrial sector has remained one of the most important parts of American capitalism. Although its size relative to the whole economy has declined since the height of the Cold War, the defense sector still absorbs hundreds of billions of tax dollars each year. Top U.S. defense contractors, including Boeing, Lockheed Martin, General Dynamics, United Technologies, and Raytheon, continue to rank among the nation's most important industrial corporations. Without considering the military-industrial sphere, we can't do an adequate job of surveying the recent history of American capitalism.

How has the military-industrial sector been shaped by American presidents, and their administrations? This question raises another one, familiar to political scientists and historians, about the extent and limits of presidential power. Might the military-industrial complex be mostly outside the control of presidents? This question was implied by President Eisenhower's 1961 farewell address, which introduced the phrase "military-industrial complex" into the national lexicon. Eisenhower, frustrated by his struggles to trim defense budgets, and offended by lobbying efforts undertaken by military contractors, warned Americans that the military-industrial complex might attain dangerous levels of autonomous power, thereby upsetting the proper balance between national security, on the one hand, and liberty and democracy, on the other.[1] The speech implied that even Eisenhower, a president with exceptional expert knowledge of the U.S. military, had found it hard to influence the military-industrial complex. It also suggested that future presidents, starting with John F. Kennedy, would likely have even more trouble.

This portrait of presidential impotence in the face of a maturing military-industrial complex was developed further, in the wake of Eisenhower's farewell address, and in the context of the Vietnam War, by numerous critics and scholars. Many of them described some version of an "iron triangle," including three major elements: for-profit military contractors, the Pentagon, and Congress.[2] Notably, the White House was not normally located on one of the three points of the triangle. Rather, the most important elected officials in military-industrial complex seemed to be members of Congress, who worked with the defense lobby and the military to translate appropriations into defense jobs in their districts.[3]

This emphasis on the limits of presidential power over the military-industrial sphere is reasonable. It may seem even more compelling when we recognize that presidents are so busy that they normally choose to delegate responsibility over this sphere to subordinates, and to the military itself, especially in wartime and other moments of crisis. However, it would be a mistake to end the discussion there. Presidents and their administrations, even if they have failed to fully control the military-industrial complex, have influenced its shape in a variety of ways.

Since World War II, several of the nation's presidents, far from being naïve pushovers when it came to the defense sector, have been true experts on its workings. These experts included not just Eisenhower but also Franklin D. Roosevelt (a former assistant secretary of the navy), Harry S. Truman (who rose to prominence as chairman of the most important congressional committee investigating the World War II economy), and Jimmy Carter (who worked on the nuclear submarine program as a young navy officer). Besides Carter and Truman, there were several other military veterans, including Presidents John F. Kennedy, Gerald R. Ford, and George H. W. Bush. Finally, several presidents, hailing from the leading "gunbelt" states of Texas and California, had significant insider knowledge of the defense industry and defense lobby. These men included presidents Lyndon B. Johnson and Richard M. Nixon, who led the nation during the Vietnam War; Ronald W. Reagan, who presided over the big defense buildup of the early 1980s; and George W. Bush, who led the nation into recent wars in Afghanistan and Iraq. In short, most U.S. presidents since World War II have qualified as savvy experts, not dupes, when it came to the operations of the defense sector.

Given that the roster of presidents with the capability to have influenced the defense sector seems to be rather large, it may be interesting to consider the question of which of them was most successful in realizing his preferences. Which American president, since 1945, was the most effective, over the long run, in influencing the shape of the military-industrial complex? Here, I would like to propose an answer that may seem surprising, if not bizarre: Herbert Hoover.

However strange this answer might seem at first glance, it is not a joke. As the first part of this chapter will suggest, since World War II, the American military-industrial complex has been reshaped in ways that accorded with the preferences of Hoover. He expressed them most clearly not during his own presidency, in the late 1920s and early 1930s, but rather during the early Cold War, when he led two presidentially appointed commissions on government reorganization. Hoover and his allies, who included many American business leaders, wanted to create a military-industrial sphere that would be far more privatized, with the military having far less in-house capacity, than it had become during the first half of the twentieth century. Hoover, like other mid-twentieth-century champions of "free enterprise," wanted the large Cold War military-industrial complex to become—to put it crudely—less socialist and more capitalist. They got their way. The military-industrial complex, contrary to the claims of many of its critics, has been neither impervious to reform nor insulated from capitalism. Rather, since the 1950s, it has been substantially privatized, deregulated, and demilitarized.[4] In the first part of this chapter, I briefly outline this transformation, which, for the purposes of this volume, may be dubbed the "Hoovering" of the American military economy.

Although it was championed during the early Cold War by a Republican ex-president, this privatization and deregulation of the military-industrial complex became a bipartisan project. Here is a second point emphasized in this chapter: from the 1960s through the end of the twentieth century, it was Democratic presidents and their administrations, no less than Republican ones, who promoted the Hoovering of the U.S. military economy. Changes in party control of the White House did little to affect the long-run trend. It seems that Democratic presidents, including Johnson, Carter, and Clinton, oversaw as much Hoovering of the military-industrial complex as did their Republican counterparts.

Finally, as the last section of this chapter suggests, several presidents after 1945 had the opportunity to reconsider the direction of defense-sector reform, as they confronted a variety of military-industrial crises. These difficult moments included the impending bankruptcies of major contractors, bitter struggles between the military and some of its leading suppliers over contracts and payments, and widely publicized scandals that pointed to systematic mismanagement and overcharging in the defense sector. But as it turned out, none of these crises, in which presidents might have chosen to pause or reverse course, caused much change in the long-run trend in the direction of deregulation and privatization. Since 1945, Hoover's vision has consistently won out.

The Hoovering of the U.S. Military Economy, 1950s–2000s: A Very Brief Sketch

Starting in the early 1930s, as the New Deal took shape, Hoover focused on what he called a "crusade against collectivism" as he battled "creeping socialism."[5] This attitude continued into the 1940s and 1950s, when Hoover led two prominent commissions on governmental reorganization. These commissions were concerned with addressing apparent inefficiencies across the whole federal government, not just in the military establishment; some of their recommendations were not especially partisan or controversial. Nevertheless, their findings were shaped by the fact that Hoover and most of his fellow commission members were pro-business conservatives, interested in reversing some New Deal initiatives in the direction of state enterprise and regulation.[6]

Hoover and his allies were greatly concerned about the way government officials handled the defense establishment, which, at the time, during the early Cold War years, was easily the biggest part of the national state. The Department of Defense (DoD) contained hundreds of government-run enterprises, which, according to Hoover and his allies, were inefficient operations, doing work that should be handled by private commercial concerns. Hoover and his fellow commissioners, like so many business leaders and conservative politicians of the mid-twentieth-century United States, touted the superiority of "free enterprise." They applied this philosophy to the task of DoD reform, which, they insisted, should consist not just of more purely technical changes such as the consolidation of duplicate functions but also of the privatization of public assets and business operations. This privatization, Hoover and his allies argued, should extend not just to small ancillary operations, such as military-run bakeries and butcher shops, but also to the largest and most important government-owned military-industrial concerns, including navy shipyards. Many of these installations and operations had been around since the earliest years of the republic. Nevertheless, according to Hoover and his allies, the government-owned facilities constituted an "alarming intrusion" into a realm that needed to be set aside for private, for-profit firms.[7]

Hoover and his contemporaries in the mid-twentieth century observed a U.S. military-industrial complex that included an enormous amount of public ownership and state enterprise. Some of this dated back to the early nineteenth century, some to the Progressive Era, World War I, and the interwar years.[8] But the "intrusion" into the private sector that so bothered Hoover and other free enterprisers was augmented during the nation's industrial mobilization for World War II. That conflict, even more than previous wars, saw the national government pour huge investments into manufacturing plants such as the Detroit Arsenal, which built tanks, and Willow Run, which produced B-24 Liberator bombers. These government-owned plants turned out most of the fighters and bombers, tanks, merchant ships, warships, explosives, and ammunition that the United States and the Allies used to win World War II. By 1945, government-owned industrial plant accounted for roughly one-fifth of the nation's total industrial capacity. Although most of this government-owned industrial plant was managed by private companies, some substantial parts of it, especially in naval shipbuilding and small arms production, continued to be run by the military itself.[9]

All of this apparent socialism in the military-industrial complex irritated both Hoover and many of the nation's business leaders and their allies in Congress. As the reports of Hoover's commissions show, these concerns continued into the 1950s, during and after the Korean War. At that time, the navy's own shipyards employed close to half of the people working in the U.S. shipbuilding industry. The government still owned many large aerospace plants. All in all, into the 1950s, the military's in-house knowledge and production capacities, when it came to weapons production, remained substantial.

However, in the long run, Hoover got his way. In the early 1960s, under Secretary of Defense Robert S. McNamara's leadership, government-owned plant was being shed at a fast pace. Between January 1961 and June 1964, the Defense Department had already made available for sale sixty-one major defense plants and nearly seven hundred thousand acres of real estate.[10] By the end of the twentieth century, most of the government-owned defense plant had been sold off. Today, in a reversal of the situation that existed in 1945, it is the private sector that owns nearly all of the nation's military-industrial manufacturing capacity.

A Bipartisan Project

One of the more remarkable aspects of the history of the Hoovering of the U.S. defense sector, during the second half of the twentieth century, is the extent to which it was implemented and advanced during the administrations of Democratic presidents, as well as Republican ones. This record is interesting, because in the mid-twentieth century, when Hoover's commissions were criticizing the DoD's public enterprises, it might not have been predicted. By that time, Hoover himself was a strongly partisan, right-wing Republican. The modern mixed military economy he and his allies were attacking had been expanded during the administrations of progressive Democratic presidents Woodrow Wilson and Franklin Roosevelt. Given this political dynamic, it seems possible that the Democratic presidents of the second half of the twentieth century, beginning with Kennedy and Johnson, might have done more to resist privatization.

In fact, however, the Hoovering of the military-industrial complex made major advances during the administrations of Democratic presidents. Indeed, it was during the mid-1960s that defense secretary McNamara, a member of Kennedy's cabinet who stayed on under Johnson, issued a series of important orders that effectively killed the military's in-house capacities for the production of small arms and warships. These steps toward privatization were more dramatic, and at least as important, as anything that had occurred during the Eisenhower years.[11]

This apparently bi-partisan effort in the direction of privatization lasted through the end of the twentieth century, from the 1970s into the early 2000s. As we think about the military-industrial complex and the parties and presidents during those years, many of us may think about evidence of military contractor–friendly behaviors by Republican administrations. Here, we might include the Reagan defense buildup; George W. Bush's Iraq War; and the activities of Republican appointees such as Dick Cheney and Donald H. Rumsfeld, who helped to shift more of the military's work toward private firms, from KBR to Blackwater.[12]

However, we need to remember that the emphasis on privatization continued through the Clinton years, as well. Indeed, as the historian Jennifer Mittelstadt has argued in her important recent book on the "military welfare state," by some measures, DoD functions were privatized more thoroughly during the Clinton administration than they had been under President Reagan.[13]

How Presidents Mattered

This record of relentless transformation in the defense sector, over the last six or seven decades, may lead us to ask whether presidents had much influence over the process. If the Hoovering of the military-industrial complex proceeded rather steadily, across multiple presidential administrations, Democratic and Republican alike, perhaps we should conclude that presidents may not have had much power in this field. Perhaps if we are interested in the drivers of this change we would be better off examining one of the three corners of the old "iron triangle." Congress, which seems to have asserted more power over military procurement since the 1950s, is surely important.[14] So too might be the military establishment itself, which for various reasons, including perhaps its growing manpower constraints after the end of the draft, assented to its own Hoovering, when it came to matters of military industry. Finally, it seems likely that business leaders and their allies played a big role, via defense industry lobbying; perhaps we need also to consider their success in reshaping the broader political environment, in the direction of making privatization and deregulation seem more natural.

The question of the relative importance of these various factors remains an open one, which future studies should do more to answer. But in this volume, we focus on the question of the influence of presidents. Here, I offer the tentative argument that we should see presidents not as impotent tools but rather as important participants in the Hoovering of the military-industrial complex. Presidents (and their inner circles) mattered in a variety of ways. First, they exerted influence via their choices of secretaries of defense and other top defense officials, who became the presidents' designated overseers of the military-industrial complex. Second, presidents also had the opportunity to be more directly influential in their management of late twentieth-century defense-sector crises, including impending financial collapses of top contractors and profiteering and corruption scandals. As it turned out, in both of these areas, presidents from both parties chose to act in ways that advanced or perpetuated the Hoovering of the military-industrial complex. This seems significant, because it is not so hard to imagine that some of them might have acted differently.

Before tackling each of these two areas in which presidential choices seem to have mattered, it is worth acknowledging that presidents also affected the sheer size of the military-industrial complex, in the short run, by their decisions regarding foreign policy. Most important, several presidents since 1945—including Truman, Johnson, and George W. Bush—caused significant medium-run increases in the defense budget by choosing to engage in major war efforts. Big budget increases also occurred during Reagan's tenure, via a major defense buildup, rather than a large overseas adventure. However, all of these presidential choices affected the size, rather than the shape, of the defense sector. So we must dig deeper, below the surface of aggregate defense budgeting, in order to assess presidential choices that may have promoted the Hoovering of the military economy.

As a first step, it is worth considering the choices presidents made when it came to appointing secretaries of defense and their top deputies. This would seem to be one area in which presidents might have had the opportunity to influence the shape of the military-industrial complex. Other than President Eisenhower, whose dissatisfaction with Secretary of Defense Charles E. Wilson caused him to do a fair bit of direct managing of defense policy, most post-1945 presidents left the management of the Pentagon to their defense secretaries.[15] Here, the record suggests that presidents of both parties overwhelmingly selected men who were sympathetic to the Hoovering of the U.S. military economy, even if they were rarely among the among the nation's most outspoken or most ideological champions of "free enterprise."

Republican presidents, faced with the problem of whom to nominate for secretary of defense, have tended to turn to executives from big corporations, conservative politicians, or some combination of the two. We can begin in 1953 with Eisenhower's choice of Wilson, the General Motors executive. One of the millionaires in a cabinet described as "nine millionaires and a plumber," Wilson is the secretary of defense still sometimes remembered for some version of his statement "I thought what was good for the country was good for General Motors and vice versa." (After Wilson stepped down in 1957, he was succeeded by another corporate executive: Neil McElroy, of Proctor & Gamble.)[16]

More recently, Republican-appointed secretaries of defense have tended to be men who started as party politicians and only became corporate executives or board members after working in Washington. These politicians turned defense secretaries include Melvin R. Laird (whose top deputy was David Packard, the Silicon Valley executive and leading Republican donor),[17] Caspar W. Weinberger (whose idol growing up was Herbert Hoover),[18] Donald Rumsfeld, and Dick Cheney.[19] As conservative Republican politicians, these men were predisposed, broadly speaking, to favor the Hoovering of the military-industrial complex.

More interesting, perhaps, is the record of Democratic presidents' choices for top Pentagon officials. Here, we might start by pointing out that some Democratic presidents have also turned to Republican politicians, including William S. Cohen and Chuck Hagel. (This was a practice that went back to FDR, who, seeking to build a broad wartime political coalition, appointed Republicans as war and navy secretaries at the beginning of World War II.) But we also find a different archetype: a man with less grassroots political experience but a strong background in high-tech enterprise. Here of course the Cold War pioneer was John F. Kennedy's choice: McNamara, the Harvard Business School professor turned army air forces analyst turned Ford Motor Co. executive. McNamara is often remembered for his role in the Vietnam War, along with his allegedly arrogant use of new quantitative analytical methods and centralization of power in his own office.[20] His Republican successors, including Laird and Weinberger, liked to emphasize their abandonment of McNamara's practices, particularly when it came to centralization of decision-making authority. Yet we need to recall that McNamara may have done more than any other secretary of defense to Hoover the military-industrial complex. In the name of economy and efficiency, McNamara shuttered much of the military's in-house production capacity.

The McNamara model, of secretary of defense as an ostensibly objective technocrat who nonetheless turned out to promote privatization, reappeared under subsequent Democratic administrations. These Democrat-appointed technocrats were ostensibly less partisan than their Republican counterparts, but in terms of defense-sector reform they were similarly committed to more privatization and commercialization.[21] In this matter, they were good Hoover Republicans—or good New Democrats. Consider the longest-serving secretary of defense in the Clinton administration, William J. Perry. A math PhD turned Silicon Valley engineer and company executive at a small defense contractor, Perry first joined the DoD as a deputy (director of research and engineering) during the Carter administration. At his nomination hearing in 1977, Perry earnestly assured conservative Senators, including Strom Thurmond, that he was a solid free-enterprise man. (In a recent memoir, Perry calls himself an "original Silicon Valley entrepreneur.")[22] As secretary of defense, Perry, along with deputies such as Jacques S. Gansler, pursued new initiatives in the direction of privatization and commercialization. This dovetailed with the Clinton-Gore administration's broader emphasis on "reinventing government," which touted the advantages of outsourcing and market competition, using a rhetoric and sensibility that was not so far removed from that deployed by Hoover and his allies four decades before.[23]

To sum up this admittedly brief and incomplete overview, the record suggests that all of our presidents since 1945, including Democrats who might have been expected to act differently, have chosen to have the Pentagon led by men who were dependable overseers, if not champions, of a Hoover-friendly military-industrial complex.[24]

We may also see some evidence of presidents' potential to shape the defense sector by examining their responses to what might be called minor military-industrial crises. Here, we may consider very briefly three disruptive episodes: the near-failure of Lockheed in the early 1970s, the government's serious standoff with its naval shipbuilders later that same decade, and the scandals over alleged corruption and profiteering in the early 1980s. In all three cases, presidential administrations, faced with crisis in the military economy, chose paths that bolstered the position of struggling contractors. These choices added to the Hoovering of the nation's military economy by avoiding options that might have shifted the balance of public and private power in the other direction.

In the case of Lockheed, one of the nation's top military contractors found itself at the brink of bankruptcy, in the very early 1970s, after it lost money on the C-5A contract it had signed with McNamara's DoD as well as on civilian aircraft projects. One of the Nixon administration's responses, which is well known, was to urge Congress to approve a controversial federal bailout.[25] Perhaps less well remembered but no less important was another aspect of the Nixon administration's response:

concluding that the lesson of the episode was that the defense sector required not more regulation but less. This was the conclusion of Treasury secretary George P. Shultz in early 1973 as he considered the Lockheed crisis.[26] Deputy Secretary of Defense David Packard agreed. As Packard explained in early 1972, profit levels in the defense sector were actually too low, especially given that the Pentagon intended to reduce progress payments to contractors, as well as the amount of government-owned plant and equipment.[27] According to top Nixon administration officials, in other words, the most important lesson to be learned from the Lockheed bankruptcy/bailout crisis was that the defense sector required less regulation and higher profits.

Struggling defense contractors emerged again as a problem for the White House only a few years later, in the mid to late 1970s, under the Ford and Carter administrations. This time the troubles involved navy contractors, including its most important suppliers of warships and submarines, such as Newport News and General Dynamics. Starting in 1976, these navy contractors threatened to stop work at their shipyards because, they claimed, the navy was not providing them with reasonable compensation, in a long-running dispute over contract claims.[28]

These threats by the contractors, which threatened to seriously delay ship deliveries and throw thousands of men and women out of work, were taken very seriously by the Ford and Carter administrations. In late 1976, navy and DoD officials proposed to meet with Ford to discuss the possibility of having the navy reenter the field of new warship construction. This was not an outlandish idea, given that the navy had left this field only a decade earlier and that standing federal laws, first enacted in the 1920s and 1930s and then re-enacted in 1965, required presidents to sign special orders if they chose *not* to have the navy make half of its own new warships. However, Ford, by then a lame duck, evidently chose not to discuss this option.[29] The navy's own shipyards were never given any orders for new warship construction, under Ford, Carter, or any of their successors. (This result in the 1970s was very different from the outcome of a similar flap between shipbuilders and steelmakers and the government in 1936–37, which ended with President Roosevelt announcing that not one but both of the first two *North Carolina*–class battleships would be built by the navy's own yards, in Brooklyn and Philadelphia.[30])

The shipbuilding crisis stretched into the presidency of Jimmy Carter, who, like Ford, was faced with the choice of how to respond to the showdown. Carter's response is especially interesting, potentially, because of his background as a navy officer involved in the production of nuclear submarines. As a young navy officer, Carter had worked under Admiral Hyman G. Rickover, whom he admired.[31] Although Rickover himself had been instrumental during the early Cold War in advancing the interests of Electric Boat, the nation's top private submarine builder, during the 1970s crisis, Rickover was highly critical of the contractors; he even suggested that the navy might have to increase its ownership, or even its management role, in the nation's naval shipyards. So, when General Dynamics threatened in 1978 to shut down its Electric Boat yards in Connecticut (and throw thousands out of work) until it obtained a more generous financial settlement with the navy, Carter might have chosen to play hardball by siding with Rickover and threatening a government takeover or even restarting new construction in navy yards that the Pentagon had considered in 1976. Instead, so far as we know, Carter chose instead to approve a negotiation being headed up by Edward Hidalgo, an assistant secretary of the navy. Hidalgo ended up recommending a generous multimillion-dollar payment to General Dynamics.[32]

What led Carter to make this choice? A full answer awaits further research; however, Carter did speak on a related matter at a press conference in 1979, when a reporter asked him about upcoming navy contract awards. Carter observed that thanks to his time as a nuclear engineer when he was a young navy officer, when he worked closely with Electric Boat, he actually knew a good deal about the industry. And, perhaps, he had a soft spot for the nation's leading private supplier of submarines: "I have a special feeling for General Dynamics," said Carter.[33] Had this "special feeling" caused him to side with the contractors, in the threatened shipyard shutdown crisis? We don't yet have good answers to this question, but at the least we can observe that here again, a president, given the opportunity to challenge or question the wisdom of the drive for a more Hoovered military-industrial complex, chose not to make waves.

Finally, we may consider the crisis faced by the Reagan administration, during widely publicized scandals in the early 1980s, over alleged waste, profiteering, and corruption, in the public and private sides of the nation's military economy. Now, to be sure, it is possible to overstate the extent of Hoovering that occurred in the defense sector during the Reagan years. As historian Jennifer Mittelstadt has pointed out, Secretary of Defense Weinberger actually increased in-house military capacities, at least by some measures, as he increased the military's civilian work force, along with the ranks of soldiers and sailors.[34]

However, the Reagan administration did promote further privatization and commercialization of the defense sector, not least in its response to the waste and profiteering scandal of the early 1980s, when the newspapers and television news programs were full of reports of the Pentagon paying thousands of dollars per unit for things like coffee pots, hammers, and toilet seats. One of the Reagan administration's main responses to this scandal crisis was the formation of the Packard Commission, led by the same David Packard who had served in the Nixon administration as deputy secretary of defense.[35] The Reagan White House hoped that this commission would help to downplay public concern about alleged contractor overcharging and fraud; instead, administration officials hoped, Packard's group would serve to tout the benefits of more privatization and commercialization.[36] Even before it started its work, the Packard Commission aimed at "substituting competition for regulation; at increasing significantly the use of commercially available components; and at other ways to reduce bureaucracy."[37] Not surprisingly, given these starting assumptions, the commission's reports, issued in 1986, favored the Hoover approach to the defense sector. As the Packard Commission put it in its reports, "when a make-or-buy decision is to be made, we believe that the presumption should be to buy. This would reverse the present procedure and bias the system in favor of commercial products and services."[38]

Furthermore, according to the Reagan administration and the commission, public criticisms of alleged defense sector profiteering were ignorant and misguided. This remained the attitude of Packard, who in the July 1986 press conference held in conjunction with the appearance of his commission's final report was asked whether it was really wise to reduce government auditing, as the commission had recommended, in favor of relying on contractors' own internal ethics programs and bookkeeping. In response, Packard replied that business leaders really cared more about integrity and reputation than they did about profits.[39] This was not just Packard's personal opinion—it was the essence of the response to the crisis by the Reagan White House: a doubling-down on the message about the superiority of free enterprise and its benefits in the military economy, even after serious questions were raised about alleged misbehavior in the private sector.[40]

Conclusion

This chapter has described a long-run transformation of the U.S. military economy, from the 1940s to the present day, in the direction of privatization, deregulation, and the degradation of the national state's in-house knowledge and capacities. To put it more crudely, over the past seven decades, the American military-industrial complex became significantly less socialist and more capitalist. This transformation represented the realization of the dreams of Herbert Hoover, who, as an ex-president at the start of the Cold War, despaired that the defense sector was an arena rife with the dangers of "creeping socialism." Hoover would surely be pleased with the developments that have occurred in recent decades, which have created a U.S. military economy in which regulation is reduced and public enterprise is largely absent.

This story should encourage questions about the relationship between developments in the defense sector and those in the broader American political economy. For some answers to those questions, readers may turn to other chapters in this volume. To some extent, it seems clear, the trend in the direction of Hoovering existed outside the military-industrial complex, as well as inside it. But we need to know more about the relationships between developments on the military and civilian sides of the economy. We also need to know more about the roles of presidents in the recent transformations of the American capitalism. As the case of the military-industrial complex suggests, presidents were far from omnipotent in the field of political economy. However, as we learn more about the record of their choices and actions—and their decisions not to act—it seems that presidents since 1945, from both parties, have done more than we might expect to promote Hoover's agenda.

Notes

1. Alex Roland, "The Military-Industrial Complex: Lobby and Trope," in *The Long War: A New History of U.S. National Security Policy since World War II*, ed. Andrew J. Bacevich (New York: Columbia University Press, 2007), 335–70; Dolores E. Janiewski, "Eisenhower's Paradoxical Relationship with the 'Military-Industrial Complex,'" *Presidential Studies Quarterly* 41, no. 4 (December 2011): 667–92; James Ledbetter, *Unwarranted Influence: Dwight D. Eisenhower and the Military Industrial Complex* (New Haven, CT: Yale University Press, 2011).

2. Seymour Melman, *Pentagon Capitalism: The Political Economy of War* (New York: McGraw Hill, 1970); Gordon Adams, *The Politics of Defense Contracting: The Iron Triangle* (New Brunswick, NJ: Transaction Books, 1982).

3. Many political scientists interested in the defense sector have focused on Congress: Kenneth R. Mayer, *The Political Economy of Defense Contracting* (New Haven, CT: Yale University Press, 1991); Rebecca U. Thorpe, *The American Warfare State: The Domestic Politics of Military Spending* (Chicago: University of Chicago Press, 2014).

4. I describe the first part of this story in Mark R. Wilson, *Destructive Creation: American Business and the Winning of World War II* (Philadelphia: University of Pennsylvania Press, 2016), 241–85. For an outstanding history of comparable developments in the field of military benefits and services, see Jennifer Mittelstadt, *The Rise of the Military Welfare State* (Cambridge, MA: Harvard University Press, 2015). Several social scientists have discussed elements of the transformation: Aaron L. Friedberg, *In the Shadow of the Garrison State: America's Antistatism and Its Cold War Grand Strategy* (Princeton: Princeton University Press, 2000); Harvey M. Sapolsky and Eugene Gholz, "Private Arsenals: America's Post-Cold War Burden," in *Arming for the Future: A Defense Industry for the 21st Century*, ed. Ann R. Markusen and Sean S. Costigan (New York: Council on Foreign Relations Press, 1999); Ann R. Markusen, "The Case against Privatizing National Security," *Governance: An International Journal of Policy, Administration, and Institutions* 16, no. 4 (October 2003): 471–501; P. W. Singer, *Corporate Warriors: The Rise of the Privatized Military Industry* (Ithaca: Cornell University Press, 2003); Deborah D. Avant, *The Market for Force: The Consequences of Privatizing Security* (New York: Cambridge University Press, 2005); Linda Weiss, *America Inc.? Innovation and Enterprise in the National Security State* (Ithaca: Cornell University Press, 2014).

5. For Hoover's own writings from the period, see George H. Nash, ed., *The Crusade Years, 1933–1955: Herbert Hoover's Lost Memoir of the New Deal Era and Its Aftermath* (Stanford, CA: Hoover Institution Press, 2013).

6. Peri Arnold, *Making the Managerial Presidency: Comprehensive Reorganization Planning, 1905–1996*, 2nd. rev. ed. (Lawrence: University Press of Kansas, 1998), 118–214; Joanna Grisinger, *The Unwieldy American State: Administrative Politics since the New Deal* (New York: Cambridge University Press, 2012), 153–250. See also Gary Dean Best, *The Life of Herbert Hoover: Keeper of the Torch, 1933–1964* (Palgrave Macmillan, 2013).

7. Wilson, *Destructive Creation*, 271–75; Mittelstadt, *Rise of the Military Welfare State*, 29, 197.

8. Merritt Roe Smith, *Harpers Ferry Armory and the New Technology: The Challenge of Change* (Ithaca, NY: Cornell University Press, 1977); Mark R. Wilson, *The Business of Civil War: Military Mobilization and the State, 1861–1865* (Baltimore: Johns Hopkins University Press, 2006); Gary E. Weir, *Building American Submarines, 1914–1940* (Washington, DC: Naval Historical Center, 1991); Mark R. Wilson, "Economic Mobilization," in *A Companion to Woodrow Wilson*, ed. Ross Kennedy (New York: John Wiley's Sons, 2013), 289–307.

9. Wilson, *Destructive Creation*.

10. McNamara to LBJ, July 7, 1964, box 174, folder ND 11, 11/22/63–11/8/64, White

House Central Files, Subject Files, LBJ Presidential Library, Austin, TX. See also Friedberg, *In the Shadow of the Garrison State*, 291.

11. Friedberg, *In the Shadow of the Garrison State*, 262–64; Wilson, *Destructive Creation*, 279–83. On the Johnson administration's promulgation of Bureau of the Budget Circular A-76, which revived and bolstered an Eisenhower administration effort to have more government operations contracted out, see Mittelstadt, *Rise of the Military Welfare State*, 29.

12. Daniel Wirls, *Buildup: The Politics of Defense in the Reagan Era* (Ithaca, NY: Cornell University Press, 1992); Paul S. Boyer, "Selling Star Wars: Ronald Reagan's Strategic Defense Initiative," in *Selling War in a Media Age: The Presidency and Public Opinion in the American Century*, ed. Kenneth Osgood and Andrew K. Frank (Gainesville: University Press of Florida, 2010), 196–223.

13. Mittelstadt, *Rise of the Military Welfare State*, 190–219.

14. Thomas L. McNaugher, *New Weapons, Old Politics: America's Military Procurement Muddle* (Washington: Brookings Institution, 1989).

15. Dale R. Herspring, "Eisenhower and the Military," in *The Eisenhower Presidency: Lessons for the Twenty-First Century*, ed. Andrew Polsky (Lanham, MD: Lexington Books, 2015), 170.

16. Bruce Geelhoed, *Charles E. Wilson and Controversy at the Pentagon, 1953 to 1957* (Detroit: Wayne State University Press, 1979); Erin R. Mahan and Jeffrey A. Larsen, eds., *Evolution of the Secretary of Defense in the Era of Massive Retaliation: Charles Wilson, Neil McElroy, and Thomas Gates, 1953–1961* (Washington, DC: Historical Office of the Office of the Secretary of Defense, 2012).

17. Laird, as a congressman in the early 1960s, wrote the introduction to *The Conservative Papers*, a volume of essays commissioned by a group of several Republican members of Congress, including Laird and Gerald Ford. According to Laird, he and others believed "that limitation of government's power is everywhere of the first order so that the individual's power is enhanced" (Melvin R. Laird, "Introduction," in *The Conservative Papers*, ed. Melvin R. Laird [Garden City, NY: Anchor, 1964], x).

18. On his affection for Hoover, see Caspar Weinberger, *Fighting for Peace: Seven Critical Years in the Pentagon* (New York: Warner Books, 1991).

19. Much of the literature on Rumsfeld and Cheney thus far concentrates on their roles in foreign policy. See, for example, James Mann, *Rise of the Vulcans: The History of Bush's War Cabinet* (New York: Viking, 2004). Their own memoirs suggest their lifelong devotion to conservative Republican politics but say little about their work on defense procurement; see Donald Rumsfeld, *Known and Unknown: A Memoir* (New York: Sentinel, 2011); and Dick Cheney, *In My Time: A Personal and Political Memoir* (New York: Threshold, 2011).

20. Lawrence S. Kaplan, Ronald D. Landa, and Edward J. Drea, *The McNamara Ascendancy, 1961–1965* (Washington, DC: Historical Office of the Office of the Secretary of Defense, 2006); Walter S. Poole, *Adapting to Flexible Response, 1960–1968* (Washington, DC: Historical Office of the Office of the Secretary of Defense, 2013).

21. One figure who may not fit easily under this general rule is Harold Brown, a scien-

tist who served under McNamara and then was president of Cal Tech before becoming secretary of defense under President Carter. We still don't know enough about Brown's administration of DoD. However, in a recent book, Brown suggested that the defense sector would benefit from more government investment and planning, rather than less. See Harold Brown and Joyce Winslow, *Star Spangled Security: Applying Lessons Learned over Six Decades Safeguarding America* (Washington: Brookings Institution Press, 2012), 225–31. Carter, who ended up admiring Brown, was careful to nominate a corporate executive, Charles Duncan Jr., of Coca-Cola, as Brown's top deputy. See Jimmy Carter, *Keeping Faith: Memoirs of a President* (New York: Bantam, 1982), 55, 82.

22. "Nominations of William James Perry and David Emerson Mann," Hearing before the Committee on Armed Services, United States Senate, 95th Cong. 1st Sess. (Washington: GPO, 1977), 9; William J. Perry, *My Journey at the Nuclear Brink* (Stanford, CA: Stanford Security Studies, 2015), 21–27.

23. James Kitfield, "How Perry Took on the Boondoggles," *National Journal*, February 1, 1997, 245; Mittelstadt, *Rise of the Military Welfare State*, 190–219; Arnold, *Making the Managerial Presidency*, 374–96. Vice President Gore highlighted the benefits of canceling special military specifications for goods, an elimination of red tape that encouraged firms such as the maker of Jockey underwear to bid on military contracts (Al Gore, *The Best Kept Secrets in Government: How the Clinton Administration Is Reinventing the Way Washington Works* [New York: Random House, 1996], 15–16).

24. Given this record, we might ask whether the post of secretary of defense is somehow inherently or traditionally reserved for pro-business conservatives. The answer is no, if we consider U.S. history before World War II. Here, it is instructive to go back to 1913, to the administration of President Wilson. Wilson's secretary of war, Newton Baker, was a progressive politician who had a record suggesting he was sympathetic to government enterprise; his secretary of the navy, the white-supremacist North Carolinian Josephus Daniels, turned out to be one of the most important champions of in-house military industrial capacity in American history. See Douglas B. Craig, *Progressives at War: William G. McAdoo and Newton D. Baker, 1863–1941* (Baltimore: Johns Hopkins University Press, 2013); and Lee A. Craig, *Josephus Daniels: His Life & Times* (Chapel Hill: University of North Carolina Press, 2013).

25. For an original, recent analysis, see Michael Brenes, "For Right and Might: The Militarization of the Cold War and the Remaking of American Democracy" (PhD diss., City University of New York, 2014), 156–68.

26. Shultz to Nixon, April 12, 1973, box 36, folder ExBE4-1 Aerospace (3 of 3), WHCF Subject Files BE, Richard Nixon Presidential Library, Yorba Linda, CA.

27. Packard memo to Laird, "Improving the Development and Procurement of New Weapons," January 14, 1972, box A79, folder Memos to Laird (2), Laird Papers, Gerald Ford Presidential Library, Ann Arbor, MI.

28. Newport News made its announcement in June 1976. See Sen. Strom Thurmond to President Ford, June 17, 1976, box 85, folder FG 15 1/1/76–6/30/76, Subject File, White House Central Files, Ford Library. See also, Rep. Thomas N. Downing to Ford, May 6, 1975, and Jack L. Bowers to Downing, June 24, 1975, both in ND 15 6/17/75–12/31/75, box 29, Subject File, White House Central Files, Ford Library.

29. Brent Scowcroft, "Schedule Proposal: To Discuss a DOD/Navy Recommendation to Resume New Ship Construction in Navy Shipyards," December 15, 1976, box 29, folder ND 15 4/1/76–12/31/76, Subject File, White House Central Files, Ford Library. Scowcroft recommended that Ford take the meeting, but another White House staff member, apparently William Nicholson, annotated the request with the words "say do not propose." In early October 1976, navy secretary J. William Middledorf II had made a public statement that some interpreted as evidence that the navy might restart in-house ship construction. See the reaction in Rep. Lionel van Deerlin to Ford, October 6, 1976, box 29, folder ND 15 4/1/76–12/31/76, Subject File, White House Central Files, Ford Library. For one example of the many documents showing that presidents had to sign special orders to avoid navy in-house shipbuilding during this era, see Laird memo to Nixon, "Proposed Construction in a Private Shipyard of Two Nuclear-Powered Attack Submarines . . . ," January 30, 1969, box A91, folder Shipyards (US Shipyard Capabilities) 1969, Laird Papers.

30. Robert H. Levine, *The Politics of American Naval Rearmament, 1930–1938* (New York: Garland, 1988), 448–66; Joe Harden Camp, "Birch Rod to Arsenal: A Study of the Naval Ordnance Plant at South Charleston, West Virginia, and the Search for a Government Industrial Policy" (PhD diss., West Virginia University, 2002), 132–33; William M. McBride, "The Unstable Dynamics of a Strategic Technology: Disarmament, Unemployment, and the Interwar Battleship," *Technology & Culture* 38, no. 2 (April 1997): 417–20.

31. Peter G. Bourne, *Jimmy Carter: A Comprehensive Biography from Plains to Post-presidency* (New York: Scribner, 1997), 75–76.

32. Jacob Goodwin, *Brotherhood of Arms: General Dynamics and the Business of Defending America* (New York: Times Books, 1985), 147–48; Patrick Tyler, *Running Critical: The Silent War, Rickover, and General Dynamics* (New York: Harper & Row, 1986), 247; Sheri Wasserman Goodman, "Legal Dilemmas in the Weapons Acquisition Process: The Procurement of the SSN-668 Attack Submarine," *Yale Law & Policy Review* 6, no. 2 (1988): 393–427.

33. *Public Papers of the Presidents of the United States: Jimmy Carter, 1979* (Washington: GPO, 1980), 2:1990. On increased defense spending in the late Carter administration, see Brian J. Auten, *Carter's Conversion: The Hardening of American Defense Policy* (Columbia: University of Missouri Press, 2008).

34. Mittelstadt, *Rise of the Military Welfare State*, 108.

35. Wirls, *Buildup*, 97–99.

36. See for example John W. Douglass to Robert C. McFarlane, April 2, 1985, box 92055, folder April 1985 Selected Documents Re: Blue Ribbon Commission; John W. Douglass and Michael B. Donley memo to John M. Poindexter, December 26, 1985, box 92048, folder Blue Ribbon Commission-3, both in John W. Douglass files, Ronald Reagan Presidential Library, Simi Valley, CA.

37. Packard "Talking Points," October 10, 1985, box 92228, folder President's Blue Ribbon Commission on Defense Management, John W. Douglass Files, Reagan Library.

38. "Draft-Acquisition Section-Packard Commission Report," March 12, 1986, box 92048, folder Blue Ribbon Commission on Defense Management Part II-1, John W. Douglass Files, Reagan Library.

39. Transcript of Packard press conference, July 2, 1986, container OA14162, folder Press Conference on the Packard Commission Final Report, Rhett Dawson Files, Reagan Library.

40. Robert B. Costello, "Acquisition Reform Moves Front and Center," *Defense* (Jan./Feb. 1988): 2–14.

5

Presidents, the Federal Budget, and Economic Good, 1946–2008

IWAN MORGAN

The Employment Act of 1946 sought to prevent another economic catastrophe on the scale of the Great Depression of the 1930s by requiring the federal government to "promote maximum employment, production, and purchasing power." While acknowledging private enterprise as the principal source of economic well-being, it placed responsibility on public policy to maintain prosperity at times when American capitalism failed to do so. The measure effectively made the president chiefly responsible for economic management by creating the Council of Economic Advisers (CEA) within the Executive Office of the President to assist in this task and requiring presidential submission of an annual report on the economy to Congress. In seeking to maintain prosperity, modern presidents never portrayed themselves as agents of American capitalism's success—even if this was their ultimate objective. Instead, they employed rhetorical symbols of economic good—such as high growth, price stability, jobs expansion, and a rising standard of living—in order to win broad support for their agenda. As Walter W. Heller, CEA chair in the John F. Kennedy and Lyndon B. Johnson administrations, observed in 1966, "the terms in which economic problems are put, even their simple semantics, have an important bearing on the fixing of political objectives and the formation of policy."[1]

This chapter explores how presidents from Harry S. Truman to George W. Bush employed the spending and taxation components of the federal budget as their principal instrument of economic management. Despite Congress holding the constitutional power of the purse, namely authority to enact budget-related legislation, presidents have broadly set the agenda for its fiscal decision-making through their obligation to present an annual budget plan estimating government costs and funding requirements. Moreover, prior to the polarization of twenty-first-century politics, legislators generally approached the budget with constituency interests in mind, while presidents regarded it as the means to manage national prosperity in aggregate terms.[2]

Presidential use of fiscal policy to manage the economy had its greatest impact during what can broadly be termed the Keynesian era. During the period from the end of World War II to the end of the 1960s, economic policy was influenced by the demand-management doctrines of British economist John Maynard Keynes (1883–1946).[3] This was the "long boom" era when U.S. economic power relative to that of other nations was at its peak and manufacturing was the ascendant sector within American capitalism. Presidents of this period regarded industries making products like automobiles, electrical goods, and steel as the principal source of prosperity, jobs, and growth. They regarded the maintenance of general economic conditions that would benefit these enterprises as a national good. To this end, Keynesian-era presidents deployed the budget with considerable success to manage aggregate consumption in support of high employment and low inflation, broadly considered the preconditions for business expansion of capital investment that would underwrite the overall growth of the economy. However, the failure of fiscal policy to overcome the menace of stagflation (the unprecedented combination of stagnant growth and hyperinflation that affected the economy in the 1970s) led to its eclipse as an instrument of short-term economic management. In the quarter-century after 1980, the Federal Reserve's monetary powers to determine interest rates charged by America's banks and financial institutions assumed greater significance as the means to combat recession and inflation. Manipulation of credit conditions enabled it to ease borrowing requirements when unemployment rose and tighten them to safeguard price stability when prosperity returned. Freed from short-term economic responsibility, fiscal policy focused instead on promoting a stronger economy in the long term. Abandoning demand management, presidents now hewed to a supply-side strategy of seeking to enhance the stock of capital available to finance American business, mainly through tax cuts that particularly benefited the investor class.[4]

Fiscal bounty took a number of forms under Harry S. Truman and Dwight D. Eisenhower, the first postwar presidents, but two elements had primary significance for American capitalism. First, national security needs gobbled up the lion's share of the budget in the early Cold War. In expanding military outlays, Truman and Eisenhower were primarily fulfilling their commander-in-chief obligations, but the benefits for their manager-of-prosperity responsibility were considerable. From fiscal year (FY) 1951 through FY1960, defense accounted for just over 60 percent of the total budget on average. This vast military spending was instrumental in Gross Domestic Product (GDP) growing over the same period from $327 billion to $535 billion.[5]

National Security Council Memorandum 68, the seminal statement of global Cold War strategy drawn up by the Truman administration in 1950, clearly identified the economic benefits of anticommunist militarization. "One of the most significant lessons of our World War II experience," it declared, "was that the American economy, when it operates at a level approaching full efficiency, can provide enormous resources for purposes other than civilian consumption while simultaneously providing a higher standard of living." Significantly, CEA chair Leon H. Keyserling was instrumental in persuading the fiscally cautious Truman that the mammoth increase in national security outlays recommended by NSC-68 would promote economic growth, business expansion, and increased employment.[6] As well as benefiting mature industries, the infusion of defense dollars stimulated the development of new ones, notably aerospace, electronics, and chemicals. It also facilitated the economic development of the so-called Sunbelt region of the West and South, where the hottest growth states were California, Texas, and Florida.

Keynesian-era presidents further contributed to the success of American capitalism through discharging their Employment Act obligations. As one commentator noted in 1962, they saw no contradiction between their "central economic management" and "the decentralization of decision" by manufacturers, investors, and consumers in a free market.[7] In the first postwar decade, the White House's economic priority was to control inflationary pressures that accompanied a buoyantly expanding economy. In the late 1950s, however, a combination of circumstances—recurrent recessions in 1957–58 and 1960, growing competition from abroad as other countries achieved recovery from World War II, and a relative slowdown in defense outlays as the Cold War eased—required policymakers to choose between promoting either employment growth or price stability. Eisenhower opted for the latter in the conviction that low inflation was essential for the interrelated issues of business profits and planning, the defense of the dollar, and the stability of the financial system. Accordingly, he insisted on balancing the budget as the surest way to achieve low inflation. In 1959–60, the president fought a largely successful battle against a heavily Democratic Congress more interested in promoting employment-boosting economic growth through new domestic spending initiatives, even at cost of fiscal deficits.[8]

Once Eisenhower's tenure ended, Democratic capture of the White House prefaced a new approach to economic management. John F. Kennedy won the presidency in 1960 with a banner promise "to get our country moving again, to get our economy moving ahead." This bespoke his conviction that government could manipulate rates of economic growth to maximize corporate profits, employment opportunities, and across-the-board improvements in Americans' standard of living, but he lacked a surefire strategy for doing so without igniting inflation. Through patient tutoring, his economic advisers in the CEA won him over to the agenda of the so-called new economics. Hitherto, the Truman and Eisenhower administrations had relied on fluctuations in tax-revenue levels produced by the business cycle to operate as an automatic stabilizer against recession and inflation. When recession struck, the resultant decline in economic activity automatically yielded a smaller volume of tax receipts that in turn produced compensatory budget deficits to boost recovery. When the economy conversely returned to prosperity, the automatic increase in tax receipts produced budget surpluses that stifled inflationary pressures. However, the Kennedy economists contended that this revenue expansion acted as a fiscal drag on consumption during periods of recovery from recession, with the consequence that the economy never reached its full potential to create new jobs. In their assessment, the retardation of employment growth was the main cause of the estimated $50 billion performance gap between potential and real GDP in 1960. To close this, the CEA advocated cutting taxes to stimulate demand in the recovery cycle, something never hitherto attempted. In this way, it hoped to get joblessness down to an effective full-employment level of 4 percent of the labor force and to keep inflation at 2 percent because the economy would be operating at its maximum productive capacity.[9]

By mid-1962 Kennedy's economists had convinced him that Keynesian demand-management could be used to accelerate economic expansion rather than merely stabilize cyclical trends of recession and recovery. The president then faced the task of persuading the corporate community that the new economics would boost business coffers rather than deplete their value by generating inflation. Beginning with his Yale commencement address in June 1962, he set out to convert the unbelievers to the gospel of what one scholar termed "growth liberalism."[10] The notion that business would be resistant to cutting taxes may strike twenty-first-century readers as paradoxical, but postwar corporate orthodoxy held that running budget deficits might be acceptable during recessions and war but never in other circumstances. The corporate elite's enthusiastic response to Kennedy's address at the Economic Club of New York in December signified the success of his public campaign. "I gave them straight Keynes and Heller," the president delightedly reported to his CEA chair, "and they loved it."[11]

With business in his corner, Kennedy included the tax cut in his 1963 legislative program but did not live to see its enactment. Lyndon B. Johnson finally piloted it onto the statute books in early 1964. The immediate consequences lived up to everything the new economists had promised. In 1965, economic expansion exceeded 6 percent, unemployment fell to 4.1 percent, inflation held steady around 2 percent, and the deficit nearly disappeared (it amounted to 0.2 percent GDP) because the lower tax rates yielded higher revenues in a growing economy. The Kennedy-Johnson economists were confident that presidents now possessed the fiscal elixir for perpetual economic growth, a budgetary prescription to manage employment and inflation levels in a way that maximized prosperity within the framework of America's ever-expanding capitalist economy. Economist Heller claimed in 1966, "Policy now centers on [performance] gap closing and growth, one realizing and enlarging the economy's non-inflationary potential."[12]

The new economists' joy soon turned to tears, however. The spike in military spending that accompanied the Americanization of the Vietnam War in 1965 put increasing strain on an economy already operating near maximum capacity. As production targets rose, the corollary growth of labor costs amid full-employment conditions brought an end to the spectacular business profits of the mid-1960s. The budget that was supposed to deliver economic good had turned into an engine of destabilization. When Vietnam outlays peaked in 1968, the fiscal deficit reached a postwar high of 3.1 percent GDP and consumer price inflation ran at 4 percent. Reflecting corporate disillusion with the economic consequences of the conflict, Bank of America chairman Louis B. Lundborg emphatically declared in 1970 that "an end to the war would be good, not bad, for business."[13]

New economists like Johnson's final CEA chair, Arthur M. Okun, hoped that the running down of the Vietnam War in the early 1970s would create the conditions for the restoration of inflation-free growth.[14] Instead, a host of new problems brought the long postwar boom to an end. In place of prosperity, Americans endured an era of stagflation, in which three recessions hit the economy (in 1970, 1974–75, and 1980) and consumer prices rose on average by 9 percent per year from 1973 to 1980. This economic misery had many causes: rapidly rising energy costs in the wake of Organization of Petroleum Exporting Countries (OPEC) oil-price hikes that led to a quadrupling of gasoline prices between 1973 and 1980; a weak dollar after the United States abandoned its fixed-convertibility value to gold in 1971; the cost-push inflationary effects of wage hikes to keep pace with rising prices; tight credit; and an inflationary psychology whereby business and consumers based their economic decisions on the expectation of unending price instability. In these circumstances, presidents seemed powerless to get the economy back on track through application of conventional fiscal remedies. The chief consequence of focusing on the battle against either stagnation or inflation was to exacerbate the other side of the stagflationary coin. Accordingly, Richard M. Nixon, Gerald R. Ford, and Jimmy Carter zigzagged uncertainly between expansion and restraint in cruel parody of their status as managers of prosperity.[15]

Addressing the American Bankers Association in 1980, investment guru Henry Kaufman called for a presidential declaration of national emergency that would permit extraordinary measures to address a runaway inflation rate that was heading into double-digits for the second year running.[16] For many business leaders, this was the greatest crisis of American capitalism since the depths of the Great Depression in 1929–33. High inflation undermined their economic planning, ate into profits, and generated labor demands for wage increases. It also created ever-tighter credit conditions, notably in the bond market, where buyers were reluctant to risk long-term investments that were liable to devaluation over time. Salvation was soon at hand for American capitalism in this particular moment of danger, but it did not come from the presidency.[17]

In July 1979 Jimmy Carter appointed Paul Volcker as chair of the Federal Reserve with effective carte blanche to conquer inflation by any means necessary. Volcker shook inflationary pressures out of the economy through the application of the castor-oil cure of monetarism—a sharp reduction in the overall quantity of money and credit in circulation—at cost of a severe recession in 1981–82. At the depth of this downturn, the jobless rate exceeded 10 percent of the labor force for the first time since the Great Depression. Only a central bank with no electoral accountability could have effected such a draconian solution. The speed with which the Fed adopted the monetarist strategy in mid-1981 and terminated it a year later in order to fight unemployment now that inflation was under control contrasted with the lengthy time presidents required to negotiate fiscal policy implementation by Congress. The central bank's decision-making advantages produced a new division of economic management responsibility between the Fed chair and the president based on their respective leadership in the monetary and fiscal domains. Henceforth the former took the lead in ensuring rapid stabilization of the economy when either inflation or recession threatened, but through incremental adjustments in interest rates that were a sufficient instrument of monetary management in the post-stagflation era, and the latter focused on laying stronger foundations for sustained economic growth.[18]

Ronald W. Reagan was the first president to operate within this new arrangement. Elected in 1980 on his promise of economic renewal, this conservative Republican attacked big government as the source of America's woes because of the high taxes needed to fund its free-spending habits. The novel doctrine of supply-side economics lent this critique intellectual legitimacy through its prognosis that increased incentive, in the form of government allowing businesses and individuals to keep more of the wealth they created, held the key to economic revival. In its credo, cutting taxes would encourage increased investment by holders of capital, a higher rate of business start-ups, and greater labor productivity. Confident that the resultant surge of economic growth would generate higher revenues for government, supply-side devotees were insistent that tax relief would close rather than enlarge the fiscal deficit. Reagan put their ideas into practice by promoting the Economic Recovery Tax Act (ERTA) of 1981, the largest tax cut in American history. This legislation immediately reduced the top marginal rate of income taxation from 70 percent to

50 percent, gave a 25 percent cut to taxpayers in other income bands in three annual tranches of 5, 10, and 10 percent, and provided a host of tax write-offs for business. However, the consequences of this largesse did not wholly conform to the comforting theory of supply-side doctrine.[19]

The Reagan economic plan, *America's New Beginning: A Program for Economic Recovery*, had assumed that ERTA-generated economic growth would result in a balanced budget by the end of his first term. Instead the deficit widened from $73.8 billion in FY1980 to $203.8 billion in FY1983 and went on to average 4.3 percent of gross domestic product yearly during Reagan's two terms compared with 2.4 percent under Jimmy Carter. These huge annual imbalances enlarged the public debt from 26.1 percent of GDP at the end of 1980 to 40.9 percent at the end of 1988. In reality, the chances of achieving a balanced budget as planned had been slim at best because Reagan had promoted the largest defense expansion since the Korean War without achieving commensurate economies in domestic programs. What blew away the rosy fiscal scenario of *America's New Beginning*, however, was the serious recession sparked by the Federal Reserve's anti-inflation strategy, which depressed tax receipts just when the Reagan plan anticipated their ERTA-influenced growth. Remarkably, the mammoth deficits of the 1980s did not have the inflationary consequences that Keynesian-era presidents had feared from the much smaller ones of their day. This was largely due to the success of the Federal Reserve's monetarist program of 1981–82 in stabilizing the value of money. Instead of price instability, the principal and unanticipated consequence of the Reagan-era deficits was their role in the restructuring of American capitalism.

The only way that the United States could meet both public and private borrowing needs in the 1980s was to import capital from abroad. To facilitate this process, the Federal Reserve kept *real* interest rates (the actual rate *minus* the rate of inflation) relatively high from 1983 onwards. With the promise of higher returns and stable money values in America, huge capital inflows from abroad helped to finance the expanding deficit and found investment opportunities on Wall Street and elsewhere. Hitherto a relatively scarce commodity, capital's increased availability accelerated the shift that had started in the 1970s toward the so-called financialization of the American economy whereby making money from money became more profitable than doing so from producing things. Undertaken in the name of free-market efficiency, shrinking government regulation of financial industry rules from the 1970s onward also assisted in boosting the profitability of the financial sector of the economy. Economic power consequently shifted from enterprises engaged in using capital to expand manufacturing to ones using it to enhance their financial resources. One measure of this vast change taking place in corporate America was the expansion of the financial sector's share of GDP from 10 percent in 1970 to 20 percent in 2010; another was the rise of its profits from less than 10 percent of total corporate profits in 1982 to 40 percent in 2010.[20]

While rising foreign demand for U.S. financial assets benefited Wall Street and other financial centers, it hurt the manufacturing sector by generating a strong dollar that made America's imports cheaper and its exports dearer. As a result of this competitive disadvantage, many U.S. manufacturing industries that had started to experience problems from foreign competition in the 1970s found recovery from the 1981–82 recession to be painful and partial. Even companies once synonymous with postwar prosperity found it expedient to focus on making still-popular brands while discarding their underperforming sectors, exemplified by General Motors' decision to cease producing medium and heavy trucks. In these circumstances, the 1980s turned out to be the first decade in American history when manufacturing jobs declined in number. The long-term continuation of this trend saw employment in this sector decline by 24 percent between 1980 and 2005.[21]

Increasingly, businesses engaged in manufacturing found greater profit from corporate buyouts, mergers, and restructuring. In total, an unprecedented $1.3 trillion of corporate assets changed hands in the 1980s. Much of the acquisition resulted in the de-conglomeration of large organizations and their replacement with smaller enterprises focused on core business. GE, whose home electrical products Ronald Reagan had once promoted on television in the 1950s, reduced its workforce from 411,000 in 1980 to 299,000 in 1985 through management reduction, shop-floor layoffs, and sell-offs of some operations. Its acquisition of other companies, some six hundred in the last two decades of the twentieth century, was the prelude to selling off their unprofitable parts to focus on so-called good units (exemplified by keeping NBC but discarding other parts of RCA acquired in a 1986 takeover). Since the wave of mergers was largely financed through borrowing, American corporations needed 56 percent of available earnings just to pay interest by 1986, compared with 33 percent a decade earlier. Debt servicing left fewer resources for other purposes—in 1988 U.S. businesses spent less in real terms on net investment in new plant and equipment than in 1979. Furthermore the need for compensatory economies to meet interest payments caused them to reduce their work forces, pare back wage structures, and transfer some operations abroad to ease debt burdens.[22]

Far more than the deficit, of course, tax reduction is what twenty-first-century Republicans remember as Reagan's principal boon to business expansion. Whether this was so in reality is debatable. The business tax breaks contained in ERTA were mainly put there not by the White House but by congressional Democrats and Republicans acting on the behest of corporate lobbyists. Many were rescinded in the Tax Equity and Fiscal Responsibility Act of 1982, enacted with Reagan's support as a deficit-control measure. The Reagan Tax Reform Act (TRA) of 1986, the most thoroughgoing overhaul of the tax system since World War II, both gave and took from business. It reduced the top corporate tax rate but increased the capital gains rate from 20 percent to 28 percent and eliminated many tax breaks that mainly benefited business and investors (among them the investment credit promoted by the Kennedy administration in 1962 and reduced depreciation allowance for new assets). These provisions meant that business largely ended up paying higher taxes to offset the revenue loss that resulted principally from the measure's simplification of the personal tax code from fourteen brackets to two, setting 28 percent for top earners and 15 percent for everyone else.[23]

The deficit that seemed to be back under some kind of control when Reagan left office began to mushroom once more under George H. W. Bush. Rising costs for Social Security and Medicare entitlements, the bill for the savings and loan industry bailout, and the effect of the 1990–91 recession on revenues were among the factors responsible for this. When Democrat William J. Clinton entered the White House in 1993, his fiscal inheritance was a budget imbalance of $292 billon in FY1992 (a current-dollar record that constituted 4.9 percent GDP) and predictions that it would rise to $653 billion (7 percent of GDP) within a decade.[24] Concern grew that this scale of U.S. borrowing would make it difficult for the Federal Reserve to preserve price stability through interest-rate adjustments. Corporate leaders worried that foreigners would flee from dollar assets unless a new dose of painful monetarism reassured them that inflation could be controlled. So anxious was the new president to maintain business confidence in the interests of sustained economic growth that he shifted his programmatic priorities in the weeks between his election and inauguration as president.

In running for the White House, Clinton had promised an ambitious agenda of "human investment" spending by government on educational and training programs to equip the nation's workforce with the skills required to make America the world leader in knowledge-based enterprises reliant on high-tech equipment. In his assessment, the United States could no longer compete with low-wage countries in traditional forms of manufacturing so it had to forge ahead in making products with computerized technology. The "Putting People First" plan that embodied this aim gave way to putting the deficit first, however. Chiefly responsible for converting him to this cause were National Economic Council chair Robert E. Rubin and Federal Reserve chair Alan Greenspan. On a courtesy visit to the president-elect in Little Rock, the latter warned that the bond market, the principal source of long-term lending to business, was raising interest rates to safeguard the value of its returns against renewed inflation produced by mammoth fiscal deficits. If the budget gap could be closed, Greenspan advised, the benefits of restored business confidence would make the economy "look awfully good" toward the end of the 1990s.[25]

Taking considerable political risk, Clinton promoted the Omnibus Budget Reconciliation Act (OBRA) of 1993 that aimed to reduce the deficit by $433 billion over five years through net revenue enhancement of $241 billion and net spending cuts of $192 billion. Sacrificed in the drive for deficit reduction was a middle-class tax cut promised in the election campaign, an omission that the congressional Republicans would exploit in their successful midterm campaign of 1994. From Clinton's perspective, however, the greatest loss was the human investment expenditures that congressional Democrats had removed from the deficit-reduction plan in order to safeguard their long-standing programmatic concerns, like antipoverty initiatives, urban aid, and public works, from large cuts. This intra-party disagreement signified tension between the president's "New Democrat" drive for modernization and the preferences of liberals for stimulus and welfare measures to help traditional Democratic constituencies.[26] Evidently not a supply-sider in the Reagan mold, Clinton had nevertheless hoped to boost the productivity and innovation of American manufacturing by improving the quality of its labor supply. Thwarted in this ambition, he reverted to the more modest supply-side objective of facilitating the availability of cheaper credit for business expansion through offering psychological insurance to the bond market and other sources of capital that the budget deficit would not become an engine of inflation. "I have a jobs program," Robert Rubin recalled Clinton telling him, "and my jobs program is deficit reduction."[27]

Measured by its effect on the bond market, Clinton's OBRA was an outright success. Long-term interest rates went into decline almost immediately following its passage. However, short-term interest rates headed in the opposite direction because Alan Greenspan was determined to stifle inflationary pressures in an economy now recovering from recession. Laying greater store on price stability than on employment growth in line with the preferences of the financial sector, he sought to manipulate interest rates to achieve a non-accelerating inflation rate of unemployment (better known as NAIRU) to ensure a steady rather than over-rapid economic recovery. Accordingly, job growth in the wake of OBRA was initially slow and fuelled Republican claims that the Clinton tax increases were to blame. Following GOP success in capturing the House and Senate in the 1994 midterms, the Democratic hold on the White House looked to be in danger for 1996. Fortunately for Clinton's reelection hopes, monetary policy changed course in mid-1995 once Greenspan was convinced that an emergent new economy, increasingly driven by the new technology of the computer revolution, was making productivity gains that kept inflation down in conjunction with presidential success in deficit reduction. As a consequence, the Fed began reducing interest rates to generate a four-year cycle of relatively cheap credit. The increasing ease of borrowing underwrote an economic boom that was accompanied by the lowest unemployment and inflation figures since the halcyon days of the 1960s. A buoyant stock market also produced a harvest of investment tax revenues for Uncle Sam, a windfall that initially accelerated the pace of deficit reduction and ultimately did much to produce four consecutive balanced budgets from FY1998 to FY2001, the longest cycle of government finances being in the black since the 1920s.[28]

Two liberal economists, Alan S. Blinder and Janet L. Yellen, who served spells in both the Clinton CEA and the Greenspan Fed in the 1990s, regarded the economic boom of the second half of the decade as proof that "tight budgets and (relatively) easy monetary policy can create a pro-investment macroeconomic climate by holding down real interest rates."[29] Greenspan himself seemingly endorsed this view in telling the president,

"If you had not turned the fiscal situation around, we couldn't have had the kind of monetary policy we've had." Testifying to the optimism of the times, official projections at century's end suggested that a run of massive surplus budgets would pay off the entire public debt by 2015. Hailing this, Clinton proclaimed on January 6, 1999, "Today, I am proud to announce that we can say the era of big deficits is over."[30] Like the new economists of the 1960s, the New Democrat of the 1990s would find that pride comes before a fall.

At a reunion of OBRA supporters in 1998, Clinton declared that "the economic plan worked, and it worked for the reasons we said it would. . . . [We] actually enacted a law of intended consequences in American life."[31] Unfortunately, there were also unintended consequences that flowed indirectly from its success. The reduction in long-term interest rates encouraged by OBRA helped to make the stock market more attractive than the bond market to increasing numbers of investors. Economic growth, cheap credit (courtesy of the Fed's monetary policy), and the prospect of making a killing in Internet start-up companies combined to transform a financial boom into an unsustainable bubble. In 1996 Greenspan famously warned that Wall Street was manifesting "irrational exuberance" but did nothing to douse it.[32] As Clinton's presidency closed, the stock market was showing worrying signs of volatility because of concerns that many so-called dot-com companies that did most of their business on the Internet, like Pixelon, Webvan, and Startups.com, were vastly overvalued. Starting early in 2001, the collapse of shares in such enterprises resulted in a financial downturn that precipitated a general economic recession. In bringing an end to the longest expansionary cycle in American economic history, the "dot-com recession" produced a sharp decline in investment tax receipts that turned the dream of perpetual surplus budgets to dust. If Clinton's fiscal policy cannot be held directly responsible for this turn of events, the late 1990s indicated that balanced budgets and low interest rates do not always have predictable or beneficial consequences.

The new Republican president, George W. Bush, brought a more orthodox supply-side tax-cutting strategy to office—and a far purer one than Ronald Reagan's. He looked to dispose of the anticipated fiscal surpluses through massive tax reduction with the aim of sustaining the 1990s boom and delivering even higher rates of economic growth. When recession hit, Bush switched to justifying his tax program in almost Keynesian terms as necessary for a rapid recovery. Nevertheless, the Economic Growth and

Tax Relief Reconciliation Act of 2001, the second-largest tax cut in American history behind the 1981 ERTA, adopted what can only be called a trickle-down approach by targeting its benefits toward the wealthy in the belief that the resultant increase in investment would generate renewed economic growth to the benefit of all. According to the Citizens for Tax Justice, a fiscal watchdog, 40 percent of its ten-year $1.35 trillion tax cuts would flow to the richest 1 percent of income earners, virtually the same share as the bottom 80 percent would get.[33]

Two years later, Bush promoted the third-largest tax cut in American history in the form of the investor-oriented Jobs and Growth Tax Reconciliation Act. In signing the measure, the president unambiguously nailed his colors to the supply-side mast by declaring that "the best way to have more jobs is to help the people who create jobs." An estimated 46 percent of its capital gains and dividend tax cuts flowed to the 0.2 percent of households with annual incomes of over $1 million a year and nearly three-quarters went to the 3.1 percent making over $200,000 a year. Other tax cuts followed, like the Working Families Tax Relief Act of 2004 and the Tax Increase Prevention and Reconciliation Act of 2006, all manifesting the same idea that tax reduction for the wealthy, with the consequent benefits for financial investment, was the best way to ensure widespread prosperity.[34]

This supply-side version of trickle-down economics did not produce the expected benefits for the American economy. Annual GDP growth only averaged 2.6 percent between the end of the dot-com recession in early 2002 and the onset of the Great Recession in early 2008. On the other hand, the loss of revenue from George W. Bush's tax cuts in combination with the costs of the military interventions in Afghanistan and Iraq produced fiscal deficits that averaged 2.5 percent of GDP over his two-term tenure and a swing from Clinton's record current-dollar surplus of $236 billion in FY2000 to a record current-dollar imbalance of $413 billion in FY2004. To finance this borrowing, the United States became even more reliant on foreign purchase of Treasury securities, with the People's Republic of China (PRC) quickly emerging as the greatest buyer. One effect of China's lending was to drive up the value of the dollar against the renminbi, thereby making its imports cheaper for Americans consumers to buy than home-produced goods. As a consequence, the U.S. trade deficit with the PRC rose from just $83 billion in 2001 to $268 billion in 2008 to the further detriment of American producers and workers. This was one reason why U.S. manufacturing accounted for only 10 percent of GDP in 2010, compared with 30 percent in the halcyon days of 1950.

Nevertheless, the greatest economic crisis of the Bush era occurred in the financial sector that had replaced manufacturing as the key driver of the economy since the 1980s. This crisis resulted from reckless lending by financial institutions on mortgages and other forms of debt in the free-and-easy credit conditions emanating from low interest rates at home and capital importation from abroad. If Bush could not be held personally responsible for the financial meltdown of 2007–8, it nevertheless marked him out on the basis of his own concept of economic good as the most unsuccessful presidential manager of the economy since Herbert Hoover.[35]

As this review indicates, U.S. presidents have actively sought to fulfill their Employment Act obligations to make American capitalism more successful and better able to deliver prosperity for the nation. Their effectiveness in the period after World War II stands in marked contrast to the limited results of their engagement with the economy from 1981 to 2008. Of course, the more advantageous structural factors of the earlier era—including the disruptive effect of World War II on industrial rivals, the very high GDP level of early Cold War defense spending, and the ascendancy of employment-intensive manufacturing—did much to underwrite presidential success. In contrast, the less advantageous conditions thereafter—including greater competition from abroad, greater reliance on foreign lending, and the financialization of the economy—helped to limit it.

Keynesian-era presidents facilitated American capitalism's postwar success in spreading the fruits of its prosperity relatively broadly throughout society. The archetypal corporate beneficiaries of their demand-management strategy in this period were the likes of U.S. Steel, General Motors, and GE. In partnership with government, businesses of this ilk generated an expanding job market, rising living standards, a growing middle class, a narrowing in income inequality, and later—with considerable help from Lyndon Johnson's Great Society—a decline in poverty. The American economy continued to grow in the supply-side era, albeit at a slower rate than in the Keynesian era, but was far less successful in the distribution of wealth created.[36] The new beneficiaries of presidential economics were the capital-rich Wall Street houses and other financial institutions whose profitability derived from making money create more money, not from the growth of jobs and consumption. According to economist James

Galbraith, the late 1970s marked "the end of normal."[37] In contrast to the broad trends of the first seventy-five years of the twentieth century and the post–World War II quarter-century in particular, income inequality has widened and median household income has stagnated since the 1970s. Although structural economic changes pertaining to the financialization of the economy, the relative decline of American manufacturing, and the broader effects of economic globalization were largely responsible for this transformation, fiscal policy was certainly a contributory factor. In other words, it was partly instrumental in promoting a new reality in which economic good had a far narrower range of beneficiaries.

Despite the differences between both periods, they shared one thing in common. Whether Keynesian or supply-side, White House efforts to accelerate economic growth were marked by blowback ill-effects, as the Kennedy-Johnson new economics, the supply-side crusades of Ronald Reagan and George W. Bush, and Clinton's boom-to-bust demonstrated. All these presidents sought the holy grail of sustained growth of widespread prosperity within the framework of American capitalism without ever truly finding it. As the United States moves further into the twenty-first century, it is arguably entering a new fiscal era. It is highly unlikely that presidents can continue offering supposedly painless agendas for maximizing growth and prosperity as in the past. Bringing under control a public debt that looks set to grow significantly faster than the economy in the second and third decades of the twenty-first century and beyond stands out as the major budgetary problem facing the United States. To achieve this end, future presidents will likely have to make tough fiscal choices in years to come instead of offering grand visions of economic growth in the manner of some predecessors in the first sixty years of the Employment Act's existence

Notes

1. Walter W. Heller, *New Dimensions of Political Economy* (New York: Norton, 1966), 18.

2. Iwan Morgan, *The Age of Deficits: Presidents and Unbalanced Budgets from Jimmy Carter to George W. Bush* (Lawrence: University Press of Kansas, 2009), 3–6.

3. For a biography, see Robert Skidelsky, *John Maynard Keynes: 1883–1946: Economist, Philosopher, Statesman* (London: Penguin, 2013).

4. Robert Lekachman, *The Age of Keynes* (New York: Random House, 1966); Greta R.

Krippner, *Capitalizing on Crisis: The Political Origins of the Rise of Finance* (Cambridge, MA: Harvard University Press, 2011).

5. Fiscal data for this chapter are drawn from *Fiscal Year 2017: Historical Tables: Budget of the US Government*, White House website, https://www.whitehouse.gov/sites/default/files/omb/budget/fy2.

6. John L. Gaddis, *Strategies of Containment: A Critical Appraisal of American National Security Strategy during the Cold War*, rev. ed. (New York: Oxford University Press, 2005), 89–91.

7. Arthur M. Schlesinger Jr., *The Politics of Hope* (Boston: Houghton Mifflin, 1962), 91.

8. Iwan Morgan, "Managing the Economy," in *A Companion to Dwight D. Eisenhower*, ed. Chester Pach (New York: Wiley-Blackwell, 2017), 227–45.

9. Iwan Morgan, "The Keynesian Consensus and Its Limits," in *The Liberal Consensus Reconsidered: American Politics and Society in the Postwar Era*, ed. Robert Mason and Iwan Morgan (Gainesville: University Press of Florida, 2017, 86–107.

10. Robert M. Collins, *More: The Politics of Economic Growth in Postwar America* (New York: Oxford University Press, 2000), 61.

11. Heller, *New Dimensions of Political Economy*, 22.

12. Heller, *New Dimensions of Political Economy*, vii–viii.

13. Allen J. Matusow, *The Unraveling of America: A History of Liberalism in the 1960s* (New York: Harper & Row, 1984), 176.

14. Arthur M. Okun, *The Political Economy of Prosperity* (New York: Norton, 1970), 130.

15. Collins, *More*, 98–165.

16. Daniel Herzberg, "Troubled Houses," *Wall Street Journal*, February 22, 1980.

17. "Fighting the Inflation 'Crisis,'" *Newsweek*, March 10, 1980.

18. Iwan Morgan, "Monetary Metamorphosis: The Volcker Fed and Inflation," *Journal of Policy History* 24 (December 2012): 545–71.

19. Robert M. Collins, *Transforming America: Politics and Culture during the Reagan Years* (New York: Columbia University Press, 2007), 59–92.

20. Judith Stein, *Pivotal Decade: How the United States Traded Factories for Finance in the 1970s* (New Haven, CT: Yale University Press, 2010); Krippner, *Capitalizing on Crisis*, 97–102; Mike Collins, "Wall Street and the Financialization of the Economy," *Forbes/Reinventing America*, February 4, 2015.

21. Patricia Atkins, Pamela Blumenthal, Adrienne Edisis, Alec Friedhoff, Leah Curran, Lisa Lowry, Travis St. Clair, Howard Wial, and Harold Wolman, "Responding to Manufacturing Job Loss: What Can Economic Development Do?" *Brookings Metropolitan Policy Report*, June 2011, 1–2.

22. Collins, *Transforming America*, 110–15. For GE, see its CEO's memoir—Jack Welch with John Byrne, *Jack: Straight from the Gut* (New York: Warner, 2003).

23. Lawrence H. Summers, "A Fair Tax Act That's Bad for Business," *Harvard Business Review* 65 (Mar./Apr. 1987): 53–58.

24. Congressional Budget Office, *Economic and Budget Outlook: Fiscal Years 1994–1998* (Washington DC: CBO, 1993), 27–29.

25. Robert E. Rubin and Jacob Weisberg, *In an Uncertain World: Tough Choices from Wall Street to Washington* (New York: Random House, 2003), 121; Alan Greenspan, *The Age of Turbulence: Adventures in a New World* (New York: Penguin, 2007), 143–45.

26. Iwan Morgan, "A New Democrat's New Economics," in *The Presidency of Bill Clinton: The Legacy of a New Domestic and Foreign Policy*, ed. Mark White (London: Tauris, 2012), 65–91.

27. Quoted in Richard Stevenson, "The Wisdom to Let the Good Times Roll," *New York Times*, December 25, 2000.

28. Bob Woodward, *Maestro: Greenspan's Fed and the American Boom* (New York: Simon & Schuster, 2000), 227; Greenspan, *The Age of Turbulence*, 164–74.

29. Alan Blinder and Janet Yellen, *The Fabulous Decade: Macroeconomic Lessons from the 1990s* (New York: Century Foundation Press, 2001), 15–24, 83–85 (quotation p. 85).

30. Woodward, *Maestro*, 221; William J. Clinton, "Remarks on the Budget Surplus for Fiscal Year 1999," Public Papers of the President (hereafter PPOP), American Presidency Project (hereafter APP), http://www.presidency.ucsb.edu/.

31. William J. Clinton, "Remarks at a Reception for Supporters of the Omnibus Budget Reconciliation Act of 1993," April 23, 1998, PPOP, APP.

32. Robert J. Shiller, *Irrational Exuberance*, rev. and expanded 3rd ed. (Princeton NJ: Princeton University Press, 2015).

33. Citizens for Tax Justice, "Year-by-Year Analysis of the Bush Tax Cuts Shows Growing Tilt to the Very Rich," June 12, 2002, http://ctj.org/ctjreports/2002/06/year-by-year_analysis_of_the_bush_tax_cuts_shows_growing_tilt_to_the_very_rich.php.

34. George W. Bush, "Remarks on Signing the Jobs and Growth Tax Relief Reconciliation Act of May 28, 2003," APP; Morgan, *The Age of Deficits*, 220–31.

35. Brad Sester and Nouriel Roubini, "Our Money, Our Debt, Our Problem," *Foreign Affairs* 84, no. 4 (2005): 198–206; Joseph Stiglitz, "The Economic Consequences of Mr. Bush," *Vanity Fair*, November 30, 2007, 227–28.

36. Robert J. Gordon, *The Rise and Fall of American Growth: The U.S. Standard of Living since the Civil War* (Princeton NJ: Princeton University Press, 2016), esp. 522–65.

37. James K. Galbraith, *The End of Normal: The Great Crisis and the Future of Growth* (New York: Simon & Schuster, 2014).

6

The Antigovernment Impulse

The Presidency, the "Market," and the Splintering Common Good

BRENT CEBUL

> The great danger is that this momentary disillusionment with government will turn into a more profound and lasting loss of faith.
>
> President Richard Nixon, 1971

> With the same energy that Franklin Roosevelt sought government solutions to problems, we will seek private solutions.
>
> President Ronald Reagan, 1981

> The era of big government is over.
>
> President Bill Clinton, 1996

President Richard M. Nixon traveled to Philadelphia in October 1972 to declare "a new American revolution." The revolution, he pledged, would be "as profound, as far-reaching, [and] as exciting as that first revolution almost 200 years ago." Nixon chose Philadelphia for its historical symbolism, which he hoped would rub off on the otherwise humdrum legislation he was there to sign. The State and Local Fiscal Assistance Act of 1972, or, in its zippier form, General Revenue Sharing, merely delivered millions of dollars in federal tax revenues to state and local governments with few strings attached. Yet Nixon insisted in framing his legislation in revolutionary terms. The founders, he said, gathered in Philadelphia "to establish the federal system. We return here in the 20th century to renew the federal system. . . . After many years in which power has been flowing away from those levels of government which are closest to the people, power will now begin to flow back to the people again."[1]

In and of itself, Nixon's legislation hardly signaled the emergence of our now well-entrenched era of antigovernment politics. Its intellectual architect, in fact, was Walter Heller, the liberal economist and advisor to Presidents John F. Kennedy and Lyndon B. Johnson. But the trickle of antigovernment political sentiment that Nixon sought to channel augured a revolutionary wave. Amidst a series of economic crises in the 1970s and the simultaneous politicization of the state itself, this drop of early antigovernment sentiment would become a rising tide.

Critical to this modern antigovernment revolution was not just trimming the influence of national government but also offering private sector actors and market solutions as alternatives to government. This sea change depended upon the popular conceptual emergence of "the market" as an *autonomous system* in which governments operated and within which citizens organized their lives. This conceptual development differed in significant ways from conservatives' earlier advocacy of "free enterprise" or "the private sector," wherein discrete markets were structured by and subordinated to larger cultural and political forces. This system of "embedded liberalism," as scholars termed it, positioned markets and market actors like businesses within political-economic boundaries set by the state, but also within social norms dictated by cultural traditions such as religious institutions.[2]

The antigovernment turn to "the market" as an alternative to public programs, particularly for fighting poverty, as this chapter suggests, represented a radical shift in the antigovernment impulse. This was particularly evident in the delivery of social provision, which had historically been routed through government, philanthropies, and faith-based organizations, or by contracting with private groups.[3] In striking contrast to these *embodied* institutions, the emergence of "market-based solutions" decoupled responsibility for social provision from specific institutions, human agency, and responsibility, offering in their place a *disembodied* and almost faith-based vision of the market as a guarantor of a variety of social and economic goods.

Presidents played a leading role in these developments. As the historian Daniel Rodgers reminds us, in their public remarks and "in the very course of the everyday acts of politics, presidents" map for the American people "an image of the nation as a collective entity over which they preside." Presidents "set into circulation mental pictures of society and its field of obligations."[4] Whether these ideas resonate, however, depends upon broader cultural factors. Successful mental pictures must tap into citizens' concerns about the major problems facing the nation. Context and history are critical. But presidential narratives must do more than simply link together a series of often highly disparate problems. These narratives also must reveal a coherent set of solutions capable of capturing the spirit of an era. As Rodgers suggests, the most commanding visions offer a "theory of society and politics" that contain the power to reshape society and its politics. "The market" as a modern form of antigovernment politics has been one such powerful vision of society, becoming, in many quarters, an encompassing metaphor for society itself.

The emergence of "the market" is the latest chapter in a long history of American antigovernment politics. The antigovernment impulse—the diagnosis that the major challenges facing the American citizenry derive from an overabundance of governance, taxes, or regulatory strictures—is hardly new. Mistrust of centralized authority spurred the nation's founding. But, in terms of its complexity, scope, and endurance, the national state that emerged from the Second World War was practically a new species. This state ensured a majority of Americans retired with a historically unprecedented degree of independence and security, enjoyed affordable mortgage rates, consumed an adequate supply of often government-subsidized calories, possessed inexpensive access to abundant energy sources, and also saw to it that many benefited from state-supported admission into a system of higher education that became the envy of the world thanks in large part to government research and defense contracts.

By 1967, public opinion pollsters Hadley Cantril and Lloyd Free published *The Political Beliefs of Americans*, in which they underscored the modern paradox of American politics. Americans, they argued, were "ideological conservatives" but "operational liberals."[5] They desired a limited government that nevertheless solved the problems of modern life. In retrospect, the citizens Cantril and Free polled may not have known how good they had it. For the three decades prior to *Political Beliefs*, the liberal state had managed to synthesize this paradox. That is, as liberals developed many of the twentieth century's most significant social policies, they factored in such ambivalence toward a powerful state. Many of the above policies, which disproportionately benefited (and helped create) the emerging white middle class, operated, in historian Margaret O'Mara's iteration of the Cantril and Free paradox, within "'strong-state-as-weak-state' frameworks."[6] These social policies functioned out of sight to most

Americans *by design*. Federal mortgage insurance enabled private banks to offer long-term loans. Government subsidization of crops and livestock occurred on the supply side, obscuring the fact that Americans' grocery bills were not paid in full until tax season. Similar subsidies or the granting of "natural" monopolies meant Americans enjoyed unfettered access to artificially affordable energy, education, and more. This enduring pattern of government working *through* market actors to deliver social goods and security obscured the state's role, often making the primary "actors appear to be those in the market or private sector."[7] Throughout the twentieth century, then, politicians and policymakers allowed political credit for many of the causes of Americans' improving standards of living to flow to the private sector rather than government, which was nevertheless often the prime mover within the systems of embedded liberalism and the mixed economy.[8] And by creating a social policy regime that fundamentally submerged the principal role of government in structuring markets, liberals inadvertently set the table for the emergence of a particularly one-sided form of antigovernment politics, one in which the positive aspects of government lacked popular understanding, let alone robust support.[9]

Compared to the antigovernment politics of the pre–New Deal United States, presidents confronting the twentieth-century state and its complex public-private social security regime thus faced a challenging balancing act. Richard Nixon inaugurated what we might call an era of "antigovernment governance," when politicians, most often from the right but also on the left, sought office not to solve problems *with* government but to solve problems *of* government. In this era of antigovernment governance, politicians spoke in increasingly clear-eyed terms about taming an unwieldy state. But their policy solutions were often and necessarily just as complex, politically muddled, esoteric, and technocratic as that state had become. These approaches included emphasizing decentralism, associationalism, and devolution—hardly zeitgeist-defining concepts capable of defining a new "theory of society."

There were good reasons for this. Upon taking office, presidents perceived the political risks of cutting programs upon which a majority of voters depended. As a result, programs like Nixon's General Revenue Sharing legitimated increasing concerns about government growth but often quietly continued that growth—whether through new regulations, spending, or increasing the ranks of government employees. This distinctly modern version of antigovernment politics would muddle along until a new vision of society offered an alternative model of antigovernment politics capable of piercing through such complexity: the "market."

The revolutionary emergence of the market idea as an alternative to government was, however, evolutionary. It emerged from earlier forms of antigovernment politics. It was nurtured by a body of economic ideas once deemed marginal to political-economic policymaking.[10] These ideas gained cultural legitimation amidst the political and economic crises of the 1970s, in which a white, working- and middle-class populism emerged, loosely organized around issues of taxation, majoritarianism, political corruption, the consumer rights of homeownership, and local neighborhood control, each of which brought the national state into the political crosshairs.[11] The emergence of the market idea as a plausible alternative to that state, however, was a highly contingent process.

* * *

Upon taking office, President Nixon confronted a sprawling federal system that, over the previous ten years, had undergone astonishing growth. The Johnson administration had already begun the process of exploring ways to simplify the explosive expansion of federal aid programs and regulations, which often had crosscutting purposes.[12] As Johnson and Nixon sought to reform the federal system, the popular antigovernment politics that emerged in the late 1960s and 1970s coalesced under the moniker "the Silent Majority." This cross-section of middle- and working-class white Americans targeted a series of highly visible attempts in the Great Society to lift a generation of marginalized Americans out of poverty, expressing frustration that government seemed beholden to minority "special interests." Hardly "free market" or touting capitalism as an alternative to government initiative, this initial expression of antigovernment politics offered majoritarianism and localism as ideal alternatives to centralized government that seemed to favor electoral and racial minorities.

Nixon's New Federalism, for which Revenue Sharing was the leading policy, responded to these grievances by institutionalizing the notion that local electoral majorities better understood local problems and their solutions than did national government experts or bureaucrats. By the end of 1976, Revenue Sharing alone had pumped more than $30 billion in federal aid to thousands of state and local governments. They, in turn, deployed the funds in ways that reflected the wishes of civic elites and middle-class voters.[13] As Nixon's speechwriter William Safire described it, Revenue Sharing was simply big government "dressed in popular conservative clothes regarding delivery systems."[14] Meant to dial back the administrative authority of the federal government, Revenue Sharing in fact left state and local governments more dependent than ever on federal funding. Nixon's version of antigovernment governance thus created new forms of federal dependencies. Further submerging these contradictions, the staggering revelations of the Watergate abuses only accelerated the popular embrace of the antigovernment impulse.

Scholars are just beginning to scratch the surface of the ways inflation and the economic shocks of the 1970s reshaped the nation's politics, discrediting the old political-economic common sense and clearing the way for something new to emerge. Since at least Franklin D. Roosevelt's fireside chats, presidents worked to interpret the economy for voters. During the postwar boom decades especially, they also sought to take political credit for economic growth. In the 1970s, however, presidents struggled to fit the various downturns, shocks, and crises into coherent narratives. The 1973 oil crisis, for instance, drove up prices at the pump and offered a stark reminder that Americans' quality of life depended upon foreign developments over which their public officials had waning influence.[15] Further undermining politicians' economic authority were stagnant wages and hiring amidst inflationary prices, "stagflation."[16] By 1975 unemployment hit 8.5 percent, reaching new postwar heights later in the decade. Simultaneously, inflation ballooned consumer prices. In 1974 alone, prices shot up by 11 percent. By 1980, inflation approached 15 percent.

The wage-price, unemployment-inflation trade-offs that confronted policymakers in the early 1970s did not offer easy solutions. But bold proclamations from President Nixon—who imposed a series of wage and price freezes—reflected the Keynesian orthodoxy that economic trouble invited macroeconomic solutions. President Gerald R. Ford, meanwhile, declared inflation "public enemy number one." But his largely voluntary approach, Whip Inflation Now, failed to assure citizens that politicians had a steady hand on the wheel.

Yet, despite such far-reaching crises eroding citizens' faith in government and politicians, cracks in the state's legitimacy did not inevitably suggest *market* alternatives. As political leaders struggled to handle worsening inflation, the nation's private sector, which still seemed to be profiting, also wrestled with consumer unrest around prices and safety, suspicion about "big" business, and frustrations with stagnant job markets.[17]

In the absence of clear solutions, Ford sought to use inflation to score partisan points by linking together government spending, broader forces buffeting the economy, and the Silent Majority's least favorite policies—a variety of welfare programs, in particular.[18] After losing the 1976 election, the outgoing president made his final budget proposal a lesson in the inflationary effects of wasteful government spending by proposing a range of cuts to Medicare, food stamps, and child nutrition programs. He pinned inflation on the ripest targets: the established political class and perceptions that government's appetite grew thanks to policies that benefited the poor and minorities. In this emerging antigovernment populism, many perceived highly visible government programs as only supporting "undeserving" minorities. Some critics argued that by flooding the market with inflationary spending, they also distorted prices, necessitated higher taxes, and undermined consumers' purchasing power, standard of living, and economic security.

Like Nixon, however, beneath his increasingly acerbic rhetoric targeting government, Ford merely entrenched government growth. Together, Nixon and Ford increased federal spending by, at minimum, $6 billion per year. Under Nixon alone, domestic spending grew from slightly more than 10 percent of GDP to nearly 14 percent. Nevertheless, Ford nurtured an emerging populist consensus that government spending and citizens' pocketbook politics existed on a zero-sum spectrum.

While the modern antigovernment impulse is often credited to an insurgent generation of conservatives, overlooked has been a parallel trajectory among a "new breed" of Democrats who came of age in the inflationary 1970s.[19] Though there was certainly overlap, Republicans tended to hammer away on the problem of government spending, while Democrats often emphasized the notion that government, particularly its bureaucracy, had grown out of touch. Colorado congresswoman Patricia Schroeder, a bona fide liberal, questioned status quo solutions for social problems. Bureaucrats, she lamented, were "not advocates of the people they are serving. . . . They are haughty and arrogant." Veteran congressman Lee Hamilton (D-IN) saw "a marked change in the ideology of younger members that reflects the mood of the country. It's much more antigovernment, maybe conservative."[20] Senator Ed Muskie (D-ME) noted that many Democrats were afraid of being seen as "budget buster[s]" and muted their demands for new social programs. "It's true," said Muskie, "it's muted me."[21] By 1980, Bruce E. Babbitt, the Democratic governor of

Arizona, complained that if the founding fathers could see the state of the union, they "would ask how we have allowed their most original creation, a carefully layered system of separate units with specified functions, to become scrambled in an undifferentiated government omelet."[22] Lyndon Johnson's protégé, Representative James Jones (D-OK), summed up the changed mood on the left: "Government can be just as excessive and obstructionist to human development as any other institution—big business, big labor." Colorado senator Gary Hart, a leader of the "new" Democrats, noted that Americans' "healthy skepticism about Government's ability to solve every problem" extended the paradox identified by Free and Cantril: "They want Government to solve the problem, but not to administer it. I don't know what you can do about that."[23]

Some commentators maintained that Democrats' limited-government posture forced Republicans' rightward tack. Congressional Republicans, a *Wall Street Journal* editorial argued, took harder stances to distinguish themselves from the "new breed of Democrat that skillfully identifies with antigovernment opinion."[24] New Republican congressmen, including Jim Jeffries, Jack Kemp, Trent Lott, Ron Paul, and David Stockman, took extraordinarily hard lines on federal spending, proposing cutting taxes even when the federal government ran a budget deficit, an unprecedented proposal.[25] Their version of antigovernment governance was premised on the notion that cuts to federal programs would encourage local governments to take up program financing in areas local majorities valued. The *Wall Street Journal*'s conservative editorial page repudiated this more aggressive conservatism: the new "Republicans have deemphasized . . . traditional fiscal conservatism in favor of a radical tax-cutting scheme, just at the time their longtime advocacy of spending restraint has become popular."[26] Fed by a general antigovernment mood, which was claiming the center of American politics, Republicans floated increasingly radical prescriptions for taming the federal beast.

Campaigning for the presidency in 1976, Jimmy Carter embraced many of the themes of Nixon's Silent Majority trope but wrapped them in a softer tone. He framed his candidacy as anti-Washington rather than antigovernment, positing a claim about the *culture* of government rather than the fact. This was a political mode he mastered in his successful 1970 bid for governor of Georgia, and Carter updated his themes for a national audience quickly losing faith in a variety of leading political institutions. In his opening years in office, President Carter often spoke in plaintive tones, offering criticism of the unwieldy and increasingly alien apparatus of government in hopes of spurring popular support for reforms that might bridge the literal and perceived divide between citizens and their state. As he put it in his 1978 State of the Union message, Americans "have seen our Government grow far from us[,] . . . almost become like a foreign country, so strange and distant."[27] As alternative explanations and visions of society emerged, however, Carter would change his tone.

Americans' quest for answers and institutions capable of explaining the decade's economic dislocations was dramatized by the popular attention to an intellectual feud that played out on public television, of all places. In 1977, the economist John Kenneth Galbraith wrote and produced *The Age of Uncertainty*, a multipart documentary that aired in Britain and the United States. The title was meant to draw a contrast with the confidence that characterized classical economic thought, and Galbraith hoped to explicate for a popular audience a number of influential social and economic thinkers, putting complex contemporary economic problems in historical context rather than offer pat solutions.[28] But viewers and critics alike found off-putting Galbraith's equivocal, self-congratulatory, and dry academic style. Meanwhile, conservative commentators found his discussion of Marx overly charitable and complained that he ignored the theories of modern economists like Milton Friedman. *Newsweek* critiqued the series for adopting a "highly personal" point of view, while the *Boston Globe* smashed Galbraith as neither "scholarly" nor "objective."[29] Friedman observed, "I looked in vain for a central idea," but, "all I could see was a man sneering at conventional solutions, without offering any of his own."[30]

Friedman took the challenge. Having recently won the Nobel Prize, the free-market economist set to work on a rebuttal. By the late 1970s, Friedman had a well-calibrated knack for communicating free-market and limited-government ideas to a broad audience thanks to his *Newsweek* column, frequent appearances on the *Phil Donahue Show*, and a popular book, *Capitalism and Freedom*, coauthored with his wife, Rose. These experiences and his clear-eyed criticism of tax-and-spend governance made Friedman something of an unlikely populist hero. Letters from daytime television viewers poured into his office at Stanford University's Hoover Institution. Many writers, like Nelda Jo Huddleston of Berryville, Arkansas, felt Friedman had given them a new, more tactful vernacular for describing their frustration with government programs like welfare: "I toss a flower to you for expressing so aptly what I've felt and believed for several years, but hadn't been able to express as adequately in words."[31] Another writer concurred: "Your personal statement agrees with my thoughts, but you were able to put it into words."[32] Another thanked Friedman, writing, "I have had the same ideas but as I am not a very good diplomatic person I am practically always in trouble with my radical ideas. [*sic*]"[33] Friedman was indefatigably committed to replying to each of his fans—their letters fill dozens of boxes in his archive—and he urged many to keep "spreading the gospel."

Having seen the popular responses to *Age of Uncertainty*, Friedman learned from his friend Galbraith's mistakes. As historian Angus Burgin described it, in his PBS series, *Free to Choose*, Friedman framed himself "as a populist who deferred to the opinions of the masses by leaving decisions to the decrees of a marketplace that was outside his control."[34] As a coproducer wrote soliciting funding from the libertarian magnate Charles Koch, in contrast to Galbraith's failed effort to appear unbiased, Friedman would offer "a strong statement on the need for a free market."[35] The thousands of letters that poured into Friedman's office following *Free to Choose* suggest he succeeded. Mrs. Joe Tom Pittard of San Antonio, Texas, spoke for many who valued the elegance of market solutions for so many of society's ills: "I appreciate the simple, concise way you present your ideas. It is so funny how time and time again the argument of how complicated the world has become is used to muddy the water of people's thinking!"[36] In Friedman's framing, the market rather than the state guaranteed genuine democracy and equality of economic opportunity.

Sensing the ground shifting beneath his feet, Jimmy Carter began to frame public policies as "market" solutions. Carter particularly highlighted associationalism—public-private partnerships—that blended government programs with nonstate actors. His urban policy, dubbed a "New Partnership," was staked on antigovernment grounds, premised on the notion that "the Federal government alone has neither the resources nor the knowledge to solve all urban problems."[37] By 1978, Carter had moved on from trying to humanize government and was instead calling for extragovernmental solutions to pressing problems. "Government," explained the president, "cannot solve our problems. It cannot set our goals. It cannot define our vision. Government cannot eliminate poverty or provide a bountiful economy or reduce inflation or save our cities, or cure illiteracy, or provide energy."[38] In beating such a strong retreat from the technocratic, Keynesian orthodoxy and optimism, Carter also offered a firmer expression of the antigovernment impulse than Richard Nixon ever had.

As Carter's top domestic advisors, Stuart Eizenstat and Bert Carp, wrote, translating the president's diminished vision for government into policy, the government's primary focus should be "developing (and/or retaining) a viable base of *private sector* activity."[39] Said Moon Landrieu, Carter's secretary of housing and urban development, "The private sector . . . built this country and . . . it was certainly capable of rebuilding it if government could create the atmosphere in which the private sector could move and . . . exercise its ingenuity and its capital and its desires."[40] Another advisor put a fine point on the increasing turn to the private sector: the "economic policy of the 1980s must place greater emphasis on the supply side of our economy."[41] Perhaps most significantly, as inflation raised concerns about consumer prices and consumer choice and simultaneously increased the cost to government of carrying out business as usual, Carter joined other liberals in pushing deregulatory policies. With Senator Edward Kennedy (D-MA) and consumer activist Ralph Nader, Carter argued that unleashing competition by limiting government regulation might drive down prices and restore consumers' purchasing power. As part of this drive to reduce government's "drag" on the economy, Carter pushed through legislation deregulating trucking, airline, and railroad rates.

When Milton Friedman's *Free to Choose* aired in 1980, Carter's presidency was approaching its end amidst the Iran hostage crisis and renewed oil shocks. Tax revolts were sweeping the country, and Friedman gleefully declared, "[The] tax revolt is no longer brewing. It is boiling over."[42] The broader right, meanwhile, particularly pro-business, limited-government conservatives, had developed a vast network of publications and think tanks, from *National Review* and *Human Events* to the Heritage Foundation and the American Enterprise Institute. These organizations, along with pro-business groups such as the U.S. Chamber of Commerce and the National Association of Manufacturers, overwhelmingly concerned themselves with government's impact on business, the wealthy, and the middle class. Limiting taxation, regulations, and red tape were their primary themes. True libertarianism, the doctrinaire vision that not only was economic liberty key to all other freedoms but also that laissez faire promised greater equality of social and economic opportunity than did a welfare state, was still a rather marginal position.

Selling the Market Idea

As Milton Friedman's fan mail suggested, Americans' search for institutions capable of delivering the economic and psychic security they had enjoyed since the Second World War was driving interest in the market idea. But an embrace of such a "simple and concise" idea as the market, as one of Friedman's writers characterized it, would take more than economic dislocation. Indeed, the notion that Americans buffeted by market forces would seek a closer embrace of those forces was hardly inevitable. While the Great Depression's dislocations cleared the way for Franklin Roosevelt's New Deal, the economic disorder of the 1970s would yield to different syntheses of state and society, new diagnoses of national ills, and, by the middle of the subsequent decade, a new and increasingly accepted metaphor for society itself. That narrative would require an author.

Ronald W. Reagan's political breakthrough came in the early 1960s when he was a tireless supporter of Barry M. Goldwater's quixotic campaign for the White House. In hindsight, the campaign's most lasting feature was Reagan's stump speech, "A Time for Choosing," in which he compared a nostalgic vision of American freedom and liberty with a breathless conflation of Soviet communism and American bureaucracy. The 1964 election, said Reagan before Kiwanis Clubs and Chambers of Commerce across the country, was a choice between preserving "for our children this, the last best hope of man on earth," or sentencing "them to take the last step into a thousand years of darkness."[43]

Reagan's posture, like Goldwater's, was largely defensive—protecting business (and the American people) from taxes and regulation. His vision was grounded in negative liberty—*freedom from* government coercion. In a time of prosperity, Reagan understood the inherent weakness of such a position. He complained,

> Any time you and I question the schemes of the do-gooders, we're denounced as being opposed to their humanitarian goals. It seems impossible to legitimately debate their solutions with the assumption

that all of us share the desire to help the less fortunate. They tell us we're always "against," never "for" anything.[44]

As a diagnosis for Goldwater's failure and, eventually, his own early difficulties with a national electorate, Reagan was spot on. His vision of a nation knit together in negative liberty included neither solutions for problems like urban and rural poverty amidst affluence nor more stirring visions, such as putting Americans in space. Beyond the specter of Soviet communism, domestically, to most Americans, Reagan's vague and dewy-eyed invocation of liberty seemed a solution in search of a problem. As a vision of the nation—a "theory of society"—Reagan had little to offer.

Yet as inflation and political scandals ate away at Americans' confidence in government, Reagan's message began to resonate. As public opinion pollster Samuel Lubell reported, by 1973, "Every use of government was becoming a tax issue." "Welfare," especially, "brought protests that 'people on relief are crushing the middle class.'"[45] Polling data made clear an arresting trend: Americans' trust in government had fallen from 76 percent in 1964 to just 32 percent in 1976.[46] By 1980, amid the cresting tide of tax revolts and a metastasizing antigovernment impulse, another poll found that just 27 percent of Americans trusted government and political officials.[47] One newspaper headline put it, "Tax Issue Can Be Booster Rocket Putting Reagan in National Orbit."[48]

As the 1980 presidential election approached, however, neither Carter nor Reagan offered coherent solutions for the staggering array of problems dogging the nation. Reagan sought to seize control of Carter's deregulatory mantle by explaining that regulatory agencies were largely responsible for the stagnant economy.[49] The nation's atrophying auto industry, Reagan charged, was "being regulated to death." He called for restoring the industry's "freedom to compete, unhindered by whimsical bureaucratic changes in energy, environmental and safety regulations." He told autoworkers their ire was better directed at Washington, not Japan.[50] After trailing for much of the campaign, however, Reagan pulled ahead for good following his lone debate with Carter just a week before the election. Though Reagan had few clear policies to offer, his sunny optimism carried the day. While pundits predicted that Reagan's victory—a "landslide"—augured a sea change in American politics, polling suggested a more complex story. Despite Reagan's nearly 10 percent victory in the popular tally (50.8 percent to Carter's 41 percent) and his overwhelming triumph in the electoral college (489 to 49, carrying 44 states to Carter's 6), more Americans "held negative attitudes toward each Presidential candidate than in any campaign" since pollsters had begun collecting such data.[51] As historian Judith Stein has argued, Reagan's victory in 1980 was largely a rejection of Jimmy Carter's indecisiveness, "not his creed," and, at best, Reagan's economic program had been "opaque."[52] If Reagan sought a mandate, he would have to manufacture one from the White House.

While Reagan confidently extolled the economic benefits of slashing taxes and regulations, his clarity offered political cover for his advisors, whose feelings about conservative supply-side economics, the administration's signature idea, ranged from wariness to an article of faith: there simply was no data to support it. As conservative commentator Jude Wanniski described it, the supply-side vision was based on a priori assumptions about "the way the world works." A range of scholars and commenters—even David Stockman, Reagan's zealous budget director, charged with implementing the most draconian cuts—described supply-side in terms of "faith." As Stockman told the *Atlantic*, "the whole thing is premised on faith." "None of us," he confessed, "really understands what's going on with all these numbers."[53]

The administration pressed on, however, and won congressional approval of a staggering set of tax and budget cuts. Its three-year, 23 percent reduction in federal income tax was the single-largest tax cut in history. Reagan also cut $35.2 billion from the federal budget, slashing 400,000 Americans' welfare benefits entirely and limiting payments to another 279,000. One million Americans were denied access to food stamps. While Democrats may have grumbled about targeting programs for the poor (60 percent of the 1981 budget savings came from antipoverty programs), there was a broad and largely bipartisan consensus on the need to address federal spending.[54] As *Newsweek* put it, Reagan's "opposition lay broken before him, so completely that he had to warn his own people against gloating."[55] The era of antigovernment governance seemed to have found its leader.

Reagan quickly faced a backlash, however, fielding charges his vision of society excluded the poor and marginalized. Criticism only escalated as he proposed more dramatic cuts, calling for "devolving" to state and local governments a variety of welfare programs. This meant the federal government would end programs, and, if lower governments valued them, they could raise taxes for state or local versions. Even Republicans offered harsh criticism of Reagan's vision. Senator David Durenberger (R-MN) called the proposals "baloney."[56] Facing this criticism, however, the best Reagan initially offered was that tax cuts benefited the poor, and, by cutting welfare, he offered "incentives" to work.[57]

Reagan soon doubled down on hard-edged rhetoric and began deploying market metaphors more frequently to defend his programs vis-à-vis the poor. "The built-in guarantee of freedom," he said, defending his dream of shifting welfare programs to the states, is "the right of a citizen to vote with his feet. If a State is badly managed, the people will . . . either use their power at the polls to redress that, or they'll go somewhere else." Americans, Reagan argued, were essentially rational, like a business: "We've seen industries driven out of some States by adverse tax policies and so forth." The value of certain policies should be tested, he argued, in "the marketplace" of states and voters.[58]

Yet, the president still struggled to articulate a vision for the nation that included solutions for problems like entrenched poverty. In seeking to present a positive program for fighting poverty, Reagan turned to the market idea. His sole urban policy, Enterprise Zones, was premised on the notion that targeted tax and regulatory relief would jumpstart growth in struggling cities.[59] Reagan offered a simple proposition: "These . . . zones [will] demonstrate that freedom of enterprise can succeed where government has failed—if given the chance."[60] The program was initially construed, like the British model upon which it was based, as a place-based development instrument. But, as one optimistic Administration memo put it, "the incentives and natural market forces thus unleashed in central cities would then be relied upon to lead to the economic redevelopment of these areas and to [create] real, private sector jobs for the disadvantaged individuals in or near these areas."[61] The *absence* of government policy would uncover and unleash latent market forces.

The concept of the market itself soon became the administration's solution for poverty. Following the bill's failure in 1982, rather than respond substantively to its internal and external critics (businesspeople were especially skeptical about the proposals), Reagan articulated a much broader potential for free markets.[62] Enterprise Zones would not just support business development and job creation. They would also generate positive *social welfare* outcomes for the nation's worst-off. When Reagan re-sent the bill to Congress in 1983, his statement reflected his new strategy to dress tax and regulatory breaks in a progressive, antipoverty rendering of the market idea. The "legislation," Reagan argued, "will be of primary benefit to America's disadvantaged citizens in our most depressed areas." Enterprise Zones "will spark the latent talents and abilities already in existence in our Nation's most depressed areas."[63]

Enterprise Zones failed again in 1983, but Reagan had found his vision, his metaphor for society. As he explained to a group of businesspeople, their societal role was no longer simply driving economic growth or jobs:

> If the dream of America is to be strengthened, we mustn't waste the genius of one mind or the strength of one body or the spirit of one soul. We must use every capability we have. And the surest way to do that is to mobilize the power of private enterprise and let you work your magic. I believe that when it comes to making sure that all Americans, from every walk of life, every color, creed, and religion have the chance to make it big, there's no better way than to keep the economy sparkling and the opportunities expanding for you and for all our citizens.[64]

Indeed, as Reagan put it on another occasion, government meddling "distort[s] the natural market forces."[65] Rather than diagnosing entrenched poverty as the result of leaving isolated urban or rural Americans unsupported and in a veritable state of nature, Reagan charged that peeling back layers of government intervention would uncover latent, natural market forces capable of driving social and economic uplift. These antigovernment, market-based claims gained further legitimacy in 1984 when Charles Murray published *Losing Ground*, a rational-choice screed targeting the social welfare state that garnered much media attention. Echoing Reagan's logic about the inherent *social* beneficence of the market, Murray provided seemingly even-handed social scientific evidence in support of a radical conclusion—eliminating the nation's social welfare programs.[66] Reagan helped mainstream the notion that the profit-driven market system itself could stand in for social policy. By the mid-1980s, Reagan's free market and antigovernment rhetoric, historian Gil Troy argues, made "prosperity patriotic—and transcendent."[67]

If Ronald Reagan popularized the market metaphor for society in 1980s, in the 1990s and following the collapse of the Soviet Union and the fall of the Berlin wall, it gained propulsive momentum with adherents left, right, and center. In those heady and optimistic years, the market offered a way of understanding a newly open and seemingly democratizing global system. Domestically, President Bill Clinton ratified the antigovernment impulse and market idea, particularly where Reagan had as well: in fighting poverty. Clinton signed the Welfare Reform Act of 1996, which, in many ways, fulfilled Charles Murray's and Reagan's conception of poverty reform. Reagan failed to secure the passage of Enterprise Zones, but the Clinton team dusted off the concept and, in the market-saturated 1990s, succeeded in passing an updated version: "Empowerment Zones." While "big-government solutions" might have been "appropriate for an earlier time," in the 1990s, as an administration memo put it, the New Democrats would deploy the "entrepreneurial spirit and enlightened self-interest of the private sector to bring new capital and jobs to communities that . . . prosperity . . . has passed by."[68] Earlier iterations of federal antipoverty policy targeted "depressed areas" or "pockets of poverty," but Clinton's legislation would "harness the power of the private market to revitalize communities," now rebranded as "New Markets."[69] Clinton even agreed with Charles Murray in blaming welfare for incentivizing out-of-wedlock pregnancies. As the president told NBC News in 1993, while he and Murray sometime disagreed, "his analysis is essentially right."[70] Like Reagan, Clinton made a political-cultural investment in market capitalism as a solution not just for poverty but for a variety of perceived social ills. This was a politically expedient move that transferred responsibility for ameliorating social ills from government to the "market."

No one, perhaps, went further in extolling the fantastic prospects of the global *system* of market capitalism than did the *New York Times*'s mandarin of neoliberalism, Thomas Friedman. Global markets, as Friedman frothily described them, had "turned the whole world into a parliamentary system" in which "people vote every hour, every day."[71] Markets had always been seen as an essential aspect of society. Unprecedented, however, was the notion that the market itself could serve as a metaphor or organizing theory of society and politics—for the entire world, in Friedman's formulation. What need would there be in the future for government if the market was the "truly democratic sphere, the state for plodding bureaucrats only."[72]

PBS updated and rereleased Milton Friedman's *Free to Choose* in the early 1990s. The aging economist received a new wave of fan mail, and this time writers joined him in extolling the market. Most no longer credited him with helping them find their new vernacular. Indeed, one particularly enthusiastic market acolyte fused the antigovernment impulse with its market alternative:

> It is now 1991, and I am convinced that Capitalism is not a "ism" but the natural order of things. Furthermore, governmental interference in the market goes against the natural order. While I knew this on an intuitive level[,] . . . your concise presentation of the emancipating principles of the market economy has made a difference and will continue to make a difference in this wonderful country of ours. God bless you in the name of Jesus Christ.[73]

Like Reagan's early supply-side advisors, this writer took the beneficence of the market as the natural order, as an article of faith—the water in which humans swim. The writer's invocation of Jesus Christ suggests not merely that the market was a natural order but that it was an expression of divine, moral intent. Ronald Reagan would not have quibbled.

* * *

The antigovernment embrace of the market as a metaphor for society itself created, on the one hand, an awkward politics for its adherents, and, on the other, a worsening crisis for the poor and marginalized—in whose name the market has most often been offered as an alternative to government solutions. Despite the overwhelming popularity of market-based solutions, the fact remained that elected officials and their constituents still operated within the paradigm articulated in 1967 by Lloyd Free and Hadley Cantril. Indeed, we no longer live in an age of Keynesian consensus, but the expectations that era created—that politicians are responsible for delivering a healthy economy as well as ensuring some degree of middle- and working-class security—are still very much with us. In practice, the result has been that the era of antigovernment governance has seen a great deal of the latter—governance—and much less of the former. While Ronald Reagan prescribed free markets for the poor, programs from the high tide of liberal social security state-building, such as Social Security and Medicare, which overwhelmingly benefitted working- and middle-class voters, saw record expansions. As only Reagan could have argued, "while I am opposed to socialized medicine, I have always felt that medical care should be available to those who cannot otherwise afford it."[74] Reagan also ballooned the federal deficit on behalf of defense spending, which, as he well knew from his time as California's governor, constituted massive local and regional economic stimulus.[75] In total, while Jimmy Carter added $483 billion dollars to the federal debt, Ronald Reagan added $1.9 trillion and raised the debt ceiling eighteen times. He increased overall federal spending by some 60 percent. Between 1962 and 2010, of the ten years with the largest executive branch payroll, seven occurred under Presidents Reagan and George H. W. Bush.

It was in this disjuncture, the dramatic fracture between rhetoric and reality, ideals and interests, that the seeds of today's fragmented politics of antigovernment governance were sewn. Beginning with Richard Nixon, presidents created ever-greater expectations of limiting government. But none had the courage to frame increased spending or new programs in terms of the valuable services they knew government performed. Instead, by failing to deliver on their promises of smaller, more efficient government, presidents frustrated the political expectations they had created. We endure the results today: an entrenched governing crisis, in which the antigovernment impulse has metastasized into kneejerk austerity, veneration of a mythical market, and a zero-sum politics. Ironically, in this paralyzed political system, the abstract "market" seems our only alternative. In the context of decades of broken promises to roll back federal growth and spending, the escalating heights of populist anger with government and politicians—first expressed in the tax revolts, updated by the Tea Party movement, and commandeered in the 2016 presidential race by Donald Trump's blend of nativism, populism, and the antigovernment impulse yoked to promises to run government like a business—should not, perhaps, be so surprising.

The only policy domain in which the market has been tried—and repeatedly so—is fighting poverty. And it is here, as well, that the market system as an article of *faith* is revealed to be most hollow. Like all matters of faith, the market idea cannot be falsified. There is always some nagging government program, some purported aspect of culture, or some legacy of past programs that inhibits *truly* free market forces from working their magic. And so, in the poorest communities, rather than invest in public institutions, the solution is more market alternatives. Public school systems wither before vouchers and charter schools. Income-support programs yield to microfinance. The very notion of a "public sphere" comes in for questioning. Inequality skyrockets.

The tragedy of the market version of the antigovernment impulse, then, is in how it has enabled political leaders, and presidents especially—possessors of the tallest bully pulpits—to abdicate responsibility for significant social problems. Earlier iterations of the antigovernment impulse posited plausible institutions, actors, and levels of government in which responsibility for managing a given societal issue would best be vested. While far from perfect, there existed means of accountability. The buck stopped with *someone*. As a more extreme version of the antigovernment impulse, the market idea, however, offers an abstract, unfalsifiable, and unverifiable system in place of specific human actors. In this schema it is all too easy and politically attractive to abjure responsibility. The emergence of the market idea—of government and other human institutions as subordinate to a market logic—emerged from the antigovernment impulse. But as a conceptual system, "the market" now exists apart from critiques of government.[76] These processes splintered authority over public life and social problems by thinning Americans' sense of personal, institutional, or societal rights and responsibilities, disaggregating and fracturing the common good.

Notes

Epigraph sources: Richard Nixon, President's Message to Congress, March 25, 1971, Executive Office of the President, *Papers Relating to the President's Departmental Reorganization Program* (Washington, DC: Government Printing Office, 1971); Ronald Reagan, "Speech before the National Alliance of Business," October 5, 1981, *Public Papers of the President: Ronald Reagan: 1981*, vol. 2 (Washington, DC: Government Printing Office, 1983) 883–87; William J. Clinton, "Address before a Joint Session of the Congress on the State of the Union," January 23, 1996, American Presidency Project, http://www.presidency.ucsb.edu/ws/?pid=53091.

1. Richard Nixon: "Statement about the General Revenue Sharing Bill," October 20, 1972, American Presidency Project, http://www.presidency.ucsb.edu/ws/?pid=3636.
2. The canonical expression of "embedded liberalism" is Karl Polanyi, *The Great Transformation: The Political and Economic Origins of Our Time* (Boston: Beacon, 2001; first published 1944).
3. See, for instance, Elisabeth S. Clemens and Doug Guthrie, eds., *Politics and Partnerships: The Role of Voluntary Associations in America's Political Past and Present* (Chicago: University of Chicago Press, 2010).
4. Daniel Rodgers, *Age of Fracture* (Cambridge, MA: Belknap, 2011), 16.
5. Lloyd A. Free and Hadley Cantril, *The Political Beliefs of Americans* (New Brunswick, NJ: Rutgers University Press, 1967).
6. Margaret O'Mara, *Cities of Knowledge: Cold War Science and the Search for the Next Silicon Valley* (Princeton: Princeton University Press, 2005), 11.

7. Suzanne Mettler, *The Submerged State: How Invisible Government Policies Undermine American Democracy* (Chicago: University of Chicago Press, 2011), 9.

8. David M. P. Freund, "Marketing the Free Market: State Intervention and the Politics of Prosperity in Metropolitan America," in *The New Suburban History*, ed. Kevin Kruse and Thomas Sugrue (Chicago: University of Chicago Press, 2006), 11–32.

9. Mettler, *The Submerged State.*

10. Angus Burgin, *The Great Persuasion: Reinventing Free Markets since the Great Depression* (Cambridge, MA: Harvard University Press, 2013).

11. See, especially, Matthew Lassiter, *The Silent Majority: Suburban Politics in the Sunbelt South* (Princeton: Princeton University Press, 2005); Robert Self, *American Babylon: Race and the Struggle for Postwar Oakland* (Princeton: Princeton University Press, 2003); and Isaac Martin, *The Permanent Tax Revolt: How the Property Tax Transformed American Politics* (Stanford: Stanford University Press, 2008).

12. Walter Heller, *New Dimensions of Political Economy* (Cambridge, MA: Harvard University Press, 1966). On the seismic shift in intergovernmental relations during the 1960s, see especially, Martha Derthick, "Crossing Thresholds: Federalism in the 1960s," in *Keeping the Compound Republic: Essays in American Federalism*, ed. Martha Derthick (Washington, DC: Brookings Institution Press, 2001).

13. Brent Cebul, *The American Way of Growth: Business, Poverty, and Development in the American Century* (Philadelphia: University of Pennsylvania Press, forthcoming).

14. William Safire, *Before the Fall: An Inside View of the Pre-Watergate White House* (Livingston, NJ: Transaction, 2005), 224.

15. Meg Jacobs, *Panic at the Pump: The Energy Crisis and the Transformation of American Politics in the 1970s* (New York: Hill and Wang, 2016).

16. On the Keynesian era's politics of economic authority, see Robert Collins, *More: The Politics of Economic Growth in Postwar America* (New York: Oxford University Press, 2002).

17. Kim Phillips-Fein, *Invisible Hands: The Making of the Conservative Movement from the New Deal to Reagan* (New York: W.W. Norton, 2009), 243–45. On the culture of skepticism more broadly, see Rick Perlstein, *The Invisible Bridge: The Fall of Nixon and the Rise of Reagan* (New York: Simon & Schuster, 2015), 174–79. See also Benjamin Waterhouse, "The Corporate Mobilization against Liberal Reform: Big Business Day, 1980," in *What's Good For Business: Business and Politics since World War II*, ed. Kim Phillips-Fein and Julian Zelizer (New York: Oxford University Press, 2012).

18. "Limits of Power," *Wall Street Journal*, January 18, 1977.

19. On "New Democrats," see E. J. Dionne, *Why Americans Hate Politics* (New York: Simon and Schuster, 1992), 270–82.

20. "Democratic Party in Transition, But the Question Is, to What?" *Washington Post*, January 14, 1979.

21. "Congress and Carter: Who's in Charge?" *New York Times*, January 30, 1977.

22. "Governors Ask Realignment of State and Federal Powers," *New York Times*, August 6, 1980.

23. "Congress and Carter: Who's in Charge?" *New York Times*, January 30, 1977.

24. "Perspective on Politics: Conservative Trend," *Wall Street Journal*, October 12, 1978.

25. Julian E. Zelizer, "Conservatives, Carter, and the Politics of National Security," in *Rightward Bound: Making America Conservative in the 1970s*, ed. Bruce J. Schulman and Julian E. Zelizer (Cambridge, MA: Harvard University Press, 2008); and Julian E. Zelizer, "Seizing Power: Conservatives and Congress since the 1970s," in *The Transformation of American Politics: Activist Government and the Rise of Conservatism*, ed. Paul Pierson and Theda Skocpol (Princeton: Princeton University Press, 2007).

26. "Perspective on Politics: Conservative Trend," *Wall Street Journal*, October 12, 1978.

27. Jimmy Carter: "The State of the Union Address Delivered before a Joint Session of the Congress," January 19, 1978, American Presidency Project, http://www.presidency.ucsb.edu/ws/?pid=30856.

28. Angus Burgin, "Age of Certainty: Galbraith, Friedman, and the Public Life of Economic Ideas," *History of Political Economy* 45 (2013): 197.

29. Burgin, "Age of Certainty," 198–99.

30. Burgin, "Age of Certainty," 200.

31. Nelda Jo Huddleston to Milton Friedman, May 14, 1980, box 8, folder 8.4, Milton Friedman Papers, Hoover Institution Archives, Stanford University, Stanford, California (hereafter MFP).

32. Jack Gellin to Milton Friedman, February 20, 1980, box 224, folder 224.21, MFP.

33. William G. Naylor to Milton Friedman, April 30, 1980, box 8, folder 8.5, MFP; Jack Gellin to Milton Friedman, February 20, 1980, MFP.

34. Burgin, "Age of Certainty," 207.

35. Burgin, "Age of Certainty," 210.

36. Mrs. Joe Tom Pittard to Milton Friedman, March 31, 1980, box 225, folder 225.23, MFP.

37. "New Partnership to Conserve America's Communities," March 27, 1978, box 309, Stu Eizenstat Papers, Jimmy Carter Presidential Library, Atlanta, GA (hereafter JCL).

38. Phillips-Fein, *Invisible Hands*, 198.

39. Quoted in Thomas J. Sugrue, "Carter's Urban Policy Crisis," in *The Carter Presidency*, ed. Hugh Davis Graham and Gary M. Fink, 148.

40. Jimmy Carter: "Urban Development Action Grant Program Remarks at a White House Reception Commemorating the Second Anniversary of the Program," October 19, 1979, American Presidency Project, http://www.presidency.ucsb.edu/ws/?pid=31561.

41. Phillips-Fein, *Invisible Hands*, 183.

42. Bruce J. Schulman, *The Seventies: The Great Shift in American Culture, Society, and Politics* (Cambridge, MA: Da Capo, 2001), 212.

43. Ronald Reagan, "A Time for Choosing," October 27, 1964, available online at the Ronald Reagan Presidential Library, https://reaganlibrary.archives.gov/archives/reference/timechoosing.html.

44. Reagan, "A Time for Choosing."

45. Rick Perlstein, *The Invisible Bridge*, 169.

46. "Is Democracy Dying? Verdict of 8 Leading World Scholars," *US News and World*

Report, March 8, 1976, attached to Bob Claxton to Newt Gingrich, January 10, 1976, box 5, folder Decentralization #2, Newt Gingrich Papers, University of West Georgia, Carrollton, Georgia.

47. Gareth Davies, "The Welfare State," in *The Reagan Presidency: Pragmatic Conservatism and Its Legacies*, ed. W. Elliot Brownlee and Hugh Davis Graham (Lawrence: University Press of Kansas, 2003), 210.

48. Jeffrey Hart, "Tax Issue Can Be Booster Rocket Putting Reagan in National Orbit," *St. Petersburg Evening Independent*, October 5, 1973.

49. Phillips-Fein, *Invisible Hands*, 206–11.

50. Phillips-Fein, *Invisible Hands*, 251.

51. Gil Troy, *Morning in America: How Ronald Reagan Invented the 1980s* (Princeton: Princeton University Press, 2007), 48–49.

52. Judith Stein, *Pivotal Decade: How the United States Traded Factories for Finance in the Seventies* (New Haven, CT: Yale University Press, 2010), 263.

53. William Greider, "The Education of David Stockman," *Atlantic*, December 1981.

54. Gareth Davies, "The Welfare State," in *The Reagan Presidency*, ed. Brownlee and Graham, 211–12.

55. "Rest in Peace, New Deal," *Newsweek*, August 10, 1981.

56. "A Rich Foe and Reagan Vex GOP Incumbent," *New York Times*, October 12, 1982.

57. Ronald Reagan Press Conference, June 16, 1981, American Presidency Project, http://www.presidency.ucsb.edu/ws/?pid=43961.

58. Ronald Reagan, Interview with Reporters on Federalism, November 19, 1981, Ronald Reagan Presidential Library, https://reaganlibrary.archives.gov/archives/speeches/1981/111981b.htm.

59. Daniel Stedman Jones, *Masters of the Universe: Hayek, Friedman, and the Birth of Neoliberal Politics* (Princeton: Princeton University Press, 2012), 315–21.

60. Ronald Reagan, Talking Points for State and Local Officials Briefing on Enterprise Zone Proposals, March 24, 1982, White House Subject Files, BE (Business-Economics), box 91, Ronald Reagan Library, Simi Valley, CA (hereafter RRL).

61. "The Administration Plan for Enterprise Zones," January 6, 1982, box 10, folder 24, George V. Voinovich Papers, Western Reserve Historical Society, Cleveland, Ohio.

62. See, for instance, Dan J. Smith to Dennis Kass and Bob Carleson, re: Enterprise Zone Panel Responses, October 28, 1981, box 05711, folder HUD Enterprise Zone Panels, Dan Smith Files, RRL.

63. Statement by the President, March 7, 1983, box 3, folder Enterprise Zones (1), OA 12999, MB Oglesby Files, RRL.

64. Ronald Reagan: "Remarks at a White House Ceremony Honoring the Minority Small Business Persons of the Year," October 11, 1984, American Presidency Project, http://www.presidency.ucsb.edu/ws/?pid=39223.

65. Kiron K. Skinner, Annelise Anderson, and Martin Anderson, eds., *Reagan: A Life in Letters* (New York: Free Press, 2003), 268.

66. Charles Murray, *Losing Ground: American Social Policy: 1950–1980* (New York: Basic Books, 1984).

67. Troy, *Morning in America*, 4.

68. "President Clinton's Challenge to Invest in America's New Markets," Domestic Policy Council, Bruce Reed, and Subject Files, "New Markets," 11, Digital Archives of the Clinton Library and Museum, http://clinton.presidentiallibraries.us/items/show/31479.

69. "President Clinton's Challenge to Invest in America's New Markets," 17.

70. Domestic Policy Council, Bruce Reed, and Welfare Reform Series, "Meetings [2]," 1, Clinton Digital Library, http://clinton.presidentiallibraries.us/items/show/31812.

71. Rodgers, *Age of Fracture*, 75.

72. Phillips-Fein, *Invisible Hands*, 264.

73. Bob Youngblood to Milton Friedman, August 1, 1991, box 226, folder 226.24, MFP.

74. David Blumenthal and James Morone, *The Heart of Power: Health and Politics in the Oval Office* (Berkeley: University of California Press, 2009), 305.

75. On Governor Reagan's reliance on defense contracting and federal bailouts for economic development, see Michael Brenes, "For Right and Might: The Militarization of the Cold War and the Remaking of American Democracy" (PhD diss., City University of New York, 2014), 156–70.

76. Fred Block and Margaret R. Somers, *The Power of Market Fundamentalism: Karl Polanyi's Critique* (Cambridge, MA: Harvard University Press, 2014).

7

From Educator to Creditor in Chief

The American Presidency, Higher Education, and the Student Loan Industry

ELIZABETH TANDY SHERMER

"The most important door that will ever open," President Lyndon Baines Johnson declared in November 1965, "is the door to education." He made that pronouncement at his alma mater, the former Southwest Texas State College, where he signed the 1965 Higher Education Act (HEA). "This legislation signed by this Congress," Johnson promised, "will swing open a new door for the young people of America." In many ways, he was right. College enrollment had increased steadily in the early twentieth century, reaching 1.5 million by the end of the 1930s. But the growth of American public and private colleges and universities in the postwar era far surpassed earlier expansion. Mass higher education became a key social guarantee, which helped improve national defense, aided business innovation, and dramatically expanded prospects for upward mobility. By the new millennium, colleges offered instruction to more than 12 million students in any given academic year.[1]

This unprecedented accessibility had a reciprocal relationship with the student loan industry. Presidents preceding and succeeding Johnson have all inadvertently contributed to the current 1.3 trillion dollars in debt obligations. The executive branch rarely sought direct support for colleges and universities. Administrations could more easily indirectly aid the academy's expansion by crafting and overseeing tuition assistance programs that let students and schools decide whether they would accept these loan and fellowship programs. This market-driven model made student debt a defining feature and product of the American higher-education system. Federal and state policymakers have rarely and inconsistently provided

Figure 7.1. President Lyndon Baines Johnson returned to his alma mater, once the Southwest Texas State Teachers College but by then the Southwest Texas State College, to sign the 1965 Higher Education Act. Johnson celebrated the promise of higher education in this speech but focused on what he considered vital to its expansion and accessibility: the new Guaranteed Student Loan program. Courtesy of LBJ Library, photo by Frank Wolfe.

direct underwriting. Business investment and philanthropic support also waxed and waned substantially over time, even for the nation's most elite stratum of schools. As a result, university administrators at both public and private schools have responded to fluctuating fortunes by augmenting tuition and fees. Unlike federal grants and personal gifts, student payments have historically had no real restrictions on their use. Enrollment income has, for example, gone toward paying faculty, modernizing classrooms, upgrading labs, and constructing new dormitories.[2]

After Johnson authorized the HEA, every university's balance sheet would come to depend on students taking out federally guaranteed college loans. That postwar assurance also became important to private lenders, whose participation in the national lending program secured a return on their investment. This government commitment, along with the recently privatized loan market for student debt, also unintentionally underwrote the far riskier loans these financiers increasingly offered privately. By the 2010s, Johnson's signature had unintentionally helped put millions of American undergraduate students and their families deeply in debt.[3]

Matchmaker in Chief

Only in the postwar era did "financial aid" come to describe student assistance. The term previously described direct business, philanthropic, or state support for private colleges, small state schools, or great public and private research universities. Donors and legislators continually proved themselves capricious. Historians have estimated that hundreds of colleges and universities went bankrupt in the nineteenth century. To remain open, university administrators needed students who paid tuition. Rates remained relatively low. Enrollees' real financial sacrifice was time, not money. They had to devote hours to school instead of work. Benefactors, moreover, tended to insist that admission be offered on the basis of merit, not social class. A few colleges earmarked funds for scholarships to be awarded first on talent and then on the basis of need. Harder to find were loans. Bankers started to offer credit after World War I, but lenders in this era generally offered borrowers short terms and high interest rates.[4]

At the start of the Great Depression, a small number of Americans requested federal loans for college, but government officials ignored their requests. Franklin D. Roosevelt certainly came into office promising Americans a new deal. But his appointees, often called New Dealers, and the social welfare legislation that he signed, collectively denoted as the New Deal, did not offer a comprehensive financial package to colleges. Thousands of tuition-dependent schools faced bankruptcy. But Roosevelt publicly demurred from helping postsecondary schools. His refusal arose partially from his governance of New York, where public institutions (as in much of the Northeast) had largely trained teachers and left the liberal arts, sciences, and engineering to private colleges and universities. Roosevelt maintained that high unemployment rates, particularly for educators, made bailouts wasteful for the entire country's patchwork system of colleges and universities. Many in his administration agreed. Few Depression-era Americans considered mass higher education possible, needed, or desired.[5]

Citizen demand led the president and his advisors to interweave educational opportunities throughout many New Deal programs. For example, Civilian Conservation Corps higher-ups assumed their all-male recruits just needed vocational training. Enlistees were, after all, only hired to help conserve and harness the nation's natural resources. Recruits worked only eight hours a day planting trees, improving parks, and building roadways. To fill their spare time, they eagerly requested courses in basic literacy and civics, and even advanced classes in the fine arts and humanities, which shocked well-educated administrators, like Grinnell graduate Harry L. Hopkins. He and other officials, whom Roosevelt broadly gave his permission to experiment, soon understood courses in literature, history, and current events to be vital. Federal officials discovered offering classes was a chance to explain policies crafted in Washington to a citizenry who, appointees had discovered, often did not understand the Constitution or federalism's long-term evolution. Roosevelt and his aides never imposed school construction, repair, or expansion on institutions or the communities surrounding them but instead let Americans decide whether to apply for support. Citizens eagerly requested school expansion and coursework. Hopkins recruited famed labor-college educator Hilda Smith to oversee the latter. Her Workers Education Program offered communities the opportunity to petition for any type of desired coursework and sent educators into hamlets, city neighborhoods, and unused college classrooms in order to offer the vocational, fine arts, and law classes students of every age sought. Grassroots demand inspired many New Dealers to consider how education might empower the citizenry. That idea shaped the Tennessee Valley Authority's (TVA) agricultural extension classes for impoverished southerners desperate for water and electricity. TVA's director continually maintained that this infrastructure project's dams, power stations, and collegiate offerings would not only improve farm yields but also put "Democracy on the March" in a region that Roosevelt famously singled out as the "Nation's #1 Economic Problem."[6]

Young American interests and needs partially shaped how the Roosevelt administration experimented with making all colleges more accessible. The president turned to southern Democrat Aubrey Williams and businessman Hans Taussig, both of whom, despite their backgrounds, agreed with the broad reformist sprit of FDR's New Deal. They convinced Roosevelt to issue an executive order creating the National Youth Administration (NYA) in 1935 because they thought sixteen- to twenty-five-year-olds needed more relief and rightly feared that FDR would be unable to persuade Congress to create another executive branch agency. Taussig insisted the New Deal offer something targeted to young people

Figure 7.2. The National Youth Administration's flagship program was work-study, an opportunity for young people to earn enough through part-time work to pay for full-time study but also a form of much-needed indirect federal aid to schools struggling to stay open during the Depression. This opportunity was open to any willing school or young person, including women, like this young Massachusetts coed sorting the mail for the State Teachers College at Fitchburg (now Fitchburg State University). Courtesy of Fitchburg State University.

Figure 7.3. Work-study had many purposes: indirectly aid schools, keep sixteen- to twenty-five-year-old Americans out of competition for jobs, and teach them skills so that they might secure better job opportunities as adults. Here a student learns the kind of woodworking knowledge that would have been hard for him to come by in Massachusetts if he had not had the opportunity to enroll in the State Teachers College at Fitchburg (now Fitchburg State University). Courtesy of Fitchburg State University.

because their high unemployment numbers seemed to make them likely converts to the youth radicalism roiling Europe. Williams, who directed the agency, placed an emphasis on educational opportunities because he had been lifted out of rural Alabama poverty by learning to read and then attending college after his WWI military service. Roosevelt gave Taussig and Williams great leeway in designing NYA programs, many of which they fashioned to keep children in schools. That goal reflected Taussig and Williams's underlying intent to educate students for better opportunities in the future. They also sought to keep young people out of competition for employment and off welfare, a job market consideration akin to the reasoning behind the Social Security's mandatory retirement at age sixty-five that Congress passed the same year.[7]

That presidential carte blanche enabled Williams and Taussig to craft a work-study program to directly help students attend college. And in that way, but indirectly, Williams and Taussig began a process of funding universities. Work-study, in short, helped applicants, both men and women, find a job and a college willing to accept them. The program also helped campuses desperately in need of students, funds, and repairs. NYA paid students directly for the work that they did. Salaries were high enough to cover living expenses and tuition fees, which schools were guaranteed to receive because a young person had to remain enrolled in order to receive work-study. This intentionally circuitous federal lifeline effectively worked around rules that federal money only be directly spent on public institutions and services or individual relief. The NYA also never imposed this opportunity on schools, which could and did decline to accept work-study. Students also had a choice. NYA gave young people the option to apply, not a presidential directive.[8]

Many campuses desperately needed students, cash, and repairs, but the program only worked because young people took this opportunity. School officials received work-study students if a young person put in for work-study at their state NYA office. Even then, appointees only matched students to willing schools offering the degree program that an applicant wanted, which was not necessarily in their home state. This executive-level directive placed state NYA directors, like Texas's young Lyndon Baines Johnson, into the business of matchmaking colleges and applicants, who could pick their course of study but not choose where they applied. After matriculation, enrollees maintained, improved, and expanded campuses, most often as a part of New Deal works projects. These on-campus, part-time positions were hence not considered jobs taken from Americans between their school and retirement years.[9]

Politics shaped work-study from start to finish. NYA appointees took great pains to ensure student jobs were not tasks that could be labeled "make-work" or "leaf-raking" because their agency, the entire Roosevelt administration, and the president himself faced fierce criticism. FDR has long been remembered as a popular president who enjoyed widespread support from Congress and the citizenry. Yet historians have demonstrated that he and his administration faced pointed outspoken skeptics, fierce opponents, and campaigns to undermine it at every step between Roosevelt's election in 1932 and his death in 1945. Many historians now contend that the limits of the New Deal reflected not just widespread disregard for racial and gender equality but also compromises Roosevelt made to get anything passed in Congress, upheld by the Supreme Court, and implemented at the local level. That reassessment has shown many southern Democrats, business leaders, and upper-class Americans to have come together to challenge the popular appeal and political power of Roosevelt and his administration. Indeed, the fact of their combined efforts helps explain why Roosevelt could and would not offer the academy genuine relief. Roosevelt, Taussig, and Williams's suspicion that FDR could not convince Congress to authorize another executive bureaucracy in 1935, for example, reflected how much the administration had to negotiate with the House and Senate over every reform measure.[10]

Political tradition, federalism, and academic hostility also prevented Roosevelt from pursuing sustained, direct funding for American universities and colleges. The Constitution's authors had left schooling as a local, state, religious, or private matter. The Supreme Court had also protected higher learning from government interference since the early republic. Leaders of the American academy in the 1930s jealously guarded this long-standing institutional autonomy and feared that federal relief or underwriting would come with intrusive oversight. Their fears reflected ivory-tower distrust of Roosevelt and his many new programs. Though much of the president's small "Brain Trust" of advisors came from the academy, many top educators in the Ivy League and at small liberal arts colleges were actually outspoken critics. The professoriate tended to attack Roosevelt for either executive overreach or federally sanctioned class antagonism. In 1935, for example, Columbia University president Nicholas Murray Butler admitted that FDR did "a great service when he took selfish, organized big business off our necks" but denounced policies that seemed poised to let "selfish organized big labor to take its place." Federal reforms also left many in the National Education Association certain that much-needed federal support would come with a dangerous sacrifice of local control or, in the case of higher education, institutional autonomy. Harvard University's James B. Conant feared such intrusions. "Nowhere is liberty and freedom more prized and more essential than in an academic community," he warned in 1934. "To coerce it is to enslave it."[11]

The controversial work-study program survived until 1943 only because of student demands, business needs, and wartime imperatives. The program was wildly popular with young people, who had done much to repair, improve, and expand schools. These students also proved that many Americans wanted and were more than capable of advanced learning. Federal support had also not proven intrusive but had in fact been a godsend, particularly to poorly endowed colleges and underfunded state universities. Schools that cooperated reaped much revenue from the $93 million Williams spent educating over six hundred thousand Americans. Yet many elite educators never stopped assailing the program and federal threats to their authority. But these professors did not necessarily convince businesses to support their attack on NYA. Instead, many executives, even those frustrated with the Roosevelt administration, applauded New Deal schooling efforts. Training was especially important as America's eventual involvement in World War II became clear. Even before Pearl Harbor, Williams, military leaders, and top manufacturers feared that the citizenry was unprepared either to fight alongside or arm the Allied powers. The money spent on education necessary for total war also helped defense contractors. A heavy-grade equipment manufacturer with operations in Illinois and Georgia even reported managers "especially pleased with these boys who . . . received machine shop training under the N.Y.A., . . . one of the finest things our present administration has undertaken."[12]

Student, military, and business enthusiasm could not save work-study, much less NYA. Congress abruptly defunded that agency and many others in 1943. This political maneuver symbolized both the continued conflict in Washington over Roosevelt's policies and policymaking and the constitutional constraints over the executive branch's power, regardless of how much it had been expanded under Roosevelt.[13]

Educator in Chief

By 1944, many in Congress and business thought that the Second World War would end in the foreseeable future. But that good news also forced lawmakers to determine what should be done to keep the millions of vets from returning to Depression-era unemployment. Memories of impoverished WWI veterans descending on Washington in the 1932 Bonus March also made that kind of payment politically impossible. Many in business circles, Washington agencies, and veterans' organizations instead wanted more guarantees for advancement and security through a college education. Moreover, the chance to pursue an advanced degree would keep veterans out of competition for jobs while they learned skills that would make them more valuable to employers and competitive on the job market. Graduating veterans found themselves with a clear pathway into the middle and professional classes. They became practicing lawyers and physicians as well as advertising and accounting wizards for large corporations. Some also used their engineering and science degrees to build the Interstate Highway System and send Americans to the moon.[14]

Few had believed veterans would be interested in education. The American Legion, Congress, and Roosevelt advisors presumed that GIs would need schooling but would prefer loans for homes, small businesses, or farms. Few subsequently thought it necessary to earmark much for schooling. Plus, leading educators opposed such guarantees. Ivy League faculty, including Conant, had certainly embraced federal support for science departments during the war, but they had no interest in welcoming working-class veterans, regardless of race or ethnicity, onto campus. To do so, the University of Chicago's Robert M. Hutchins declared, would turn colleges and universities into "hobo jungles." Cost also concerned the conservative coalition of congressmen who had written key components out of the 1943 budget. These senators and representatives were deeply skeptical of offering generous entitlements to education.[15]

Such opposition necessitated presidential compromise to secure more opportunities for schooling. Roosevelt and his advisors found allies among two staunch critics, the American Legion and the Hearst newspapers. Legionnaires and other veteran organizations insisted upon robust programs to help GIs readjust. There was no guarantee that such aid would get through Congress, particularly provisions for advanced learning. So

Legionnaires went to the aging William Randolph Hearst, whose papers stood out at the time for their open, strident criticism of the Roosevelt administration. The publisher spared no expense or editorial page space on promoting the Legion's preferred bills. Coverage insisted that returnees had earned these benefits. Reporters spent far less time reporting the particular difference between the Legion's preferred legislation and the Roosevelt administration's proposals, which most often differed in the amounts earmarked as well as who would oversee the program. The Legion, the Hearst papers, and their congressional allies wanted the Veterans Administration (VA) to oversee all programs. Williams and other Roosevelt officials championed the Federal Security Administration's oversight. They feared that the VA's authority would permanently wall off these social guarantees from the rest of the citizenry, whereas FSA control might eventually enable veterans' entitlements to be offered to the entire citizenry.[16]

Roosevelt lost that fight, but the Servicemen's Readjustment Act that he signed included his preferred method of underwriting higher education. That 1944 omnibus bill, usually referred to as the GI Bill, empowered the VA to oversee a tuition plan that liberals had intentionally designed to further their efforts to indirectly fund the expansion of schools willing to accept ordinary Americans. Supporters in Congress and the Roosevelt administration considered institutional growth necessary for advanced learning, of which many Americans had proven themselves capable and desirous in the 1930s. The GI Bill was unlike work-study in that schools billed the federal government for enrolled veterans' fees, and the stipend for living expenses went directly to students. Policymakers intentionally set the maximum reimbursement far higher than most schools charged. Roosevelt staffers considered that five-hundred-dollar ceiling a means to encourage schools to raise rates. They hoped extra revenue would encourage and underwrite the expansions needed to accommodate the tidal wave of GI applicants. That growth would ready schools to accept subsequent generations of applicants, who Roosevelt insiders rightly predicted would need and demand more learning.[17]

This approach also intentionally enabled the Roosevelt administration to sidestep accusations that its programs ran afoul of federal restraint in matters pertaining to local control, religion, class, and race. Directly funding the needed college and university expansions would have launched a debate about federal funds paid to private institutions, a key concern during the drafting of NYA's work-study program. However, by the mid-1940s, there was also widespread concern about public money going toward religious, historically black, all-white, or men- or women-only institutions. Their most basic selection criteria ran against the ethos of the All-American war effort that the federal government promoted, as well as the rallying cry of labor and civil rights organizations that the war end with victories over fascism abroad and racism at home. Just like work-study, the GI Bill instead left federal funding for such schools contingent on the choices of the prospective students and the willingness of schools to accept them. Neither the executive branch nor the VA interfered with where an applicant enrolled. The federal government determined whether a school could be considered a reputable institution of higher learning, which generally left only trade schools, not established colleges and universities, scrambling to prove their programs' merits. But with the GI Bill, in an important difference from how work-study operated, veterans ultimately decided where they applied and hence which institutions received a check from the VA for their tuition. Hence, the VA did not so much act as a matchmaker, as NYA had done, but as an accreditation agency in the market for advanced learning.[18]

But neither VA officials nor the president of the United States were responsible for the GI Bill's success—veterans were, especially in regard to education. Soldiers shocked everyone with their eagerness to enroll as well as their general disinterest in loans to start farms or small businesses. GIs instead clamored to continue their education because many considered schooling a better avenue out of the working class. Plus, they could apply elsewhere for a home or small business loan. The schools most in need of funding readily accepted them, less so the elite schools, such as Harvard, Northwestern, and Columbia, which then operated under a quota system, which generally kept Jews, Catholics, and racial minorities out. Yet more schooling, wherever GIs matriculated, has been unquestionably shown to have transformed the earning power and respectability of blue-collar veterans. They excelled. Within two years of the bill's passage, faculty continually and publicly praised GIs for being eager, capable students. Congress also had to increase the money earmarked for this provision because of demand.[19]

But Capitol Hill was also responsible for the Servicemen's Readjustment Act's faults. There was never enough federal or state funding to adequately expand educational opportunity. Pictures of veterans crowded

Figure 7.4. No one, including President Franklin Delano Roosevelt, predicted how popular the 1944 Servicemen's Readjustment Act's educational benefits would be. Roosevelt and his aides put in a great effort shaping the bill and securing its passage, but the veterans eager to take advantage of the so-called GI Bill were the ones really responsible for its success. Here Chicago-area soldiers stand in line for hours to register at the city's makeshift Navy Pier Campus, quickly built to accommodate the many local GIs who couldn't secure a place in existing area schools or leave their families behind to study elsewhere. Photograph by Thomas Fehr. Photograph UA_96_033_018.jpg. 003-09-00-01-02 (UA 96-33). University Archives. University of Illinois at Chicago.

into classrooms only eventually yielded some small direct federal outlays to make more room for the unexpected number of applicants. Tuition remittance also did not provide enough immediate capital for the improvements needed. Instead, the five-hundred-dollar fee cap had the unintentional consequence of putting higher education out of reach for ordinary Americans. Schools eagerly raised tuition but had to do so for everyone. Only veterans' tuition was guaranteed, which had the effect of easing their ability to get into schools in need of tuition revenue. Colleges subsequently became more expensive for every American, few of whom had GI benefits. In effect, Roosevelt's inability to keep Congress from charging the VA with implementing this legislation restricted working-class civilians from being able to afford this pathway into the middle classes.[20]

Would-Be Educators in Chief

The short-term overwhelming success and popularity of these educational guarantees also made expanding access important to later presidents. FDR's successor, Harry S. Truman, was the first to consider an expansive federal guarantee. Family finances and work obligations had stopped his collegiate dreams. In 1946, Truman created the Presidential Commission on Higher Education to study and write a comprehensive report on what Washington should and could do. He also purposely chose educators amenable to federal aid, including American Council of Education president George F. Zook. However, Truman's involvement largely ended there. Zook oversaw the commission, whose six-volume 1947 recommendations, entitled *Higher Education for American Democracy*, offered ambitious plans to guarantee at least two years of postsecondary schooling to every young person. That goal hinged on direct federal aid for colleges and universities. But the so-called Zook Report never garnered much congressional support, even with Truman's public endorsement.[21]

Opposition to the very spirit of these reforms could also be found outside Congress. For example, key members of the American business community who disliked the New Deal and its legacy yearned to protect American free enterprise and feared the continued expansion of the federal government. These so-called business conservatives conflated preserving American capitalism and federalism with expanding private higher education and conscribing public schooling. Their key allies were to be found in the Ford Foundation, which the automaker Henry Ford started as a means to evade taxes in the Roosevelt era. By the late 1940s, this philanthropy had expanded its projects outside Michigan but also taken up the cause of improving private schooling options. Businessmen enjoyed an early victory in New Jersey, where the courts ruled that corporate donations to colleges could be tax deductible. This win encouraged Ford Foundation higher-ups to reach out to representatives from the Carnegie and Rockefeller Foundations to coordinate fundraising efforts among American CEOs. Among the amenable businessmen were U.S. Steel's Irving S. Olde, Procter & Gamble's Neil McElroy, and General

Electric's Gerald L. Phillippe, all of whom feared that the earlier growth of the federal government had weakened the American commitment to their definition of "free" enterprise.[22]

They and similarly minded business executives joined Ford, Carnegie, and Rockefeller executives to found and direct the Council on Financial Aid to Education (CFAE). This organization did not concern itself with student assistance but instead fundraised on behalf of private schools. CFAE promotional materials routinely declared business support critical to ensuring that advanced learning remained the purview of private schools. They feared for the health of small, private schools, which could not compete for federal research grants underwriting university science departments. Yet CFAE's steering committee also recognized that the top private schools (such as MIT, Harvard, and Stanford) were already receiving such federal awards. These institutions still needed corporate support in order to compete with growing public schools, such as the University of California's campuses, for the students and tuition dollars to keep doors open.[23]

A deeply divided Congress prevented the public schooling expansion that CFAE leaders had opposed. Disagreements included fears of federal intrusion into a historically state, local, or private matter as well as the thorny issue of dedicating national resources to bolster schools that were private, religious, or exclusively for minorities, women, or whites. Discord traversed party lines. Liberal Democrats had been insisting on federal assistance since the 1940s. Only a handful of southern Democrats considered advanced learning important. Most of their support stemmed from education's importance to their own personal advancement. But these congressmen, chief among them Alabama's Lister Hill, generally wanted federal assistance without interference, particularly if the strings attached to aid might be used to reshape southern race relations. Republicans were also divided on the issue. Some liberal Republicans agreed with their counterparts in the other party. But conservative Republicans, including Senator Barry M. Goldwater, judged schooling best left to colleges and states. Republicans like Goldwater proposed federal tax breaks for tuition payments. These congressional representatives considered such concessions enough to encourage and help more Americans pursue advanced degrees. Moderate Republicans, including President Dwight D. Eisenhower's advisors, flatly rejected that idea on the grounds that it would ensure college education remained the exclusive purview of elites.[24]

Higher education policies remained divisive even after Sputnik's 1957 launch, which shocked ordinary Americans. The Soviet Union's Sputnik, an orbiting satellite (the likes of which the United States did not have at the time) failed to produce an immediate sea change in federal support for higher education; Congress actually spent a year hammering out the 1958 National Defense Education Act (NDEA).[25]

Eisenhower eventually intervened to ensure passage but still chose to act more as a hands-off moderator in chief than an involved educator in chief. His administration confronted an array of domestic and foreign issues and did not prioritize NDEA's passage. For example, Eisenhower turned to his advisor Marian B. Folsom for advice. The former Kodak executive advised against the conservative Republicans' tax deduction proposal. But Eisenhower did not concur with Folsom in a meeting called to discuss only the omnibus bill. The president made that decision in a high-level meeting where policymakers had made room on the docket for this pending legislation alongside the foreign policy concerns that Ike considered more pressing.[26]

International tensions were not the only reasons Eisenhower did not focus on NDEA. Historians have noted that the president had shown himself restrained in his efforts to corral Congress. His trust in Folsom also reflected Eisenhower's approach to circumscribing, not dismantling, Roosevelt's New Deal. That approach stood behind Goldwater's damnation that Ike had offered Americans a watered-down New Deal but that modus operandi also reflected the president's decision to approach Folsom, an executive whose direct involvement in constructing the Social Security Act had limited how much the federal government would underwrite social welfare. Similarly, Eisenhower made clear to Congress that he would sign only a limited education bill.[27]

Educators at the time recognized NDEA's shortcomings. The law improved instruction in science, math, and foreign languages, encouraged students to pursue a college degree, and provided both fellowships and small short-term loans for students promising to pursue a course of study important to the nation. But Congress and the Eisenhower administration also did not consider the relatively small grant and lending programs a means to fully expand schools, as work-study and the GI Bill authors had aimed to do. The earmarks were too small. Plus, the lending schema was a limited self-perpetuating program. Federal officials generally provided most of the funding for the loan funds that schools had to set up in order for financial aid officers to give applicants' these ten-year, low-interest loan offers. Borrowers paid back these loans with interest, which incrementally increased the amount of money available. Applicants had to apply for specific degree programs at schools that they chose. Once again, student choice enabled policymakers to navigate the thorny issue of federal funds going toward private schools or those that considered race, creed, or sex in the admissions process. But NDEA loans also gave recipients leeway after matriculation. Students could easily change their degree program. The only undergraduates and graduates beholden to stay with a particular course of study were the ones who found funding through the National Institutes of Health (NIH) and the National Science Foundation (NSF), the agencies also offering a lot of the targeted research money that built the medical schools, science departments, and engineering labs. This federal money available from NIH, NSF, and NDEA did much to expand the programs and buildings tied to science, health, and national defense at well-established state and private universities, such as the University of California, Berkeley, and the University of Chicago. However, this revenue could not be used to underwrite university growth broadly, since this money had to go toward specific projects, labs, and departments.[28]

These various public and private pots of money accelerated the competition between colleges and universities. Administrators across the country vied for federal research money, private business investment, philanthropic support, and also students. Only undergraduates were a guaranteed source of unrestricted revenue. Tuition dollars (whether or not they were paid or loaned by the federal government) did not have to go to a specific research project or academic discipline. Campus fees could be used where needed and did go toward expanding the faculties, classrooms, and labs needed to apply for the more lucrative public and private money available.[29]

NDEA earmarks, grants, donations, and student tuition payments did not sufficiently prepare colleges for the arrival of the Baby Boomers in the 1960s. Many of these new arrivals were the children of WWII veterans who had clamored to take advantage of the GI Bill's education provisions. Schools needed professors, classrooms, and dorms; and yet President John F. Kennedy's efforts to directly fund hiring professors, building dormitories, and constructing classrooms died in Congress. Eisenhower's tepid interventions in the long-standing debates about federal aid to education had hardly yielded a congressional accord. His successor also lacked coattails from his narrow 1960 victory. Kennedy hence found himself able to do little for advanced learning even though he had in fact campaigned on expanding higher education. He certainly tried. He turned to academics for advice, even appointing professors eager for expanding federal support for college campuses, such as Harvard Education School's Francis Keppel. But Kennedy's aides could not get these bills through Congress until February 1963. Senators and representatives remained bitterly divided on the constitutionality of direct federal support, particularly to historically black institutions, religious schools, and segregated universities.[30]

Broker in Chief

"Assisting smaller, undernourished colleges" was but one component of the Higher Education Act that Kennedy's successor celebrated in 1965. But LBJ mentioned that provision after outlining the scholarships, part-time jobs, and "loans, free of interest and free of any payment schedule until after you graduate, to worthy, deserving, capable students." Indeed, his remarks managed to encapsulate much about this sweeping legislation, his ambitious plans for a Great Society, and his personal life. This bright southerner had few options but to attend the teachers college to which he had returned to sign this bill. He was accordingly candid about how his own schooling had been a pathway out of poverty to which few had access. He learned that lesson during his brief stint teaching at a predominantly Mexican American school. That experience benefitted the thousands of Texans who applied for NYA's work-study program. But LBJ's position as the director of the NYA in his home state was but a steppingstone during his political ascent. This young New Dealer famously caught the attention of FDR, who proclaimed him capable of someday becoming the nation's next southern president. Many historians maintain that Johnson's years in the Senate helped him secure passage of the sweeping legislation behind the ambitious War on Poverty and Great Society to complete the New Deal.[31]

Johnson, like his predecessors, faced a divided Congress that refused to bow to presidential will. In theory, HEA's passage should have been easy. The 1964 Civil Rights Act had removed concern about public money going toward segregated institutions. No institution could receive federal aid if it discriminated. Controversy instead surrounded how and what the national government would underwrite. Tax breaks remained the rallying cry of conservative Republicans in Congress. Liberal Democrats tended to support both institutional aid and student assistance. Educators also stepped forward to make the case for generous support. For example, one of the leading educators of the era, well-known University of California president Clark Kerr, openly opposed the loans and tax credits discussed. He publicly warned that continuing to put an emphasis on using tuition to fund higher education in effect muddied colleges' and universities' status as a *public good*, threatening to keep it a private luxury when advanced learning was now a civic necessity.[32]

Johnson, however, had emphasized lending within his administration but had publicly gone back and forth on tax breaks over the years. He was likely following precedent and strategizing politically. Federally guaranteed loans and tuition assistance programs were hardly innovative in the mid-1960s. Johnson had learned during World War II that working with private businesses contracting with the federal government, like Brown and Root, could pay real political dividends. But decades of pork-barrel politics had not brought much awareness of the building postwar conservative movement, which took many Americans by surprise in the mid-1960s. Senator Barry Goldwater's 1964 presidential bid reflected the foreign policy, social concerns, and free-enterprise principles at the core of this challenge to modern liberalism. Leading businessmen, as with CFAE, did much to bankroll this insurgency. Hence, as historians have recently noted, LBJ rightly feared his opponent. The president accordingly reached out to executives in order to shore up business support, which included closed-door meetings during which LBJ promised to extend Kennedy's corporate tax cuts.[33]

But Congress did not give Johnson a student tax break to sign into law in 1965. HEA's fifty-seven pages had just eight titles. The first promised direct support to underwrite programs that would turn schools into modern multi-versities that served a range of constituents, not just students and faculty. Such sprawling research institutions needed better repositories and more librarians, both of which the second title funded. The third section provided direct aid to "developing institutions," a polite way of referring to historically black colleges and universities. The first three parts pleased many university administrators, including Kerr. Money would go to any institution, regardless of whether it was a private, public, religious, or women's only institution. These early sections also reflected educators' widespread sense that financial aid still meant direct assistance to schools, which they considered far more important to expanding opportunity and ensuring the needed revenue. Robust funding was also a means to prevent the burden of paying for colleges and universities from falling on students and parents. But sandwiched between those titles and the final four dedicated to teacher training, undergraduate instruction, and amendments to earlier legislation was "Student Assistance."[34]

That fourth section, particularly its loan provisions, pleased both the Johnson administration and Congress. Johnson had even singled out that body's role in crafting this law at the start of his signing statement. Lawmakers also publicly crowed that they had provided three basic forms of student assistance to make up an individually tailored "package": grants, revived work-study opportunities, and low-interest loans insured by the federal government (like most American mortgages had been since the New Deal). Liberals and conservatives prided themselves on protecting school autonomy because campus financial aid officers would get to determine the amount of each type of aid a student received. Conservatives and liberals also celebrated that no student would receive a "free ride" because grants were too small to cover tuition, books, and living expenses. It was presumed by conservatives and many liberals, like Republican New York governor Nelson A. Rockefeller, who had also been active in New Deal circles, that students must pay something toward their own education.[35]

Yet no one explained or lauded HEA's scholarships, work-study opportunities, and loans in the context of providing students with a choice. Since the 1930s, Congress and the executive branch had used student preference to navigate what the entire federal government could not do in regards to education. This shift in the 1960s partly reflected no longer needing to fear public support for segregated schools. But this linguistic evolution also highlighted the crystallization of the then uniquely American approach to financing higher education. Even though colleges and universities, whether public or private, could receive direct support, they could make up budget shortfalls by courting private donors, competing for government contracts, and raising tuition rates, or some combination thereof. Educators were, after all, guaranteed that students would be able to take out a loan if they could not pay out of pocket.

The administration's records reveal that securing that revenue stream may have taken place after Congress approved the Higher Education Act. In closed, top-level meetings, the president, his top economic and political aides, Douglass Cater and James C. Gaither, and leading figures from the American Bankers Association discussed how to implement the federal guaranteed student loan program. That plan intrigued leading bankers because a handful of states, most notably New York under Rockefeller, had also started and successfully administered higher education agencies to broker credit agreements between students and local lenders.[36]

Epilogue

Creditor in Chief

Since HEA's passage, the manner in which presidents have played the role of creditor in chief has been far more indirect. Fluctuating loan rates, new payback plans, and increased campus fees need to be attributed to the Department of Education's staffers, school administrators, financial aid officers, state legislators, and higher-ups in the sprawling financial aid industry, not just private lenders but intermediaries between federal appointees and the students and schools that they were supposed to serve. They all spent time lobbying for both the periodic direct congressional reauthorizations of the Higher Education Act and the indirect modifications by the estimated seven thousand sections of federal regulations just pertaining to loans. Many of those changes do not require presidential signatures, robbing presidents of the chance to once again celebrate what higher education means to the citizenry.[37]

In fact, HEA's periodic mandatory reauthorizations unintentionally lessened presidential purview over education policy and increased the reliance on loans. The 1972 changes, for example, introduced two important measures. The more famous was the direct federal grant program for impoverished students later called Pell grants after the Rhode Island senator who championed them. But Democrat Claiborne Pell's efforts to add a fourth part of the federal student aid package alienated lawmakers. Oregon congresswoman Edith Green disliked the idea of a guaranteed federal handout to students. This former educator wanted colleges to determine who was worthy. She subsequently left the House education subcommittee in order to join the budget committee, where she could ensure that Pell grants never received the full amount earmarked in the 1972 reauthorization. That legislation also created Sallie Mae, a recently privatized clearing house for student loan debt modeled off of the New Deal's Fannie Mae and earlier state level experiments. Richard M. Nixon's advisors had urged this government-sponsored enterprise in order to encourage lenders to participate in the nascent student loan industry just as Fannie Mae had coaxed banks into the mortgage sector.[38]

But this addition, congressional control of the budget, as well as 1970s revisions to the allocation process, unintentionally eroded congressional and presidential control over the academy's fortunes and the student loan industry. By the early 1990s, presidents and legislators made the most substantive changes to financial aid for students and for schools through either other laws or riders to other bills. For example, Bill Clinton had hoped to get rid of the guaranteed loan program. However, he was only able to make permanent the small direct loan program first introduced in the 1992 reauthorizations. A more important fulfillment of his promise to aid education came when he signed off on a separate revision to the tax code, which included a tuition benefit that some southern governors had already begun to adopt at the state level. But the 1997 Taxpayer Relief Act also finally put into law the kind of higher-education tax credits and deductions that conservative Republicans and a handful of Democrats (like LBJ) had been publicly championing since the 1950s. The guaranteed indirect loan program only ended in 2010, when President Barack Obama signed the Health Care and Education Reconciliation Act, which included provisions to cut out the middlemen between the education department, universities, and students. Nevertheless, past borrowers still had to repay the federal loans offered through banks and most often sold by the now privatized Sallie Mae.[39]

Not many Americans took note of that end-run around a now long-overdue and stalled reauthorization of the higher education law. Most Americans consider the tuition tax write-offs far more sacrosanct. But this new third rail in American tax write-offs does not really ease alumni's financial burdens. Experts have shown that only the wealthiest Americans earned enough to get the full benefit of a so-called reform that actually privileged enrollment in the country's most expensive schools.[40] Nonetheless, Obama echoed LBJ's 1965 remarks when he traveled to a Northern Virginia community college where Vice President Joe Biden's wife taught. "That's two major victories in one week," Obama noted. The first was, of course, health care. The second was the end of the once-revered Guaranteed Loan Program that LBJ had signed into law, "a sweetheart deal in federal law that essentially gave billions of dollars to banks." But neither Congress nor Johnson had intended federal student loans to become the center of a massive, supposedly nonprofit industry whose financial products recently have seemed to many a pathway into, not out of, poverty.[41]

Notes

1. Lyndon Baines Johnson, "Remarks on Signing the Higher Education Act of 1965," November 8, 1965, Texas State Common Experience website, http://www.txstate.edu/commonexperience/pastsitearchives/2008-2009/lbjresources/higheredact.html; Roger Geiger, *To Advance Knowledge: The Growth of American Research Universities* (New York: Oxford University Press, 1986); Christopher Loss, *Between Citizens and the State: The Politics of American Higher Education in the 20th Century* (Princeton: Princeton University Press, 2012); Thomas D. Snyder, *120 Years of American Education: A Statistical Portrait* (Washington, DC: U.S. Department of Education, Office of Educational Research and Improvement, 1993), http://nces.ed.gov/pubs93/93442.pdf.

2. Roger Geiger, *Knowledge & Money: Research Universities and the Paradox of the Marketplace* (Stanford: Stanford University Press, 2004); Martin Trow, "American Higher Education: Past, Present, and Future," *Educational Researcher* 17 (April 1988): 13–23; David Larabee, "A System without a Plan: Emergence of an American System of Higher Education in the Twentieth Century," *Bildungsgegeschichte: International Journal for the Historiography of Education* 3 (2013): 46–59; Martin Trow, "From Mass Higher Education to Universal Access: The American Advantage," *Minerva* 37 (December 1999): 303–28; Christopher Newfield, *Unmaking the Public University: The Forty-Year Assault on the Middle Class* (Cambridge, MA: Harvard University Press, 2008).

3. Geiger, *Knowledge & Money*; Trow, "American Higher Education"; Larabee, "A System without a Plan"; Trow, "From Mass Higher Education to Universal Access"; Newfield, *Unmaking the Public University*.

4. Merle Curti and Roderick Nash, *Philanthropy in the Shaping of American Higher Education* (New Brunswick, NJ: Rutgers University Press, 1965); Laurence Veysey, *The Emergence of the American University* (Chicago: University of Chicago Press, 1970); Jackson Toby, "How Scholarships Morphed into Financial Aid," *Academic Questions* 23 (September 2010): 298–310; Loss, *Between Citizens and the State*, 19–52.

5. Ronald Story, "The New Deal and Higher Education," 272–96, in *The New Deal and the Triumph of Liberalism*, ed. Sidney Milkus and Jerome Mileur (Amherst: University of Massachusetts Press, 2002); Paula Fass, "Without Design: Education Policy in the New Deal," *American Journal of Education* 91 (November 1982): 36–64; only letter asking for loans found in file 107, box 1, President's Official File, FDR Presidential Library and Archive, Hyde Park, NY (hereafter FDRL).

6. Fass, "Without Design"; Story, "New Deal and Higher Education"; David Lilienthal, *TVA: Democracy on the March* (New York: Harper & Brothers, 1944); Bruce Schulman, *From Cotton Belt to Sunbelt: Federal Policy, Economic Development, and the Transformation of the South, 1938–1980* (New York: Oxford University Press, 1991), 3–38, quoted 3.

7. Loss, *Between Citizens and the State*, 53–90; Story, "New Deal and Higher Educa-

tion"; Fass, "Without Design"; Richard Reiman, *New Deal and American Youth: Ideas and Ideals in a Depression Decade* (Athens: University of Georgia Press, 1992).

8. Loss, *Between Citizens and the State*, 53–90; Story, "New Deal and Higher Education"; Fass, "Without Design"; Reiman, *New Deal and American Youth.*

9. Loss, *Between Citizens and the State*, 53–90; Story, "New Deal and Higher Education"; Fass, "Without Design"; Reiman, *New Deal and American Youth*; National Advisory Committee, *Report of the National Advisory Committee of the National Youth Administration to the President of the United States* (Washington, DC: Government Printing Office, 1942), 1–5, 37–80.

10. Taussig expressed those concerns in minutes/correspondence, box 6, Charles Taussig Papers, FDRL; on historiography and recent reconsiderations of the New Deal see Jason Scott Smith, *A Concise History of the New Deal* (New York: Cambridge University Press, 2014); on choice to use executive order see Reiman, *New Deal and American Youth*, 97–122.

11. Fass, "Without Design"; Larabee, "A System without a Plan"; Story, "New Deal and Higher Education"; "Freedom of Press and Schools Urged," *New York Times*, June 6, 1934; "'Big Labor' Called Threat by Butler," *New York Times*, March 2, 1935.

12. National Advisory Committee, *Report of the National Advisory Committee*, 6–36; John Salmond, *A Southern Rebel: The Life and Times of Aubrey Willis Williams, 1890–1965* (Chapel Hill: University of North Carolina Press), 141–61; Loss, *Between Citizens and the State*, 91–120; Guy B. Arthur Jr. to Kelly Barnes, October 17, 1942, box 6, folder "Advisory Committee, 1935–1942," Aubrey Williams Papers, FDRL. For continued university opposition see files 1–4 (Senator Byrd Joint Committee on Reduction of Non-essential Federal Expenditures), box 10, Aubrey Williams Papers, FDRL.

13. Salmond, *A Southern Rebel*, 162–78; Reiman, *The New Deal and American Youth*, 175–81.

14. Keith Olson, "The G.I. Bill and Higher Education: Success and Surprise" *American Quarterly* 25 (December 1973): 596–610; Susan Mettler, *Soldiers to Citizens: The G.I. Bill and the Making of the Greatest Generation* (New York: Oxford University Press, 2005); Kathleen Frydl, *The GI Bill* (New York: Cambridge University Press, 2009); Glenn Altschuler and Stuart Blumin, *The GI Bill: The New Deal for Veterans* (Oxford: Oxford University Press, 2009).

15. Quoted in Mettler, *Soldiers to Citizens*, 71; Altschuler and Blumin, *The GI Bill*, 51–84.

16. Altschuler and Blumin, *The GI Bill*, 51–84; David Nasaw, *The Chief: The Life of William Randolph Hearst* (New York: Houghton Mifflin, 2000), 576–603.

17. Altschuler and Blumin, *The GI Bill*, 51–84.

18. Mettler, *Soldiers to Citizens*, 15–23, 41–58; Altschuler and Blumin, *The GI Bill*, 35–50, 85–116.

19. Mettler, *Soldiers to Citizens*, 41–58; Olson, "The G.I. Bill and Higher Education."

20. Mettler, *Soldiers to Citizens*, 1–14, 41–86, 163–76.

21. Michael Fabricant and Stephen Brier, *Austerity Blues: Financing for the Soul of Public Higher Education* (Baltimore: Johns Hopkins University Press, 2016), 46–60;

James G. Harlow, "Five Years of Discussion," *Journal of Higher Education* 24, no. 1 (January 1953): 17–24.

22. Curti and Nash, *Philanthropy in the Shaping of American Higher Education*, 238–58; Council for Financial Aid to Education, Inc., *Twenty-Fifth Annual Report* (New York: Council for Financial Aid to Education, 1978). On these executives and the nature of business thinking about "free enterprise" see Elizabeth Tandy Shermer, *Sunbelt Capitalism: Phoenix and the Transformation of American Politics* (Philadelphia: University of Pennsylvania Press, 2013), 1–16, 147–224; and Kim Phillips-Fein, *Invisible Hands: The Businessmen's Crusade against the New Deal* (New York: W.W. Norton, 2009), ix–xii, 26–52.

23. Curti and Nash, *Philanthropy in the Shaping of American Higher Education*, 238–58; Council for Financial Aid to Education, Inc., *Twenty-Fifth Annual Report* (New York: Council for Financial Aid to Education, 1978).

24. Barbara Clowse, *Brainpower for the Cold War: The Sputnik Crisis and the National Defense Education Act of 1958* (Westport, CT: Greenwood, 1981); Janet Kerr-Tener, "Eisenhower and Federal Aid to Higher Education," *Presidential Studies Quarterly* 17 (Summer 1987): 473–85; January 17, 1958 Meeting, box 10, Cabinet Series, Dwight Eisenhower Papers as President, Dwight Eisenhower Presidential Library and Archive, Abilene, KS (hereafter DEP).

25. Clowse, *Brainpower for the Cold War*.

26. Clowse, *Brainpower for the Cold War*, esp. 54–65; January 17, 1958 Meeting, box 10, Cabinet Series, DEP.

27. Robert Griffith, "Eisenhower and the Corporate Commonwealth" *American Historical Review* 87 (February 1982): 87–122; Elizabeth Tandy Shermer, "Origins of the Conservative Ascendancy: Barry Goldwater's Early Senate Career and the De-legitimization of Organized Labor," *Journal of American History* 95 (December 2008): 678–709; Sanford Jacoby, *Modern Manors: Welfare Capitalism since the New Deal* (Princeton: Princeton University Press, 1997), 57–94; Clowse, *Brainpower for the Cold War*, 128–38.

28. Clowse, *Brainpower for the Cold War*, 139–51; George Kizer, "Federal Aid to Education, 1945–1963," *History of Education Society* 10 (Spring 1970): 84–102.

29. Larabee, "A System without a Plan"; Trow, "American Higher Education"; Martin Trow, "From Mass Higher Education to Universal Access: The American Advantage," *Minerva* 37, no. 4 (December 1999): 303–28.

30. Hugh Davis Graham, *Uncertain Triumph: Federal Education Policy in the Kennedy and Johnson Years* (Chapel Hill: University of North Carolina Press, 2011).

31. Johnson, "Remarks on Signing the Higher Education Act of 1965," November 8, 1965, http://www.txstate.edu/commonexperience/pastsitearchives/2008-2009/lbjresources/higheredact.html; Loss, *Between Citizens and the State*, 53–90, 165–213; Christie L. Bourgeois, "Stepping over Lines: Lyndon Johnson, Black Texans, and the National Youth Administration, 1935–1937," *Southern Historical Quarterly* 91 (October 1987): 149–72.

32. Graham, *Uncertain Triumph*, 53–131; Paddy Riley, "Clark Kerr: From the Industrial to the Knowledge Economy," 71–87, in *American Capitalism: Social Thought and Political Economy in the Twentieth Century*, ed. Nelson Lichtenstein (Philadelphia: Univer-

sity of Pennsylvania Press, 2006); Francis Keppel, "Higher Education Acts Contrasted, 1965–1986: Has Federal Policy Come of Age?" *Harvard Educational Review* 57 (February 1987): 49–67; Sally Ann Davenport, "Smuggling-In Reform: Equal Opportunity and the Higher Education Act, 1965–80" (PhD diss., Johns Hopkins University, 1983), 113–50; Muhammad Attaullah Chaudhry, "The Higher Education Act of 1965: An Historical Case Study" (PhD diss., Oklahoma State University, 1981), 67–122.

33. Stephen Crawford Brock, "A Comparative Study of Federal Aid to Higher Education: The Higher Education Act of 1965 and Project Upward Bound" (PhD diss., Cornell University, 1968), 21–50; Jordon Schwartz, *The New Dealers: Power Politics in the Age of Roosevelt* (New York: Alfred A. Knopf, 1993), 264–84; Phillips-Fein, *Invisible Hands*, 115–49.

34. Keppel, "Higher Education Acts Contrasted, 1965–1986."

35. Keppel, "Higher Education Acts Contrasted, 1965–1986"; Davenport, "Smuggling-In Reform," 113–50; Leonard Manning, "Aid to Education—State Style" *Fordham Law Review* 29, no. 3 (1961): 525–52; Richard Norton Smith, *On His Own Terms: A Life of Nelson Rockefeller* (New York: Random House, 2014), 349–75.

36. Graham, *Uncertain Triumph*, 53–131. See boxes 34 and 43, Douglass Cater Paper, LBJ Presidential Library, Austin, TX (hereafter LBJL); boxes 227 and 229, James Gaither Papers, LBJL; box 37, folders marked LE/FA2, White House Central Files, LBJL; J. D. Boyd, "History of State Involvement in Financial Aid," *Perspectives on Financial Aid* (New York: College Entrance Examination Board, 1975), 118–28; Manning, "Aid to Education—State Style."

37. Patrick Mungovan, "Role of the U.S. Federal Government in the Student Loan Industry" (master's thesis, MIT Sloan School of Management, 2005).

38. Lawrence E. Gladieux and Thomas R. Wolanin, *Congress and the Colleges: The National Politics of Higher Education* (Lexington, MA: Lexington Books, 1976).

39. Barbara Sinclair, "Congressional Reform," 625–37, esp. 635–37, and Eric Patashnik, "Congress and the Budget Since 1974," 668–86, both in *The American Congress: The Building of Democracy*, ed. Julien Zelizer (New York: Houghton Mifflin, 2004); Susan Hannah, "The Higher Education Act of 1992: Skills, Constraints, and the Politics of Higher Education," *Journal of Higher Education* 67 (Sept./Oct. 1996): 498–527; Peter Baker and David Herszenhorn, "Obama Signs Bill on Student Loans and Health Care," *New York Times*, March 30, 2010, http://thecaucus.blogs.nytimes.com/2010/03/30/obama-signs-bill-on-student-loans-health-care/.

40. Jacqueline King, ed., *Financing a College Education: How It Works, How It's Changing* (Phoenix: Oryx, 1999); Derek Price, *Borrowing Inequality: Race, Class, and Student Loans* (Boulder, CO: L. Reinner, 2004).

41. Baker and Herszenhorn, "Obama Signs Bill on Student Loans and Health Care."

PART II

SECTORS

The Way Politics Organizes Business and the Economy

8

Parallel Ladders to the Glass Ceiling

Presidential and Corporate Executive Appointments

PAMELA WALKER LAIRD

Imagine Wonder Woman flying up to a glass ceiling and *smashing* it. That is the image that expressions about conquering the glass ceiling conjure—*crack* and *shatter*! Yet, despite meritocratic rhetoric about fulfilling ambitions by grit and determination, the reality is that glass ceilings only yield to pull from above, not force from below. Moreover, long before ambitious people can approach a glass ceiling, they must get onto the right ladder, for not all ladders lead to the top. Yet only their supporters and employers, acting as gatekeepers, can place people on tall ladders and then pull them through glass ceilings. Therefore, women's progress toward and through glass ceilings, whether in business or presidential politics, reflects historical changes in both gatekeepers' incentives and their perceptions of women's abilities.[1] The different levels of women's success on corporate and political ladders highlight significant differences between gatekeepers' incentives and expectations in the two arenas. The similarities follow from how people—all people—climb both sets of ladders. Looking at power relations on professional ladders through the lens of gender and compared across capitalist and governmental institutions reveals strong parallels that remain obscured otherwise. Through this comparison, we can see opportunities and limits for ambitious people within systems in which meritocratic ideals are often eclipsed by less noble realities.

Professional ladders in both political and business arenas carry strongly gendered associations. Traditional ladders for women focus on constituencies' needs as humans, be those social, physical, or psychological. In businesses, these are called "staff" functions, in contrast to the "line" functions that promote organizations' core missions. Thus, top executives, and

Figure 8.1. Superhero women smash, crack, and shatter glass ceilings from below—but only in cartoons. In the real world, no one rises above glass ceilings unless pulled from above by influential people, such as presidents and corporate leaders. Courtesy of Shelmal/Dreamstime.com.

especially CEOs, climb through the ranks on ladders attending to production, marketing, or finance. In government, the ladders women typically climb also attend to constituencies' well-being, such as health, education, and working conditions. As important as these functions are, rarely do people on those service ladders reach corporations' or governments' top echelons. The tallest ladders advance their organizations' core missions, such as production and marketing for corporations or international relations or finances for governments. Gatekeepers control access to ladders, and only when women get on and get pulled up the ladders that gatekeepers value most can they approach and pass through the highest glass ceilings.

For most of modern history, women have tried to climb nontraditional ladders, such as those in engineering, science, business, politics, and the military, but at their peril. The risks they took included raw discrimination—"push" discrimination that works through deliberate rejection and harassment, plus more subtle "pull" discrimination, by which gatekeepers and possible mentors failed to recognize women's potential and did not pull them into powerful networks and high-potential opportunities.[2] Over the half-century since the 1964 Civil Rights Act, legal and cultural changes have gradually made nontraditional choices less risky. Women on nontraditional ladders have increasingly come to appear "normal"; gatekeepers and mentors have come to appreciate their potential to contribute, thereby increasing women's successes. Access to and encouragement on core ladders has increased over the last half century, and the highest glass ceilings have come into view, and, increasingly, they shatter.

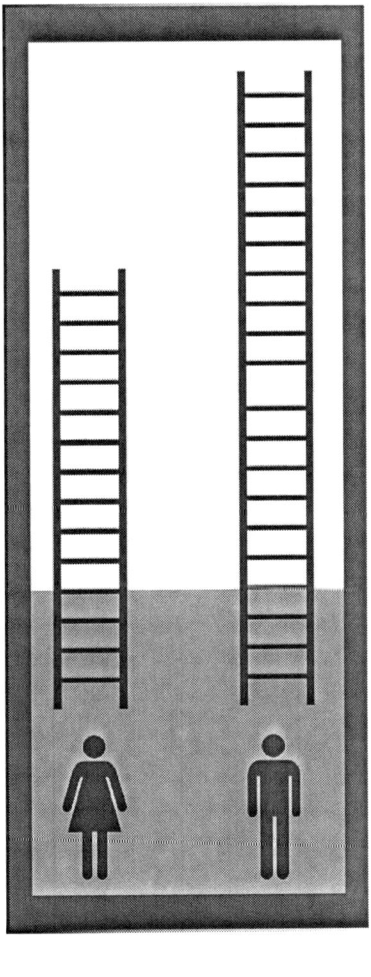

Figure 8.2. Until recently, women did not have access to ladders that reach to the top of major political or corporate institutions. Ladders traditionally associated with women serve social, physical, or psychological needs, whereas the ladders that political and business leaders value most promote their organizations' core missions, such as finance in business or foreign affairs in government. Courtesy of Eleanore S. Lewis.

Back in the 1970s, Katherine Hudson understood the differences among corporate ladders. She set a target, in her words, to "be the first woman corporate officer in a job that was not OK for a woman to be in. That meant not human resources, not public relations, not advertising." Instead, she got a job in Eastman Kodak's corporate communications; through that channel she met the firm's head, Walter Fallon. The first time Fallon met her, he asked her boss, "What's she doing here?" Soon, though, Hudson proved her mettle and justified several mentors' confidence, rising to chief information officer by 1988. When her mentors retired and the glass ceiling at Kodak turned to brick, she left to head the Brady Corporation in 1993. Within seven years, its sales doubled, and its worth almost tripled.[3]

Hudson began her climb in the 1970s, in the peak intensity of the feminist movement that had surged the previous decade. Today's numbers of women in corporate management reflect five decades of progress after the 1964 Civil Rights Act. According to Catalyst, Inc., a research and advocacy organization for professional women, in 2014, 36.8 percent of lower- and mid-level managers in Standard & Poor 500 companies were women. Nonetheless, in 2015 only twenty-three, not quite 5 percent, of Fortune 500 CEOs were women.[4] One of those women, Jacqueline Hinman, pursued her ambitions as a skilled engineer and manager. Now she heads CH2M, one of the world's leading engineering and construction firms. Climbing such a nontraditional ladder required the help of mentors to recognize and value her merits and to pull her up. For instance, Hinman's predecessor at CH2M, Ralph Peterson, emphasized pulling women up through the firm with the result that it won the prestigious Catalyst Award in 2009. According to the citation, CH2M "leverages women employees by ensuring they are placed in important positions . . . and are responsible for high-profile projects, linking their expertise to business success."[5]

That CH2M "leverages women employees" by "linking their expertise to business success" typifies the language of "diversity" that business leaders have adopted since the 1990s. Gatekeepers' acceptance of diversity's business advantages has driven what is in effect affirmative action, despite the decline of government support since the 1980s and the lack of legal requirements for it. This rhetoric emphasizes maximizing the business benefits of expertise, competence, productivity, and creativity best found along a broad spectrum of employees. Significantly, CH2M was the first engineering and construction firm to receive the Catalyst Award, and that happened the first year it entered the ranks of the Fortune 500. Jacqueline Hinman's ambition, abilities, and timing meshed well with this corporation's innovative culture and, in turn, within the context of a larger business culture that has increasingly valued workforce diversity for what it has brought to firms' competitiveness.[6]

Glass ceilings have functioned differently in government agencies. In particular, American presidents select their top administrators, including their cabinet members, according to different criteria and methods than do corporate gatekeepers. Rather than use expertise to build profits, politicians must build political support—political capital—to accomplish their goals. Their successes depend on marshaling support among a range of constituencies, including other politicians. As a result, they often appoint agency heads less for their expertise and administrative experience than for what they bring in political assets or personal loyalty. Moreover, presidents' initial cabinet appointments typically attract widespread attention, so those appointees, male or female, tend to bring less expertise and more political capital than do later rounds of appointments, especially second-term appointments.[7] This prominent feature of presidential strategies has resulted in a higher proportion of women, as well as underrepresented minorities, in top government positions than in business. Thus, when presidents and other government leaders have sought "diversity," they have often done so for reasons other than to expand their pool of competent, productive, and innovative talent.

The presidential side of this story of parallel ladders began in 1929 when Franklin D. Roosevelt began pulling the high-profile social reformer Frances Perkins up administrative ladders while he was governor of New York. Four years later, President Roosevelt appointed her secretary of labor—the first female presidential cabinet member and the first woman in the line of presidential succession. Among key factors defining that historical context, women had recently become voters, and, therefore, Perkins brought a wealth of political capital to the New Deal, even at the risk of offending the male-dominated labor organizations. Decades of work for laboring people also brought her administrative experience into an arena of critical importance to FDR's presidency. As a result of this confluence of factors, plus her friendship with Eleanor Roosevelt, this labor secretary achieved "inner cabinet" status rarely afforded that department. So anomalous was her situation that she had to create a title for herself—"Madam Secretary." And she admitted to feeling "odd" in her new role.[8] Nonetheless, for six decades no woman again entered the inner cabinet of secretaries with whom presidents consult most closely.

Fast forward to the feminist resurgence in the 1960s and 1970s, which reflected and affected attitudes toward women and their eligibility for the upper rungs of important ladders, including presidential cabinets. For forty-two years after FDR pulled Perkins up through the presidential cabinet's glass ceiling, only Dwight D. Eisenhower had appointed a woman, Oveta Culp Hobby in 1953, to head the newly created Department of Health, Education, and Welfare. In 1975, Gerald R. Ford appointed Carla Anderson Hills to Housing and Urban Development as the third female cabinet secretary. However, Jimmy Carter and the next five presidents appointed at least three women to their cabinets, and, equally important, into increasing numbers of nontraditional posts, such as Transportation and State, recognizing and advancing women's professional stature.

Even though Richard M. Nixon appointed no women to cabinet ranks, he advanced women to tall government ladders in response to women's growing political and cultural stature. For example, as he and President Eisenhower left the White House in 1961, Vice President Nixon wrote to commend Margaret Garrity for her work on the President's Committee on Government Contracts. He offered the highest praise imaginable then: "You have certainly proved that a woman can handle a top executive assignment with as much, and many times more, effectiveness than a man!"[9] Lest we snicker at this encomium, I hasten to point out that such praise and recognition were exactly what women needed to move up and forward in professional arenas, given the identity and attitudes of most gatekeepers controlling access to tall ladders then. Moreover, Nixon seemed genuinely to encourage women to participate in executive government roles then and later as president.[10]

In 1969, as the women's movement intensified, the recently inaugerated Nixon had to field widespread criticism for including only three women among his first two hundred policy position appointments, and all in traditional, human service areas. Statements from various officials denying "discrimination" met with angry demands that "equal opportunity" called for actively seeking out qualified women for executive positions. In response, by the middle of Nixon's first year, he instructed his cabinet to increase the numbers of women in positions of authority and responsibility. With little success in response to that first vague directive, he next created the Citizens' Advisory Council on the Status of Women. Top advisors urged the president to press forward, pointing out the political capital to be gained by addressing women's concerns. Daniel Patrick Moynihan, another Nixon aide, contended that "we have educated women for equality in America, but have not really given it to them." Therefore, this was "a subject ripe for creative political leadership and initiative," and he argued for appointments as well as "pronouncements." John D. Ehrlichman, one of Nixon's two closest advisors, likewise noted that "politically this is a golden opportunity and that we should, whenever possible, champion female equality."[11] These influential policymakers and the president thus encountered and responded to a type of public pressure to which corporate leaders have largely been immune.

President Nixon took the many urgings to heart. Following several efforts to diversify with little success, recruiting women accelerated in April 1971 when Barbara Hackman Franklin entered the White House, charged with recruiting women for high-level jobs. Franklin had a strong professional record, with an MBA from the Harvard Business School in the first class that had included women plus several years of business experience, including as an assistant vice president for corporate planning for a major bank. Even so, as a measure of the level of linguistic insensitivity then, her new title was proclaimed as "Staff Assistant to the President for Executive Manpower." To be sure, that title soon changed. With White House support, Franklin's work as liaison between federal supervisors and qualified women quickly improved the rate of female appointments, in one year overtaking that of the Kennedy administration and tripling the number of female policymakers.[12] Adding fuel and authority to the efforts, later that same month, President Nixon circulated the "Memorandum for the Heads of Executive Departments and Agencies." Beginning with a statement about his "desire to attract the ablest and most talented people in the country," Nixon continued with an assertion and call for action that did not become commonplace in the corporate world for another twenty years, namely that the "Nation's many highly qualified women represent an important reservoir of ability and talent that we must draw on to a greater degree." He required that each head "develop and put into action a plan for attracting more qualified women" to top positions within a month and report directly to the White House on their progress.[13]

The press took notice, and a year later *Newsweek* praised Franklin's achievements under her presidential mandate. A *Newsweek* writer even asserted that "the person in Washington who has done the most for the women's movement may be Richard Nixon."[14] As a male staff member noted years later, many of the women who arrived during those years "developed into very senior accomplished women." He concluded that Nixon had cultivated "an environment that apparently fostered that sort of growth." Within that climate, Franklin used her position to help start Executive Women in Government, which still thrives as a nonpartisan networking organization for women in federal government executive positions, including in the military. Another founding member worth noting was Elizabeth Hanford, later Elizabeth Dole. Franklin and Dole learned well the networking lessons of that era's women's activism. Under later presidents, they both became cabinet secretaries in nontraditional fields, Franklin as the second female secretary of commerce and Dole as the first female secretary of transportation. Dole later headed the Department of Labor, where her programs pointedly challenged glass ceilings in every profession.[15]

In the meantime, during the 1970s and 1980s, women in the business world, like African American men, experienced grave frustrations with their lack of progress up corporate ladders. During the first decade after the 1964 Civil Rights Act, millions of formerly excluded people entered corporations' lower levels. Exclusionary discrimination had become illegal, and despite ongoing rejection and harassment, progress on those entry levels encouraged efforts. However, progress onto nontraditional ladders and up tall ladders to powerful positions moved imperceptibly, so women and African American men began to search for explanations and seek solutions. Within women's groups like the National Organization for Women (NOW), founded in 1966, older but expanding groups like Business and Professional Women's, Inc., and countless discussion and support groups within their firms, women at all levels of American businesses read sociologists and other scholars in the 1970s, quickly building a social capital lexicon. These words and phrases that once only sociologists and educators used include most prominently "network" and "mentor," along with "gatekeeper" and "role model." With these conceptual tools to guide and inspire them, outsiders figured out how to become insiders. Today, of course, these social capital terms are ubiquitous. Yet it was only four decades ago when women and other outsiders brought awareness of these ancient but previously unacknowledged professional dynamics into our everyday language and actions.[16]

Even with these concepts and the newly discovered tools for building social capital and fulfilling career ambitions, another decade passed of growing frustrations for many. In order to explain and surmount the sources of their frustrations, advocates for women and underrepresented minority men learned yet another term—"glass ceiling." That newly approachable but still impervious barrier to executive positions received its name in an article in *Adweek* in 1984, and the term went viral two years later following a *Wall Street Journal* special report on "The Corporate Woman." For thirty pages, this report analyzed the glass ceilings that frustrated outsiders who had advanced far enough to whet their ambitions for managerial ranks in business and government but who could not climb there. As the lead article explained, quoting a Catalyst director, "up to a certain point, brains and competence work, [then] barriers against women set in." A consultant in banking explained that the barrier "often happens when a woman approaches a key managerial position where she'll affect company policy."[17] As glass ceilings obstructed progress in business, they did so in government, where "affect[ing] company policy" lies at the fore of all activity. Consequently, twenty-one of the thirty-one women who have served in cabinet positions to date have headed departments with missions analogous to corporate personnel and community service departments, as for instance Sylvia Mathews Burwell at Health and Human Services, President Obama's second female appointment for that position. Progress in conquering the cabinet's remaining glass ceilings requires moving beyond this pattern.

In 1989, three years after the *Wall Street Journal* report, George H. W. Bush's secretary of labor, Elizabeth Hanford Dole, confronted this growing problem and instituted the Glass Ceiling Initiative. Its analyses revealed that women and underrepresented minority men had little access to the ladders in business or government that reached top positions. Secretary Dole's own success at building social capital, political capital, and administrative credibility ever since her work with Barbara Franklin in Nixon's administration had attracted mentors who pulled her through several glass ceilings, including helping her become the first woman to head the Department of Transportation, in Ronald W. Reagan's administration. She knew what it took to climb ladders and to reach beyond glass ceilings, and she worked to institutionalize her understandings on others' behalf. She said in 1990, "I have made this issue a top priority, and it will remain so during my service as Secretary of Labor. For me, it is a matter of fairness and equity, born out of personal experience." In addition to policy, Dole added practice. Twenty of her first thirty-two top executive appointees were women, black, or Hispanic, or fell into more than one of these categories. Only the Department of Health and Human Services under Secretary Louis W. Sullivan, an African American medical doctor, surpassed Labor's 63 percent achievement with a 70 percent record as of mid-1990.[18]

One of Elizabeth Dole's own important connections, her husband, Senator Robert J. Dole, cosponsored legislation that created a Glass Ceiling Commission as part of Title II within what became the 1991 Civil Rights Act. Provisions included a "National Award for Diversity and Excellence in American Executive Management" that Senator Dole described as one that presidents would bestow on firms that made "substantial efforts to promote opportunities for women and minorities to advance to top levels." The legislation that finally emerged included the "Frances Perkins/Elizabeth Hanford Dole Award" to recognize these two secretaries of labor and their conquering of cabinet-level glass ceilings.[19]

On the corporate front in 1990, Fortune 500 corporations included only three women as CEOs, and all three owned major stakes in those firms.[20] As owners, they had not had to rely on gatekeepers to pull them up ladders and into leadership positions in their own corporations. Although the cabinet's one woman out of fourteen positions left much to be desired in 1990, the differential between that 7 percent and the corporate six-tenths of one percent that year merits examination. The current contrast between those institutions points to progress in both spheres, but corporations still lag behind with less than 5 percent women CEOs in contrast to 25 percent—eight of thirty two—cabinet appointments during Barack Obama's two terms. Or, counting departments, since 2009, women have headed eight out of fifteen cabinet departments, slightly more than half.[21] Although there are many complicated reasons for these contrasting proportions of women at the top of important ladders in business and government, the gatekeeper factor figures in each of them, determining both access to ladders and how high anyone can climb on them. Gatekeepers, with their expectations about the gendered nature of various ladders, thereby regulate how close anyone can get to glass ceilings and who gets pulled through them.

Why do presidents appoint *anyone* to their cabinets? Cabinet appointments are among a new president's highest-profile decisions, attracting levels of scrutiny that exceed their administrative weight. Most often, presidents seek to build political capital among constituents—repaying electoral debts, looking to future elections, or seeking support for their administrations' policies. Therefore, cabinet appointees of any demographic often have little administrative experience or relevant training for their positions. Their roles serve a strongly symbolic and representational purpose, especially as the Executive Office of the President has grown in administrative responsibilities. Even President Eisenhower, who rather disliked the whole realm of politics and notably sought administrative competence, appointed Oveta Hobby in 1953 primarily to draw in support from her southern roots and from women generally. Even so, Hobby's administrative credentials exceeded those of many of Eisenhower's male appointees, who had also been pulled into place for their political capital.[22]

The parallels and contrasts among women's differential progress up leadership ladders across corporations and presidential cabinets highlight how presidents and other gatekeepers understand the sources and dynamics of their own power and authority. Those perceptions of necessity reflect and shape their incentives. As gatekeepers concerned about public opinion and electoral support, American presidents since 1964 have become vastly more motivated toward gender equality than businessmen, whose primary constituencies are stockholders, and whose main judges are their own peers. In contrast, although many indications point to Richard Nixon's genuine interest in moving women up government ladders, we also know that his advisors urged him to do so for electoral reasons, for building political capital. Women voters provided Bill Clinton with the edge in his presidential electoral victories, and he acknowledged their importance as the first president to appoint five women as cabinet secretaries, each to a different department. Moreover, three of those appointments were firsts in nontraditional positions—Janet Reno to attorney general, Hazel R. O'Leary to Energy, and Madeleine Albright to State. George W. Bush, in turn, appointed six women, two of whom were firsts—Gale Norton to Interior and Ann Veneman to Agriculture. And, as mentioned above, Barack Obama appointed eight women to his cabinet, including Janet Napolitano as the first woman to head the relatively new and highly visible Department of Homeland Security. A measure of the "new normal" was the lack of extensive press commentary on the genders of Obama's appointments.[23] Growing popular expectations of diversity across ranks, including in leadership, has even encouraged political candidates to proclaim more progressive attitudes than their actions warrant, such as 2012 presidential candidate Mitt Romney's misguided and misleading assertion that he had sought to build "whole binders full of women" from which to make high-level appointments.[24]

Thus, because of electoral pressures, glass ceilings in political positions have crumbled faster than those in corporate America. Yet when presidents select women primarily for their symbolic identities rather than for their expertise or experience, their stature and effectiveness suffer. When women's departments fall outside of a president's key policy areas, their marginalization deepens, as Secretary Hobby experienced as Eisenhower's secretary of health, education, and welfare. Conversely, the more women are appointed to cabinet posts primarily because of their expertise instead of their symbolic usefulness, the more they approach the legitimacy of women CEOs. Madeleine Albright's highly respected expertise as the first female secretary of state serves as a case in point. Thus, the most meaningful shattering of federal glass ceilings began when Presidents Bill Clinton and George W. Bush each named more women with expertise and experience than any previous presidents had done. President Obama exceeded those records with his appointments of women with expertise and ability.[25] Of course, all of these presidents have enhanced the symbolic value of their female cabinet heads when they named women with strong credentials, such as when Obama nominated Loretta Lynch to become the second female attorney general—and therefore a member of his inner cabinet—because of her substantial credentials as a strong federal prosecutor.

The next major test of whether a president will exchange women's political capital for men's will come with the remaining cabinet bastions of Defense, Treasury, and Veterans Affairs. Apropos of these still-resistant glass ceilings is Obama's appointment of Janet Yellen to chair of the board of governors of the Federal Reserve System in 2014. Although the Federal Reserve is not a cabinet department, its chair is unquestionably one of the most powerful people in the world. Yellen is the first woman to lead the Fed, and only now at the beginning of its second century. This triumph caps her lifelong string of successes at conquering glass ceilings, in step with the women's movement and its progress through recent decades. As

Obama said when he nominated Yellen, her contributions as a role model are important. Yet her successes have required not only brilliance and dedication but mentors and colleagues who recognized those qualities and their value. For instance, in 1994 a male academic colleague recommended Yellen to President Bill Clinton for a vacancy on the Federal Reserve's board of governors. This decision drew her onto the Fed's very tall ladder, where her abilities could take her through the glass ceiling. Political capital played a part in her triumph, however, as the National Organization for Women and many other activists, including Gloria Steinem, lobbied hard for her appointment, their fervor fueled in part because Lawrence H. Summers, who was well-known for offensive remarks on women's "innate" abilities, was Obama's initial preference.[26]

Although the language of meritocracy dominates corporate culture as much as ever, social and cultural variables continue to carry as much weight as expertise and abilities. That is, if gatekeepers hold prejudices that make it impossible for them to recognize any group's abilities, they will not invite members of those groups into their networks nor pull them up ladders that reach and pass through glass ceilings.[27] Therefore, growing acceptance of women's capabilities across the national culture has built the foundation for advances toward integrating executive suites. This recognition has encouraged gatekeepers and mentors to see beyond traditional, gendered stereotypes to appreciate and cultivate women's abilities. In order for that progress to continue, women will have to choose carefully among the array of ladders that might take them to their goals. Like women in the military who seek combat duty, Katherine Hudson and Jacqueline Hinman understood that women who take care of others' needs do so on ladders that do not lead to the top. Ignoring stereotypes about women's affinity for caregiving, they, instead, trained for and climbed ladders in areas of expertise that relate to firms' core missions and bottom lines. With the pull of increasingly supportive gatekeepers, a few women have climbed those ladders to the tops of corporations.

Overall, the statistics on the current cohort of female CEOs of Fortune 500 firms reinforce Hudson and Hinman's career choices. Many, like Hinman, are engineers by training. Others have trained and excelled in economics, finance, accounting, marketing, computer science, physics, chemistry, math, law, systems analysis, and business management. Among the current twenty-three women CEOs, twenty worked their way up ladders performing line and core functions rather than staff and support functions. The other three worked on both types of ladders.[28] Ilene Gordon, CEO of Ingredion, a $5 billion food ingredient manufacturer, summed up the importance of selecting the right kind of ladders. She observed in 2013 that "a lot of women go into staff roles," but she had benefited from a mentor who urged her "to run a business" and "pushed [her] to leave the safe staff role and [to go] into line management. Most women would like that chance, but perhaps companies haven't provided it or women have shied away from the risk." Gordon also advised "the next generation of leaders" regardless of gender to "get the operating, line experience. Don't just stay in staff roles. Find a mentor who will give you advice, who's not emotionally involved and isn't going to be biased. People will need different mentors at different stages in their careers." She concluded, "Get your hands dirty."[29]

Although everyone has to make choices that match ladders with ambitions, as did Hudson, Hinman, and Gordon, the long history of intense resistance to women's ambitions among incumbents has only just begun to abate. Despite being extraordinarily talented, trained, and hard-working, none of these twenty-three women could have climbed their ladders and conquered their glass ceilings two decades ago. None had. In addition to overcoming gatekeepers' refusals to allow women into powerful networks and onto nontraditional ladders, as well as possible mentors' shortsightedness about women's "potential," outsiders have had to overcome resistance from peers. All of the current female CEOs of Fortune 500 firms tell stories of the social and cultural barriers that slowed or impeded their climbs. Much of the pride that they express about their achievements emphasizes overcoming those barriers. With their successes, and those of other previously excluded categories of people, corporate America may finally be approaching the meritocracy it has always claimed to be.

In both civic and business arenas, the constraints affecting women on these parallel ladders show that the meritocratic pretensions so vigorously proclaimed to justify both American capitalism and politics still collide with glass ceilings in almost every professional arena. Nonetheless, whether in corporations or government offices, the direction of change is clear, as the formerly excluded slowly acquire gatekeepers' approval, influential mentors, and access to powerful networks. However, even these smart, strong women could not have succeeded as they have until the civil rights and feminist movements generated both legal and cultural changes. The legal changes aimed to end exclusionary discrimination, and the cultural changes have made it possible to redistribute "pull"—social capital—across a broad spectrum of Americans. In a high-profile illustration of these dynamics across parallel ladders in corporations and presidential cabinets, former secretary of the treasury Lawrence Summers pulled Sheryl Sandberg into powerful networks and opportunities, seeing in her an exception to his notorious disparagement of women's "innate abilities." She is now chief operating officer of Facebook and a vocal advocate of women's deliberate development of social capital. Only by those means can outsiders become insiders and, as such, be pulled up tall ladders and through glass ceilings.

Not Yet the Conclusion

The highest glass ceiling in America is the office of the president itself. Although there are many reasons for Hillary Clinton's being the first truly viable female presidential candidate, in the context of this analysis of cabinet glass ceilings, her having served as secretary of state seems more than a happenstance. In a nontrivial sense, her own history replicates the broader history summarized here. When her husband ran for president in 1992, she and Barbara Bush competed for the nation's heart with their chocolate chip cookie recipes. As first lady, Hillary Clinton's primary project addressed the nation's health care system, a key and highly contentious initiative, but still one analogous to leadership in corporate support areas and governmental human and social services. One of the greatest challenges of her 2016 campaign was how to balance the friendliness and nurturing that many people still expect of a woman with the toughness voters expect of a national leader. Stereotypes die hard, but the nation has come a long way since a woman's merit hinged on her cookie recipe. Nonetheless, despite her accomplishments and the nation's progress, Clinton's challenge to this highest of glass ceilings did not succeed.

Clearly one of Clinton's most significant qualifications resulted from her having served as the nation's third female secretary of state. Back in 1997, President Bill Clinton had appointed the first, Madeleine Albright, pulling that accomplished and highly respected foreign policy expert through a key glass ceiling. Bill Clinton put Albright on the world stage and brought her into the inner cabinet, along with Attorney General Janet Reno, as the first women to work there since Frances Perkins. President Clinton's confidence in these two exceptional women highlighted both their expertise and representational symbolism.[30] President Obama, in turn, had many reasons to appoint his former presidential opponent Hillary Clinton to this most senior of cabinet positions with its international profile and immense responsibilities. From her perspective, the effect was less complicated, namely pulling her up one of the nation's tallest political ladders. With all of her former professional accomplishments, plus her social and political capital, Hillary Clinton still had to establish her professional credentials in prominent national and international arenas.[31] Performing impressively in that top cabinet position served her well as she looked to yet another glass ceiling to conquer.

How much, if any difference will it make to "add women and stir" in elite leadership positions, as the phrase goes? That depends, of course, on more variables affecting both business and politics than this short chapter can address. As it stands, women appointed to the U.S. cabinet strongly resemble their male predecessors and colleagues in origins, training, and, importantly, perspectives.[32] That stands to reason because the qualities that identify "potential" for leadership are not likely to change any time soon. The homogeneous business and political settings in which former and current leaders have operated and into which they have begun to pull newcomers have valued standards and rewarded characteristics, backgrounds, and training that are not likely to change anytime soon. Thus, the women most likely to conquer the highest glass ceilings will have attributes and experiences more similar to those of incumbent male gatekeepers than to those of women with experience and reputations gained on social welfare ladders. Gatekeepers' incentives and the willingness of mentors will always determine individual aspirants' success at approaching and climbing professional ladders, as well as conquering glass ceilings.

Notes

I am very grateful to Mark H. Rose and Roger Biles for their invitation to develop this project and their generous guidance in improving it. I also greatly appreciate advice and support from Frank N. Laird, Chad Pearson, and, especially, Jarett Zuboy for his invaluable research assistance.

1. Both sets of changes resulted from a complex evolution of legal and cultural conditions. See Pamela Walker Laird, *Pull: Networking and Success since Benjamin Franklin* (Cambridge, MA: Harvard University Press, 2006); and Laird, "Entangled: Civil Rights in Corporate America Since 1964," in *Capital Gains: Business and Politics in Twentieth-Century America*, ed. Kim Phillips-Fein and Richard R. John (Philadelphia: University of Pennsylvania Press, 2016).

2. Laird, *Pull*, 4–6.

3. Katherine M. Hudson, "Unexpected Career Path Cracks Glass Ceiling," *Denver Rocky Mountain News*, September 3, 2000; Katherine M. Hudson, "Transforming a Conservative Company—One Laugh at a Time," *Harvard Business Review* 79, no. 7 (2001): 45–48, 51–53, 143; Joshua Shapiro, "Profile: An Unusual Climb at Kodak Wins Her a Place at the Top," *New York Times*, January 30, 1994. Brady's fiscal 2016 sales were $1.12 billion (Brady Corp website, "Company Overview," accessed May 3, 2017, http://www.bradycorp.com/en/about/company-overview).

4. Catalyst website, "Women in S&P 500 Companies," April 25, 2017, http://www.catalyst.org/knowledge/women-sp-500-companies; "At No. 6, GM CEO Mary Barra is Fortune 500's highest ranked woman ever," *Fortune* website, accessed June 29, 2015, http://fortune.com/2015/06/29/female-ceos-fortune-500-barra/?iid=sr-link9.

5. "CH2M Hill—Constructing Pathways for Women through Inclusion," Catalyst website, accessed January 14, 2016, http://www.catalyst.org/knowledge/ch2m-hill.

6. Laird, "Entangled"; Kristen Leigh Painter, "Jacqueline Hinman Engineers Her Rise to Top at CH2M Hill," *Denver Post*, October 20, 2013; "Awards," CH2M website, http://www.ch2m.com/newsroom/awards, and "CH2M Hill," Catalyst website, accessed January 14, 2016, http://www.catalyst.org.

7. Margaret Jane Wyszomirski, "Presidential Personnel and Political Capital: From Roosevelt to Reagan," in *Pathways to Power: Selecting Rulers in Pluralist Democracies*, ed. Mattei Dogan (Boulder, CO: Westview, 1989), 45–73, esp. 65–66; MaryAnne Borrelli, *The President's Cabinet: Gender, Power, and Representation* (Boulder, CO: Lynne Reinner, 2002), ch. 2.

8. Arthur M. Schlesinger Jr., *The Coming of the New Deal* (Boston: Houghton Mifflin, 1958), 300; Wyszomirski, "Presidential Personnel," 65–66.

9. Letter from Richard Nixon to Margaret Garrity, January 17, 1961, in possession of Scott Sandage.

10. Lee Stout, *A Matter of Simple Justice: The Untold Story of Barbara Hackman Franklin and a Few Good Women* (University Park: Pennsylvania State University Libraries, 2012).

11. Stout, *Matter of Simple Justice*, chs. 2, 4; quotations 22–23.

12. Stout, *Matter of Simple Justice*, 58–76, 84–85.

13. Richard Nixon, "Memorandum about Women in Government," April 21, 1971, American Presidency Project, http://www.presidency.ucsb.edu/ws/?pid=2989.

14. "The Administration: Help Wanted (Female)," *Newsweek*, August 21, 1972.

15. Stout, *Matter of Simple Justice*, 76. On executive women in government, see Executive Women in Government website, "About Us: Who We Are," accessed March 23, 2016, http://execwomeningov.org/about.

16. Laird, *Pull*, ch. 7.

17. Nora Frenkiel, "The Up-and-Comers; Bryant Takes Aim At the Settlers-In," *Adweek* (Magazine World) special report, March 1984; Carol Hymowitz and Timothy D. Schellhardt, "The Glass Ceiling," *Wall Street Journal*, March 24, 1986.

18. Peter T. Kilborn, "Labor Dept. Wants to Take on Job Bias in the Executive Suite," *New York Times*, July 30, 1990.

19. U.S. Senate, Subcommittee on Employment and Productivity, *Women and the Workplace: The Glass Ceiling* (Washington, DC: GPO, October 23, 1991), 10–11.

20. Prior to the feminist movement of the 1970s, the only way for a woman to head a corporation was to start it, inherit it, or buy into it. Similarly, the first three female governors succeeded their husbands, and the first woman elected governor in her own right was Ella Grasso of Connecticut in 1975, in the peak of that era.

21. Catalyst, "Historical List of Women CEOs of the Fortune Lists: 1972–2015," November 2015, 24.

22. Jeffrey E. Cohen, *The Politics of the U.S. Cabinet: Representation in the Executive Branch, 1789–1984* (Pittsburgh: University of Pittsburgh Press, 1988), 169–78; Wyszomirski, "Presidential Personnel and Political Capital"; MaryAnne Borrelli, *The President's Cabinet*, 65.

23. Borrelli, "Gender Desegregation and Gender Integration in the President's Cabinet, 1933–2010," *Presidential Studies Quarterly* 40, no. 4 (December 2010): 734–49.

24. Maria Cardona, "Romney's Empty 'Binders Full of Women,'" October 18, 2012, accessed March 22, 2016, http://www.cnn.com/2012/10/17/opinion/cardona-binders-women/.

25. Wyszomirski, "Presidential Personnel and Political Capital"; Borrelli, "Gender Desegregation," 744–46.

26. Yian Q. Mui, "New Fed Chief Janet Yellen Lets a Long Career of Breaking Barriers Speak for Itself," *Washington Post*, February 2, 2014.

27. Laird, *Pull*, esp. chs. 1, 3, 5.

28. Jarett Zuboy, online research of CEO biographies. In some cases, such as Deanna Mulligan's, her career prior to becoming CEO of Guardian Life Insurance might have been considered support in the manufacturing industry but it was core in the insurance field.

29. Jenna Goudreau, "The CEO of $5 Billion Ingredion Reveals Her Secret to 'Having It All,'" *Forbes/Leadership*, March 18, 2013, http://www.forbes.com/sites/jennagoudreau/2013/03/18/the-ceo-of-5-billion-ingredion-reveals-her-secret-to-having-it-all/-4c4f696616fa.

30. Borrelli, *President's Cabinet*, 72.

31. Alison Mitchell reinforces this point by comparing Clinton's campaign to Geraldine Ferraro's 1984 vice presidential campaign in "To Understand Clinton's Moment, Consider That It Came 32 Years After Ferraro's," *New York Times*, June 11, 2016.

32. Maria Escobar-Lemmon and Michelle M. Taylor-Robinson, *Women in Presidential Cabinets: Power Players or Abundant Tokens?* (New York: Oxford University Press, 2016); Paul Burstein, "Political Elites and Labor Markets: Selection of American Cabinet Members, 1932–1972," *Social Forces* 56, no. 1 (September 1977): 189–201.

9

"Equality as a Result"?

Affirmative Action and the Stubbornness of Sex Segregation

ALLISON ELIAS

Introduction

At Howard University's commencement ceremony in 1965, President Lyndon B. Johnson proposed, "You do not take a person who, for years, has been hobbled by chains and liberate him, bring him up to the starting line of a race and then say, 'you are free to compete with all the others,' and still justly believe that you have been completely fair." Positing that "freedom [was] not enough," Johnson issued Executive Order 11246 in 1965 to address past injustices that had left many people of color at a disadvantage in the present-day labor market. With this directive, Johnson was seeking "not just equality as a right and a theory but equality as a fact and equality as a result."[1] Employment policies must address not only "push" discrimination, or overt exclusion, but also "pull" discrimination, or disparate access to social capital.[2]

Historically, presidential directives regarding employment, like 11246, along with federal employment legislation such as Title VII of the Civil Rights Act of 1964, have been designed to remedy labor market barriers faced by black men.[3] At times white women and women of color have confronted similar limitations (such as reduced access to higher education), but also they have encountered specific problems because of socially embedded norms about gender, work, and family. The tendency to prioritize race in fair employment policy, and thus bolster the earning potential of black men who had been denied fair employment practices for generations, reflected a long-standing family wage ideal from the nineteenth century: men required higher wages, or so ran the reasoning, because they had dependents. But women, many Americans wanted to believe, participated in paid labor force only temporarily to supplement family income.[4] For much of the twentieth century, the state protected female wage earners from the harsh conditions of the industrial workplace, citing women's primary role as mothers as crucial to the success of current and future generations.[5] Yet by the 1960s, an organized feminist movement exposed the social construction of gender roles that had cast women as biologically destined to serve as caretakers. Greater numbers of women—in particular white, educated, married women—entered the paid labor force, some seeking opportunities for fulfillment beyond their roles as mothers.[6]

In 1967, amid mounting pressure from feminist groups, and accompanied by the urging of Assistant Secretary of Labor Esther Peterson, Johnson signed a new order, Executive Order 11375, which added "sex" to the list of protected classes previously outlined in 11246. The benefit for women: they were now a category of workers entitled to affirmative action guidelines. The shortcoming: President Johnson, and previous presidents who had designed fair employment directives, had issued the executive orders with black men in mind.[7] They constructed guidelines to allow minority men access to male-dominated defense and construction work.

Adding women to legislation designed to advance black men proved problematic given long-standing ideas about gender. Although some women gained access to higher-paid, male-dominated jobs, many women lacked the education and sponsorship necessary to transition into new fields. Or they needed flexibility to enter and exit the labor market, flexibility that was found in in sex-segregated jobs designed for temporary workers. Thus, affirmative action did not promise "equality as a result" for women due to the occupational structure of gendered labor markets. To use Johnson's footrace analogy from Howard University, women and men were running races on different tracks. Within corporations, job ladders were gendered, and women were assigned to clerical ladders, which were shorter than male-dominated managerial job ladders. The separateness of the two ladders—experience on the clerical ladder was not considered training for the managerial ladder—emphasized the inferiority of clerical jobs in terms of pay and status.[8] In fact, certain types of clerical experience often disqualified women from managerial positions.[9]

In the 1970s, as government and business leaders were interpreting and implementing affirmative action, one-third of working women were employed in clerical positions. Many female office workers were forming collective movements—some localized within their own firms and others at a more national level—using the strategies and goals of both the labor and feminist movements. The most visible organization was 9to5, the National Association of Working Women, cofounded by Karen Nussbaum, a Harvard University clerical who eventually would lead the Women's Bureau under President William J. Clinton. 9to5 leaders such as Nussbaum argued that clerical pay scales and promotional opportunities did not reflect the knowledge, skills, and abilities of women office workers. Clerical work, which was women's work, wrongly was characterized as marginal, as not essential, to the functioning of the firm.

Nussbaum sought to change the way that corporations compensated and promoted female office workers, and in turn she wanted to alter broader cultural norms that devalued administrative support work. In the 1970s and 1980s sex segregation began to diminish as federal equal employment opportunity (EEO) policies gave women more occupational choices. Yet a striking degree of segregation still existed by the 1990s: women remained overrepresented in low-paying, administrative support positions that offered little opportunity for advancement. The percentage of women who worked as secretaries actually increased from 1970 to 1990.[10] Many support and caregiving occupations remained more than 95 percent female.[11] The feminist movement had destroyed formal barriers to upward mobility, but it had left many women in low-paid, female-dominated jobs, isolated from legal recourse.

Scholars often point to President Ronald W. Reagan's 1980 election when accounting for the shortcomings of affirmative action, and indeed the Reagan administration did weaken affirmative action.[12] Yet during the earlier administrations of Presidents Richard M. Nixon and Gerald R. Ford, affirmative action hardly provided a substantial remedy for sex discrimination. In the early 1970s, the Equal Employment Opportunity Commission's (EEOC) consent decree with American Telephone & Telegraph (AT&T) aimed to destabilize gendered job stereotypes. Not only should women gain access to men's jobs, EEOC attorneys claimed, but also men should move into women's jobs. The final settlement established statistical goals for integrating clerical work: 10 percent of all new operators and 25 percent of all new clericals hired should be male.[13]

While government attorneys intended for the AT&T decree to serve as a best practice for other employers, affirmative action programs, even before the alleged conservative turn of the 1980s, did little to remedy the crowding of women into low-paid clerical work.[14] Many working women wanted affirmative action to bridge the clerical ladder to the managerial ladder so that clerical experience would be considered valuable when applying for managerial positions. Yet the opposite actually occurred: legal and cultural definitions of fair employment narrowed such that by the 1990s sex-based equality meant allowing women access to men's jobs. The private sector did not alter its gendered ladders so that clerical work constituted training for managerial work, which meant that women's work remained dead-end.

Implementing Affirmative Action: Toward Underutilization

In the late 1960s, Nixon began to implement Executive Order 11246 by requiring employers in Philadelphia's building trade to set numerical targets for hiring black men. In 1970, labor secretary George P. Shultz issued Order No. 4, which required all federal contractors, not just construction contractors, to submit goals and timetables for hiring racial minorities. The following year, James Hodgson, also a Nixon appointee, assumed the post of labor secretary. Hodgson claimed that Order No. 4 was not intended to resolve "the often different, more difficult and more elusive problem of sex discrimination." After facing pressure from several congressional representatives including Representatives Patsy Mink (D-HI) and Edith Green (D-OR), he issued Revised Order No. 4 to include women.[15]

The Nixon administration's Labor Department instructed employers to gather data about the availability of women and minorities in both internal and external labor pools when determining goals and timetables. Employers should aim to establish statistical parity between the percentages of women and minorities in the surrounding areas and the percentages of women and minorities in underutilized job categories within their firms.[16] This model of underutilization pushed employers to devote resources to increasing the percentage of women and minorities in job categories where historically they had not worked.

Although the underutilization approach seemed to standardize affirmative action compliance, in reality, individual employers retained much interpretative power when setting their own goals and gathering their own data. First, when constructing targets, employers had the authority to delineate the boundaries of their own job categories. Akin to gerrymandering of voting districts, employers could label employees as managerial when in reality they had extremely low salaries and worked in positions with scant mobility. Thus, employers could submit data that obscured the segregation of women and minorities into certain roles with low pay grades or onto certain ladders. And most compliance efforts used job titles instead of salaries to categorize employees, which often obscured job quality and created faulty statistical representations of equity.[17] In compliance reviews of the nation's largest banks, some employers reported a 50 percent increase in numbers of managerial women and a corresponding 50 percent decrease in clerical women within one year! According to one vigilant regulator, such "games make for lots of paper work, but no progress; they are simply means of preserving the status quo."[18]

Once employers classified employees internally, those same employers—not regulators—defined the potential labor pool for underutilized positions. When determining availability of women and minorities in the population, some used national data while others relied on local data. Some included all women and minorities while others included only women and minorities who were considered qualified or interested. Data might not account for women and minorities who would be high-potential if offered training. Also, data might not assume that some women and minorities failed to express interest in certain types of work because institutional discrimination and social norms discouraged them from reaching for positions that historically had been the domain of white men. Also, employers considered "historical flows" or the pipeline into underutilized jobs, when determining the potential labor pool.[19] In other words, employers remained wedded to the traditional structure of taking applicants from certain feeder jobs, which meant that most female-dominated jobs on clerical ladders were not considered appropriate for management positions.

Labor feminist leaders like Karen Nussbaum recognized that employers could conceal the severity of occupational segregation in their compliance reports, but still she saw potential in affirmative action as a remedy for gender-based pay inequity. A student at the University of Chicago, Nussbaum left college in the late 1960s to devote herself to the New Left. She and 9to5 cofounder Ellen Cassedy took clerical jobs at Harvard

University. In 1973, they launched 9to5 as an informal lunchtime discussion group for women office workers. As 9to5 expanded across Boston, and eventually throughout the nation, its members voted in 1975 to make affirmative action, more so than maternity benefits or even cost-of-living raises, the issue of primary concern on their agenda.[20] 9to5 members wanted affirmative action to remedy overutilization, or the clustering of women in low-paying clerical positions; in other words, overutilization should also trigger compliance reviews.[21] They wanted affirmative action to force employers to redesign "historical flows" so that female workers on the clerical ladder would be considered part of the pipeline for management positions. Nussbaum believed that "there should be no such thing as a dead-end job for *anyone*."[22] With 9to5's vision of affirmative action, "so-called dead end jobs such as many clericals now feel they have would be opened up for promotion to positions of increased responsibility."[23]

However, personnel practices, even when legally in compliance with affirmative action directives, failed to benefit clerical workers by addressing overutilization. When 9to5 activists investigated the contemporary policies of eleven Boston insurance firms regarding internal job postings, written job descriptions, employee training, and promotions, the distinction between under- and overutilization became clear. Most companies did not offer promotional training to their clerical workers. At Travelers Insurance, "jobs [were] filled from the outside" and at John Hancock "promotions [occur] from outside, not [from] within." Training for promotions was available for those working in sales, management, or underwriting, but not for clerical work. And job postings were common for "lower level positions" or "lower level clerical positions," but not for managerial openings.[24] 9to5's data revealed that higher-paid positions remained elusive for clerical women even within their own companies. Many companies preferred to hire externally for professional positions rather than to train or promote internal clerical workers. 9to5 activists judged insurance companies' practices to be unfair, but, in truth, most of their practices were legal. Companies did not have to promote clericals to managerial positions as long as they could find external female candidates to fill these underutilized positions.

Other records confirmed that overrepresentation of women in clerical positions did not trigger compliance reviews. Honeywell Information Systems reported in 1974 that it had no EEO problems—meaning it had not violated Title VII of the Civil Rights Act of 1964 nor had it violated affirmative action guidelines—in the clerical category because underutilization of women was not a problem there.[25] The Cabot Corporation reported similar findings. Only areas with too few women or minorities were marked as problematic and in need of remedy. Cabot claimed to have a "general policy of promoting from within" although it had no formal training programs to move women out of clerical positions.[26] A female human resource officer from the Norton Simon conglomerate explained the ways that she fulfilled government mandates in companies such as Max Factor, Canada Dry, Hunt's Tomato Paste, and Avis Rent-a-Car. Each of her nine companies had to report EEO statistics quarterly to show that they were working toward more equitable distributions of women and minorities in underutilized categories. No numerical goals, however, had to be established to increase the percentages of men in female-dominated jobs.[27]

Personnel practices often favored younger workers, and many affirmative action programs privileged new college graduates over current employees. An executive vice president noted that Mobil recruited at colleges to fill new openings for professional positions.[28] Similarly, at the Polaroid Corporation, personnel officers recruited talented minorities and women from college campuses, advertising in publications such as *Black Collegian* and *Collegiate Women's Careers*, as well as female- and minority-specific issues of *MBA* and *New Engineer* to reach graduates. Seasoned Polaroid employees complained about lack of mobility, citing personnel's focus on younger talent from external labor markets.[29] The Honeywell Affirmative Action Plan declared that recruiters should solicit applicants at local minority employment agencies. Yet concerning the recruitment of internal applicants for internal positions, Honeywell promised only to publicly post its commitment to EEO laws in the lobby and in the company newspaper.[30] Programs at these companies offered new openings to young, well-educated women and minorities. Yet managers overlooked the potential internal pool of talent, perceiving seasoned office workers as lacking in managerial potential. Nussbaum and her supporters wanted affirmative action to eliminate dead-end jobs. In reality, however, affirmative action failed to change the status of clerical work, offering few opportunities for women in clerical positions to move into management.

Enforcing Affirmative Action: Toward Individual Onus

Besides lobbying for attention to the overutilization of women in clerical jobs, Nussbaum wanted systematic affirmative action reviews of all firms with federal contracts. When firms were reviewed, they showed that women were underutilized in higher-paying managerial positions and overutilized in the lower-paid clerical positions. However, because presidential administrations, regardless of party affiliation, allocated few resources to compliance, reviews remained infrequent, forcing activists like those in 9to5 to use their own resources to lobby the Labor Department to investigate potential violators.[31] And if reviews were conducted, often they were mismanaged, which compelled activists to scrutinize each step of the Labor Department's investigation. The failure of the Labor Department to systemically review industries shifted the burden of enforcement to individual workers and their advocates.

9to5 activists found an ally in Carol Greenwald, the Massachusetts banking commissioner, who took her duty to oversee the industry seriously. She investigated banking employment practices, working tirelessly to ameliorate ongoing sex and race discrimination. Greenwald claimed that the U.S. Department of the Treasury, which was charged with monitoring affirmative action compliance in the banking industry, rarely conducted reviews or forced meaningful action. In fact, in 1974 only thirty-five people nationwide were charged with enforcing affirmative action in the banking industry. And only 2 percent of all banks were reviewed in 1974.[32] The General Accounting Office (GAO), an independent, nonpartisan, investigative arm of Congress (later renamed the Government Accountability Office), reported in 1976, "Treasury had not only failed to enforce the law, but had undermined the credibility of all affirmative action efforts by its record of nonenforcement."[33] Inertia at the federal level meant that Greenwald and 9to5 activists were fighting an uphill battle in Boston-area workplaces.

When 9to5's attorneys filed formal charges of sex discrimination against New England Merchants National Bank of Boston in 1976, the U.S. Treasury mismanaged the compliance review. 9to5 had charged the bank with denying women access to managerial training programs, forcing women to train men to be their supervisors and denying women equal pay for comparable work. Treasury officials began to investigate Merchants soon after 9to5 submitted their complaints, finding that the bank was not in compliance and had refused to conciliate. However, no government action was taken against Merchants because Treasury reported that it lost its own work records while moving regional offices. The initial stages of the investigation began a second time in 1978 when the Labor Department's contract compliance officers gained enforcement authority from the Treasury Department. Four years later, the investigation was still in its initial stages. Greenwald perceived the federal government's delaying tactics as "[undercutting] the credibility of 9to5 as an effective organization."[34] 9to5 activists expressed outrage at the handling of the investigation, declaring that "this case [has been] mismanaged to the point where it is unclear whether the Dep. Of Labor or Merchants is conducting the investigation."

When complaining to contract compliance officers about the investigation, Nussbaum and the 9to5 attorneys pointed to three events that it perceived as inequitable. First, in 1977 when Treasury found that Merchants was not in compliance, Treasury nonetheless continued to grant numerous extensions to Merchants, claiming that it was allowing the bank to decide whether it wanted to conciliate. Yet 9to5 claimed that Merchants was not moving toward conciliation; thus, a finding of noncompliance should have been just cause to begin enforcement proceedings. Second, when the contract compliance officers took over the case in 1978, Leonard Biermann, regional officer for the Office of Federal Contract Compliance Programs (OFCCP), allowed Merchants to submit entirely new data. 9to5 had evidence that Merchants submitted revised records to Biermann. These records claimed that employees had received promotions and raises although the employees themselves were not aware of receiving these benefits. Third, Biermann claimed that he lost the records of the Treasury interviews with Merchants employees; still, he did not conduct new interviews, which meant that the new investigation omitted the employees' perspectives.[35] Employees had lost the opportunity to formally contradict Merchants managers' statements on the record.

While Nussbaum was outraged over the mishandling of the Merchants investigation, these and other types of dubious practices like title inflation (changing job titles to raise women into underutilized categories) were occurring routinely, according to Greenwald. Yet the U.S. Treasury rarely took action against nonconforming banks, which, according to Greenwald, "implicitly condoned" the practice of manipulating or even falsifying facts.[36] Furthermore, Treasury found banks in compliance even if they did not have the required affirmative action data on file. The GAO reported that from 1971 to 1975, Treasury had not once sanctioned a bank for noncompliance. It had never removed any federal deposits, which should have been the penalty implemented as a "potent sanction."[37]

This pattern of weak enforcement held true in the insurance industry as well. The Department of Health, Education, and Welfare (HEW) was responsible for monitoring the insurance industry, and within HEW, the Social Security Administration (SSA) was assigned to conduct reviews.[38] Although all insurance companies with federal contracts were required by executive order to have an affirmative action plan, only if SSA officials decided to review the company did the corporation have to submit its plan. Thus, unless the SSA requested the plan, no one really knew whether the company had a plan or whether it was effective or substantial. The SSA reviewed companies depending on the time and staff available, or it might pursue a company if given a reason to investigate.[39] Sometimes companies resisted the review process, arguing that personnel information was private, even if eventually they submitted the necessary information.[40] Such disputes cost the SSA and HEW time and money, given their scarce human and financial resources.[41]

9to5's officers believed that the SSA should have developed more comprehensive data among a larger number of insurance firms. Nussbaum sent a copy of her 1974 report on the condition of women office workers to the SSA, presenting data about low salaries and sex segregation in the Boston insurance workforce.[42] According to the report's authors, almost 60 percent of the Boston insurance labor force consisted of women, but 86 percent of female employees held low-wage clerical positions. 9to5 wrote, "No one could accuse the Insurance Industry in Boston of not *hiring* women. . . . But where are these many women employed *within* the companies?" Only 2 percent of women in insurance earned over $10,000 while 51 percent of men earned more than that amount. 9to5 blamed weak affirmative action enforcement for the continued clustering of women in low-paying jobs. Sex segregation existed because federal guidelines had failed to require firms to remedy overutilization for clerical work. Nussbaum regularly asserted that hiring and promotional practices at these firms were not just unfair but also illegal.[43]

But all was not yet lost: SSA officials agreed to take the 9to5 report into account when selecting offices for reviews.[44] Furthermore, the SSA sent two compliance officers to Boston in early 1975 to meet with 9to5 insurance committee members, advising them how to initiate complaints. The

SSA officers disclosed that "the best way to get action" was to file a charge with the SSA, the Labor Department's OFCCP, or both, and then to lobby the SSA to launch the review. Although 9to5 officers had a "good" meeting with the SSA, they remained dissatisfied with the overall investigation model.[45] The SSA was primarily investigating complaints that had been forwarded by specific charging parties; 9to5 wanted more systemic review of all insurance companies to achieve more far-reaching change.

Seeking government support, 9to5 issued a complaint against the affirmative action plan at Marsh & McLennan (Marsh), at that time the world's largest insurance brokerage firm. Nussbaum and leaders of two related organizations launched a coordinated campaign in several cities, insisting that Marsh "begin obeying the equal opportunity laws." Nussbaum and her energetic 9to5 officers argued that the goals and timetables set by Marsh's personnel managers were inadequate to remedy the existing discrimination. They claimed that Marsh was not in compliance because women were clustered in the lowest-paying clerical positions. Only 4.4 percent of the 1,101 officials, managers, and supervisors in all of Marsh's offices worldwide were women. However, 82 percent of the women employed by Marsh were in low-paying clerical jobs. And of the almost 6,000 total employees, only 214 were black women (and 181 of those were clericals).[46] In its 1974 affirmative action plan, Marsh declared that it would try to fill 19 percent of all positions that paid $10,400 or more per year with women. Nussbaum and other activists were outraged. "That means 81% of those jobs will remain in the male domain. The [Affirmative Action] Guide goes on to say that this 19% 'goal' need not even be accomplished in one year!"[47] Nussbaum perceived the Marsh plan as inequitable and as not in compliance with affirmative action guidelines. However, Marsh's plan did in fact fulfill Department of Labor requirements: it reported current underutilization areas and set goals for improvement based on Marsh's data about the available labor pool.

There was clearly a disconnect between what Nussbaum saw as fair, even as legal, and what businesses were required to do to avoid penalty. 9to5 and its advocates viewed Marsh as engaging in illegal employment practices because its affirmative action plan sought gradual change, with a target of filling 19 percent of higher-paying jobs with women over a period of several years. Women Employed Chicago, an advocacy group similar to 9to5, wrote, "[Marsh's] discriminatory employment practices are clearly illegal. We may not be able to change their basic philosophy about women, but we can force them to obey the laws." Marsh should develop "meaningful goals and timetables for training and promoting women and minorities" unlike its current affirmative action plan. Women Employed Chicago also recommended regular salary reviews and raising the pay range for many jobs as well as establishing written job descriptions, internal job postings, and on-the-job training. In addition, "[career] ladders should be instituted with bridge positions allowing clericals to move into professional positions."[48] When Nussbaum and leaders of other women's groups like Women Employed Chicago met with a Marsh vice president of personnel, they received answers that were only partially satisfactory. The vice president claimed that Marsh was committed to affirmative action, but then he refused to make the 1976 Affirmative Action Guide available to employees. When asked about written job descriptions, he claimed that written descriptions seemed too "rigid." And although he agreed to begin a job posting system on January 1, 1976, he would post non-management jobs only. Clericals would continue to lack access to managerial positions, and the Marsh vice president signaled that clericals were not qualified to apply for them anyway.[49]

Following the Marsh campaign, the 9to5 insurance committee devised a three-month plan to improve affirmative action enforcement. One of the campaign's goals was to lobby officials at the Massachusetts Commission Against Discrimination and at the Labor Department's OFCCP, placing pressure on both state and federal agencies to review reported offenders regularly. Second, the 9to5 committee wanted additional employees to evaluate their own affirmative action plans. Nussbaum and others decided to create and distribute an insurance newsletter for office workers, which would encourage women to assess and discuss their own company's affirmative action practices.[50] 9to5 would establish task forces at certain Boston insurance firms to assist employees in constructing "criteria for what *we* [the employees] view as an acceptable a.a. plan." Then the employee task forces could present recommendations to personnel management. To pressure companies with weak practices to strengthen their plans, the 9to5 insurance committee publicly lauded companies with strong plans while condemning those with weak plans.[51]

In the 1976 newsletter distributed to women office workers, "How to Evaluate your Company," 9to5 insurance committee members explained how to assess personnel practices at their own companies. Employees should urge their managers to implement "job posting," recommended the newsletter. According to 9to5, affirmative action mandated that "*all* jobs should be conspicuously posted," preferably internally for two weeks. For clericals who were told that their experience was not relevant for internal openings, employees should make sure that the company was using "fair requirements" when choosing applicants to hire. In other words, employers might have required certain irrelevant skills or experience purposely to exclude clerical women from changing jobs. "The company should look at *related* job experience, and periodically survey to find qualified women in the company," according to 9to5. If clericals had lacked mobility for numerous years, employees should suggest that "training programs" become part of the company's affirmative action plan. Training programs should "bridge clerical and other jobs . . . in order to eliminate dead-end positions."[52]

Several Boston insurance companies, when pushed to implement affirmative action, started to alter their policies regarding job postings and job descriptions. Two firms, Frank B. Hall and Massachusetts Mutual, began internal job postings in 1976.[53] Also the OFCCP began to negotiate with Prudential in 1976, pushing the company to institute more equitable hiring and promotion policies. Employees from Liberty Mutual, Blue Cross, and Aetna gathered to read and discuss their affirmative action plans and to make suggestions for improvements. At Aetna, several women met with company managers and secured job postings.[54] 9to5 filed charges against Travelers for failing to institute job postings, provide accurate job descriptions, and offer job training for promotions.[55] Once 9to5 filed complaints with the SSA, Travelers started posting some jobs on the lunchroom bulletin board.[56] By early 1977, change was occurring in a piecemeal fashion.

Conclusion

To be sure, 9to5 influenced personnel procedures in the insurance industry, as well as in banks, publishing houses, and other private firms during the 1970s. It helped to win internal job posting, written job descriptions, and paid job training in workplaces across the nation as employers moved toward EEO compliance. Yet to what extent would these practices offer mobility to female office workers if overutilization remained legal? Internal job postings mattered little if clerical work still was not considered experience for a management position. Written job descriptions mattered little if all clerical descriptions included "ad hoc" language. Paid job training mattered little if employers interpreted "job-related" so narrowly as to exclude training for higher-paid, higher-status positions.

The implementation and enforcement of affirmative action in most companies did not effectively address the separation of clerical and managerial job ladders, which meant that women who entered clerical work remained confined to dead-end positions. EEO law allowed many women to access male-dominated occupations, increasing female representation in fields like medicine, law, and engineering. But from 1964 to 1979, the density of women in clerical occupations actually increased.[57] As the 1970s became the 1980s, federal support for affirmative action languished: President Reagan attempted to rescind Executive Order 11246 and reduced the OFCCP's budget, which essentially stalled affirmative action enforcement. The appointment of Clarence Thomas, a fervent opponent of affirmative action, to lead the Equal Employment Opportunity Commission also weakened implementation.[58] The promise of bridging clerical and managerial ladders that arose in the 1970s as activists, policymakers, employers, and employees negotiated the boundaries of EEO law abruptly ended as the Reagan administration assumed power in 1981s.

In a 1976 speech, Nussbaum had expressed dissatisfaction at government attentiveness and corporate response to affirmative action. "It seems that a good amount of federal money, company action, and public attention has focused on progress in hiring women and minorities in occupations where they have traditionally been shut out." Nussbaum continued, "We, in *offices* throughout Boston, would like to share in some of [the] improvement. It's time to reexamine government priorities and see that we move to the top of the list."[59] After serving as director of the Women's Bureau in the 1990s, Nussbaum broadened her labor rights agenda beyond women office workers. In 2003 she cofounded Working America, an AFL-CIO affiliate, to mobilize working-class Americans to vote for labor-backed political candidates.

By the turn of the twenty-first century, the private sector was embracing the underutilization model of affirmative action. Many corporations actively recruited the most talented women and minorities into managerial and executive roles as human resource leaders argued that diverse organizations enjoyed competitive advantages.[60] Although a business case for diversity has succeeded, the call to use affirmative action systemically to remedy sex segregation has failed. In turn, many regulators, corporate leaders, and even professional women judged the dead-end nature of clerical work perfectly fair as long as women had access (or seemed to have access) to male-dominated jobs. The unrealized promise of affirmative action in the 1970s sheds light on the endurance of the gender wage gap. As women became more likely than ever to serve as sole or primary breadwinners for their families starting in the 1970s, the jobs available to many remained low paid and without the promise of mobility. Few recognized the president's hidden hand in women's employment.

Notes

1. President Lyndon B. Johnson, Commencement Address at Howard University, "To Fulfill These Rights," June 4, 1965, American Presidency Project, http://www.presidency.ucsb.edu/ws/?pid=27021.

2. Pamela Walker Laird, *Pull: Networking and Success since Benjamin Franklin* (Cambridge, MA: Harvard University Press, 2006), 1–10.

3. Anthony Chen, *The Fifth Freedom: Jobs, Politics, and Civil Rights in the United States, 1941–1972* (Princeton: Princeton University Press, 2009), 170–229.

4. Alice Kessler-Harris, *Out to Work: A History of Wage-Earning Women in the United States* (New York: Oxford University Press, 1982), 45–74.

5. Nancy Woloch, *A Class by Herself: Protective Laws for Women Workers, 1890s–1990s* (Princeton: Princeton University Press, 2015), 54–84.

6. The idea of paid labor as providing fulfillment for women emerges from Betty Friedan, *The Feminine Mystique* (New York: W.W. Norton, 1963).

7. Serena Mayeri, *Reasoning from Race: Feminism, Law, and the Civil Rights Revolution* (Cambridge, MA: Harvard University Press, 2011), 1–40.

8. For a rich body of sociological literature about internal labor markets and gender see work by Andrea Beller, Patricia Roos, William Bielby, James N. Baron, Barbara Reskin, Heidi Hartmann, and Thomas DiPrete, among others.

9. Rosabeth Moss Kanter, *Men and Women of the Corporation* (New York: Basic Books, 1977); Allison Elias, "Learning to Lead: Women and Success in Corporate America," *Business and Economic History—Online* 13 (2015) https://www.thebhc.org/sites/default/files/Elias_BEHO_Final%20Draft_0.pdf.

10. Francine Blau, Patricia Simpson, and Deborah Anderson, "Continuing Progress? Trends in Occupational Segregation in the United States over the 1970s and 1980s," *Feminist Economics*, Fall 1998, 29–71.

11. Christine Jolls, "Accommodation Mandates," *Stanford Law Review* 53 (2000): 223, 292.

12. See, for example, Nancy MacLean, *Freedom Is Not Enough: The Opening of the American Workplace* (New York: Russell Sage Foundation, 2006); Dennis Deslippe, *Protesting Affirmative Action: The Struggle over Equality after the Civil Rights Revolution* (Baltimore: Johns Hopkins University Press, 2012).

13. Harvey D. Shapiro, "Women on the Line, Men at the Switchboard: Equal Employment Comes to the Bell System," *New York Times*, May 20, 1973.

14. Affirmative action did allow some women to move from female-dominated work into male-dominated, blue-collar jobs. Although the number of women in the skilled trades has grown, women hold only 2 percent of the well-paying skilled jobs. See Nancy MacLean, "The Hidden History of Affirmative Action: Working Women's Struggles in the 1970s and the Gender of Class," *Feminist Studies* 25, no. 1 (Spring 1999): 66.

15. Dean Kotlowski, *Nixon's Civil Rights: Politics, Principle, and Policy* (Cambridge, MA: Harvard University Press, 2002), 240–45.

16. Patricia J. Snider, "External Data for Affirmative Action Planning," in *Affirmative Action Planning*, ed. George Milkovich and Lee Dyer (New York: Human Resource Planning Society, 1979), 6; Chen, *The Fifth Freedom*, 220–21.

17. Author interview with former in-house counsel of MNE in 1980s, January 21, 2016.

18. Carol S. Greenwald, *Banks Are Dangerous to Your Wealth* (Englewood Cliffs, NJ: Prentice-Hall, 1980), 10–11.

19. Jerry Newman and Frank Krzystofiak, "Toward Internal Availability: Intra-Organizational Roadmaps," in *Affirmative Action Planning*, ed. Milkovich and Dyer (New York: Human Resource Planning Society, 1979), 32.

20. Minutes of Executive Board, November 17, 1975, 79-M16–81-M121, carton 1, folder 6, 9to5, National Association of Working Women (U.S.) Records, 1972–1980 (hereafter NAWWR), Schlesinger Library, Radcliffe Institute, Harvard University, Cambridge, MA (hereafter SchL).

21. *Women's Insurance News* 1, no. 1, n.d. [1976], 88-M96–89-M104, carton 3, folder 111, 9to5, National Association of Working Women (U.S.) additional records (hereafter NAWWa), 1972–1986, SchL.

22. Text of speech from Karen Nussbaum, "Women at Work," May 23, 1978, 88-M96–86-M104, carton 2, folder 47, NAWWa, 1972–1986, SchL.

23. 9to5, "Enforcement Research Committee Report" (concerning affirmative action), n.d. [early 1980s], 88-96-89-M104, carton 4, folder 144, NAWWa, 1972–1986, SchL. Although most 9to5 members were white women, 9to5 recognized that women of color faced discrimination "both by sex as well as race" and declared, "[We] need to unite all discriminated women if we ever plan to eliminate sex discrimination."

24. 9to5, Attachment to Demands to SSA, January 27, 1977, 82-M189–86-M213, carton 16, folder 1033, NAWWa, 1972–1985, SchL.

25. Honeywell Affirmative Action Plan, 1974, 79-M16–81-M121, carton 3, folder 92, NAWWR, SchL. Overall women constituted 87 percent of its office workforce.

26. Dorothy G. Curnane (manager of personnel and EEO coordinator), "Affirmative Action Program," Cabot Corporation of Boston, May 1, 1976, 82-M189–86-M213, carton 16, folder 1037, NAWWa, 1972–1985, SchL.

27. Evelyn Ray (EEO compliance at Norton Simon), Women at Work Exposition, October 1979, box 92, folder 31, Women's Action Alliance Records, Sophia Smith Collection, Smith College, Northampton, MA (hereafter WAAR).

28. P. C. Krist (executive vice president, Mobil Oil Corporation), Women at Work Exposition, October 1979, box 93, folder 3, WAAR. While he acknowledged that Mobil

provided career counseling and training opportunities for current employees, Mr. Krist was more enthusiastic to explain Mobil's recruitment of the most talented college women for professional work (including a college internship program).

29. Polaroid Corporation Corporate Services Division, "Affirmative Action Plan," July 1979 to July 1980, HR-18, I.388, Baker Library, Harvard Business School, Cambridge, MA. For employee complaints about external hiring, see Minutes from Employees Committee (EC)-Personnel Policy Committee (PPC) meeting, April 15, 1976, and Minutes from EC-PPC meeting, May 20, 1976, HR-5, I.377, Baker Library, Harvard Business School, Cambridge, MA. See March 31, 1977, meeting, HR-5, I.377, for Employees Committee slideshow presentation on the problems of external hiring.

30. Honeywell Affirmative Action Plan, 1974, 79-M16–81-M121, carton 3, folder 92, NAWWR, SchL.

31. Economist Jonathan S. Leonard examined the record of compliance reviews from 1974 to 1980 in "Affirmative Action as Earnings Redistribution: The Targeting of Compliance Reviews," *Journal of Labor Economics* 3, no. 3 (July 1985): 363–84. He reported "no evidence of a systematic government policy for reviewing contractor firms." In other words, enforcement was essentially a random process. The OFCCP maintained that it had formal targeting systems that selected establishments for review with a low proportion of minorities or women relative to other establishments in the same industry. But interviews with OFCCP officials in Washington and in the field suggested to Leonard that these formal targeting systems were rarely used.

32. Text of speech from Karen Nussbaum, 1976, 79-M16–81-M121, carton 1, folder 3, NAWWR, SchL.

33. Greenwald, *Banks Are Dangerous to Your Wealth*, 7.

34. Greenwald, *Banks Are Dangerous to Your Wealth*, 9.

35. Letter from Ruth Olds, Banking Chair, 9to5 to Weldon J. Rougeau, Director of OFCCP, December 18, 1979, 82-M189–86-M213, carton 16, folder 1028, NAWWa, 1972–1985, SchL.

36. Greenwald, *Banks Are Dangerous to Your Wealth*, 10–11.

37. Greenwald, *Banks Are Dangerous to Your Wealth*, 17.

38. Until 1978 the OFCCP (originally named the Office of Federal Contract Compliance, or OFCC, until 1975) only supervised the various agencies that conducted compliance reviews in each industry. See Bernard E. Anderson, "The Ebb and Flow of Enforcing Executive Order 11246," *American Economic Review* 86, no. 2 (Papers and Proceedings of the 108th Annual Meeting of the American Economic Association, May 1996): 299.

39. Letter from Janet Selcer, 9to5 Staff, to Insurance Committee Members, July 30, 1974, and Attachment to letter, "Boston Insurance Companies and Affirmative action Requirements," 1974, 88-M96–89-M104, carton 3, folder 105, NAWWa, 1972–1986, SchL.

40. For instance, when Everette Friedman, SSA chief compliance officer, was planning to review Prudential in Boston, Prudential fought to keep its records confidential. See –Letter from Janet Selcer, 9to5 Staff, to Insurance Committee Members, July 30, 1974, and attachment to letter, "Boston Insurance Companies and Affirmative action Requirements," 88-M96–89-M104, carton 3, folder 105, NAWWa, 1972–1986, SchL; and

–9to5 chart, Insurance Committee Activity with the Social Security Administration, n.d. [1976], 88-M96–89-M104, carton 3, folder 110, NAWWa, 1972–1986, SchL.

41. In addition, Frank B. Hall and Marsh & McLennan maintained that they did not have to submit information to the SSA. Both claimed that they did not have more than $50,000 in federal contracts, which was the minimum required for a company to be subject to affirmative action guidelines. Despite delays and disputes, the SSA scheduled reviews at Blue Cross Blue Shield and Travelers Insurance; eventually 9to5 convinced the SSA to review both John Hancock and Liberty Mutual. See –9to5 chart, Insurance Committee Activity with the Social Security Administration, n.d. [1976], 88-M96–89-M104, carton 3, folder 110, NAWWa, 1972–1986, SchL. John Hancock review mentioned in 9to5, *Women's Insurance News* 1, no. 2, n.d. [Summer 1976], 88-M96–89-M104, carton 3, folder 111, NAWWa, SchL. Liberty Mutual mentioned in 9to5, *Women's Insurance News*, n.d. [Summer 1977], 88-M96–89-M104, carton 3, folder 111, NAWWa, SchL.

42. 9to5 chart, Insurance Committee Activity with the Social Security Administration, n.d. [1976], 88-M96–89-M104, carton 3, folder 110, NAWWa, 1972–1986, SchL.

43. 9to5 Boston, Finance Committee, "Claim against Boston's Insurance Industry: A Study of the Treatment of Women Office Workers in Insurance," September 1974, 88-M96–89-M104, carton 3, folder 110, NAWWa, 1972–1986, SchL.

44. 9to5 chart, Insurance Committee Activity with the Social Security Administration, n.d. [1976], 88-M96–89-M104, carton 3, folder 110, NAWWa, 1972–1986, SchL.

45. 9to5 chart, Insurance Committee Activity with the Social Security Administration, n.d. [1976], 88-M96–89-M104, carton 3, folder 110, NAWWa, 1972–1986, SchL.

46. 9to5, Marsh & McLennan Newsletter for Women Employees, vol. 1, no. 1, October 1975, 88-M96–89-M104, carton 3, folder 111, NAWWa, 1972–1986, SchL.

47. 9to5, Marsh & McLennan Newsletter for Women Employees, vol. 1, no. 1, October 1975.

48. 9to5, Marsh & McLennan Newsletter for Women Employees, vol. 1, no. 1, October 1975.

49. 9to5, Marsh & McLennan Newsletter for Women Employees, vol. 1, no. 1, October 1975.

50. 9to5, Committees Three Month Plan, Insurance, 1976, 79-M16–81-M121, carton 1, folder 7, NAWWR, SchL.

51. 9to5, Planning Committee, 3 Month Plan, July, August, September 1976, 82-M189–86-M213, carton 16, folder 1024, NAWWa, 1972–1985, SchL.

52. "How to Evaluate Your Company," n.d. [1976], 82-M189–86-M213, carton 16, folder 1034, NAWWa, 1972–1985, SchL.

53. 9to5, *Women's Insurance News* 1, no. 1, n.d. [1976], 88-M96–89-M104, carton 3, folder 111, NAWWa, 1972–1986, SchL.

54. 9to5, *Women's Insurance News* 1, no. 2, n.d. [Summer 1976], 88-M96–89-M104, carton 3, folder 111, NAWWa, 1972–1986, SchL.

55. However, at Liberty Mutual an employee relations manager refused to speak with 9to5 about job postings; Liberty remained one of the last major Boston companies that refused to alter its posting practices. See –9to5, *Women's Insurance News*, n.d. [1976/1977], 88-M96–89-M104, carton 3, folder 111, NAWWa, 1972–1986, SchL.

56. 9to5, *Women's Insurance News*, n.d. [Summer 1977], 88-M96–89-M104, carton 3, folder 111, NAWWa, 1972–1986, SchL. For more on campaigns and potential campaigns in specific offices see 9to5, Minutes of the Women's Insurance Forum Steering Committee, September 15, 1976, 88-M96–89-M104, carton 3, folder 110, SchL.

57. Ruth Blumrosen (Rutgers Law professor), Equal Pay Workshop, Women at Work Exposition, October 1979, box 91, folder 32, WAAR.

58. Deslippe, *Protesting Affirmative Action*. At the state level by the 1990s, affirmative action further unraveled, particularly as California voters passed Proposition 209 in 1996, effectively prohibiting affirmative action in state education and employment.

59. Text of speech from Karen Nussbaum, 1976, 79-M16–81-M121, carton 1, folder 3, NAWWR, SchL.

60. Frank Dobbin, *Inventing Equal Opportunity* (Princeton: Princeton University Press, 2009).

10

Executive Stewardship of America's Credit Card Economy

SEAN H. VANATTA

Introduction

Presidential portraits adorn our nation's paper money. But in many consumer wallets, pride of place has long since gone to plastic. Most credit cards lack overt national symbolism; instead, they carry corporate logos, bank brands, and images depicting sports teams, airlines, Roman soldiers—my wife's favored card has a picture of our family dog. As credit cards, and later debit cards, became central to consumers' experience of buying and borrowing in modern America, we might wonder, were contemporary presidents made uneasy by the replacement of their forebears on the central media of consumption?

We ask this question not out of concern for executive vanity but rather because as changing financial practices and credit technologies reshaped the American economy in the postwar era, they in turn reshaped executive stewardship of that economy. Since World War II, consumption has been the driving force of economic growth in the United States, and credit has been central to facilitating that consumption. Yet the unsecured revolving credit offered by credit cards differed from forms like auto loans and mortgages, which concretely linked consumption to production and with it cherished values of work and thrift. As credit card use expanded, cards quickly became symbolic of irresponsible borrowing, for both individuals and a nation awash in debt. And in the postwar era, credit card use did nothing but expand. One—admittedly imperfect—measure, the amount of revolving debt outstanding, grew from almost nothing in the late 1960s to more than a trillion dollars before the financial crisis of 2008

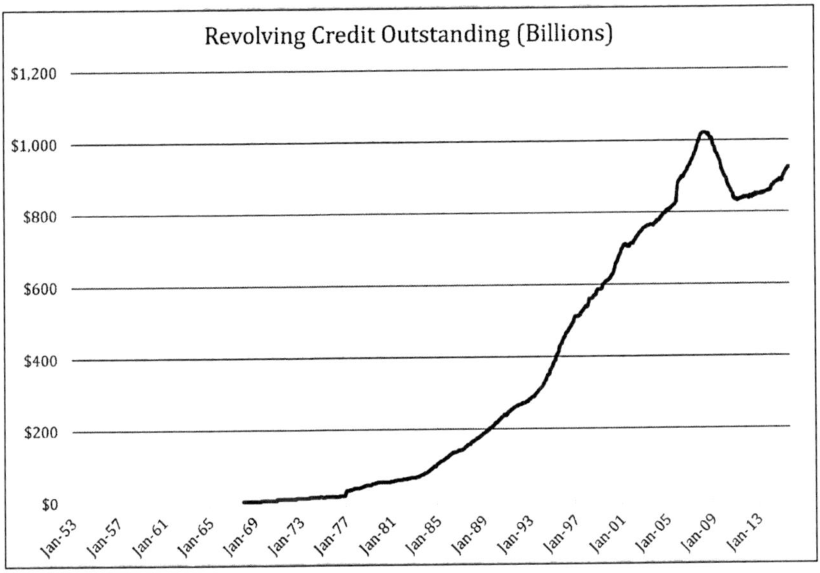

Figure 10.1. Seasonally Adjusted Revolving Credit Outstanding. From Board of Governors of the Federal Reserve System, Series G.19, "Consumer Credit," http://www.federalreserve.gov/releases/g19/current/.

(see figure 10.1). Credit card use also expanded relative to other forms of credit and when compared to the economy as a whole. As wages stagnated beginning in the 1970s, credit cards continued to fuel America's consumption engine, filling the gap between the promise of American prosperity and its realization. For better or worse, unsecured borrowing became an essential component of the economy, a fact that presidential administrations eventually had to confront, even as Americans bought with credit cards rather than dead presidents.[1]

At its most basic, this chapter plots the trajectory of this graph in a narrative of America's postwar presidencies. It does so by examining both how presidents talked about credit cards and how their administrations addressed the public policy challenges posed by credit cards, as an economy driven by unsecured credit emerged and took shape.[2] Starting in the 1950s with Dwight D. Eisenhower, presidents used cards as a metaphor for profligate government spending, even as they tried, beginning with John F. Kennedy and Lyndon B. Johnson, to broaden credit access and with it access to prosperity. During the 1970s credit card markets grew rapidly, but through the Richard M. Nixon and Gerald R. Ford presidencies executives did little to directly shape them; such growth was primarily the product of competitive and regulatory dynamics within the credit industry, while credit card policy was developed in Congress.

The benign neglect ended with Jimmy Carter. Carter stood at a pivot joining his predecessors, who had sought to promote broad-based credit access, to his successors, who would urge consumers to keep spending even as they accrued larger and larger debts. For a brief moment, Carter charted a different path. Using authority granted by the Credit Control Act (1969), Carter tried to slow the advance of the credit card economy, combining a policy aimed at reducing credit card lending with a moral critique of card use. Carter's intervention, this chapter argues, might have been a turning point: a countermovement against the credit card economy. But it came too late. The economy was (and ordinary consumers were and remained) too dependent on credit card spending. Until the financial crisis of 2008, every president after Carter urged consumers to make use of their individual cards and keep buying, even as their collective debts piled up.

The financial crisis, as the chart indicates, was a major disruption; we must leave it to later historians to tell whether it was a break, a pause, or something new altogether.

Credit Cards in the Postwar Era

The modern credit card owes its existence to presidential action. Before the Second World War, payment cards—at the time embossed metal plates—were part of larger accounting and billing technologies that retailers, gasoline companies, and other large consumer-oriented firms were gradually adopting to manage consumer charge accounts, a form of credit that consumers paid off every month. With the outbreak of the war, Roosevelt sought to restrict credit buying in order "to keep the cost of living from spiraling upward." To achieve this goal, he charged the Federal Reserve with designing and instituting controls on consumer credit, known as Regulation W. This policy required retailers to keep close tabs on their customers' credit spending, and payment card technology made it easier for retailers to comply with Federal Reserve regulations. During the war, retailers also experimented with new modes of granting credit. Credit controls placed limits on the prevailing forms of retail credit, both charge accounts, which consumers paid off every month, and installment lending, which consumers paid in fixed installments over time. To skirt controls, retailers developed revolving credit, which gave consumers a fixed credit limit—like a charge account—but allowed them to pay over time—like installment credit. Wartime credit controls thus linked revolving credit and credit card technologies. Still, after the war, credit cards spread slowly, and cards remained a minor part of the language and practice of credit during the 1940s and early 1950s.[3]

Credit cards became more prominent during the Eisenhower administration, when, in the context of a broad credit expansion, several major firms initiated card programs. These plans, in turn, drew the administration's attention to the rhetorical power of the credit card as a symbol for unrestrained credit spending. By the beginning of Eisenhower's tenure in 1953, borrowing, by both individuals and the federal government, had become central to economic growth. Eisenhower and his economic team worried that the ebbs and flows of consumer credit could play havoc with the postwar commitment to ensuring "stable economic progress." These concerns were borne out by a credit-fueled expansion in 1955 and 1956, which was followed by a major slowdown in 1957 and 1958 as the Federal Reserve raised interest rates, credit conditions tightened, and consumers retreated from credit buying. In the midst of these swings, Eisenhower commissioned an extensive report from the Fed on how consumer credit was reshaping the nation's economy. The report noted the presence of revolving credit in the context of overall consumer credit expansion, but it was issued before a veritable flourishing of new credit card plans in 1958, when executives at American Express, Bank of America, and the Chase Manhattan Bank all initiated large-scale card plans. These, in turn, spurred retailers to expand their existing card programs. As credit cards entered the national consciousness, Eisenhower worried about out-of-control borrowing. Taking a metaphor first employed by his budget director, Maurice H. Stans, Eisenhower warned the incoming Kennedy administration, "If . . . we deliberately run the Government by credit cards, improvidently spending today at the expense of tomorrow, we will break faith with the American people."[4]

Eisenhower believed that public and private indebtedness were a weak foundation for U.S. economic expansion, and his critique of government by credit card was a rallying cry for conservatives likewise worried about America's expanding debts. Yet while Eisenhower was reluctant to champion credit-driven prosperity, his Democratic successors—and Americans more broadly—were more willing to accept credit as a necessary adjunct to the wage-driven prosperity of the era. Congressional leaders, like Senator Paul H. Douglass (D-IL), spurred on by a growing consumer movement seeking safety in the marketplace, sought to focus federal credit policy first on making credit safe and then on expanding credit access. During the Kennedy and Johnson administrations, credit cards became central to these larger policy debates, most importantly those surrounding Douglas's Truth-in-Lending Act (1968). Both Kennedy and Johnson supported Truth-in-Lending, but as the bill finally gained traction in Congress in the late 1960s, credit cards were the most nettlesome sticking point. Retailers, led by firms like J. C. Penney and Sears, were still the dominant card issuers, and their representatives argued that cards were too difficult to regulate and should be excluded from the bill. Consumer advocates, like the National Consumers League's Sarah H. Newman, disagreed, arguing that "to give the fastest growing segment of consumer credit preferential treatment would . . . strike a blow at the very heart of the protection this legislation should be extending." Ultimately, Johnson's legislative staff was instrumental in convincing financial firms, like banks and credit unions, to support the inclusion of credit cards, because otherwise the law would have awarded the retailers a regulatory advantage.[5]

While the Johnson administration advanced the consumer and congressional agenda of making the credit card market safe, Nixon's administration instead sought to temper Congress's regulatory ambitions so cards could continue their unimpeded growth. At the moment consumers won on Truth-in-Lending, for instance, banks began aggressively entering the credit card market, mailing millions of unsolicited credit cards directly to consumers. Many congressional Democrats, fearing inflation, moral corruption, and the financial safety of both consumers and banks, moved to ban this aggressive credit marketing technique. At first Nixon's consumer staff publicly supported this solution. As legislation moved forward, however, members of other executive departments, like the Council of Economic Advisers, argued internally that the policy would constrain the growth of an important form of consumer credit, forcing the consumer staff to abandon their position. Many members of Congress were likewise reluctant to limit the growth of the card market, especially as they became increasingly interested in broadening credit access for groups of

Americans, such as women, minorities, and the poor, who card firms were excluding from middle-class credit. Senator William Proxmire (D-WI), for example, embraced credit cards as a solution to urban poverty that would allow poor consumers to shop away from the high-cost "ghetto" merchants. At the same time, lobbying by women and minorities for access to credit cards—and with them full economic citizenship—was the driving force behind the Equal Credit Opportunity Act (1974), which extended new credit rights to these groups.[6]

Still, during the 1960s and 1970s, the presidents themselves had little to say publicly about credit cards, even as the Nixon administration marked a transition toward a political economy where consumption was maintained by access to credit, not rising wages. The credit card market expanded significantly under the Nixon and Ford presidencies. Though we lack clear data for retailer card plans, when Nixon was sworn in in January 1969, banks held $2.3 billion in credit card receivables. When Jimmy Carter took the oath of office eight years later, that number had grown to $14.3 billion. Relatively speaking, these were still small figures. Over the same period, non-revolving credit (primarily auto loans) held by banks grew from $60 billion to $114 billion. But for both the Federal Reserve and Congress, the rapid expansion of cards and the prospects for continued growth were worrying.[7]

That worry would soon spread to the Oval Office.

Jimmy Carter and America's Crisis of Credit

When Carter came into office in January 1977, the credit card industry was poised for a new round of frantic growth. This process was initiated by New York's Citibank, which, under the leadership of its aggressive Chairman Walter B. Wriston, began a massive, nationwide card marketing campaign in August 1977. To protect their local markets, rival banks stepped up their solicitation efforts as well. Bank credit card debt had grown by 15 percent a year from 1974 to 1977, but over the next two years it leapt up at a 30 percent annual rate. The expansion of credit card lending renewed long-standing concerns that credit cards increased consumer demand for goods, enabled anticipatory buying, and fueled inflation psychology. "We wonder whether the proliferation of credit cards is actually plastic inflation," a House Banking Committee staffer told the *Los Angeles Times*, adding, "We have a time bomb situation here." At first, renewed credit card expansion was a minor current in the sea of economic problems facing the Carter administration, but as cards continued to flood the market, the administration began to consider active steps to stem the tide.[8]

Administration officials began discussing the possibility of renewing World War II–style credit controls as a way to constrain card growth in early 1979 as both card use and inflation were advancing rapidly. "Many credit card companies—practically all of them, in fact," one official warned, "are actively promoting long-term debt by credit card, at 18% interest." Such promotions fed the anticipatory buying and "inflation psychology" the administration feared. As policy memos moved between the Treasury Department and the Council of Economic Advisers, administration staff first focused on instituting minimum down payments and shortened repayment periods, the mode of credit control employed during World War II and the Korean Conflict. The policy was shelved in May 1979 because Carter's advisors thought such measures were "essentially unworkable." Indeed, these were the very controls revolving credit had been designed to circumvent.[9]

Cards presented an economic policy challenge, but they were also, as Charles L. Schultze, Carter's chairman of the Council of Economic Advisers, recalled, symbolic of the individual irresponsibility that, in Carter's view, made collective problems like inflation and energy dependence intractable for his administration. The moral tone of Carter's presidency is well documented. Beginning in early 1979, Carter, through his chief pollster Patrick H. "Pat" Caddell, was influenced by a cadre of social theorists who decried American's drift into self-indulgence and urged national renewal of self-restraint, religiosity, and communal values. A vein of this concern was directed at consumer debt. Caddell lamented to Carter in his famous memo "Of Crisis and Opportunity," "The public . . . is spending as if there is no tomorrow," while "live for today, financed by greater and greater debt has replaced the stable rock of steady, prudent future planning in America." These concerns meshed well with Carter's own evangelical views and found expression in his famous "malaise" speech in July 1979, where Carter implored Americans to understand "that owning things and consuming things does not satisfy our longing for meaning."[10]

The "malaise" speech triggered brief national self-reflection while also setting in motion a series of events that would lead to the administration's direct confrontation with the credit card economy in March 1980. Following the speech, Carter reshuffled his cabinet, moving Federal Reserve chairman G. William Miller to secretary of the treasury and appointing Paul A. Volcker as chairman of the Federal Reserve. In August, seeking to break the nation's inflationary psychology, Volcker ended direct Fed control over market interest rates, sending them into the stratosphere. Rising rates, in turn, led to renewed calls for credit controls, which Volker initially rejected as counterproductive to his own monetary policy agenda. But when inflation spiked in February 1980, Carter's economic team returned to controls, looking to the Fed for a new implementation strategy. Fed officials shifted the emphasis of the program away from consumer credit and toward business lending. But, at Carter's insistence, credit cards remained part of the package.[11]

Introducing credit controls on March 14, 1980, Carter came back to the rhetoric and tone of the "malaise" speech, admonishing Americans for their irresponsible buying habits: "Our whole society, the entire American family, must try harder than ever to live within its means. As individuals and as a nation," Carter continued "we must begin to spend money according to what we can afford in the long run and not according to what we can borrow in the short run." In essence, Carter had returned to the position staked out by Eisenhower, expressing concern about individual and government borrowing. But while Eisenhower worried about building postwar prosperity on a foundation of sand, by Carter's term the edifice had already been built.[12]

Carter's plea for credit austerity was simple, but the credit control policy was exceedingly complex. Instead of strictly mandating credit terms in an effort to increase the price of credit for consumers, and thus manipulating the demand for credit as the World War II controls had done, Carter's economic team decided to increase the cost of extending credit for lenders, thus manipulating the supply. To do so, the Fed required lenders who extended unsecured consumer credit, and who had $2 million or more of such credit outstanding, to deposit 15 percent of all *new* credit extended with the Federal Reserve in non–interest bearing accounts. Under this plan, for each new dollar lent to consumers that earned interest, the lender also had to set aside 15 cents that did not. Because lenders still had to pay a high rate of interest to their depositors on money that simply sat at the Fed, this special deposit significantly increased the cost of credit card lending. At the same time, state usury limits, which largely restricted credit card interest rates to 18 percent, meant that card firms could not easily pass higher costs on to borrowers.[13]

Consumers did not see these complex mechanisms; what they saw was Carter confronting the credit card economy and debt-driven insecurity, and they responded. "I'm in full support of President Carter's anti-inflationary attack on the use of credit cards," one citizen wrote to *Newsweek*. "I am glad to see someone has intervened in this craze." A *New York Times/CBS News* poll taken in April 1980 found that 58 percent of Americans claimed to be using credit cards less than they had been the previous year, while only 5 percent claimed to be using them more. By May, the Federal Reserve Bank of New York found that 90 percent of banks in its district reported that demand for consumer credit had weakened since March. Though controls were not designed to influence consumer behavior directly—they were meant to influence the supply, not the demand, for credit—the American Retail Federation found that "Americans are trying to cut back, have intended to for some time, and foresee a day when they can live their lives in a more manageable economic setting."[14]

Within the White House, Carter's advisors met the apparent success of the credit control program with a complex mix of pleasure and dread. By early May, CEA chairman Charles Schultze worried that the controls might have gone too far, prompting an economic slowdown as consumers withdrew from the marketplace. In preparation for a May 6 meeting of the administration's economic team, Schultze expressed concern that "many consumers believe the use of credit cards is now illegal or unpatriotic," and asked whether the administration ought to counter these notions. The meeting did little to allay Schultze's fear, and a subsequent memo notified Carter that Fed chairman Volcker was looking into whether consumers were overreacting to the credit controls. By May 15, Schultze was still reporting "substantial consumer withdrawal from the use of *credit cards*."[15]

Consumers were not the only ones responding. The control policy, by increasing the cost of lending, exacerbated dislocations already unfolding in credit card markets. With the dramatic rise of market interest rates and stickiness of state usury laws, by late 1979 it was no longer profitable for firms to lend through credit cards. On March 7, 1980, a week before credit controls were implemented, a member of the Federal Reserve Board's policymaking committee, Thomas M. Timlen, nonchalantly observed, "There is also a good deal of concern regarding losses on consumer credit cards, but that's news to no one." Retailers and banks were looking to withdraw from the market. Carter's credit control policy gave them cover. In consultations with the administration before the policy went into effect, business leaders predicted, "Credit controls would shift the blame of denial of credit to the President when, because of market forces, credit institutions would have to deny credit anyway." In subsequent months, they turned prophesy into reality.[16]

As consumers turned away from cards and retailers and banks withdrew credit, the White House's fears manifested. As Carter explained to a town hall meeting at Temple University in May, "We put some constraints on consumer spending . . . including a slight restraint on credit card use. The results," he continued, "have been many times greater than what we thought they would be." That was putting it mildly. During the second quarter of 1980, with credit controls fully in effect, gross domestic product declined at an annual rate of 7.9 percent. Unemployment rose from 6.3 in March, to 7.5 in May before peaking at 7.8 in July. Consumers may have wanted to "cut back" and "live their lives in a more manageable economic setting," but their lives—and the American economy—were dependent on credit cards.[17]

None of this, by the way, helped Carter's reelection chances. His successors, perhaps wisely, made peace with the credit card economy.

Post-Carter Paradox: We Won't Go into Debt so You Can!

The credit card economy withstood Carter's intervention. Following his victory in the 1980 election, Ronald W. Reagan began a new phase of executive credit card rhetoric, renewing Eisenhower's criticism of government by credit card while at the same time indirectly suggesting that consumers should use their cards as they wished. His successors would be more explicit, encouraging credit card buying to spur continued economic growth. Eventually, discussion of government and consumer debt would meld, so that efforts to reduce the former were pitched as a means to help consumers increase consumption through the latter. There was only so much credit in the world, the logic went, and if the government gobbled it up, there would be little left for consumers. This argument, however, was undermined by the continued expansion of all debts, public and private, during the 1980s, 1990s, and 2000s. In card markets specifically, new financial strategies like securitization, where banks and other issuers packaged and sold credit card debts to investors, made it easier and more profitable for firms to pour ever more capital into credit card plans.

Although presidential administrations had worried throughout the postwar years about expanding consumer credit use and attendant rising consumer debt, these concerns were not in evidence during the Reagan administration. Instead, Reagan's economic team was largely committed to deregulatory absolutism, and almost certainly saw the growth of credit card and other consumer credit markets under his administration as a clear expression of the success of these policies. For his part, when Reagan invoked credit cards, he did so in ways that foregrounded the individual card user as the preeminent judge of their own finances, free to make consumption choices without concern for wider repercussions. This framing began with Reagan's critique of Carter's credit control policy, which rejected any government intervention meant to bend individual actions to the common good. Under Carter, "we could hardly adjust our thermostats or use our credit cards," Reagan explained at a Heritage Foundation dinner in October 1983, "without checking first with Washington." Reagan, who constantly projected a dreamy optimism about America's economic future, implied that consumers didn't need to check with anyone before making spending choices. And spend individuals did. From Reagan's inauguration in January 1981, to when he left office in the same month in 1989, credit card indebtedness grew by more than 16 percent a year.[18]

As credit card use expanded, cards returned as a metaphor for out-of-control government spending, but now divorced from its paired concern with individual debt. During the 1986 mid-term elections, Reagan targeted congressional Democrats in stump speeches from Wisconsin to Florida, joking, "When it comes to spending your hard-earned money, those liberals act like they've got your credit card in their pocket. And believe me, they never leave home without it." Here, Reagan drew on advertising language from up-market American Express cards, bringing an anti-elitist edge to his unrelenting attacks on "tax-and-spend liberals." Further, like his criticism of Carter's credit control policy, these remarks made clear his view that Americans were the best judges of their individual credit use. The administration's criticism of out-of-control spending cut both ways, however. Reagan was perfectly comfortable demonizing Congress while borrowing-to-buy his own priorities, like increased military spending—so much so that his own advisors complained bitterly about the administration's inconsistent commitment to reining in deficits. In turn, Reagan's Democratic presidential opponents, candidates Walter F. Mondale in 1984 and Michael S. Dukakis in 1988, tenaciously attacked the administration's "credit card mentality."[19]

Following Reagan, George H. W. Bush and William J. "Bill" Clinton went further, urging the credit industry to make it easier for consumers to use credit cards. In one sense, this was an extension of the goal of broad credit access advanced since the Johnson administration. It carried a new emphasis, however, driven not by the desire to enable marginalized citizens to consume through democratic and equable distribution of credit but instead focused on convincing already indebted consumers to keep using cards to boost the economy. In remarks at a fundraising luncheon in November 1991, Bush told attendees, "I'd frankly like to see the credit card rates [come] down. I believe that would help stimulate the consumer and get consumer confidence moving again." Bush's remarks sparked an unexpected uproar. Members of Congress, like Senator Alphonse M. D'Amato (R-NY), took the president at his word and tried to institute a national interest rate ceiling on credit card loans. Bush rejected this idea, but he stuck to his jawboning strategy. "Earlier this week, I called for lower credit card rates to take some of the sting out of consumer debt, and I'm pleased to see some banks responding," Bush explained to a group of prominent executives. Less burdensome consumer debt, Bush hoped, would "revive consumer confidence" and "give this economy a little kick."[20]

Bill Clinton was likewise optimistic that lower interest rates would stimulate increased consumer spending, and he made interest rate reduction a centerpiece of his economic strategy. Clinton promised to reduce government borrowing, which, by reducing overall demand for credit, would lower interest rates for consumer loans on all fronts. "As interest rates fall," Clinton explained to the U.S. Chamber of Commerce, "more people will be able to save money on business loans, home loans, car loans, credit card transactions; all these things will free up cash to get the economy moving again." Clinton introduced this theme to promote his administration's economic plan in 1993, and he returned to it during the elections of 1996 and 2000 as a way to challenge Republican tax-cut plans that would undercut his administration's success at reducing the federal deficit. As the 2000 election developed into a national debate over how to deploy the new federal surplus, Clinton, working to protect his legacy, continued to argue that the best way to help families was to pay down the federal debt, which would keep interest rates low on the bundle of consumer loans—credit cards, mortgages, and auto loans—that were essential for economic citizenship and general prosperity.[21]

On the other side of this debate was George W. Bush, who recognized that the extraordinary growth of credit card indebtedness during the Clinton years—from $281 billion to $687 billion—made credit card debt into *the* significant debt burden of working families. Or at least the most politically salient one. So as Bush campaigned for his tax cut plan in the first year of his presidency, he argued that instead of using the surplus to pay down the government's debts, it would be better to let consumers pay off their own obligations. "Part of the remedy for people who have got a lot of credit card debt," Bush told a crowd in Lafayette, Louisiana, in March 2001, "is to make sure people get some of their own money back." Once he had achieved his tax priorities, however, credit cards largely dropped out of Bush's speech. But the credit card debt he worried over did not subside. It continued its relentless climb, though at a reduced pace, growing at only 5 percent a year during his presidency. This number, however, understates the expansion, because consumers were now consolidating credit card debts into home mortgages, entwining formerly separate forms of indebtedness in their efforts to fully participate in the nation's prosperity.[22]

Still, the good times were good—until they weren't.

An End to the Credit Card Economy?

By the end of his term, with the 2008 financial crisis unfolding, Bush emphasized credit card debts in new calls for individual fiscal discipline. In a commencement address at Furman University in May 2008, Bush warned graduates that they may "find it tempting to amass more debt, particularly from credit cards," and urged them "not to dig a financial hole that you can't get out of." "There are no shortcuts to the American Dream," Bush warned. But if the American Dream was a high-paying job and sustainable borrowing as part of a lifecycle of asset accumulation, it had been shortcut and shortchanged for some time, as the economy came to depend more on expanding debt than on expanding wages. Barack H. Obama confronted this fact soon after he took office, telling Americans, "The days when we are going to be able to grow this economy just on an overheated housing market or people spending—maxing out on their credit cards, those days are over." The end of days were reflected, again, in the numbers. Beginning in July 2008, seasonally adjusted revolving credit outstanding—our proxy for credit card debt—began its first sustained decline, falling 18.5 percent from its $1.02 trillion peak to $832 billion in April 2011.[23]

The financial crisis was a shock to the credit card economy. At least four factors contributed to the steep decline in consumer indebtedness: increased repayments as consumers deleveraged their household balance sheets, increased defaults as other consumers could no longer meet their debt obligations, reduced lending to all borrowers because of tight credit markets, and reduced lending to more risky borrowers because of legislative reforms that made it more difficult to lend profitably to these individuals. On this last point, the financial crisis also spurred forward a long-developing congressional effort to rein in the credit card industry, especially what members viewed as predatory lending to marginal borrowers and college students. The incoming Obama administration made action on this front a priority. The resultant legislation, the Credit Card Affordability Responsibility and Disclosure (CARD) Act (2009), created new rules for billing transparency, regulated credit card fees, and protected consumers from unexpected interest rate increases. In touting this achievement, Obama invoked the credit card far more than any other president. Yet while the CARD Act made credit card markets less expensive and safer for many consumers, for others it reduced their access to credit without reducing their need to borrow. This trend has been especially clear in student loan markets, where many students have substituted loan debt for credit card debt. As one consequence of this dramatic change, student debt emerged as a major issue for presidential candidates Bernie Sanders and Hillary R. Clinton as they jockeyed for the 2016 Democratic Party nomination.[24]

For his part, new president Donald J. Trump has yet to make any substantive statements about consumer debt. As of April 2017, his likely approach to these issues remains anyone's guess. At the same time, however, Trump's education secretary Betsy DeVos's early moves to liberalize student loan regulations suggest his administration might return to pursuing economy in government while promoting the indebtedness economy.[25]

Conclusion

What this chapter has found exceptional is not that presidents talked about credit cards but that before the 1990s they talked about them—and through this talk addressed credit cards' role in the U.S. economy—so seldom. During the postwar years, presidential administrations moved from discovery to confrontation to acceptance and even encouragement of credit card spending. But credit cards also remained on the margins of presidential speech, cropping up first as a metaphor for out-of-control government borrowing and later when America's chief executives hoped to prod consumers into "[giving] this economy a little kick." Historians have shown how economic policies pursued since the 1970s undermined the finances of working families, and more broadly historians of capitalism have a sense that consumers continued to accrue debt to maintain consumption in the face of declining real wages and increasing economic inequality.[26] In this narrative, credit spared policymakers—and presidents especially—from confronting growing inequality and its political consequences, which might have emerged more forcefully in a less financialized economy. This makes Carter's action, coming early in the long, steep climb of credit card spending and indebtedness, remarkable. But Carter's stand was just a notch on this long rise. We are left to wonder whether the momentum for reform emerging from the financial crisis will help bring about a more lasting reevaluation of the credit card economy or whether we have merely experienced a similar, if larger, divot.

Because, as our chart makes clear, credit card debt is back on the rise.

Notes

1. Throughout this chapter, I'll use the Federal Reserve's G-19 consumer credit series as a proxy for credit card debt, although the series contains other minor forms of revolving credit. The Federal Reserve began measuring revolving credit in 1968 and revised the series in 1977. For the relationship between credit, wages, and the promise of prosperity, see Dirk Krueger and Fabrizio Perri, "Does Income Inequality Lead to Consumption Inequality? Evidence and Theory," *Review of Economic Studies* 73, no. 1 (2006): 163–93; Colin Crouch, "Privatized Keynesianism: An Unacknowledged Policy Regime," *British Journal of Politics & International Relations* 11, no. 3 (2009): 382–99; and Dan Herman, "The Missing Movement: A Polanyian Analysis of Pre-Crisis America," *International Journal of Social Economics* 39, no. 8 (2012): 624–41. Some economists reject the idea that debt has had negative consequences, for example see Thomas Durkin, Gregory Elliehau-

sen, Michael Staten, and Todd Zywicki, *Consumer Credit and the American Economy* (New York: Oxford University Press, 2014), 34–38.

2. By focusing on presidential speech, this chapter follows Daniel T. Rodgers (*Age of Fracture* [Cambridge, MA: Harvard University Press, 2011], 15–40).

3. Franklin D. Roosevelt, "Message to Congress on an Economic Stabilization Program," April 27, 1942, American Presidency Project, http://www.presidency.ucsb.edu (hereafter APP); Louis Hyman, *Debtor Nation: A History of America in Red Ink* (Princeton, NJ: Princeton University Press, 2011), 100–127.

4. Federal Reserve, *Consumer Instalment Credit*, 1957, vol. 1, 1; Robert M. Collins, *More: The Politics of Economic Growth in Postwar America* (New York: Oxford University Press, 2000), 45; *Economic Report of the President* (Washington: Government Printing Office, 1956), 94; Gilbert Burck and Sanford Parker, "The Coming Turn in Consumer Credit," *Fortune*, March 1956; Dwight D. Eisenhower, "Annual Budget Message to the Congress: Fiscal Year 1962," January 16, 1961, APP; Maurice H. Stans, "Fiscal Delusions: Fallacies About U.S. Spending Threaten Nation's Solvency," *Wall Street Journal*, August 2, 1960.

5. Lizabeth Cohen, *A Consumers' Republic: The Politics of Mass Consumption in Postwar America* (New York: Vintage Books, 2003), 123–24, 345–63; *Consumer Credit Protection Act: Hearings on H.R. 11601 before the Subcommittee on Consumer Affairs of the House Committee on Banking and Currency*, 90 Cong., part 2, 683 (1967) (Statement of Sarah H. Newman); Memo, Barefoot Sanders to Lyndon Johnson, January 26, 1968; Memo, Barefoot Sanders to Lyndon Johnson, January 30, 1968; Memo, Barefoot Sanders to Lyndon Johnson, February 1, 1968; "Fact Sheet on Truth-in-Lending," February 1, 1968; Memo, Joseph Barr to Lyndon B. Johnson, February 7, 1968, all in White House Central File, Legislation, box 50, Lyndon Baines Johnson Presidential Library, Austin, TX.

6. Memo, Jonathan Rose to Peter M. Flanigan, December 11, 1969, White House Central Files, Finance, box 41, Richard M. Nixon Presidential Library, Yorba Linda, CA; Hyman, *Debtor Nation*, 184; "Credit Task Force Correspondence," boxes 44–45, Records of the National Organization for Women, Schlesinger Library, Harvard University, Cambridge, MA

7. The early 1970s are often pointed to as the turning point when postwar wage gains stalled for most Americans, but there seems to be little research on the economic mechanics of continued GDP growth in the wake of wage stagnation. The conventional academic wisdom is that credit filled in this gap—and that finance grew as this gap widened—but the literature remains thin. For the best I've found, see Crouch, "Privatized Keynesianism," and Herman, "The Missing Movement."

8. Priscilla Meyer, "Citicorp Is Apparently Trying to Become a Major Force in the Credit Card Industry," *Wall Street Journal*, August 19, 1977; Roger Smith, "Citibank Blitz: Credit Cards Dealt in Game for Big Money," *Los Angeles Times*, March 9, 1978.

9. Memo, Charles B. Holstein to Ester Peterson, March 12, 1979, box 13, Special Advisor—Inflation, Kahn; "Selective Controls of Consumer Credit," March 13, 1979, box 14, Staff Office—CEA; Memo, Charlie Schultze to Jimmy Carter, May 25, 1979, box 54,

Staff Office—CEA, all in Jimmy Carter Presidential Library (hereafter Carter Library), Atlanta, GA.

10. Author interview with Charles Schultze, July 25, 2013; Daniel Horowitz, *The Anxieties of Affluence: Critiques of American Consumer Culture, 1939–1979* (Amherst: University of Massachusetts Press, 2004), 205–6; Kevin Mattson, *"What the Heck Are You Up To Mr. President?": Jimmy Carter, America's "Malaise," and the Speech That Should Have Changed the Country* (New York: Bloomsbury, 2009); Memo, Pat Caddell to Jimmy Carter, April 23, 1979, box 40, Staff Offices: Press, Jody Powell, Carter Library; Jimmy Carter: "Address to the Nation on Energy and National Goals: 'The Malaise Speech,'" July 15, 1979, APP.

11. Thomas Karier, *Great Experiments in American Economic Policy: From Kennedy to Reagan* (Westport, CT: Praeger, 1997), 40; Stacey L. Schreft, "Credit Controls: 1980," Federal Reserve Bank of Richmond, *Economic Review* 76 (Nov./Dec. 1990), 33; Memo, Lyle Gramley to Charlie Schultze, January 25, 1980, box 14, Staff Office—CEA; Memo, The CEA and Treasury Staff to The Economic Planning Group, February 26, 1980, box 95, Staff Office—CEA; Memo, William Miller to Jimmy Carter, February 28, 1980, box 172, Presidential Handwriting File; Meeting Notes, February 28, 1980, box 172, Presidential Handwriting File; Memo, William Miller to Jimmy Carter, February 29, 1980, box 173, Presidential Handwriting File; Draft Speech, March 14, 1980, box 175, Presidential Handwriting File; Inflation Announcement, March 14, 1980, box 175, Presidential Handwriting File, all in Carter Library. Carter does not reflect on this decision, and the explanation given for the controls—that Labor favored them—does not come through in the archives.

12. Jimmy Carter, "Anti-Inflation Program Remarks Announcing the Administration's Program," March 14, 1980, APP.

13. Memo, William Miller to President Carter, February 28, 1980, box 172, Presidential Handwriting File; Memo, Alfred Kahn to Betsy Hamilton, February 2, 1980, box 13, Special Advisor—Inflation, Kahn, Carter Library; "Withdrawal Pain for Credit-Card Holders," *Newsweek*, March 31, 1980, 29; Memo, Burke Dillon to Charlie Schultze, February 27, 1980, box 147, Staff Office—CEA, Carter Library; Roger S. White, Federal Reserve, "Federal Reserve System Special Anti-Inflation Programs Announced March 14, 1980: A Brief Description," Report 80–73 E, April 2, 1980.

14. Jerry L. Hunter, "Letters," *Newsweek*, April 14, 1980; Steve Lohr, "Buying Habits Found Unexpectedly Curbed by Controls on Credit," *New York Times*, May 9, 1980; Memo, James Fergus and Charles Luckett to Prell, May 14, 1980, Federal Reserve Bank of New York Archives; "Americans View Inflation, the Public Policy Response, and the Retail Industry," Cambridge Reports, Inc. (April 1980), box 25, Special Advisor—Inflation, Kahn, Carter Library.

15. Memo, Charlie Schultze to Jimmy Carter, May 5, 1980; Memo, Charlie Schultze to Jimmy Carter, May 12, 1980; Memo, Charlie Schultze to Jimmy Carter, May 15, 1980, box 54, Staff Office—CEA, Carter Library.

16. Thomas Timlen, Federal Reserve, Federal Open Market Committee, "Meeting of Federal Open Market Committee: March 7, 1980," http://www.federalreserve.gov/mon-

etarypolicy/files/FOMC19800307confcall.pdf; Memo, Al McDonald and Anne Wexler to EPG Steering Group, box 25, Special Advisor—Inflation, Kahn, Carter Library.

17. Jimmy Carter, "Philadelphia, Pennsylvania Remarks and a Question-and-Answer Session at a Townhall Meeting at Temple University," May 9, 1980, APP; U.S. Bureau of Economic Analysis, "Real Gross Domestic Product [A191RL1Q225SBEA]," retrieved from FRED, https://research.stlouisfed.org/fred2/series/A191RL1Q225SBEA; U.S. Bureau of Labor Statistics, "Labor Force Statistics from the Current Population Survey," March–July 1980, http://data.bls.gov/pdq/SurveyOutputServlet. Other economic factors were certainly at play, which I am not qualified to disentangle, but the administration and subsequent commentators (Schreft, "Credit Controls: 1980") alike blame credit controls for the timing and force of the 1980 downturn.

18. See, for example, CEA Staff Files, Ronald Reagan Presidential Library, Simi Valley, CA; Ronald Reagan, "Remarks at a Dinner Marking the 10th Anniversary of the Heritage Foundation," October 8, 1983, APP. Although as of the time of this writing many administration records dealing with finance and banking remain closed. However, in the *Economic Report of the President*, for instance, searching for "consumer credit" yields one result (excluding standard tables) for the entire eight years.

19. Ronald Reagan, "Remarks at a Campaign Rally for Senator Robert W. Kasten Jr. in Waukesha, Wisconsin," October 23, 1986, APP; Ronald Reagan, "Remarks at a Campaign Rally for Senator Paula Hawkins in Tampa, Florida," October 24, 1986, APP; Memo, Martin Feldstein to Ronald Reagan, December 13, 1983; Memo, Martin Feldstein to Ronald Reagan, October 22, 1983, box 2, Martin Feldstein Files, Ronald Reagan Presidential Library; Paul Taylor, "Candidates Joust Over Deficit," *Washington Post*, September 9, 1984; Michael Dukakis, "Presidential Debate at the University of California in Los Angeles, October 13, 1988," APP.

20. George Bush, "Remarks at a Bush-Quayle Fundraising Luncheon in New York City," November 12, 1991, APP; Jerry Knight and Albert Crenshaw, "Senate Votes to Cap Rates on Credit Cards," *Washington Post*, November 14, 1991; Bush, "Teleconference Remarks with the Fortune 500 Forum," November 15, 1991, APP.

21. Bill Clinton, "Remarks to the U.S. Chamber of Commerce National Business Action Rally," February 23, 1993, APP.

22. George W. Bush, "Remarks in Lafayette, Louisiana," March 9, 2001, APP; Hyman, *Debtor Nation*, 251–80.

23. George W. Bush, "Commencement Address at Furman University in Greenville, South Carolina," May 31, 2008, APP; Barack Obama, "Remarks Following a Meeting with President's Economic Recovery Advisory Board Chairman Paul A. Volcker and an Exchange with Reporters," March 29, 2009, APP.

24. Consumer Financial Protection Bureau, *CARD ACT Report: A Review of the Impact of the CARD Act on the Consumer Credit Card Market*, October 1, 2013, http://files.consumerfinance.gov/f/201309_cfpb_card-act-report.pdf; Federal Reserve, "Survey of Consumer Finances," 2007, 2013, http://www.federalreserve.gov/econresdata/scf/scfindex.htm. More research on the relationship between credit card and student loan debt is necessary.

25. Stacy Cowley and Jessica Silver-Greenberg, "DeVos Halts Obama-Era Plan to Revamp Student Loan Management," *New York Times*, April 14, 2017.

26. Judith Stein, *Pivotal Decade: How the United States Traded Factories for Finance in the Seventies* (New Haven, CT: Yale University Press, 2010).

11

Computerizing America

Presidents, Business, and Politics in a Digital Age

ANDREW MEADE MCGEE

Certain technologies slot naturally into the narrative of the American presidency. The United States' legacy as a nuclear-armed power is predicated on a series of executive decisions. Whistle-stop tours by train and the romanticization of Air Force One link the inhabitant of the Oval Office to the technological ascendance of rail and the boundless promise of the Jet Age. Presidents burnished reputations and secured historical legacies by mastering the radio and television as communication devices. From Jefferson the tinkerer and Lincoln the promoter of land-grant "mechanic arts" to Hoover and Carter the engineers, Roosevelt and Eisenhower the infrastructure builders, and Kennedy the prophet of rocket ships to the moon, presidents are linked in popular imagination and historical record with many of the key technological shifts in the nation's past.

The computer does not neatly slot into this narrative.[1] Electronic computers and the modern digital communications, data management, and information technology systems they make possible are ubiquitous in early twenty-first-century America, but no clear line directly links the Oval Office to the rise of Silicon Valley.[2] Harry Truman never swapped out vacuum tubes in the Philadelphia basement that housed the ENIAC, the first general-purpose electronic digital computer unveiled in 1946. Lyndon B. Johnson and Richard M. Nixon never personally inserted punch cards into mainframes to prosecute the War on Poverty or the war in Vietnam. For that matter, Jimmy Carter never soldered microchips in a California garage with Steve Jobs. The stories Americans tell themselves about the spread of digital society feature entrepreneurial engineers and hackers, college students such as Michael S. Dell and Mark E. Zuckerberg, working in garages and dorm rooms and Radio Shacks, but not the executive branch of the federal government.

While the Oval Office can in no sense be construed as the progenitor of the electronic computer; in significant ways the actions of American presidents created the environment that made possible the computer and the entire digital era. The American presidency presents a compelling lens through which to understand the intertwining of the federal government and capitalism in an emerging digital society. Decisions made by the figures who occupied the White House and historical tendencies they embodied in that position connect the presidency to the rise of electronic computing and a broader digital society. The relationship of presidents after 1945 to the emergence of America's modern digital society in fact mirrors that of the federal state to the story of the computer in the second half of the twentieth century: structural, largely invisible, and deeply enmeshed with market interests, changing societal forces, and other political actors such as Congress, state governments, and the federal bureaucracy.

Just as the parameters of presidential power and the applied functioning of computing systems evidence change over time, so too did the intersections of presidents with digital systems reflect an evolution shaped by political context and broader proliferation of information technologies. Immediate postwar presidents encountered the computer within the context of Cold War national security institutions; their successors in the 1960s and 1970s took advantage of the administrative proliferation and technological flexibility of general-purpose mainframe systems to experiment with governmental reorganizations and new policy-development techniques centered on the computer. Presidents at the turn of the millennium extended this impulse to press for bureaucratic efficiency and citizen accountability through the harnessing of online databases and mobile computing. For the last three decades, presidents have moved beyond considering computers as tools of federal governance, acting as evangelists at home and abroad for advanced digital technologies and the idea of America as a postindustrial, information society. With the diffusion of computing technologies and digital conceptualizations of information throughout American society and economy, presidents in the twenty-first century have found that the dual endeavors of politics and policy require explicit attention to digital technologies. In campaigning, crafting policy, communicating with the American public, and articulating their political visions, recent presidents "get down to business" in a context explicitly shaped by digital technologies their predecessors fostered and normalized.

Institutional Frameworks

The best entry to understanding the structural, albeit out-of-sight, role American presidents played in shaping the computer age can be found in a joke from the turn of millennium: the widespread popular merriment surrounding the meme that Vice President Al Gore had claimed in 1999 to have "invented the Internet." Columnists, comedians, late night talk show hosts, online commentators, and families over dinner tables alike gleefully derided the out-of-context misquote stemming from Gore's description of his sponsorship of the High Performance Computing Act of 1991. The appellation burnished the vice president's reputation as a stiff technocrat, ascribing to the federal state what most Americans saw as a technological triumph of the market.[3] The logic undergirding a nation's belly laughs and rolled eyes was direct: politicians and government agencies didn't develop things, technologists and entrepreneurs did. Political pundits lambasted the Democratic presidential contender for overreach, and Republican nominee George W. Bush ridiculed the line by name in his acceptance speech at his party's summer convention in 2000.[4] Only tech-savvy markets invented—government just intruded.

And yet Gore was onto something, however tangentially. The electronic digital computer, and the seventy years of digital innovation that followed its development, was fundamentally the product of contexts that presidents created. The digital era was a child of the total war commitment of the U.S. scientific establishment during World War II, and its first avatars were birthed during a nascent Cold War.[5] The United States government was the first—and single most influential—patron of early computer construction, and the decision to pursue costly, untested mainframe computer installations in the 1940s and 1950s derived directly from the strategic policy directives of Presidents Harry S. Truman and Dwight D. Eisenhower.

The Truman-guided restructuring of the military under the National Security Act of 1947 coalesced several of the most computer-inclined defense constituencies in a single, well-funded branch and created conditions under which "systems" approaches to complex weapon purchases might flourish. The IBM/MIT-developed "Project Whirlwind" would by the mid-1950s feed into SAGE (the multibillion-dollar "Semi-Automatic Ground Environment" network of interlinked computers). In his 1957 radio and television address to Americans on the subject of "Science in National Security," Eisenhower explicitly listed "electronic computers" as a cornerstone of a continental defense system, along with radar, missiles, supersonic aircraft, and the atomic bomb.[6] Four years later, in his televised farewell message, the former general included "hundreds of new electronic computers" as an element in the military-industrial complex against which he cautioned.[7]

Concurrently, expansion of the federal government's central role in the economy fueled dissemination of computing technologies and practices from the Pentagon to civilian agencies. Computers designed as naval targeting aids and perfected as installations overseeing complex nuclear deterrence had by the late 1950s been adopted as tools of mundane administration—processing payrolls, cutting government checks, managing inventory. Beginning in 1958, Eisenhower ordered the Bureau of the Budget to conduct comprehensive surveys of the number, location, and purpose of all computer installations owned or leased by the federal government. The resulting picture revealed just how crucial governmental patronage was to leading firms of the emerging computer industry. Washington, DC, in particular the Department of Defense, the Atomic Energy Commission, the Bureau of the Census, and the National Bureau of Standards, essentially underwrote the entire computing divisions of firms such as IBM, Sperry-UNIVAC, General Electric, and Honeywell. In a decade when even the most data-hungry corporations—insurance firms, aerospace consortiums, multinational conglomerates—were hesitant to front the multimillion-dollar, multi-year outlays required to research advances in computer hardware, memory, and programming techniques, federal spending underwrote the high cost of early research and development. This massive outlay of governmental funds and attention was only possible because computer-assisted systems methodologies were seen as the most viable solutions to the elaborate national security agendas of the Truman and Eisenhower White Houses. Coordinating bombers, missiles, nuclear weapons, far-flung military installations, and civil defense authorities proved a task of such complexity that the promise of computerized efficiency seemed the only answer to presidential mandates for comprehensive, high-technology national defense networks.

The special relationship between computer manufacturers and reliable federal contracts provided the capital that enabled those firms' executives and engineers to conduct crucial research and expand their private-sector marketing and sales. Money flowed from federal coffers to computer manufacturers, data-processing consultants, and quasi-public think tanks charged with devising digital tools and methods suitable for their largest client—the government. IBM's narrative—a firm whose origins lie with Herman Hollerith's mechanical processing of the 1890 Census and whose fortunes were secured with the prolific mid-1930's contracts to supply analog data keypunches to the new Social Security program—made them ideal partners for the data processing associated with continued expansion of Social Security and implementation of Medicare and Medicaid during the Great Society. The complex, big-ticket leasing and purchasing protocols associated with acquiring computers for governmental uses embody the emerging contract state that came to define Cold War federal expenditures.[8] In his 1960 Budget message to Congress, for example, Eisenhower called for a substantial $29 million increased appropriation for the Internal Revenue Service to fund a new electronic computer system, "the first step in a long-range plan."[9]

Later presidents solidified the centrality of the computer as an element of the U.S. national security state. Ronald Reagan in 1981 suspended exports of American computing technology to the Soviet Union in retaliation for the Kremlin's role in the crackdown on Solidarity labor protests in Poland, reiterating the link between the U.S. defense ecosystem and digital information technologies. George H. W. Bush, commemorating the seventh anniversary of the Strategic Defense Initiative (the computer-controlled orbital laser system nicknamed "Star Wars" by the national press), explicitly credited defense agency contracts for advances in computing speed and miniaturization: "SDI has pushed back the frontier of technology."[10] Presidents George W. Bush and Barack H. Obama prioritized cybersecurity initiatives that reiterated to the world the intertwining of America's technological sector and its national security priorities.

Tools of Presidential Policy

Beyond their status as backbone of the Cold War national security apparatus, computers came to fuel huge swathes of domestic policy in the administrations of John F. Kennedy, Lyndon B. Johnson, and Richard M. Nixon. For presidential administrations with grand policy ambitions, electronic data-processing technologies offered seemingly limitless potential to sift through information and identify optimal solution paths for thorny policy issues. Key advisors and allies to presidents made it known that the occupants of the Oval Office in the 1960s favored technology-abetted contributions to the New Frontier, Great Society, and New Federalism policy regimes. One early proponent of such techniques, secretary of defense for Kennedy and Johnson Robert S. McNamara, was referred to in the halls of Washington as "a human computer"; the technocratic Whiz Kids he recruited in the early 1960s from universities and the RAND Corporation to restructure the Pentagon shared backgrounds in operations research, systems analysis, game theory, complex economic modeling, and organizational management—all fields dominated at the time by a fascination with computers and complex information technologies. Their influence trickled into Congress and civilian agencies. Key presidential allies on Capitol Hill, such as one of Johnson's fellow Texans, Rep. Jack B. Brooks, saw to it that appropriations facilitated presidential requests for expensive investments in computing technology across government.

By the late 1960s, leaders of the American Association for the Advancement of Science could herald "an increasing devotion . . . to the systematic use of information in public and private decision-making, as is exemplified by the President's Council of Economic Advisors."[11] From the Johnson administration onward, mid-level bureaucrats tasked with policy-formulation had also been increasingly exposed to computer-based principles of operations research and systems analysis, as public policy degree programs and administrative training outlets (including the Department of Agriculture's graduate school and the Federal Executive Institute) featured computer themes in their curricula. Computer techniques permitted collection of impressive quantities of data, provided some analytical framework for assessment, and resulted in numbers and organizational schema well-suited to tailoring to match presidential policy priorities.

Reflecting perhaps the convergence of rapid mainframe dissemination and the personal paranoia of a chief executive obsessed with accumulating information, President Nixon initiated a number of proposals for computerized policy initiatives, even if many fizzled or never came to ultimate fruition. Among assorted Nixon proposals were "a computerized organized crime intelligence system . . . developed to house detailed information on the personalities and activities of organized crime nationally" and federal grants for cities supporting "flexible bus service based on computer-forecast demands."[12] Under Nixon and Secretary of State Henry A. Kissinger's foreign policy, computers could even become tools of statecraft. The Nixon White House also sponsored a delegation of American computer scientists visiting the People's Republic of China in 1973, and as an example of Cold War détente Nixon envisioned the United States and the Soviet Union "collaborating in the use of computers in management" for the betterment of both peoples.[13]

Jimmy Carter directly conveyed the understanding a president might have of the potential of computers in enhancing citizen-government relations. Carter proposed to "frame information policy for the 1980s" by dramatically expanding federal support for the nation's school and public libraries, which he saw as gateways to providing technological access, aggregated information, and information-derived services for millions of Americans. He said,

> New technologies are revolutionizing the ways in which we create, store and disseminate information. . . . My Administration is actively encouraging the creative application of these technologies for the benefit of all individuals. As the largest user of computer technology in the world, the Federal government plays a major role in deciding how this technology is applied everywhere.[14]

Subsequent presidents promoted the computer as a device to find jobs for the unemployed. The prospect of computer-assisted job training likewise played a central role in the Clinton administration's second-term welfare reforms. Under the 1997 Federal Welfare-to-Work Hiring Initiative, the Department of Housing and Urban Development, the navy, and the Office of Personnel Management all promoted computer skill training as a pathway for welfare recipients to full-time employment.[15] For the millions of Americans subject to diminished governmental benefits under welfare reform, computers were presented both as the impartial devices administering the databases that defined their eligibility and as the gateways to career prospects in a postindustrial society.

As computers became more central to the daily functioning of the president's inner circle, both information-processing technologies and staffers expert in use of digital technologies moved closer in space to the Oval Office. Jimmy Carter had a mainframe room installed in the Old Executive Office Building. George W. Bush occasionally accessed a staffer's computer in a room adjacent to the Oval Office. Barack Obama, outfitted with a specially secured Blackberry handset, became the first chief executive to regularly make use of an e-mail account.

The rapidity with which personal computers had come to dominate implementation of presidential agenda-setting can be seen in the transition from the Bush 41 administration to the Clinton administration, where, thanks to a subpoena by Independent Counsel Joseph diGenova investigating potential improper activities by the outgoing administration, the Department of Justice seized all government-owned computers within the White House administrative offices. As one newspaper account reported, "as a result, Clinton staffers arrived at their new offices only to find gaping holes in computers everywhere in the White House complex . . . that crippled the computers the officials were counting on using. . . . Without full use of the computers, Clinton staffers struggled to accomplish even the simplest tasks."[16] The Clintonian bridge to the twenty-first century would be delayed until executive-office employees could be provisioned with functional data-processing equipment. Clinton staffers, of course, famously pranked the incoming George W. Bush administration by removing the "W" keys from keyboards of West Wing desktop computers.

Government Reorganization

Beginning with Truman, presidents put computers at the center of their many efforts to remake the vast federal bureaucracy. Starting in 1966, Robert C. Weaver, the first secretary of housing and urban development, predicated his organization's administrative structure on Johnson's directives that the new cabinet agency incorporate computer-savvy techniques of accumulating, processing, and analyzing the data required for addressing multifaceted urban issues. President Nixon enlisted Roy L. Ash, head of the technology conglomerate Litton Industries, to direct his Executive Committee on Reorganization and eventually his Office of Management and Budget. In 1982 President Reagan charged the Private Sector Survey on Cost Control—popularly referred to as the Grace Commission—with identifying inefficiency and waste in executive branch operations. Computers undergirded two key goals of this ongoing postwar drive to enhance federal government operations: efficiency and improved service to citizens. Presidents of both parties concurred that computers, as seemingly nonpolitical devices, could highlight paths to improved federal organization, increased budgetary savings, and enhanced citizen services.

"The use of automatic data processing equipment during the past ten years," President Johnson informed Congress in 1965, "has contributed significantly to increased effectiveness and rising productivity in governmental operations. The electronic computer," Johnson added, "has enabled the Government to carry out programs which otherwise would have been impossible."[17] If presidents in the 1960s and 1970s did not understand the inner workings of mainframe computers, they surely grasped the importance of presenting an impartial, technological solution to what were fundamentally problems of political analysis. At times this calculation backfired. A mere six years after Lyndon Johnson's paean to the computer as a tool of presidential will, his successor, Richard Nixon, railed to congressional allies about executive agencies that deployed computers to report economic trends and declining job numbers inimical to the Oval Office's preferred narrative. Nixon's hapless successor, Gerald R. Ford, pleaded with the White House press corps to disregard prospects for persistent stagflation "as some of the computer readouts tend to lead you to believe."[18]

From Nixon onward, every president has agitated for leaner, more efficient, and more technologically savvy government. Enhanced digital systems became a weapon in the struggle against bureaucracy, with speedier punch card processing or better-managed computer printouts evidence of a president's successful combatting red tape with magnetic tape. Nixon with the Veterans' Administration, Reagan with the Internal Revenue Service, Clinton with the Department of Health and Human Services, and George W. Bush with the Social Security Administration and Environmental Protection Agency—all saw agency restructuring couched in terms of information management.

No grand reorganization proposal more thoroughly illustrated this impulse than the Lyndon Johnson–backed Planning-Programming-Budget System (PPBS) put in place by Robert McNamara that came to dominate the government budget from the mid-1960s.[19] Contemporaries drew a straight line between the impact of Johnson's PPBS ambitions and the computers that that made such detailed organizational and budgetary analysis possible. The 1971 edited volume *Information Technology in a Democracy*—widely disseminated among academics, members of the media, and government officials—included an entire multi-essay section on the implications of presidentially mandated computerized budgeting, featuring contributions by business management theorist John T. Diebold, RAND Corporation official Daniel J. Alesch, and Assistant Secretary of Defense Alain C. Enthoven, among others.

A slew of digitally focused reconceptualizations of government agency organization and public outreach followed during the Clinton and Bush administrations. One of Bill Clinton's earliest official acts in 1993 was the establishment of the National Performance Review, later renamed the National Partnership for Reinventing Government. This interagency task force was charged with streamlining the federal government, and it explicitly encouraged federal employees to seek out technological means of doing so. Information became a tool for remaking the federal government in a post–Cold War world. Such attitudes tied well in to the ascent of Silicon Valley high-technology firms in the nation's economy and cultural imagination. The Government Printing Office was ordered to provide to the American public electronic access to federal information, including explicit "on-line computer access" to the Congressional Record and Federal Register.[20]

The National Partnership for Reinventing Government in 1997 issued a report entitled "Access America: Reengineering through Information Technology" that referred to the notion of "electronic government" as a means of "serving the public on its terms." Calling for shifting all federal payments to computerized fund transfers; providing the public with access to digitized environmental, criminal justice, and public health databases; and transforming web portals into viable sites for public access to governmental services, the president's agenda essentially re-envisioned the relationship between citizen (as customer) and government employee (as service provider) as one that in the near future could be mediated by computer and conducted online.[21]

Calling "interconnecting computers and databases . . . integral to many of the Access America initiatives," the report to the president asserted that "the government's electronic information and information technology is essential to creating government services that are more accessible, efficient, and easy to use." Ironically, the report concluded that in order to streamline bureaucracy and implement more responsible e-governance, the government would need to establish "a corresponding policy and management structure" well versed in the nuances of computer technologies.

Clinton and Gore's calls for a streamlined, digitally savvy government responsive to the citizen as consumer both hearkened back to the Cold War government-market context that birthed the computer and an emerging, globalization-era economic mindset that embraced digital techniques as pathways to growth:

> These systems must also be able to support the government's responsibilities to provide for national security, support law enforcement, enhance global competitiveness and productivity for U.S. business and industry, and protect privacy and civil liberties. All this must be done in a flexible, cost-effective manner, through a collaboration among the public, industry, academia, and the government.[22]

Federal agencies soon created public-oriented websites; government offices that dealt heavily in grant dispersal (such as the Departments of Transportation and Housing and Urban Redevelopment) transitioned to electronic submission of application forms as the federal government sought to match presidential imperative for e-government.

Evangelists for a Digital Future

Presidents both reflect and shape the temper of their times. As central figures of the digital age, their frequent invocations of computers and associated digital practices legitimate and contextualize the place of the computer in American government and broader society. They can do this on a personal level, by exhibiting familiarity with newer digital technologies (even if public office security protocols prohibit them fully making use of certain vulnerable digital communication tools) and on a political level by articulating their visions for the computerization of the United States.

The American public, especially over the past twenty five years, has evidenced a desire to understand the ways in which presidents have interacted with the rapidly evolving digital technologies transforming daily life in the United States. Recent presidents have been happy to oblige—to humanize themselves and link their administrations to the era's zeitgeist. Photo-opportunities with computer systems proved a natural draw to presidents as candidates and office-holders, offering an opportunity to pose with compelling, futuristic technology. John Kennedy gleefully posed with model rockets before banks of gleaming mainframes when he toured NASA facilities. On a visit to the Social Security Administration headquarters in Baltimore, Lyndon Johnson inspected the agency's computer center with the same enthusiasm he might christen an aircraft carrier. Thirty years apart Gerald Ford and George W. Bush sat down at classroom computers on visits to inner-city schools. Bill Clinton, master of the layered narrative, posed for White House photographers as he pressed the button dispatching the first e-mail sent by a president in his official capacity: a brief note to former Sen. John Glenn, then orbiting the earth on the space shuttle *Discovery*.

In popular press accounts, presidential relations with—or comments about—computer technologies became lenses into the chief executive's personality, a rare chance for an ordinary citizen to compare his or her own encounters with computer devices to those reported for the president. Thus the *Washington Post* could in 1991 run a tongue-in-cheek article titled "All the President's Modems" that referred to the forty-first president as the "nation's top DOS man" and inquired, "Does the president do Windows?" before concluding, "None of this will make sense yet to George Bush."[23]

More crucial than posing with computers were official references to an emerging information society. Presidents deployed language that deliberately linked their economic and social policy proposals to the presumed nonpolitical, impartial expertise exuded by the electronic computer. At the same time they acknowledged, often enthusiastically, the transformative aspects of digital technologies on American culture and commerce.

Presidential rhetoric invoked computers in soaring, generic fashion, ascribing to digital technologies great promise and bright futures, cementing the linkage in media coverage and popular perception between the presence of the computer as a device and the notion of technological advancement as an integral element of general American identity. Kennedy referenced such "vital new industries as electronic data processing and computers" in his descriptions of the American economy.[24] Thus, in 1964, Johnson could position the electronic computer as a pivotal tool of the Great Society agenda: "All the human knowledge stored in computers will be available in seconds to help solve problems half-a-world away."[25]

Audiences, particularly elite listeners in the business community, favored presidential optimism about computers. The same year as Johnson's speech, David Sarnoff, president of Radio Corporation of America (RCA), echoed virtually identical words to the American Bankers Association. The computer, Sarnoff asserted, could make the nation's chief executive more responsive to the needs of American citizens. The computer would permit a capable president to function more effectively and implement grander ambitions:

> The use of the computer provides a vast opportunity for finding answers to many of our most complex social problems—in education, conservation of natural resources, air and water pollution, urban planning and renewal, the retraining of persons displaced by automation, the reduction of poverty. . . . The computer will make it possible to restore a direct dialogue between the people and their political leaders, in the tradition of an Athenian assembly or a New England town meeting. Democracy is the highest form of government ever developed, but the magnitude and complexities of our society have made us poor practitioners. . . . Far from downgrading the political, social and spiritual leader, the rapid progress of the computer places a higher premium upon his abilities, understanding and courage.[26]

Befitting his public persona of eternal optimist, Ronald W. Reagan perhaps best exemplified this tendency, elevating his home state of California's microchip industry and the nation's burgeoning software market into exemplars of American ingenuity and enterprise in the midst of exacerbated Cold War tensions. A year after the seminal 1984 commercial that introduced the Macintosh computer to the world, Reagan presented Steve Jobs with the National Medal of Technology. Of the twelve recipients of that year's inaugural award, seven—including Jobs, his Apple Computer compatriot Steve Wozniak, and Fred Brooks of IBM—were distinguished in their citations for computer or computer-derived technologies. These technologies—these new forms of knowledge—in Reagan's eyes became exemplars of the strength of the American economic system. As he observed, "in the computer industry, for instance, miraculous advances in productivity are now almost commonplace."[27]

The computer was an economy-rejuvenating "product" and "tool" made possible by presidential geopolitical vision. Shortly before his term concluded, Reagan addressed the students of Moscow State University on a state visit to the Soviet Union. He invoked Steve Jobs and Steve Wozniak as exemplars of American ingenuity and harbingers of a technology-driven future, presenting himself as ambassador of a United States fundamentally being remade by information technology. Reagan noted,

> Standing here before a mural of your revolution, I want to talk about a very different revolution that is taking place right now, quietly sweeping the globe without bloodshed or conflict. Its effects are peaceful, but they will fundamentally alter our world, shatter old assumptions, and reshape our lives. It's easy to underestimate because it's not accompanied by banners or fanfare. It's been called the technological or information revolution, and as its emblem, one might take the tiny silicon chip, no bigger than a fingerprint. One of these chips has more computing power than a roomful of old-style computers.
>
> As part of an exchange program, we now have an exhibition touring your country that shows how information technology is transforming our lives—replacing manual labor with robots, forecasting weather for farmers, or mapping the genetic code of DNA for medical researchers. These microcomputers today aid the design of everything from houses to ears to spacecraft; they even design better and faster computers. They can translate English into Russian or enable the blind to read or help Michael Jackson produce on one synthesizer the sounds of a whole orchestra. Linked by a network of satellites and fiber-optic cables, one individual with a desktop computer and a telephone commands resources unavailable to the largest governments just a few years ago. . . . Think of that little computer chip. . . . We're breaking through the material conditions of existence to a world where man creates his own destiny.[28]

George H. W. Bush and Bill Clinton continued this generalized promotion. References to the seemingly unlimited potential of a computerized future in presidential addresses in the 1990s both reinforced contemporary business attitudes on the theme and validated the lofty goals of private sector interests driving the boom in the information technology sector. Bush, touring a suburban Virginia high school in 1989, expressed his appreciation at the school's personal computer–stocked labs: "I think it is important that people be computer literate."[29] Clinton routinely structured his bridge to the twenty-first century around girders of digital technology, praising young people for their increasing proficiency with computers and touting the expected savings to the American economy.

Under George W. Bush and Barack Obama, "innovation" became a byword for a particular, Silicon Valley–influenced understanding of technological progress. Throughout his term, Bush explicitly framed expansion of broadband Internet access and preservation of federal online commerce tax exemptions as essential elements of national economic competitiveness in a wired, globalized world.[30] Obama endorsed software-coding education and suggested that government support of high-technology small-business hubs could revolutionize domestic new industries centered on three-dimensional printing, wearable electronics, and "the internet of things."[31] Expressions of presidential enthusiasm about the role of computers and digital technologies in broader American society themselves became functional means of implementing broader policy agendas relating to technology and markets in the post-1945 world.

Presidents and Computers Get Down to Business

The last three decades have seen the presidency directly confront policy implications resulting from the proliferation of computer technologies across American society and the broader globe. By the early 1990s, "Information" and "Technology" would ascend to capital-letter policy category status and become catalysts for hot-button political debate, much as Trade, Health Care, Immigration, and Labor had in preceding generations. With increased usage of the electronic computer in everyday American life came growing prominence of information technology–related issues themselves as drivers of the policy cycle and topics of political debate upon which presidents were expected to comment.

Inklings of the stature of "digitized" issues as drivers of policy debate can be seen as early as the Kennedy administration, where the president expressed concern over "office and clerical workers . . . increasingly being displaced by automatic computers and processes."[32] Gerald Ford devoted considerable energy to establishing federal guidelines for security of digital information, culminating in his lobbying Congress for an under-the-wire midnight passage of the Privacy Act of 1974 before the legislative branch adjourned for its session. Jimmy Carter devoted an entire section of his final State of the Union address to the need to implement a national privacy policy in response to the rise of massive computerized databases maintained by public and private organizations. In the same speech, he articulated a link between digital flows of information and his administration's push for deregulation of crucial sectors of the economy: "Technological advances, such as satellites, computers, and microwave relays,"

Carter asserted, "have made it practical to move much of the telecommunications industry from a regulated monopoly to a deregulated, competitive market."[33] A month after the September 11 attacks, George Bush issued Executive Order 13231 on "Critical Infrastructure Protection in the Information Age," acknowledging the centrality of the digital to the functioning of business and government alike. "The information technology revolution," Bush argued, "has changed the way business is transacted, government operates, and national defense is conducted."[34]

Both Presidents Clinton and Obama highlighted medical information technologies as core components of their health care reform proposals.[35] The former proclaimed a "National Health Information Management Week" in November 1993 and suggested the key to controlling national health care costs lay in better technological management of hospitals.[36] Nearly two decades later his Democratic successor faced a number of controversial issues linked to the digital realm: electronic government surveillance, leaking of classified electronic files, computer-guided drone warfare, Internet neutrality, and technological solutions to public health and energy concerns. The proliferation of digital technology–themed offices, appointments, and proclamations within the Obama administration reflected the increasing centrality of the modern information society to the policy priorities of the modern White House; in 2009 he appointed the nation's first "chief technology officer" and elevated another executive office post to the Silicon Valley–inspired title "chief information officer of the United States."

Beyond their status as grist for emerging policy debate, digital technologies have over the past three decades also become an increasingly integral component of the act of running for president in the first place. Computers are hardly newcomers to the business of presidential electoral politics. CBS News famously deployed early UNIVAC mainframes to predict Dwight Eisenhower's victories over Adlai Stevenson in 1952 and 1956.[37] National campaigns soon adopted similar tools, harnessing information to suss out any political advantage.

Presidential candidates from Kennedy and Johnson onward consciously operated in a setting in which computers acted as intermediaries for the aggregation of crucial polling and donor data, and in which electronic technology itself predicted, processed, and disseminated results from polling booths. Thus a month before his landslide 1964 election, Lyndon Johnson could address a rally of campaign supporters on an airport tarmac in Boise, conflating electoral choice a month hence with the authority of computer-aggregated vote tallies: "The collective judgment of 75 million people will be recorded that night by the computers of the Nation."[38]

By the mid-1970s, "mailing lists, stored on computer tapes," had become the backbone of dynamic presidential campaigns seeking to target carefully sliced demographic (and donor) constituencies.[39] By 1988, the *New York Times* could declare that "from laptop to mainframe, computers have established a firm hold on the business of politics. They have been integral to every 1988 Presidential campaign[,] . . . tracking convention delegates, writing fundraising letters and thank you notes, processing donations, drafting news releases, maintaining electronic news libraries, and communicating between field and headquarters."[40]

Barack Obama's dramatic 2008 primary and general election victories were arguably as much a product of his sophisticated social media and digital voter roll operations as they were the resonance of his call for "hope and change." Building on the first tentative social media and online meetup strategies pioneered by unsuccessful Democratic presidential candidate Howard B. Dean four years earlier, Obama met with Silicon Valley executives in 2007 and 2008 to plot a voter mobilization and fundraising strategy rooted in electronic communications and Big Data analysis.[41] The 2016 presidential election cycle saw traditional media outlets, web-based pundits, and campaign operations themselves increasingly invest in the computerized parsing of Big Data even as digital mastery of online fundraising and social media promotion reshaped the fundamental tenets of electioneering for a new generation.

Summing Up the Computer and the White House

The relation between the presidency and the computer is not a direct linkage but rather a subtler reflection of the ways in which an emerging technology can embody the context and changing nature of the post-WWII federal government. A product of the Cold War and the postwar contract state, the computer ascended to a position of prominence in the executive branch as a result of successive presidentially dictated governmental reorganization schemes. Though not knowledgeable in the technical specifics—or even the functional usage—of data-processing and information systems, American presidents perceived in the touted potential of the computer a means of gaining enhanced authority over a scattered, sometimes recalcitrant bureaucracy. The data aggregation, analysis, and dissemination capabilities that made computers ideal instruments of scientific research and office administration gradually seeped into the realm of policy formulation and implementation, from the 1960s onward composing integral elements of ambitious executive branch proposals—even if the success of actual computer-abetted implementation of such agendas varied.

Over the course of the twentieth century, the office of president of the United States has assumed a remarkable array of additional obligations beyond its traditional roles of head of state, commander in chief, and party leader. The era of the "imperial presidency" saw Oval Office inhabitants become wagers of undeclared war, trade negotiators, overseers of a vastly expanded federal state, mourners in chief, commentators on popular culture, and conduits of action for coalescing social movements.[42] Presidents and their circles have articulated social progress and regression, codified new fashions and cultural trends, and reshaped the environmental, social, and economic landscapes of the United States. With the evolution of presidential libraries, they have even become the first line of assessment on their own historical legacies. Americans, as both voters and citizens, demand their presidents have trenchant and satisfying opinions on a staggering range of issues: economics, national security, foreign relations, cultural values—and the place of science and technology. In the seven decades since the close of World War II, this augmented set of responsibilities has increasingly meant that presidents hold opinions on, make decisions regarding, and respond to the influence of the electronic computer and the digital information society that has arisen around it. No one expects the president to be the nation's "IT Guy," but over the past half-century in particular the occupancy of the Oval Office has entailed a heightened attention to the role of information technology as a central element of American government, economy, and identity.

Notes

1. Given that the computer is a technological device so rooted in the mid-twentieth-century American state, it is surprising how little has been written on the interlinkages between it and established U.S. political institutions, a theme discussed in this author's own "Stating the Field: Institutions and Outcomes in Computer History," *IEEE Annals of the History of Computing* 34, no. 1 (Jan.–Mar. 2012): 104. The most comprehensive work

on the political context of American computing remains Paul N. Edwards, *The Closed World: Computers and the Politics of Discourse in Cold War America* (Cambridge, MA: MIT Press, 1996). James W. Cortada has produced a detailed and highly useful overview of the introduction of computing to several executive branch agencies in his *The Digital Hand*, vol. 3, *How Computers Changed the Work of American Public Sector Industries* (New York: Oxford University Press, 2008).

2. From the American perspective, John Laprise has been the scholar most directly addressing the theme of computers and the presidency, most notably in "White House Computer Adoption and Information Policy from 1969–1979" (Northwestern University, Ph.D. diss., 2009) and "Kissinger's Computer: National Security Council Computerization, 1969–1972," *IEEE Annals of the History of Computing* 33, no. 1 (Jan.–Mar. 2011): 38–51.

3. As portrayed in contemporary American media and popular culture, such as the popular volumes by Walter Isaacson, the computer revolution is a market-driven narrative of "technological wizards." Silicon Valley idols Bill Gates, Steve Jobs, and Mark Zuckerberg merge the roles of celebrated industrial-age material object innovators such as Thomas Edison and Alexander Graham Bell with the corporation-building savvy of Andrew Carnegie or John D. Rockefeller to transform the technological landscape, build vast fortunes, and create gizmos that deeply embed themselves into the daily lives of ordinary Americans. The federal state is absent in the narrative, and presidents appear only in the coda to present a medal to the technologist-entrepreneurs.

4. For more on the history of the role of government and individual politicians in the development of the Internet, see Janet Abbate, "Privatizing the Internet: Competing Visions and Chaotic Events, 1987–1995," *IEEE Annals of the History of Computing* 33, no. 1 (Jan.–Mar. 2010): 10–22.

5. Among early U.S. government–commissioned computers were the ENIAC (1946); Mark II (1948); Mark III, SEAC, SWAC, and ERA ATLAS (all 1950); and the EDVAC and ORDVAC (1951). The first commercially viable electronic computer, the UNIVAC I, was sold to private firms after its design had been funded by a contract from the Census Bureau.

6. Dwight Eisenhower, "Radio and Television Address to the American People on Science in National Security," November 7, 1957, *Public Papers of the Presidents of the United States: Dwight D. Eisenhower*, vol. 5, *January 1, 1957 to December 31, 1957* (Washington, DC: U.S. Government Printing Office, 1962), 230.

7. Dwight Eisenhower, "Farewell Radio and Television Address to the American People," January 17, 1961, *Public Papers of the Presidents of the United States: Dwight D. Eisenhower*, vol. 8, *January 1, 1960 to January 20, 1961* (Washington, DC: U.S. Government Printing Office, 1962), 421.

8. This echoes tendencies in postwar military procurement explored by Mark R. Wilson in another chapter in this volume.

9. Dwight Eisenhower, "Annual Budget Message to the Congress: Fiscal Year 1961," January 18, 1960, *Public Papers of the Presidents of the United States: Dwight D. Eisenhower*, vol. 8, *January 1, 1960 to January 20, 1961* (Washington, DC: U.S. Government Printing Office, 1962), 101.

10. George H. W. Bush, "Statement on the Seventh Anniversary of the Strategic Defense Initiative," March 23, 1990, *Public Papers of the Presidents of the United States: George Bush, 1990,* bk. 1, *January 1 to June 30, 1990* (Washington, DC: U.S. Government Printing Office, 1991), 421–422.

11. Emmanuel G. Mesthene, "How Technology Will Shape the Future," *Science* 161 (July 12, 1968), 135.

12. Richard Nixon, "Special Message to the Congress on a Program to Combat Organized Crime in America," April 23, 1969, and "Special Message to the Congress on Public Transportation," August 7, 1969, both in *Public Papers of the Presidents of the United States: Richard M. Nixon: Containing the Public Messages, Speeches, and Statements of the President, 1969* (Washington, DC: U.S. Government Printing Office, 1971).

13. Richard Nixon, "Fourth Annual Report to the Congress on United States Foreign Policy," May 3, 1973, *Public Papers of the Presidents of the United States: Richard M. Nixon: Containing the Public Messages, Speeches, and Statements of the President, 1973* (Washington, DC: U.S. Government Printing Office, 1975).

14. Jimmy Carter, "Libraries and Information Services Message to the Congress," September 28, 1980, *Public Papers of the Presidents of the United States: Jimmy Carter, 1980/1981,* bk. 3, *September 29, 1980 to January 20, 1981* (Washington, DC: U.S. Government Printing Office, 1982).

15. Al Gore, Letter to the President, in *The Federal Welfare-to-Work Hiring Initiative: Second Annual Report* (Washington, DC: Government Printing Office, 1999), 2.

16. Jeffrey Birnbaum and Barbara Rosewicz, "Prosecutor's Move Disables Computers at White House," *Wall Street Journal*, January 22, 1993.

17. Lyndon Johnson, "Letter to the President of the Senate and to the Speaker of the House on Government Use of Automatic Data Processing Equipment," March 2, 1965, *Public Papers of the Presidents of the United States: Lyndon B. Johnson*, vol. 2, bk. 1, *January 1, 1965 to May 31, 1965* (Washington, DC: U.S. Government Printing Office, 1970).

18. Gerald R. Ford, "News Conference," February 4, 1975, *Public Papers of the Presidents: Gerald R. Ford*, vol. 2, *1974–77* (Washington, DC: Government Printing Office, 1979), 72.

19. David R. Jardini. "Out of the Blue Yonder: The Transfer of Systems Thinking from the Pentagon to the Great Society, 1961–1965," in *Systems, Experts, and Computers: The Systems Approach in Management and Engineering, World War II and After*, ed. Agatha C. Hughes and Thomas P. Hughes (Cambridge, MA: MIT Press, 2000).

20. Bill Clinton, "Statement on Signing the Government Printing Office Electronic Information Access Enhancement Act of 1993," June 8, 1993, in *Public Papers of the Presidents of the United States: William J. Clinton, 1993*, bk. 1, *January 20 to July 31, 1993* (Washington, DC: U.S. Government Printing Office, 1994).

21. National Partnership for Reinventing Government, "Access America: Reengineering through Information Technology" (Washington, DC: U.S. Government Printing Office, February 1997).

22. National Partnership for Reinventing Government, "Access America: Reengineering through Information Technology" (Washington, DC: U.S. Government Printing Office, February 1997), sect. A14.

23. Richard Leiby, "All the President's Modems," *Washington Post*, April 26, 1991. DOS here refers to Microsoft Disk Operating System (MS-DOS), a prominent text-based computer operating system prevalent in the 1980s and early 1990s.

24. John F. Kennedy, "Statement by the President Announcing a Contract for a Materials Research Laboratory at the University of North Carolina," October 12, 1961, *Public Papers of the Presidents of the United States: John F. Kennedy*, vol. 1, *January 20, 1961 to December 31, 1961* (Washington, DC: U.S. Government Printing Office, 1964), 417.

25. Lyndon Johnson, "Remarks to Members of the Communications Satellite Corporation Board," August 17, 1964, *Public Papers of the Presidents of the United States: Lyndon B. Johnson*, vol. 1, bk. 2, *July 1, 1964 to December 31, 1964* (Washington, DC: U.S. Government Printing Office, 1970), 517.

26. David Sarnoff, "The Social Impact of Computers," *Union Seminary Quarterly Review* 21, no. 4 (May 1966): 377.

27. Ronald Reagan, "Remarks at the Presentation Ceremony for the National Medals of Science and Technology," March 12, 1986, *Public Papers of the Presidents of the United States: Ronald Reagan, 1981–1989*, vol. 10, *January 1 to June 27, 1986* (Washington, DC: U.S. Government Printing Office, 1992). The other medal recipients that year were Erich Bloch and Bob Evans, Brooks's co-contributors to development of the influential IBM System/360 mainframe, and Harold Rosen and Allen E. Puckett of Hughes Electronics, for their work on the first geostationary communications satellite.

28. Ronald Reagan, "Address at Moscow State University," May 31, 1988, *Public Papers of the Presidents of the United States: Ronald Reagan, 1981–1989*, vol. 14, *January 1 to July 1, 1988* (Washington, DC: U.S. Government Printing Office, 1992).

29. George H. W. Bush, "Remarks and a Question-and-Answer Session with Students at James Madison High School in Vienna, Virginia," March 28, 1989, *Public Papers of the Presidents of the United States: George Bush, 1989*, bk. 1, *January 20 to June 30, 1989* (Washington, DC: U.S. Government Printing Office, 1990).

30. George W. Bush, "Statement on Senate Action on Proposed Internet Tax Nondiscrimination Legislation," April 29, 2004, *Public Papers of the Presidents of the United States: George W. Bush, 2004*, bk. 1, *January 1 to June 30, 2004* (Washington, DC: U.S. Government Printing Office, 2007).

31. Barack Obama, "Remarks at the Techmer PM, LLC, Manufacturing Facility in Clinton, Tennessee," January 9, 2015 (Washington, DC: U.S. Government Printing Office, 2015), https://www.gpo.gov/fdsys/pkg/DCPD-201500017/pdf/DCPD-201500017.pdf.

32. John F. Kennedy, "Remarks at a Civic Luncheon in Chicago," March 23, 1963, *Public Papers of the Presidents of the United States: John F. Kennedy*, vol. 3, *January 1, 1963 to November 22, 1963* (Washington, DC: U.S. Government Printing Office, 1964), 110.

33. Jimmy Carter, "The State of the Union Annual Message to the Congress," January 21, 1980, *Public Papers of the Presidents of the United States: Jimmy Carter, 1980/1981*, bk. 1, *January 1, 1980 to May 23, 1980* (Washington, DC: U.S. Government Printing Office, 1981).

34. George W. Bush, "Executive Order 13231—Critical Infrastructure Protection in the Information Age," October 16, 2001, *Public Papers of the Presidents of the United*

States: George W. Bush, 2001, bk. 2, *July 1 to December 31, 2001*(Washington, DC: U.S. Government Printing Office, 2003).

35. Clinton's call for increased use of electronic data in reshaping the national health care system may have indirectly inspired one of the more peculiar artifacts of the era. In 1994, during the height of the debates over health care reform, the wonkish social welfare policy–focused Markle Foundation commissioned the Silicon Valley firm Maxis Software, creators of the popular *SimCity* lines of games, to design *SimHealth,* a game for the personal computer in which players could channel their inner Hillary Rodham Clinton or Newt Gingrich and simulate varied data-driven national health care policies. (*Entertainment Weekly* rated the game a C-minus.)

36. Bill Clinton, "Proclamation 6620: National Health Information Management Week, 1993," November 3, 1993, *Public Papers of the Presidents of the United States: William J. Clinton, 1993*, bk. 2, *August 1 to December 31, 1993* (Washington, DC: U.S. Government Printing Office, 1994).

37. Lyle R. Johnson, "Coming to Grips with Univac," *IEEE Annals of the History of Computing* 28, no. 2 (Apr.–Jun. 2006): 32–42; Paul Attallah, "Of Homes and Machines: TV, Technology, and Fun in America, 1944–1984," *Continuum: Journal of Media & Cultural Studies* 4, no. 2 (Jan. 1991): 58–97; James Coleman, Ernest Heau, Robert Peabody, Leo Rigsby, "Computers and Election Analysis: The New York Times Project," *Public Opinion Quarterly* 28, no. 3 (Fall 1964): 418–46.

38. Lyndon Johnson, "Remarks upon Arrival at the Airport in Boise," October 12, 1964, *Public Papers of the Presidents of the United States: Lyndon B. Johnson*, vol. 1, bk. 2, *July 1, 1964 to December 31, 1964* (Washington, DC: U.S. Government Printing Office, 1970), 659.

39. Christopher Lydon, "How a Man Decides He'll Run for the Presidency," *New York Times*, January 5, 1975; Andrew Rosenthal, "Politicians Count on Computers," *New York Times*, May 9, 1988.

40. Andrew Rosenthal, "Politicians Count on Computers"; Birnbaum and Rosewicz, "Prosecutor's Move Disables Computers at White House."

41. David Carr, "How Obama Tapped into Social Networks' Power," *New York Times*, November 9, 2008.

42. The concept of the "imperial presidency," shorthand for the tendency of mid-century presidents to absorb extraconstitutional powers through the expanding scope of executive-branch attention and function, was popularized by Arthur M. Schlesinger Jr., one of the twentieth century's few academic historians to operate in close proximity to the Oval Office. See Arthur M. Schlesinger Jr., *The Imperial Presidency* (Boston: Houghton Mifflin, 1973).

12

The President and American Retirement Planning

PAULA K. GAJEWSKI

In the mid-twentieth century, private retirement plans operated at the discretion of employers, many of whom still regarded the pension as a gift granted to long-serving employees in return for loyal service—the proverbial gold watch. In the absence of comprehensive federal regulation of how funds should be collected or invested, employees had no guarantee that the pensions they expected would be paid. By the late 1960s, many workers faced the prospect of post-work life either without retirement funds or with drastically less than they had been led to expect.

In 1971, President Richard M. Nixon proposed legislation that would become part of the Employee Retirement Income Security Act (ERISA), the landmark legislation that changed American private retirement practices. Nixon proposed allowing individuals to create their own retirement accounts. In September 1974, President Gerald R. Ford signed ERISA into law, creating the Individual Retirement Account, commonly known as the IRA.[1] At a moment when federal lawmakers spoke volubly about devolving authority away from Washington, DC, ERISA's authors preempted state retirement legislation. Creation of the IRA, now a cornerstone of modern retirement planning, demonstrates the presence of an oft-decisive presidential hand in policymaking.

ERISA's authors also fostered changes that no one at the time foresaw. The IRA was only a single provision, inserted in the bill to appease a small, market-oriented group of Nixon advisors. During the next decades, corporate and individual retirement accounts created billions of dollars that had to be invested in stocks and bonds, thus both buoying and also profoundly reshaping financial markets. Retirement planning, a seemingly personal event, came to rest on federal legislation that has remained invisible to ordinary Americans. In this imperceptible fashion, ERISA encouraged Americans to believe that they alone bore responsibility to finance their retirement. In truth, retirement within the American version of capitalism was intimately personal and increasingly corporate.

In early twentieth-century America, "retirement" was an unhappy situation forced upon those too disabled or enfeebled to continue working. Pensions served the dual function of securing a stable workforce and removing individuals from that workforce at a predetermined age. As industry evolved, the increasing depersonalization of the workforce made the pension a useful key to control workers' behavior. The fundamental characteristic of early pensions was that the choice of how long to work was a decision made by the company, not by the worker. Through the first half of the twentieth century, the promise of pension income convinced workers to retire, and employers in turn achieved significant savings by replacing older, higher-wage employees with entry-level workers.[2]

President Franklin D. Roosevelt's advisors embraced the insistence of pension reformers that every worker should have some form of guaranteed old-age security. In 1935, congressional authorization of Social Security legitimized the idea of retirement by acknowledging the necessity of financial support during the period between the end of work and death. The question facing both management and employees was whether the pension could continue as a gift from employer to loyal employee, or whether an adequate retirement income should be considered a fundamental right of the workingman. The advent of Social Security converted provision for old age from a personal responsibility into "a social requirement."[3]

The idea of "retirement"—a period of well-deserved leisure following a lifetime of work—developed after World War II. While one's career or profession conferred social status, quality of life began to be measured by how Americans spent their free time. Retirement during the 1950s was the frontier of leisure and consumption. Insurance companies promoted retirement as a period for life to be enjoyed, courtesy of the pensions they sold. Unions pushed to expand pension coverage, by making pensions a primary point of contention in collective bargaining. At the same time, the elderly found it necessary to present themselves as active and purposeful, in order to qualify for health insurance coverage. According to contemporary writers, retirement gave the middle class an opportunity to "build new lives on a foundation of leisure."[4]

As retirement became "a permanent paid vacation," retired persons discovered they had time to buy and enjoy consumer goods, and the manufacturers of those goods found a new, potentially very profitable market.[5] "Free time" was not free; in 1958, Americans spent more than $60 million on golf equipment.[6] By 1960, retirement was the pinnacle of the American dream, an enjoyable and enviable time of life.[7] Pensions were necessary to pay for that dream. The purpose of retirement changed as society moved from acceptance of a guarantee of subsistence income to the idea of a retirement in which one's highest achieved standard of living could be maintained. The demands placed on private pensions grew in kind.[8]

With Social Security poised to cover a retiree's basic needs, the private pension became supplemental. The majority of plans were noncontributory—that is, employees did not pay in to them. By integrating pensions into corporate financial planning, businesses were able to use that money to fund growth.[9] Traditionally, pension money had been invested with insurance companies, but as the stock market boomed in the 1960s, many corporate officials moved their firms' pensions to financial institutions, such as investment companies or trust foundations, trading the safety of insurance plans for riskier but potentially more profitable stock investments. By the late 1960s, those fast-growing institutions controlled half of all outstanding common shares.[10] As pension funds, collectively, grew into billions of dollars, politicians began to pay more attention to how that money was being used, or potentially misused.

The faults of private pensions became obvious. First, the war in Vietnam and 1960s-era social programs pushed large amounts of money into the economy, producing a rapid uptick in inflation. Traditional pensions did increase in value, however. Second, the shift of pension money from secure fixed instruments to uncertain common stock exposed millions to risks many judged inappropriate for a pension fund. As the right to an enjoyable retirement became an extension of the right to an "American standard of living," federal pension regulation became not only legitimized but also required. Congress recognized that retirement had become a collective social promise, and that Americans had nowhere to turn when that promise was broken. And yet no single law or group of laws governed private pension implementation and maintenance until the

Employee Retirement Income Security Act of 1974.[11] Even more, many in and out of Congress had begun to argue, the older pension system was actually bad for employees and for business.

Prior to ERISA, the pension system confined workers' choices about employment. In this respect, businesses and unions were exercising a form of public political power, which put the private pension system in limbo between private operation and public purpose.[12] To resolve this dilemma, Congress needed either to reclaim that power for itself or cede it entirely to the private sector.[13] Accepting that provision for retirement is a social responsibility of business, and that business plays a vital role in society that extends beyond its function as a conduit of shareholder returns, the policy question that emerged was the extent to which pensions should be subject to regulation. Members of Congress needed twelve years to answer that question.

In 1962, President John F. Kennedy created the cabinet-level Committee on Corporate Pension Funds, in response to advice from Walter W. Heller, chair of the Council of Economic Advisors. When the committee presented its findings in 1965, President Lyndon B. Johnson was reluctant to endorse wholesale reforms that might endanger his relationships with the business community, although many in the administration supported reform. By the late 1960s, leaders of important business groups including the National Association of Life Underwriters, the National Association of Manufacturers, and the U.S. Chamber of Commerce were lobbying for pension reform. However, no single person or organization was spearheading the effort. With so many groups desiring a voice and so little concrete research on private pension operations, lawmakers approached the issue of reform with extreme caution.[14]

In 1967, Senator Jacob K. Javits (R-NY) introduced a comprehensive pension reform bill, which drew criticism from all sides because it was so expansive. Javits recruited help from Senator Harrison A. Williams (D-NJ), who wielded significant political power. With help from other pro-reform congressmen and consumer activists like Ralph Nader, the senators used the public press and popular media to rally support for their proposal, the Williams-Javits Bill. The issue of private pension reform represents one of the first times that politicians purposely fed news stories to the national media with the intent to shape public opinion. In particular, an NBC documentary titled "Pensions: The Broken Promise" put the pension reform bill in the national spotlight.[15] The refashioning of the pension from a problem of labor relations to an issue of social welfare enabled the eventual passage of ERISA.[16]

The American public was frustrated and dissatisfied. Abroad, Vietnam had become a deadly and expensive quagmire, and at home, President Johnson's Great Society was already losing its appeal. Americans were disenchanted with both parties' leadership.[17] The general malaise of American society found one form of expression through calls for an improved retirement. In a period when many workers faced a grim future of repetitious work for a lifetime, the promise of retirement became the light at the end of a long tunnel.[18]

In 1969, when Nixon became president, the main legislative activity regarding old-age security remained centered on Social Security. Nixon was not particularly interested in pension reform; and for that matter, he preferred to leave most domestic policy under the supervision of senior advisor John Ehrlichman. But pensions were an important issue to blue-collar voters, and, with nationwide publicity and billions of dollars involved, the administration had to take part in the pension debate. Also, Nixon feared that Senator Williams would steal his thunder.[19]

Chief Domestic Advisor Arthur F. Burns led an initial review of pension policy as part of Nixon's transition to office, but he ran into the same problems of jurisdiction that hobbled congressional plans. No one was sure which department should oversee pension regulation, since up to that point only the Internal Revenue Service had taken an official hand in reviewing pension plans, and then only with an eye toward taxation.

Burns submitted his proposal to the Labor and Commerce Departments. Labor referred a bill back to the administration; senior aide Peter M. Flanigan submitted that bill to the Treasury Department. Treasury officials were at work on their own plan, but despite their objections the administration submitted the Employee Benefits Protection Act of 1970, which focused predominantly on changes to the tax code.[20]

In 1971, Nixon charged Flanigan, a former investment banker, with the creation of an interagency task force to put together new pension reform legislation. Nixon shied away from the more expansive recommendations included in the Senate Labor Committee bill (Williams-Javits). The task force focused on individual retirement accounts and on vesting, which is the term for the extent of employee ownership of pensions. Only when an employee is 100 percent vested does the entire pension legally belong to that person and not to the company. The task force did not fully address the other goals of Williams-Javits, which included the question of how companies should allocate money to pensions (funding), how employees might take pensions with them if they moved jobs (portability), and how pensions could be insured in case a company could no longer make payments (termination insurance).

The administration would lose the support of the business community if it supported these provisions, all of which required additional employer costs. But many of those same business leaders supported a method by which workers took responsibility for their retirement. When Flanigan presented the task force recommendations in late 1971, the centerpiece was a new investment vehicle, the Individual Retirement Account. The IRA embodied the president's intention that "individuals be encouraged in the American tradition of helping individuals to help themselves."[21]

By August 1972, Nixon had grown impatient with the seemingly endless pension reform debate. Flanigan cautioned the president that if he urged action, it might be seen as support for the Williams-Javits bill. One device to avoid lending support to Williams-Javits was to involve the Senate Finance Committee, because the bill involved taxes. Powerful chair Russell B. Long (D-LA) was adamant that the Labor Committee not usurp his jurisdiction, and after a week of closed-door deliberations, finance members struck every key provision, crippling the bill. Williams angrily blamed Nixon, but the accusation was hard to support when Democrats controlled the Senate.[22]

With reform so visibly stymied in Congress, state officials began to develop their own proposals for pension legislation. The fear of creating as many as fifty sets of pension rules encouraged business leaders to support the creation of uniform federal legislation. This concession reinvigorated the Williams-Javits bill, because the Labor Committee held jurisdiction over employment laws. Meanwhile, Finance Committee members were creating their own reform bill. This move benefited the administration, because one of the senators working on the new bill was Lloyd M. Bentsen. A Democrat from Texas, Bentsen was also the founder of an insurance company, president of a financial holding company, and, most important, a protégé of former Texas governor John B. Connally.[23]

Connally was one of few people whom Nixon actually respected. His competent and confident attitude had led Nixon to include Connally in his administration. In late 1970, Nixon replaced Treasury secretary David M. Kennedy with Connally. Although not as close to Nixon as Ehrlichman or chief of staff Bob Haldeman, Connally was still part of the inner circle, at one time considered for Nixon's vice president in the 1972 election. Nixon appointed George P. Shultz Treasury secretary in 1972, but Connally remained more influential than many of Nixon's other advisors and encouraged the president to take bold action to achieve his goals.[24]

While Finance was working on its new bill, a group of conservative Republican senators led by Senator Carl T. Curtis (R-NE) introduced the Nixon administration's version of pension reform legislation, now titled the Individual Retirement Benefits Act of 1973.[25] One of the main features of the plan, which was appended to the Finance bill and ultimately to ERISA, was an increase to the amounts individuals could set aside in Keogh plans, which were self-funded retirement accounts available to the self-employed. The bill outlined the creation of a similar investment vehicle with more widespread availability, the IRA, and adopted a Treasury recommendation to allow IRAs to be used for pension portability, that is, rollovers.[26]

Bentsen helped persuade potential critics not to derail the evolving legislation. One of the biggest fears among pension and insurance industry insiders was the prospect of a government takeover of the private system and the evolution of some sort of "super Social Security." They feared both the growth of federal bureaucracy and the potential loss of control by the private sector.[27] In his introductory remarks on the Finance bill, Senator Bentsen argued against these objections, saying, "Some individuals will argue that enactment of this legislation would result in excessive Federal interference with the private retirement system. I strongly disagree. . . . I strongly oppose efforts toward a Federal takeover of the private pension system." The primary goals of the Finance bill included vesting and funding provisions similar to those in the Williams-Javits Bill, but it emphasized that the main idea was to change the Internal Revenue Code in such a way that more people would be encouraged to save for their own retirement. The promotional rhetoric assuaged conservative fears by affirming that the purpose of reform was to help the free enterprise system operate more efficiently and effectively.[28]

Bentsen put forth a number of reasons why the Finance bill was superior to that proposed by the Labor Committee, chiefly that vesting and funding provisions would be better administered by the IRS than by the Labor Department. The Finance plan actually proposed better protections for workers by including both smaller plans and union-administered plans financed solely by member contributions. Bentsen called for both earlier vesting (after five years instead of eight) and tax credits for employee contributions. In another move to limit bureaucratic expansion, the Finance bill proposed that the termination insurance program be operated by a federally chartered nonprofit corporation.[29]

The Senate combined the Finance bill with the Williams-Javits bill and began debate on the new bill, S. 4, in late 1973. S. 4 was 227 pages long, and many senators complained about the hurried nature of debate and the length of the bill, which was provided for review at short notice. Senator Gaylord Nelson (D-WI), an ally of reform on the Finance Committee though not part of the conservative faction, sponsored S. 4 for debate. He took the lead in defending the bill against its most persistent critic, Senator Vance Hartke (D-IN). Ironically, Hartke was one of the original proponents of retirement reform; he had sponsored the Federal Reinsurance of Private Pensions Act in 1964.[30] The fact that Hartke, a staunch advocate of pension reform, was the most critical opponent of S. 4 reveals much about the confusing compromise that became ERISA. The majority of Hartke's objections centered on points where he thought the law was not far-reaching enough. His opinion was that if Congress could not do the right thing, it was better to wait until his proposed goals could be achieved. After their previous failures, Javits and Williams determined that something was better than nothing, and that new retirement regulations could only pass if they included provisions acceptable to the conservative side of Congress.

Bentsen rose to again support the idea that the new bill was intended to supplement the existing system, not supplant it. He reiterated, "I strongly oppose efforts toward a Federal takeover of the private pension system. I believe that the free enterprise system can work effectively in this area but only if a proper balance is reached between the interests of employers and employees." The Finance Committee Republicans argued less about the protection of the rights of workers and instead called for businesses and individuals to be treated the same way by the tax code with regard to money intended for pensions.[31]

The legislative history of ERISA shows no actions taken between October 1973 and February 1974. At another legislative moment, this delay could have signaled the bill's demise. In fact, Congress had bigger fish to fry, and President Nixon was not paying attention to domestic policy. Congressional leaders, worried that impeachment hearings would bump

ERISA consideration until the next Congress, pushed hard to get the final bill ready before Congress became embroiled in the Watergate hearings. However, pension scholar Fran Hawthorne contends, the Watergate scandal and the lack of normalcy during 1974 saved ERISA by diverting the attention and criticism of Congress.[32]

The Senate passed the bill by a vote of 93 to 0.[33] The next step in the process was a joint House and Senate conference, to iron out the differences between the Senate's new H.R. 4200 and the House's version, H.R. 2. A final vote in the House produced only two dissenting votes. New president Ford signed ERISA into law on Labor Day, September 2, 1974.

ERISA first and foremost called for stringent standards of fiduciary responsibility, applicable to both pension fund management and to the businesses sponsoring plans. Legislative authors provided vesting standards, so that employees would legally own their own pensions, and portability rules, so workers could take their pensions with them if they moved jobs. Under ERISA, all plans would have to meet minimum funding requirements and purchase plan insurance through a new agency, the Pension Benefit Guaranty Corporation. The one element all of ERISA's provisions had in common was the increased complexity and supervision they required of pension management.[34] ERISA changed the emphasis of federal pension legislation from maintaining plan assets to protecting the rights of individual employees.

What Congress did not foresee was how new regulation of retirement and concurrent changes at the New York Stock Exchange would, in combination, drive employers and stockbrokers to promote retirement planning as an individual, rather than a corporate, responsibility. ERISA and securities regulations mutually discouraged the growth and expansion of traditional defined benefit pension plans.

America of the early 1970s was undergoing massive change. Civil rights and equality for women still commanded headlines. But a revolution was taking place within the halls of American business. The end of the Bretton Woods monetary system marked the end of the gold standard in 1971 but also signified a new conception of money.[35] Americans' ways of measuring value came to embrace a greater range of attributes than sheer monetary worth. The concept of value became increasing fluid as consumers began to consider whether a purchase or investment was safe, family-friendly, fairly traded, environmentally conscious, or some combination thereof. Money was no longer meant only to be spent or saved, invested or donated. Money became something to be managed, and it was the job of the managers of new and powerful institutions to make money work.[36] Money management was surely an uncertain business.

Employers reacted to the 1974 passage of ERISA with extreme caution. The economy was still reeling from the 1973 oil crisis and the effects of stagflation, and the stock market's poor performance reflected the general malaise. The rate of inflation for 1973 was 8 percent, and pension obligations were growing at twice the average rate of earnings.[37] ERISA's expanded definition of fiduciary responsibility extended liability to anyone with any measure of authority or control over any part of the pension itself or any decisions relating to it.[38] This definition meant that virtually any person involved in pension management decisions might face litigation in response to a loss suffered by the pension, if that loss could be traced to a failure to uphold fiduciary standards.[39]

The legislation was so unclear that the executive director of the Association of Private Pension and Welfare Plans, Joseph Leary, remarked that "except for a handful" no one in Congress understood what they had just done. Many companies had difficulty finding people willing to serve as pension plan trustees in the months following ERISA's passage; no one wanted the job until Congress clarified the responsibilities and potential penalties associated with it. Pension management became more an issue of avoiding failure than of achieving success.[40] Pension fund managers needed to develop a statement of plan objectives and investment policy. Once that step was completed, however, managers were "largely off the hook" if they delegated further decision-making to investment professionals.[41]

Industry experts had predicted in the 1960s that the vast majority of plans would be noncontributory within twenty years. As late as December 1968, insurance analyst John Kittredge predicted that most plans would be noncontributory by 1975.[42] After ERISA, pension experts began predicting a shift to more profit-sharing plans. Defined contribution plans were more flexible and better suited to worker mobility, something recognized as the new normal. And defined contribution plans gave employers a way to subvert ERISA. Replacing defined benefit plans that paid an expected amount on a regular schedule with a form of profit-sharing simplified administration, removed part of the burden of liability from managers, and did not necessitate termination insurance payments.[43]

One of ERISA's often overlooked requirements was for pension plan portability. In order to address the problem of employees changing employers and losing their accumulated pension credits, Congress mandated that employees be able to effectively take their pensions with them. This posed an immediate challenge to defined benefit plans. Administrators could arrange a transfer of funds in such a situation, but the money in their pension funds was not individually earmarked, which made for challenging calculations.[44] The other option was to standardize plans between companies so that employees could transfer credits, but that would still involve a monetary transfer at some point and left managers scratching their heads as to how widespread that standardization would need to be, whether within an industry or beyond. Defined contribution plans avoided the issue entirely because it was an easy matter for employees to transfer their own individual accounts or roll them over into IRAs. Because vesting provisions gave employees ownership of their funds, the burden was on them to ensure that such transfers took place, removing that step from employers' termination procedures.[45]

ERISA produced a fundamental change in the nature of retirement planning for individual American workers. Retirement was an issue of private and individual circumstances, which provided the impetus for reform. But retirement was also a public problem. Pension funds amounting to billions of dollars went into privately managed funds, where managers did not answer to regulators or to public officials. Although Congress forced the business community to change their pensions, either by complying fully with ERISA or by converting defined benefit to defined contribution, the response to ERISA still perpetuated traditional profit-seeking behaviors. The inventiveness and resilience of the system was such that executives of pension-sponsoring companies and their stockbrokers found ways to circumvent the new regulations, specifically by creating plans in which employees directed the investment of their own retirement funds.

The Securities Acts Amendments, passed in 1975, symbolically supported individual rights; mandating negotiated commissions at the New York Stock Exchange gave the appearance of democratizing the stock market. Pension managers began to realize that lower commission rates not only made investing more affordable for individuals but also that the consequences of that change, chiefly greater access to information and to investment options like IRAs and mutual funds, meant that corporations could justify shifting more retirement responsibility to employees.[46]

The IRA was never intended to be an escape route for companies to shrug off their pension responsibilities, although some used it in just that way. At its introduction, the IRA was more important as a concept than as an actual financial tool. The IRA gave government sanction to self-directed, self-controlled retirement planning. The IRA provided all the advantages of employer-sponsored plans plus immediate full vesting and easy portability.[47] Participation in employer-sponsored pension plans stabilized in the 1970s and then decreased; personal retirement accounts have become the dominant choice of American workers since 1980.[48] IRA growth began slowly, going from $3 billion invested in 1975 to $20 billion by 1980, but took off during the early 1990s. By 2016, IRAs contained more than $7 trillion, with just under half of that amount invested in mutual funds.[49]

The story of ERISA, the death of the traditional defined benefit pension, and the growing power of Wall Street and financial institutions prompts a reconsideration of the nature of American capitalism. Management consultant Peter F. Drucker pointed out in *Unseen Revolution* (1976) that, following a strict definition of ownership of the means of production, the United States was the first truly socialist country in the world. Through the stock ownership offered in defined contribution and personal retirement accounts, the workers of America have in fact become capitalist owners. But although retirement account holders do have ownership, they do not have *power*.[50]

If we define ownership as the degree to which someone can exert control over the thing they own, then the distribution of American stockholding does not make the country socialist, because most stockholders' control is minute. The power of stock ownership resides with those who can control sizeable amounts of stock, for example, mutual fund companies. Congress neglected to take into account the reactions and behaviors of those who were involved in the pension system other than those who were workers expecting pensions. The executives, the plan managers, and the financial institutions that managed pension money all reacted to ERISA in predictable ways. The implementation of regulation proposed a decrease in their power.

By divesting themselves of the operations of their pensions, corporations turned over a measure of their power to the financial institutions now doing the retirement investing for them. In order to exercise their power, these institutions are dependent on having a market in which to operate, which is exactly what the New York Stock Exchange provides. This is one reason why American retirement planning is so very dependent on the success of the stock market. However, a crucial difference remains between investing through defined contribution plans versus through IRAs. Under defined contribution plans such as the 401(k), employee choice is still confined by employer decisions, but Nixon's IRA left the often unprepared individual to make retirement investment choices. The invisible authority wielded by Richard Nixon created a fundamental change in the way Americans prepare for retirement. Nixon's creation of the IRA demonstrates a powerful presidential influence on the evolution of American capitalism.

Notes

1. ERISA made the IRA available only to those individuals not covered by a retirement plan through their employer; this restriction was removed in the early 1980s.

2. Daniel Béland, *Social Security: History and Politics from the New Deal to the Privatization Debate* (Lawrence: University Press of Kansas, 2005), 51; Dora L. Costa, *The Evolution of Retirement: An American Economic History, 1880–1990* (Chicago: University of Chicago Press, 1998), 3–35; William Graebner, *A History of Retirement: The Meaning and Function of an American Institution, 1885–1978* (New Haven, CT: Yale University Press, 1980), 13; Steven A. Sass, *The Promise of Private Pensions: The First Hundred Years* (Cambridge, MA: Harvard University Press, 1997), 14, 40–42, 54; James A. Wooten, *The Employee Retirement Income Security Act of 1974: A Political History* (Berkeley: University of California Press, 2004), 34–39.

3. Béland, *Social Security*, 4; Lizabeth Cohen, *Making a New Deal: Industrial Workers in Chicago, 1919–1939*, 2nd ed. (Cambridge, UK: Cambridge University Press, 2008), 267–68, 272; Graebner, *A History of Retirement*, 199–200; Sass, *The Promise of Private Pensions*, 9–10. See also Jennifer Klein's argument about the provision of supplemental benefits as the "American way," in Jennifer Klein, *For All These Rights: Business, Labor, and the Shaping of America's Public Private Welfare State*. See Paula K. Gajewski, "The New York Stock Exchange and the Transformation of Retirement in America" (PhD diss., Vanderbilt University, 2016).

4. W. Andrew Achenbaum, *Shades of Gray: Old Age, American Values, and Federal Policies since 1920* (Boston: Little, Brown, 1983), 59; Graebner, *A History of Retirement*, 227–25; Gregory Wood, *Retiring Men: Manhood, Labor, and Growing Old in America, 1900–1960* (New York: University Press of America, 2012), 84. Examples include Irving Salomon, *Retire and Be Happy* (New York: Greenberg, 1951); Theodor Greene, *How to Enjoy Retirement for the Rest of Your Life* (New York: Exposition, 1957); Ray Giles, *How to Retire and Enjoy It* (New York: McGraw-Hill, 1949); Walter B. Pitkin, *The Best Years: How to Enjoy Retirement* (New York: Current Books, 1946).

5. Gary S. Cross, *An All-Consuming Century: Why Commercialism Won in Modern America* (New York: Columbia University Press, 2000), 187.

6. Wood, *Retiring Men*, 199.

7. Graebner, *A History of Retirement*, 240, 214.

8. Julian Gumperz, "Pension Funds in an Age of Discontinuity," *Financial Analysts Journal* 26, no. 6 (Nov./Dec. 1970): 24.

9. Graebner, *A History of Retirement*, 219; Lichtenstein, *The Most Dangerous Man in Detroit: Walter Reuther and the Fate of American Labor* (New York: Basic Books, 1995), 282; James E. McNulty, *Decision and Influence Processes in Private Pension Plans* (Homewood, IL: Pension Research Council, Wharton School of Finance and Commerce, University of Pennsylvania, by R. D. Irwin, 1961), 36–37; Sass, *The Promise of Private Pensions*, 86. The tax treatment of private plans encouraged the use of pensions as executive rewards.

10. Ralph and Estelle James, *Hoffa and the Teamsters: A Study of Union Power* (Princeton, NJ: D. Van Nostrand, 1965), 238; Mark B. Smith, *The Equity Culture: The Story of the Global Stock Market* (New York: Farrar, Strauss, and Giroux, 2003), 165.

11. Achenbaum, *Shades of Gray*, 130; Meg Jacobs, *Pocketbook Politics*: Economic Citizenship in Twentieth-Century America (Princeton, NJ: Princeton University Press, 2005), 5–8; Sylvester J. Schieber and John B. Shoven, "The Economics of US Retirement Policy: Current Status and Future Directions," in *Public Policy toward Pensions*, ed. Sylvester J. Schieber and John B. Shoven (Cambridge, MA: MIT Press, 1997), 1–39. Postwar Americans fully absorbed the Keynesian idea that thrift was no longer a virtue; see Robert Collins, *The Business Response to Keynes, 1929–1964* (New York: Columbia University Press, 1982).

12. Grant McConnell, *Private Power and American Democracy* (New York: Alfred A. Knopf, 1966), 296.

13. Examined within a vacuum, ERISA could have put private pensions under federal control. This did not happen, in part because the system was too well entrenched but also because Congress was simultaneously creating securities legislation that defeated this purpose. See Gajewski, "The New York Stock Exchange and the Transformation of Retirement in America," 245–46; and Meg Jacobs and Julian Zelizer, "The Democratic Experiment: New Directions in American Political History," in *The Democratic Experiment: New Directions in American Political History*, ed. Meg Jacobs, Julian E. Zelizer, and William J. Novak (Princeton, NJ: Princeton University Press, 2003), 1–19.

14. Wooten, *The Employee Retirement Income Security Act of 1974*, 77–87. The committee was established in response to recommendations made by the Commission on Money and Credit; Kennedy understood pension issues well because of his time as chair of the Senate Subcommittee on Welfare and Pension Plan Legislation. See Sass, *The Promise of Private Pensions*, 213; and Theodore Schuchat, "Washington Letter," *Pensions & Investments*, October 1971.

15. David L. Altheide, *Creating Reality: How TV News Distorts Events* (Beverly Hills: Sage, 1976), 2–6, 25–27; Jacob K. Javits and Rafael Steinberg, *Javits: The Autobiography of a Public Man* (Boston: Houghton Mifflin, 1981), 380; Wooten, *The Employee Retire-*

ment Income Security Act of 1974, 169. See Ralph Nader and Kate Blackwell, *You and Your Pension: Why You May Never Get a Penny—What Should Be Done about It* (New York: Grossman, 1973); NBC News, "Pensions: The Broken Promise," aired September 12, 1972 (New York: NBC Universal), transcript from NBC Learn, accessed January 17, 2015, https://archives.nbclearn.com/portal/site/k-12/browse/?cuecard=57200accessed.

16. Fran Hawthorne, *Pension Dumping: The Reasons, the Wreckage, the Stakes for Wall Street* (New York: Bloomberg, 2008), 44; P.L. 93–406, 88 Stat. 829 (September 2, 1974). ERISA is codified at §§1001 to 1453 of title 29, United States Code and in §§ 401–15 and 4972–75 of the Internal Revenue Code.

17. Donald T. Critchlow, *The Conservative Ascendancy: How the GOP Right Made Political History* (Cambridge, MA: Harvard University Press, 2007), 78.

18. See Jefferson Cowie, *Stayin' Alive: The 1970s and the Last Days of the Working Class* (New York: New Press, 2010); Bruce J. Schulman, *The Seventies: The Great Shift in American Culture, Society, and Politics* (New York: Free Press, 2001); Bruce J. Schulman and Julian E. Zelizer, eds., *Rightward Bound: Making America Conservative in the 1970s* (Cambridge, MA: Harvard University Press, 2008).

19. Nigel Bowles, *Nixon's Business: Authority and Power in Presidential Politics* (College Station: Texas A&M University Press, 2005), 65; Larry W. DeWitt, Daniel Béland, and Edward D. Berkowitz, *Social Security: A Documentary History* (Washington, DC: CQPress, 2008), 17; John Robert Greene, *The Limits of Power: The Nixon and Ford Administrations* (Bloomington: Indiana University Press, 1992), 31, 70; Sass, *The Promise of Private Pensions*, 214; Melvin Small, *The Presidency of Richard Nixon* (Lawrence: University Press of Kansas, 1999), 156; Wooten, *The Employee Retirement Income Security Act of 1974*, 169.

20. Theodore Schuchat, "Washington Letter"; Wooten, *The Employee Retirement Income Security Act of 1974*, 153–55. For a good explanation of Nixon's convoluted management see Joan Hoff, "The Nixonian System of Corporate Governance," ch. 2 in *Nixon Reconsidered* (New York: Basic Books, 1994).

21. Wooten, *The Employee Retirement Income Security Act of 1974*, 169–76.

22. Wooten, *The Employee Retirement Income Security Act of 1974*, 179–88.

23. Javits and Steinberg, *Javits*, 382–84; Wooten, *The Employee Retirement Income Security Act of 1974*, 191–94; David E. Rosenbaum, "Lloyd Bentsen Dies at 85; Senator Ran with Dukakis," *New York Times*, May 24, 2006, http://www.nytimes.com/2006/05/24/washington/24bentsen.html.

24. Michael A. Genovese, *The Nixon Presidency: Power and Politics in Turbulent Times* (New York: Greenwood, 1990), 64–65; J. R. Greene, *The Limits of Power*, 60; Hoff, "The Nixonian System of Corporate Governance," 51; Allen J. Matusow, *Nixon's Economy: Booms, Busts, Dollars, and Votes* (Lawrence: University Press of Kansas, 1998) 84–87, 108–9; Small, *The Presidency of Richard Nixon*, 37.

25. See the Biographical Directory of the United States Congress, http://bioguide.congress.gov; Legislative History of the Employee Retirement Income Security Act of 1974: Public Law 93–406 (hereafter ERISA History), 325. The other senators were Clifford Hansen (R-WY), a far-right Republican; Wallace Bennett (R-UT), former president

of the National Association of Manufacturers; Peter Dominick (R-CO), a Yale law graduate born in Stamford, CT; and Paul Fannin (R-AZ), a former petroleum distributor and governor of Arizona.

26. ERISA History, 325; Wooten, *The Employee Retirement Income Security Act of 1974*, 198–99.

27. "Washington Letters," *Pension and Welfare News*, 1972–73.

28. ERISA History, 215; Wooten, *The Employee Retirement Income Security Act of 1974*, 196.

29. ERISA History, 217–19; Wooten, *The Employee Retirement Income Security Act of 1974*, 207. Much of the administration bill was incorporated in the Finance bill.

30. Wooten, *The Employee Retirement Income Security Act of 1974*, 78.

31. ERISA History, 1637, 1621–32.

32. Bowles, *Nixon's Business*, 175; Genovese, *The Nixon Presidency*, 74; Hawthorne, *Pension Dumping*, 45; Wooten, *The Employee Retirement Income Security Act of 1974*, 241–45, 261.

33. ERISA History, 1881.

34. "Practically every plan will have to be revised to meet the standards." See Alfred M. Skolnik, "Private Pension Plans, 1950–74," *Social Security Bulletin* 39, no.– 6 (June 1976): 3–17, 5. Most of the new standards required by ERISA took effect January 1, 1976.

35. Bowles, *Nixon's Business*, 164–65.

36. John K. Kittredge, "Group Insurance and Pensions in 1975," *Pension and Welfare News*, December 1968, 36: "Economists quite confidently predict an increasing level of affluence for the American public during the '70s."

37. Dana L. Thomas, "Escalating Pensions: They're a Mounting Threat to Corporate Finances," *Barron's National Business and Financial Weekly* 54, no. 11 (March 18, 1974): 3.

38. Dan McGill, *Preservation of Pension Benefit Rights* (Homewood, IL: Irwin, 1972), 49; Wooten, *The Employee Retirement Income Security Act of 1974*, 257.

39. William M. O'Barr and John M. Conley, with economic analysis by Carolyn Kay Brancato, *Fortune and Folly: The Wealth and Power of Institutional Investing* (Homewood, IL: Business One Irwin, 1992), 99.

40. "Editorially Speaking: Finding Replacement Isn't Trustee's Job," *Pensions & Investments*, March 14, 1977, 12; McGill, *Preservation of Pension Benefit Rights*, 32, 39. The result of this policy was an overfunding of pensions, which led to pension raiding in the late 1990s and early 2000s; see Hawthorne, *Pension Dumping*.

41. Joseph M. LaMotta, "ERISA Is Having a Bad Effect on Traditional Investment Practices," *Pensions & Investments*, July 4, 1977, 19.

42. John K. Kittredge, "Group Insurance and Pensions in 1975," *Pension and Welfare News*, December 1968, 37; Howard M. Koster, "Current Trends in Retirement Plans," *Pension and Welfare News*, May 1968, 26–28; Carolyn S. Winkler and Charles E. Selinske, "The 1970 Study of Industrial Retirement Plans," *Pensions & Investments*, March 1971, 29–34, 54.

43. "The Push for Pension Reform" *Business Week*, March 17, 1973, 46–58; Michael Clowes, "Is ERISA Just an Excuse Plans Use to Terminate?" *Pensions & Investments*, September 12, 1977, 19–20.

44. "A Straitjacket for Pensions?" *Nation's Business* 61, no. 9 (September 1973): 74.

45. William A. Dreher, "Deadline for Private Pensions," *Pension and Welfare News*, September 1971, 16–24.

46. See William G. Shepherd, "Swinging with the New IRA Plans," *Business Week*, June 30, 1975, 92; Ingo Walter, ed., *Deregulating Wall Street: Commercial Bank Penetration of the Corporate Securities Market* (New York: John Wiley & Sons, 1985); "The Bulls Trample May Day Worries," *Business Week*, May 10, 1976, 88; "The Popularity of IRAs and Keoghs," *Pensions & Investments*, January 3, 1977.

47. Norman B. Ture and Barbara A. Fields, *The Future of Private Pension Plans* (Washington DC: American Enterprise Institute for Public Policy Research, 1976), 9, 95.

48. E. Philip Davis, *Pension Funds: Retirement-Income Security, and Capital Markets, an International Perspective* (Oxford: Clarendon Press, 1995), 100; Schieber and Shoven, "The Economics of US Retirement Policy," 12, 18.

49. Investment Company Institute, *2016 Investment Company Fact Book: A Review of Trends and Activities in the U.S. Investment Company Industry*, 151, http://www.ici.org/research/stats/retirement; "The Popularity of IRAs and Keoghs," *Pensions & Investments*, January 3, 1977.

50. Peter Drucker, *Unseen Revolution: How Pension Fund Socialism Came to America* (New York: Harper & Row, 1976). See also Peter F. Drucker, "The Governance of Corporations," in *A Functioning Society: Selections from Sixty-Five Years of Writing on Community, Society, and Polity*, ed. Peter F. Drucker (New Brunswick: Transaction, 2003), 129; O'Barr and Conley with Brancato, *Fortune and Folly*, 22–23; William G. Roy, *Socializing Capital: The Rise of the Large Industrial Corporation in America* (Princeton, NY: Princeton University Press, 1997), 259.

PART III

ENVIRONMENTS

The Larger Setting

13

The Postindustrial City

TRACY NEUMANN

In 1964 Lyndon B. Johnson delivered the commencement address at the University of Michigan. In early May, he had first used the term "Great Society" in a speech at Ohio University, a few hundred miles south of Ann Arbor. Addressing the Michigan graduates three weeks later, Johnson elaborated on his vision for an ambitious set of domestic reforms aimed at eliminating poverty and racial inequality. He predicted that urban populations would double by the end of the century, saying, "In the next 40 years, we must rebuild the entire urban United States."[1] In northeastern and midwestern cities, infrastructure was overloaded, adequate housing was in short supply, the movement of people and businesses to the suburbs had begun in earnest, and industrial decentralization out of manufacturing centers was well underway.[2] "Our society will never be great until our cities are great," Johnson proclaimed. "Today the frontier of imagination and innovation is inside those cities and not beyond their borders. New experiments are already going on." He told the class of 1964 that it was incumbent upon them "to make the American city a place where future generations will come, not only to live but to live the good life."[3]

When Johnson delivered his commencement address, the headline-grabbing rebellions that took place in Watts in 1965 and Newark and Detroit in 1967 were still on the horizon. Cities were losing residents to the suburbs, but not at the alarming rate captured in the 1970 census. The so-called "urban crisis" that preoccupied reporters and pundits later in the decade and through the 1970s had not permeated the national imagination. Neither had the idea of a "post-industrial society," a term coined by sociologist David Riesman in 1959 to describe a society organized around leisure rather than work and popularized by another sociologist, Daniel

Bell, in his 1973 book, *The Coming of Post-Industrial Society*.[4] Yet it was these related factors—racial conflict borne out of centuries of white supremacy, physical decline in aging central cities, and the decentralization of people and jobs across increasingly sprawling metropolitan areas—that Johnson proposed to address through welfare, civil rights, and educational reforms.

Many of the people listening to Johnson's speech in Michigan Stadium likely had firsthand knowledge of the urban problems he described. Ann Arbor is a mere forty-five miles west of Detroit, which by 1964 had been losing industry and residents for nearly two decades. The city was struggling, to be sure, but its decline was not a foregone conclusion. In the mid-1960s, Hudson's, Detroit's iconic department store, still attracted urban and suburban shoppers to the central city. Mies van der Rohe's Lafayette Park, part of an urban renewal project that razed a working-class African American neighborhood to make way for middle-class housing near downtown, had just been completed. With the support of African American voters, handsome young Democrat Jerome Cavanaugh had been elected mayor two years earlier, drawing comparisons to John F. Kennedy. Under Cavanaugh, Detroit became one of Johnson's first Model Cities.

In the ensuing decades, Detroit's future and that of other manufacturing centers looked much less hopeful. Seismic shifts in the geography of production after World War II, in which American manufacturing moved first to the suburbs, then to the American South and Sunbelt, and finally to the Global South, were felt earliest and most intensely in what would eventually come to be known as the Rust Belt—the economically devastated region that stretched across the northern United States from New England to the Midwest. In anticipation of industrial restructuring, entrepreneurial mayors, civic leaders, and businessmen in those places implemented urban redevelopment and economic diversification strategies intended to reinvent cities for a postindustrial economy. They sought to attract corporate headquarters buildings and luxury housing designed to meet the needs of the financial and commercial service sectors, they removed industrial detritus from residential neighborhoods, they built state-of-the-art sports stadiums and convention centers, and they supported culture and leisure activities that would appeal to tourists and suburbanites.[5]

Some places, like Pittsburgh, achieved moderate success in realizing local leaders' visions. Many others, such as Detroit and Youngstown, did not. In Pittsburgh, by the mid-1980s, public subsidies for private development led to the construction of several skyscrapers downtown, a new cultural district, makeovers of working-class neighborhoods, and the conversion of a mill site to an advanced technology center. In Detroit, too, mayors and business elites wanted to address the city's social and economic problems through physical redevelopment. There, however, parts of the city lay in ruin after the 1967 rebellion; the Renaissance Center commercial complex, Henry Ford II's solution to Detroit's woes, was a massive financial failure when it was completed in 1981; and Hudson's shuttered its flagship store in 1983, demolishing the landmark building fourteen years later.

The activities of mayors, urban planners, and civic leaders to remake their cities may seem at first glance to be local issues, the kind of quotidian land use and zoning concerns that are the purview of city halls, not the White House. From the New Deal to the Great Society, however, the federal government took a direct role in shaping urban development through public policies and new agencies devoted to housing, highway construction, and urban renewal. Mortgages underwritten by the Federal Housing Authority spurred suburban development at the expense of central cities by "redlining" urban neighborhoods and classifying them as poor investments based on their racial and ethnic composition. The federal government subsidized highway construction and the renewal of downtrodden residential and commercial districts, which more often than not destroyed African American and working-class white neighborhoods and displaced their residents. Johnson intended his urban-focused Great Society initiatives—most notably Community Action Programs and Model Cities, which sought to foster citizen participation in response to backlash against top-down urban renewal models—to reorient federal policy toward comprehensive planning, social service provision, and rehabilitation rather than the wholesale destruction of distressed neighborhoods.[6]

The Great Society did not end inequality, halt suburban flight, or remake cities as places most Americans associated with the "good life," and the political consensus that had allowed Johnson to push his domestic programs through Congress was short-lived. By 1968, Democrats criticized him for underfunding social programs while Republicans denounced them as too expensive, civil rights leaders demanded a "Marshall Plan for cities," local officials and community groups demanded a more streamlined federal bureaucracy, and urban violence had increased rather than decreased. When Richard M. Nixon replaced Johnson in the White House, he parlayed broad, bipartisan dissatisfaction with the relationship between the federal government and the nation's cities into a mandate to reorient federal urban policy. Gerald R. Ford, Jimmy Carter, and Ronald Reagan followed suit, and the federal government withdrew from urban redevelopment. But even as successive presidential administrations retreated from Johnson's more capacious vision of government intervention in urban problems, the White House pursued formal and de facto urban, economic, and industrial policies that shaped the conditions in which state and local government officials, civic and business leaders, and grassroots activists made decisions that affected the lives of millions of urban residents.

Between 1968 and 1988, federal officials presided over a shift from manufacturing to services and finance as the basis of the national economy, and a related shift from government spending on liberal social programs to a greater reliance on free-market, individualistic approaches to solving social problems. Policymakers emphasized moving residents from declining cities to jobs in booming regions, reduced social welfare spending, and removed or failed to enforce protectionist measures for domestic industry. This federal retrenchment meant that the fate of cities and their residents was increasingly dependent on the good intentions of corporations and local political leaders. The net result was to foster a shift from cities as pluralistic places where skilled, high-wage manufacturing took place alongside commercial and financial enterprises to urban centers that served as entertainment zones, where white and middle-class suburbanites went for a convention or for dinner and a baseball game.

Nixon, New Federalism, and Urban Crisis

In an early presidential address, Nixon reminded Americans that the nation faced "an urban crisis, a social crisis—and, at the same time, a crisis of confidence in the capacity of government to do its job."[7] His speech tapped into popular anxieties about the nature of cities. In the wake of the perceived failure of the Great Society, congressional delegates, academics, and federal, state, and local policymakers from across the political spectrum questioned the government's proper role in urban development. At academic conferences and in the pages of daily newspapers, they debated the causes of and potential solutions to a diffuse "urban crisis." When policymakers first used the phrase in the late 1950s and early 1960s, they meant uncontrolled metropolitan growth. By the late 1960s, however, talk of an urban crisis almost always referred to urban racial uprisings, "white flight" from central cities to suburbs, and deindustrialization.[8] Nixon contended that these urban, social, and government crises were the legacy of three decades of failed social experiments emerging from the New Deal. The government institutions established under Franklin D. Roosevelt and expanded under successive Democratic presidents, he insisted, had become a "bureaucratic monstrosity," whose "entrenched" social programs were no longer relevant. It was time, he declared, for "a New Federalism," which would decentralize authority away from the federal government and return power and money to the "states and the people."[9]

Nixon's New Federalism was premised on a seemingly benign and ultimately popular model of revenue sharing, which he used to direct federal aid away from socially and economically distressed central cities like New York, Detroit, and Pittsburgh and toward constituents in prosperous suburbs and the Sunbelt. Nixon coopted bipartisan support for streamlining administrative requirements for his more ideological project of realigning intergovernmental relations and weakening federal agencies that administered liberal social programs. In 1972, Nixon signed a general revenue sharing bill into law. General revenue sharing returned a portion of taxes collected by the federal government to state and local governments with few restrictions on how the money could be used, which made it popular among state and local officials. For decades, federal agencies had administered social programs through "categorical" grants, which required state and local governments to apply for federal funding for a specific project. The number of these categorical grants had nearly doubled between 1962 and 1967, and Nixon set out to replace them with special revenue sharing "block grants." Block grants transferred federal aid to state and local government for types of activities, such as community development or public health, without reference to a specific project. Compared to categorical grants, block grants had few conditions attached, required little federal oversight, and promised to dramatically reduce the number of applications city and state governments needed to file to receive federal aid in any given year.[10]

Nixon achieved success in two program areas germane to struggling manufacturing centers interested in remaking themselves as postindustrial cities: community development and job training. The 1973 Comprehensive Employment and Training Act (CETA) consolidated a variety of federal employment programs instituted after the Great Depression and provided block grants for public and private job training programs to states and localities. Ford signed Community Development Block Grant (CDBG) legislation into law the week after Nixon's resignation, and it went into effect in January 1975. CDGB supported initiatives ranging from housing and infrastructure to antipoverty programs. The funds went disproportionately to central cities, and federal officials formulated CDBG as a "hold harmless" program, which meant that urban areas had access to the same level of funding they had received through categorical grants. As a result, the program received substantial political support.[11] What the mayors and governors who embraced revenue-sharing may not have anticipated was that Nixon's efforts laid the groundwork for his successors' retreat from urban development.[12]

Though Nixon maintained federal outlays for cities, an anti-urban bias clearly took root during his administration. Nixon disliked the Department of Housing and Urban Development (HUD), and he set out to "streamline" the agency much as he had the federal grant process. He reorganized and decentralized HUD and called for federal personnel cuts in 1971. In January 1973, he hobbled the agency through a moratorium on federal funding for housing and community development programs. Two months later, in a State of the Union message to Congress on Community Development, Nixon declared that the urban crisis was over. "Not long ago we became accustomed to the constant rhetorical drumbeat of the 'crisis of our cities,'" he said. "Many of these problems still persist, but I believe we have made sufficient progress in recent years that fears of doom are no longer justified."[13]

Nixon's moratorium on HUD programs led to a new kind of urban program: housing vouchers. One of the most pressing policy debates of the 1970s was about whether to aid "people" or "places"—to provide direct federal funding to individuals or to help people in need indirectly by funding struggling cities. Proponents of "people-based" aid assumed that individuals were the root of urban problems, and their arguments reflected a conservative, market-based approach to service provision; proponents of "place-based" aid saw political and economic institutions and practices as the cause of the urban crisis and wanted to combat it with a liberal, government-based approach.[14] Nixon's block grants provided place-based aid, but his freeze on funding for public housing projects in favor of providing Section 8 vouchers to citizens who qualified for housing assistance, which could then be used as a subsidy for market-rate housing, was a seminal example of people-based aid. Under the new program, the federal government stopped constructing public housing and instead provided individuals who qualified for aid with a voucher that represented the difference between what the federal government determined they could afford to pay and "fair market" rent in their area.[15] When Nixon left office, the debate between aiding people versus aiding places remained unsettled, but the institutions and mechanisms through which the federal government provided aid had been completely overhauled to direct federal aid away from the declining Northeast and Midwest and toward the booming Sunbelt.

Self-Help Urbanism

At the same time Nixon set about renegotiating the relationship between the federal government, state houses, and the nation's cities, a powerful "neighborhoodism" was emerging to challenge city and federal government control over urban life. Disparate groups of local activists—African Americans who came of age with the Black Power movement, young liberals who worked with Great Society programs, intellectuals on the left such as urbanists Jane Jacobs and William Whyte, and white-collar gentrifiers—formed a loose neighborhood movement. Its members rejected the centralized planning and technocratic expertise typical of New Deal liberalism, trusting neither the government nor corporations. Politicians with roots in the neighborhood movement formed coalitions among white-collar professionals, blue-collar white ethnics, and black activists. Neighborhoodism also ruled in Washington, as federal policy shifted toward volunteerism, individual choice, local control, and market-driven reform under Carter.[16]

With urban constituencies irate over nearly a decade of federal neglect, the formulation of a national urban policy to support socially and fiscally distressed cities had featured prominently in Carter's campaign promises to mayors and civil rights groups. Those promises were at odds with a worldview that led Carter to distrust "special interests" and express concern for the "forgotten" white middle class. After taking office, Carter announced that he would develop the nation's first comprehensive urban policy even as he retreated from expansive liberal social programs, opposed increased federal urban spending, and promoted the capacity of the private sector (including both for-profit and nonprofit entities), rather than the government, to address urban problems.[17]

Carter's much-anticipated national urban policy, delivered to Congress in a 1978 report, *A New Partnership to Conserve America's Communities*, did not initiate major new federal programs or substantially increase funding levels for existing urban programs. His first year in office, he had introduced Urban Development Action Grants (UDAGs) to stimulate private-sector urban redevelopment and instituted a countercyclical assistance program as part of an economic stimulus package to provide federal aid to states and localities hit particularly hard by the recession. His administration also transferred a greater share of CDBG funds to northeastern and midwestern cities. In general, however, Carter's approach toward cities generally and UDAGs in particular were an amplification of Nixon's New Federalism.[18]

Carter wanted his urban policy to emphasize public-private partnerships, and he supported programs that encouraged self-help, voluntarism, and incentives for private sector activity, which were less of a political liability in the suburbs and the Sunbelt than increased direct federal expenditures in cities. His policy advisors, like Nixon's, were divided over people- versus place-based aid. When it was released, Carter's urban policy unequivocally signaled to mayors that the national government would no longer provide large federal outlays to reverse urban decline or temper the effects of industrial restructuring but neither would it entirely abandon cities. Cities were "more than just simply centers of jobs, communications and commerce," *A New Partnership* reminded its readers. They were also "centers of learning, centers of culture, centers of social services."[19] It was this latter—postindustrial—assemblage of services that the Carter administration wanted to emphasize.

The most tangible outcomes of the national urban policy, four executive orders issued in 1978, directed federal agencies to locate facilities in urban areas, emphasize procurement set-asides in areas with high unemployment, consider the impact of programs on urban areas, and establish an interagency council to implement federal urban policy. The legislative package attached to *A New Partnership* failed to gain traction because liberal Democrats were unhappy about limits to federal oversight, because of bipartisan political opposition to targeting aid to distressed cities, and because of concern over the financial implications of the proposed programs in a time of stagflation and tax revolts. With his focus more fully on foreign policy and the weak economy, Carter did not push Congress to support the proposed legislation, and the impact of his national urban policy was negligible.[20] John Gunther, the executive director of the U.S. Conference of Mayors, complained that the federal budget was "based on economic and social principles which are a disappointment to the cities." Mayors may have been displeased, but they seemed to understand the new urban policy landscape: in 1978, they had pressed Carter to add $11.3 billion to the federal budget for new urban and job programs; in 1979, they asked for neither new programs nor money.[21]

If big-city mayors were disappointed with the national urban policy, they were incensed by the recommendations of what turned out to be Carter's last urban-related initiative. The year after he delivered *A New Partnership*, Carter appointed a Presidential Commission for a National Agenda for the Eighties to offer policy recommendations for what he likely hoped would be his second term. Chaired by former Columbia University president William McGill, the commission's recommendations were profoundly anti-urban and recommended intensifying policies that accelerated the decline of northern cities. McGill established nine thematic panels, including one on "policies and prospects for metropolitan and non-metropolitan America." Agricultural economist Charles Bishop chaired the subcommittee created to study "Urban America in the Eighties," a panel that also included League of Women Voters president Ruth J. Hinerfeld, CEOs Frank Pace Jr. and Robert S. Benson, and University of Chicago urban policy professor Pastora San Juan Cafferty. All of the commissioners except Cafferty held MBAs and had long corporate resumes.

The panel's report, *Urban America in the Eighties: Perspectives and Prospects*, drew on Daniel Bell's research to determine that the United States was "on a trajectory toward an increasingly consumer-oriented, postindustrial society where employment growth rates in service sectors are higher than those in the manufacturing sectors." In fact, Carter had appointed Bell as a member of the McGill Commission, though he did not sit on the urban panel. The report's first section was subtitled, "The Emergence of Postindustrial Urban America," a fitting introduction to a series of recommendations that federal aid should be used to ease the transition to a new economy rather than attempt to reverse market forces. Panelists urged Carter to create programs that accelerated, rather than resisted, the "transformation" of the national economy from manufacturing to service- and finance-sector employment, noting at the outset that "this report seeks to underscore the long-term inevitability and desirability of this transformation."[22]

For the urban panel, the future lay not in old industrial centers, ravaged by decades of systematic plant closures and disinvestment, but in the "new" cities of the South and Southwest. To panelists, the "industrial heartland" had reached maturity in the early twentieth century and, in 1980, represented nothing more than "bricks-and-mortar snapshots of a bygone era." If the federal government thought about urban revitalization as an "attempt to restore our older industrial cities and regions to the influential positions they have held through the industrial era," they cautioned, "then urban revitalization will surely fail." Northeastern and midwestern manufacturing centers had been damaged beyond repair by industrial restructuring, racial conflict, and fiscal crises, the panel suggested, and to successfully revitalize cities the nation should strive "to assist all urban centers to assume newer, more specialized social and economic roles . . . [as] specialized service and consumption centers within larger urban economic systems."[23] As they saw it, the only practical course of action was to make labor as mobile as capital and encourage workers to follow industry as it relocated to more "geographically desirable" areas.[24]

The panelists clearly favored people-based aid, writing that while both people and places suffered as the United States became a postindustrial society, "the primary responsibility of the federal government is to assist people, and to do so as directly as possible." They treated industry and labor as mobile, albeit unequally so, and equated any expansion of U.S. industry—inside or outside of national borders—with national economic health. While it was necessary to enforce a "measure of social responsibility" by corporations, the panelists suggested, industry must remain geographically unfettered to "retain as much flexibility as possible for responding to shifting national and international economic crosscurrents."[25] A "flexible" framework reinforced long-term federal policies that directed public resources to the Sunbelt and suburbs and promoted decentralization and deindustrialization. Nearly four decades of de facto federal urban and regional development policy, from federal mortgage subsidies to revenue sharing programs, had privileged the suburbs over cities, and the South and West over the North and East. The panelists suggested that the national economy would suffer if "the newly prospering regions that historically have been economically depressed are defined as inimical to historically prosperous regions that are now experiencing relative economic decline."[26]

Dismissing efforts to reverse industrial or physical decline as a nostalgic "attempt to preserve [cities] under glass," McGill Commission staffer Donald Hicks said that "the physical forms of the older urban centers in this nation and in the Western world generally were laid down in the 19th century" and not suited to twentieth-century social and economic organization. Instead, Hicks reported that the panel believed federal officials should try to "ameliorate the consequences" of economic restructuring on local governments and laid-off manufacturing workers.[27] The verdict in the final report that "public policy should seek to loosen the tie between distressed people and distressed places just as a variety of technological developments loosened the ties between industry and its traditional urban location" reflected a decisive shift to people-based policies over place-based policies.[28]

By 1980, the decline of basic industry in northeastern and midwestern manufacturing centers had been underway for at least twenty years, leaving many urban economies near collapse. Northeastern and midwestern mayors were infuriated by the recommendations: New York deputy mayor Nathan Leventhal told the *New York Times* that Mayor Ed Koch's reaction to the report was "unprintable." Leventhal, more measured than Koch, called the report's recommendations "dumb" and "destructive."[29] Carter, all but out of office by the time McGill delivered the final report in December 1980, immediately tried to distance himself from the recommendations of the commission he had appointed two years earlier. He thanked the commissioners for their service but chided, "We cannot abandon our older urban areas."[30] Despite Carter's move away from the urban policy recommendations, the McGill Commission's deliberations clearly reflected his administration's agenda of decentralized government, increased privatization, and "self-help."

The Reagan Revolution

Programs established under Nixon and Carter, as well as a shift in national policy directions and public discourse about cities in the 1970s, left Reagan well positioned to implement his more ideologically driven agenda. For Nixon, a new federalism meant reduced federal oversight and an increased role in program management for local elected officials, in part stemming from a desire to transfer blame for urban problems away from the federal government. Carter, too, had been interested in community control, but he was not terribly concerned with reducing federal oversight of grant funding; his primary goal was to transfer the financial burden of urban problems away from the federal government. Reagan, by contrast, pursued policies that forced state and local governments to shoulder both the moral and fiscal responsibility for urban problems.

Nixon and Carter had pragmatically reoriented national urban policy so that the private sector, civic groups, and lower levels of government carried it out. In doing so, they laid the foundation for Reagan's more ideologically driven version of New Federalism, which contracted the welfare state, changed federal tax policy to favor large corporations over small businesses and the more affluent over the disadvantaged, further decentralized federal programs, and reduced federal regulation of business. Nixon and Carter had both responded to municipal fiscal distress in times of recession by providing some type of countercyclical aid. During the 1981–83 recession, the Reagan administration refused to enact similar measures to help struggling local governments. For all practical purposes, Reagan settled the debate over people-based versus place-based aid by eliminating both and insisting that there was no compelling evidence that economic development programs actually created jobs or new capital investment. He also mounted an attack on federal urban programs, with catastrophic results for old manufacturing centers.[31]

In his first inaugural speech, Reagan announced his intention "to curb the size and influence of the Federal establishment and to demand recognition of the distinction between the powers granted to the Federal Government and those reserved to the States or to the people" through a "new" New Federalism.[32] Through the privatization of public programs and institutions, and the offloading of oversight and financing of urban programs to state and local governments, Reagan sought to eliminate any federal urban development initiatives that did not marshal public resources in support of private enterprise. Where mayors had widely supported Nixon's New Federalism and the block grants on which it was premised, they strongly criticized Reagan's version. Detroit mayor Coleman A. Young dismissed as "simplistic and naïve" Reagan's claims that the private sector and civic organizations would "pick up the responsibilities abdicated by the Federal Government," and New York's Ed Koch charged that Reagan had "set forth a litany of destructive actions and call[ed] it an urban policy."[33]

Reagan had eliminated Nixon's popular general revenue sharing program and Carter's UDAGs as expediently as possible, but block grants were of paramount significance to his version of New Federalism. His Omnibus Budget Reconciliation Act of 1981 eased federal restrictions on education and urban programs and established or revised block grants for public health, social services, education, and community development. Under Reagan, block grant funds were allocated to state governments with virtually no federal oversight. New regulations for CDBGs shifted funds away from the neediest communities and slashed federal funding by a quarter. Reagan substantially cut employment and training programs by replacing CETA with the more restrictive and poorly funded Jobs Training Partnership Act in 1982. He also reversed Carter's targeting and procurement policies, which required that federal contractors and facilities be located in urban areas whenever feasible, by instituting defense contracting procedures that delivered federal outlays to the suburbs, small cities, and the South and Southwest. Between 1980 and 1985, aid to cities like Detroit, St. Louis, and Pittsburgh, which the federal government classified as "distressed," fell by 18 percent, while aid increased by 23 percent in areas it classified as "healthy." Reagan's efforts did not go entirely unchallenged by Democrats (particularly in the House of Representatives), but they proved unable to muster a compelling case for maintaining existing programs.[34]

The Reagan administration also threw its support behind legislation for Enterprise Zones, modeled on a similar program Margaret Thatcher introduced in Britain in 1979, which would have provided tax abatements and other incentives for private-sector economic development in impoverished areas. Enterprise Zones required no federal appropriations, and Reagan described them as "the direct opposite" of liberal social programs like Model Cities, which relied heavily on federal subsidies to distressed cities. "The Enterprise Zone concept is based on utilizing the market to solve urban problems, relying primarily on private sector institutions," Reagan noted in a message to Congress. "The idea is to create a productive, free market environment in economically depressed areas by reducing taxes, regulations and other government burdens on economic activity."[35]

The proposal Reagan supported never made it out of committee, but by 1985, at least forty states had implemented enterprise zone legislation in anticipation that Reagan would succeed in pushing through a federal version. In the wake of the Enterprise Zone failure, Reagan pursued no new federal urban or economic development programs for the remainder of his presidency.[36] For many cities in the emerging Rust Belt, the shift was catastrophic. Chicago Mayor Harold Washington accused Reagan of waging a "war on the cities" and scoffed at the idea that local taxes or the private sector would compensate for the loss of federal funding. "How can there be a public-private partnership when we have nothing to bring to the table?" he asked.[37]

Washington's antipathy toward Reagan underscored the fact that neither city nor state governments were financially or administratively prepared to accommodate the loss of federal aid to cities between the late 1970s and the end of the 1980s. In 1978, federal funds as a percentage of municipal revenue reached a high of approximately 17 percent; that percentage declined steadily across the 1980s, with federal funds accounting for less than 5 percent of municipal revenue by 1992. Between 1981 and 1993, the federal government cut CDBG funding by 36.5 percent, eliminated general revenue sharing and UDAGs at a combined loss of $8.6 billion in federal aid to cities, cut mass transit funds by 49 percent, and slashed federal aid for job training programs by 71 percent. State governments found themselves unable to meet their increased financial responsibilities for urban development: state aid to local governments as a proportion of local revenues decreased from 25 percent to 21 percent of local revenues between 1977 and 1992. HUD's budget dropped from more than $30 billion in 1980 to around $10 billion in 1988.[38]

Conclusion: The Rise of Entrepreneurial Cities

As the American economy became increasingly oriented around service and finance industries and less reliant on manufacturing—as it became "postindustrial"—once-powerful industrial centers like Detroit, Pittsburgh, Cleveland, and Baltimore lost their economic engines. After 1968, at all levels of government and in the academy, the private sector, and the nonprofit world, a loose consensus took shape around the idea that local governments and the free market were best equipped to confront urban problems. This broad agreement led to incremental decentralization, devolution, and privatization. In other words, the fate of its cities was no longer the responsibility of the federal government. The economic malaise of the 1970s accelerated corporate disinvestment in American manufacturing and by the 1980s had contributed to fiscal crises in many American cities. Local governments and workers were left to their own devices, as the states struggled, after decades of being cut out of urban policy, to come up with plans to deal with distress more or less overnight.

States repurposed economic development policy as urban policy by implementing fiscal strategies to make their metropolitan areas appealing as business locations and as residences for executives. They assumed economic development functions previously carried out by the federal government by acting as development banks to provide direct subsidies or industrial development bonds to encourage corporations to relocate to or expand in their state. State governments also sponsored research and development, and at least twelve states established venture capital funds. State-level personal tax reductions, discretionary business tax incentives, changes in corporate and banking regulations, enterprise zones, educational and job training programs, and technology development programs served dual functions as economic stimuli and physical redevelopment tools.[39]

Public-private partnerships, and particularly government-industry-university partnerships, became governors' and legislators' answer to what they understood to be an overreliance on manufacturing industries; public-private partnerships were also the preferred mechanism for shifting public funds into technology-based sectors. Business elites found the public-private partnership model politically palatable because it encouraged state governments to cater to business interests within their state. Business leaders were less concerned about the regulatory reach of state governments than with that of the national government, and in what one critic described as a "mercantilist system of competing states," subsidies to businesses supplanted both people- and place-based aid.[40]

In 1964, when Lyndon Johnson called on University of Michigan students to make American cities places to live "the good life," he unveiled an ambitious (if underfunded) set of federal programs to help them do so. His successors, however, rejected large-scale federal subsidies for declining central cities. Faced with federal aid reductions, cash-strapped local governments were increasingly unable to provide basic services or make much-needed infrastructure improvements. Combined with plant closures and crises in the manufacturing sector, the federal government's withdrawal from funding and regulating urban development between Nixon and Reagan spurred municipalities to become "entrepreneurial" by offering their own incentives to the private sector, particularly for job-creating enterprises and new construction. These incentives included revenue bonds, tax abatement, tax increment financing, and lease financing, as well as an increasing redirection of CDBG funds toward attracting private investment.[41] Economic development initiatives that privileged advanced technology, medical complexes, and leisure, culture, and tourism opened up new, decentralized concentrations of economic activity, new areas for residential development, and new uses for sites once devoted to heavy industry. As manufacturing centers were transformed into postindustrial cities, they came to be characterized by hollowed-out manufacturing zones, the gentrification of blue-collar neighborhoods, and the perpetual rebuilding of commercial, leisure, and entertainment districts—a transformation that was in no small part the result of the urban policies of American presidents between the late 1960s and mid-1980s.

Notes

1. Lyndon B. Johnson, "Remarks at the University of Michigan," May 22, 1964, American Presidency Project, http://www.presidency.ucsb.edu.

2. Barry Bluestone and Bennett Harrison, *The Deindustrialization of America: Plant Closings, Community Abandonment, and the Dismantling of Basic Industries* (New York: Basic Books, 1982); Jefferson R. Cowie, *Capital Moves: RCA's Seventy-Year Quest for Cheap Labor* (Ithaca: Cornell University Press, 1999); Allen Dieterich-Ward, *Beyond Rust: Metropolitan Pittsburgh and the Fate of Industrial America* (Philadelphia: University of Pennsylvania Press, 2015); Howard Gillette, *Camden after the Fall: Decline and Renewal in a Post-Industrial City* (Philadelphia: University of Pennsylvania Press, 2005); Andrew R. Highsmith, *Demolition Means Progress: Flint, Michigan, and the Fate of the American Metropolis* (Chicago: University of Chicago Press, 2015); Guian A. McKee, *The Problem of Jobs: Liberalism, Race, and Deindustrialization in Philadelphia* (Chicago: University of Chicago Press, 2008); Thomas J. Sugrue, *The Origins of the Urban Crisis: Race and Inequality in Postwar Detroit* (Princeton: Princeton University Press, 1996).

3. Johnson, "Remarks at the University of Michigan."

4. Daniel Bell, *The Coming of Post-Industrial Society: A Venture in Social Forecasting* (New York: Basic Books, 1976). On the genesis of the term "postindustrial society," see Howard Brick, "Optimism of the Mind: Imagining Postindustrial Society in the 1960s and 1970s," *American Quarterly* 44, no. 3 (September 1992): 348.

5. Tracy Neumann, *Remaking the Rust Belt: The Postindustrial Transformation of North America* (Philadelphia: University of Pennsylvania Press, 2016).

6. On federal urban policy since 1945, see Roger Biles, *The Fate of Cities: Urban America and the Federal Government, 1945–2000* (Lawrence: University Press of Kansas, 2011).

7. Richard Nixon, "Address to the Nation on Domestic Programs," August 8, 1969, American Presidency Project, http://www.presidency.ucsb.edu.

8. On the urban crisis, see especially Robert A. Beauregard, *Voices of Decline: The Postwar Fate of U.S. Cities* (New York: Routledge, 2003); and Sugrue, *The Origins of the Urban Crisis.*

9. Richard Nixon, "Address to the Nation on Domestic Programs."

10. William R. Barnes, "Beyond Federal Urban Policy," *Urban Affairs Review* 40, no. 5 (May 2005): 581; Wendell E. Pritchett, "Which Urban Crisis? Regionalism, Race, and Urban Policy, 1960–1974," *Journal of Urban History* 34, no. 2 (January 2008): 279. On the development of block grants, see Timothy J. Conlan, "The Politics of Federal Block Grants: From Nixon to Reagan," *Political Science Quarterly* 99, no. 2 (Summer 1984): 247–70.

11. Conlan, "The Politics of Federal Block Grants."

12. For a detailed history of Community Development Block Grants, see Daniel Amsterdam's chapter in this volume.

13. Richard Nixon, "State of the Union Message to the Congress on Community Development," March 8, 1973, American Presidency Project, http://www.presidency.ucsb.edu.

14. On people- versus place-based aid, see Roger Bolton, "'Place Prosperity VS. People Prosperity' Revisited: An Old Issue with a New Angle," *Urban Studies* 29, no. 2 (1992): 185–203.

15. Biles, *The Fate of Cities*, 191.

16. Tracy Neumann, "Privatization, Devolution, and Jimmy Carter's National Urban Policy," *Journal of Urban History* 40, no. 2 (March 1, 2014): 283–300; Suleiman Osman, "The Decade of the Neighborhood," in *Rightward Bound: Making America Conservative in the 1970s*, ed. Bruce J. Schulman and Julian E. Zelizer (Cambridge, MA: Harvard University Press, 2008), 106–27.

17. On Carter's campaign, governing style, and worldview, see Jefferson R. Cowie, *Stayin' Alive: The 1970s and the Last Days of the Working Class* (New York: New Press, 2010); Laura Kalman, *Right Star Rising: A New Politics, 1974–1980* (New York: W.W. Norton, 2010); Judith Stein, *Pivotal Decade: How the United States Traded Factories for Finance in the Seventies* (New Haven, CT: Yale University Press, 2010); Thomas J. Sugrue, "Carter's Urban Policy Crisis," in *The Carter Presidency: Policy Choices in the Post-New Deal Era*, ed. Gary M. Fink and Hugh Davis Graham (Lawrence: University Press of Kansas, 1998), 137–57.

18. Biles, *The Fate of Cities*, 237; Sugrue, "Carter's Urban Policy Crisis," 149–50.

19. President's Urban and Regional Policy Group, *A New Partnership to Conserve America's Communities: A National Urban Policy* (Washington, DC: Department of Housing and Community Development, 1978), 1.

20. Biles, *The Fate of Cities*, 237; Stuart Meck and Rebecca Retzlaff, "President Jimmy Carter's Urban Policy: A Reconstruction and an Appraisal," *Journal of Planning History* 11 (August 2012): 257.

21. Susanna McBee, "Mayors Criticize Carter for Retreat on Urban Aid," *Washington Post,* January 25, 1979.

22. Panel on Policies and Prospects for Metropolitan and Nonmetropolitan America, *Urban America in the Eighties: Perspectives and Prospects* (Washington: President's Commission for a National Agenda for the Eighties, 1980), 3.

23. Panel on Policies and Prospects for Metropolitan and Nonmetropolitan America, *Urban America in the Eighties*, 4, 13.

24. Panel on Policies and Prospects for Metropolitan and Nonmetropolitan America, *Urban America in the Eighties*, 24.

25. Panel on Policies and Prospects for Metropolitan and Nonmetropolitan America, *Urban America in the Eighties*, 3–4.

26. Panel on Policies and Prospects for Metropolitan and Nonmetropolitan America, *Urban America in the Eighties*, 99–100.

27. Testimony of Donald A. Hicks before the Subcommittee on Intergovernmental Relations, February 26, 1981, p. 3, 24, box 11, folder Panel 5 Met/Nonmet Subcommittee Hearing 2/26/81, Records of the National Commission on an Agenda for the Eighties, RG 220, Jimmy Carter Library and Museum, Atlanta, GA.

28. Panel on Policies and Prospects for Metropolitan and Nonmetropolitan America, *Urban America in the Eighties*, 62.

29. Robert Pear, "Panel on Goals Proposes U.S. Aid for Migration to Sunbelt," *New York Times*, December 27, 1980; Clyde Haberman, "Koch's Office Criticizes the Idea of U.S. Aid in Moves to Sun Belt," *New York Times*, December 29, 1980.

30. Jimmy Carter, "President's Commission for a National Agenda for the Eighties Statement on Receiving the Commission's Final Report," January 16, 1981.

31. Richard Child Hill, "Market, State, and Community National Urban Policy in the 1980s," *Urban Affairs Review* 19, no. 1 (September 1, 1983): 7; Harold Wolman, "The Reagan Urban Policy and Its Impacts," *Urban Affairs Quarterly* 21, no. 3 (March 1986): 328.

32. Ronald Reagan, "Inaugural Address," January 20, 1981, American Presidency Project, http://www.presidency.ucsb.edu.

33. Robert Pear, "Mayors Call Reagan Urban Policy an 'Abdication' of Responsibility," *New York Times*, July 14, 1982.

34. F. J. James, "President Carter's Comprehensive National Urban Policy: Achievements and Lessons Learned," *Environment and Planning C: Government and Policy* 8 (1990): 38; Norman Fainstein and Susan S. Fainstein, "The Ambivalent State: Economic Development Policy in the U.S. Federal System under the Reagan Administration," *Urban Affairs Review* 25, no. 1 (1989): 37; James, "Carter's Comprehensive National Urban Policy," 38; Wolman, "The Reagan Urban Policy and Its Impacts," 328.

35. Ronald Reagan, "Message to the Congress Transmitting Proposed Enterprise Zone Legislation," March 23, 1982, American Presidency Project, http://www.presidency.ucsb.edu.

36. Biles, *The Fate of Cities*, 325–30; Karen Mossberger, *The Politics of Ideas and the Spread of Enterprise Zones* (Washington, D.C.: Georgetown University Press, 2000).

37. Steven V. Roberts, "Budget Panel, Visiting Chicago, Hears Complaints," *New York Times*, February 11, 1986.

38. Barnes, "Beyond Federal Urban Policy," 582; Biles, *The Fate of Cities*, 260–64; Peter K. Eisinger, "City Politics in an Era of Federal Devolution," *Urban Affairs Review* 33, no. 3 (1998): 310–11.

39. Peter K. Eisinger, *The Rise of the Entrepreneurial State: State and Local Economic Development Policy in the United States* (Madison: University of Wisconsin Press, 1988); Jon C. Teaford, *The Rise of the States: Evolution of American State Government* (Baltimore: Johns Hopkins University Press, 2002).

40. Fainstein and Fainstein, "The Ambivalent State," 55–56, 59.

41. David Harvey, "From Managerialism to Entrepreneurialism: The Transformation in Urban Governance in Late Capitalism," *Geografiska Annaler. Series B, Human Geography* 71, no. 1 (1989): 3.

14

The President, Congress, and Federal Social Policy in the 1970s

DANIEL AMSTERDAM

Federal legislation passed in the 1970s shaped American social policy for years to come. Community Development Block Grants, implemented in 1974, became the federal government's main mechanism for funding urban redevelopment. Facets of the Section 8 subsidized housing program, adopted in the same year, remain central to federal housing policy. Supplemental Security Income, which provides cash assistance to the disabled and elderly poor, was also created in 1974. A year later, President Gerald R. Ford signed the Education for All Handicapped Children Act, requiring public schools that receive federal aid to provide equal educational access to disabled students. Today, the Earned Income Tax Credit is the largest federal program offering cash benefits to Americans living in poverty. It, too, was created in the 1970s. The Community Reinvestment Act of 1977 helped make more loans available to minority borrowers than ever before—an attempt to address years of discriminatory lending in the housing market. Meanwhile, the minimum wage rose, and social programs like food stamps expanded dramatically.

With important exceptions, historical overviews of the 1970s either ignore or pay only passing attention to most of these programs. Instead, their authors generally pursue different agendas when it comes to domestic politics and policy, especially tracing conservatism's rise and documenting the economy's drift away from manufacturing and toward finance and service. The titles and subtitles of many recent books on the 1970s suggest these priorities: "Rightward Bound," "Right Star Rising," "The Fall of Nixon and the Rise of Reagan," "The Crisis of the 1970s and the Rise of the Populist Right," "How the United States Traded Factories for Finance," and "The Last Days of the Working Class," meaning, for the most part, a manufacturing-based working class.[1]

There is no doubt that various dynamics in the 1970s helped provoke a "great shift" in American politics—to quote the subtitle of yet another book about the decade.[2] But fully grasping the importance of the era demands more than unearthing how the 1970s helped usher in the comparatively conservative, pro-market, and finance- and service-driven age that followed. The years separating Lyndon B. Johnson's presidency from Ronald W. Reagan's also saw the continuation, extension, and elaboration of important trends that had gained strength in earlier years, including the attempt to use federal government programs to address many of modern capitalism's most glaring shortcomings—from poverty and urban blight to the private market's failure to provide affordable housing—efforts that had, of course, been on the front burner of American politics during Johnson's presidency.

Historians have been more apt to note how Richard M. Nixon grappled with these issues. But too often they have given short shrift to the role that congressional Democrats played in reshaping federal social policy during the Nixon years. Democrats enjoyed majorities in both houses of Congress throughout Nixon's term, as they would throughout the 1970s. Historians often portray Nixon's "New Federalism"—which sought to reorder the relationship between federal, state, and local governments—as the first sally in a conservative push to devolve public responsibility away from Washington and toward statehouses and city halls, a cause Reagan later championed. Yet as political scientists have underscored, major social policies associated with Nixon's New Federalism grew from bipartisan frustrations with the status quo and passed only due to liberal, Democratic support in Congress. At the same time, in another pattern that political scientists have highlighted more than historians, Nixon's New Federalism did not focus exclusively on devolution. Rather, Nixon sought to centralize certain policies in Washington, such as public assistance to the poor, as part of his New Federalism. As these examples begin to suggest, the political history of the 1970s has yet to benefit fully from the cross-fertilization of scholarship among political scientists, historical sociologists, and historians that has become the hallmark of fields like policy history and the study of government development more generally in recent years. Meanwhile, other initiatives frequently associated with American social policy's conservative drift under Nixon, such as the

Section 8 housing program, originally included often forgotten initiatives, such as funding to construct new subsidized housing, and also grew from bipartisan trends.[3]

Issues like poverty, housing, and urban development remained in the foreground of Washington politics well into the Jimmy Carter years. Similar to facets of Nixon's, Carter's approach to social policy is sometimes depicted as presaging Reagan's, especially when it comes to urban America, but this, too, is inaccurate. The Carter administration made adjustments to existing federal programs to better serve cities and expanded a number of other social programs in ways that ran sharply against Reagan's ideals. In fact, Carter embraced a measure that even Johnson had rejected: funding the first federal jobs program since the New Deal. Carter cut appropriations to many social programs as his presidency progressed. But he did so largely amid a broader fight against inflation, not necessarily because he opposed them outright, as Reagan did.[4]

To be sure, there were aspects of Reagan's and his successors' approaches to governance that built on earlier patterns. But fully appreciating the 1970's long-term impact on the development of American social policy—and, in turn, how the decade shaped American government more generally—demands paying heed to these other patterns as well.

The Nixon and Ford Years

By the time Richard Nixon assumed the presidency in January 1969, a number of developments that would reshape federal social policy over the next decade were already in full swing. First, even among liberal Democrats, frustration was growing with the sheer number of social initiatives and related mandates that federal policymakers had created during the 1960s. Second, displeasure with the existing system of "welfare"—specifically cash assistance to poor families—had become widespread. Finally, both Democrats and Republicans had already begun to advocate with new fervor public-private partnership as a mode of program delivery in major social policy areas such as subsidized housing.

Much has been made of how Nixon's "New Federalism" helped encourage the devolution of American social policy from the federal to the state and local levels in areas like community development and job training. Importantly, however, Nixon's vision dovetailed with sentiments that transcended party loyalties. During the Johnson years, complaints among

Democrats about the structure of the Great Society, including the War on Poverty, quickly spread. Mayors, governors, federal agencies, and leading White House officials expressed displeasure at the inefficiency and inflexibility of the War on Poverty's and Great Society's emphasis on creating new "categorical" programs—in other words, policies that offered federal funding only for specific purposes. One local official, for instance, complained that his city had "become a battleground among federal Cabinet agencies." At the federal level, top officials in the Budget Bureau and the Government Accounting Office, as well as entities focused on intergovernmental relations, all called for consolidating and increasing flexibility in a variety of existing federal social programs. When it came to job training initiatives, for instance, few in the federal bureaucracy saw merit in the status quo, which entailed thirteen federal agencies negotiating "30,000 separate contracts with 10,000 local governments and community organizations." Leading figures in the Johnson administration, like budget director Charles L. Schultze and onetime head of the Council of Economic Advisers Walter W. Heller, called for streamlining federal programs and giving officials on the ground greater discretion in spending federal funds. Well before leaving office, Johnson himself embraced such a strategy in certain policy areas. In 1966, for instance, Johnson and Congress approved legislation that combined several existing categorical health initiatives into a single block grant. Johnson took similar steps in the realm of criminal justice two years later. When Johnson's tenure came to a close, members of his administration were considering reshaping a number of other policy areas through block grants as well.[5]

This relatively broad base of support for block grants—which above all aimed to increase the efficiency of the federal bureaucracy and give state and local officials greater flexibility in spending federal funds—was essential to their adoption during the Nixon years. Nixon and Congress began negotiating over early incarnations of what would become the two main block grants focused on social policy created under Nixon—the Comprehensive Employment and Training Act and Community Development Block Grants—during Nixon's first term. Among other changes, the Comprehensive Employment and Training Act bundled together funding for a number of existing job training and related federal manpower programs. Community Development Block Grants did much the same for federal urban and community redevelopment initiatives. Neither passed until after Nixon's reelection in 1972 but not due to differences between

Democrats in Congress and the White House over block grants per se. To be sure, there were congressional Democrats who resisted block grant legislation because they opposed ending categorical programs that they especially supported. When it came to job-training policy, such resistance eventually led to the adoption of "hybrid" legislation that created new block grants while retaining certain categorical programs. Even so, the failure of both the community development and manpower block grants to pass earlier in Nixon's presidency was primarily rooted in other dynamics. In the case of the federal job training block grant that eventually became the Comprehensive Employment and Training Act, liberal Democrats attempted to include a new federal public employment program that Nixon initially refused to approve. Similarly, conflicts between the White House and Congress over funding formulas especially delayed the adoption of Community Development Block Grants, not Democratic opposition to the block grant idea in itself. Indeed, the legislation that created Community Development Block Grants passed in the House 351 to 25 and in the Senate 76 to 11. In the end, congressional Democrats coalesced around the Community Development Block Grant legislation despite the fact the bill reduced appropriations to American cities, especially in the Rust Belt, while redirecting control over federal funds away from community groups toward elected officials. Democrats and Republicans alike shared responsibility for these shifts. The Comprehensive Employment and Training Act passed by similarly lopsided majorities.[6]

Meanwhile, Nixon's "New Federalism" focused on more than moving power away from Washington toward statehouses and city halls. Nixon also envisioned centralizing certain policy areas in Washington in new ways. When it came to social policy, Nixon especially sought to centralize and consolidate responsibility for "welfare"—that is, cash assistance for the indigent. Nixon proposed what would become known as his Family Assistance Plan (FAP) within months of taking office. The FAP promised to give all families with children a guaranteed minimum income funded by the federal government, specifically $1,600 along with food stamps for a four-member family earning up to $720. This minimum would apply to families headed by either working or unemployed adults, with payments diminishing as beneficiaries earned more in the labor market. Among other goals was the Nixon administration's hope to redesign the nation's system of public assistance to encourage work and marriage. Nixon agreed with critics of existing public assistance programs, especially Aid to Families with Dependent Children (AFDC), that those policies encouraged dependence on government rather than on the private labor market and incentivized the growth of single-family homes. Proponents of the FAP within the Nixon administration also sought to equalize benefits across the states. As Nixon himself put it, welfare payments "were grossly unequal" at the time, varying widely from state to state across the nation's decentralized federalist system. Payment levels were especially low in the South. Nixon hoped that having the federal government assume the cost of public assistance in southern states while raising benefits would bolster his political support in the region. He also reportedly embraced the FAP because it promised to debilitate the network of generally liberal social workers and other community activists involved in the nation's existing welfare apparatus whose political strength had grown during the Great Society years.[7]

Nixon attempted to implement two variants of the FAP during his first term but failed both times largely due to resistance in the U.S. Senate. Still, the debates surrounding Nixon's plan resulted in two new federal social assistance programs of major long-term consequence. Senators could not agree on a plan providing a guaranteed minimum income to *all* Americans. Nonetheless, a majority of senators proved open to creating new income floors for certain categories of the indigent: the working poor, the elderly, and the disabled. In October 1972, the Senate rejected the second iteration of Nixon's FAP but created Supplemental Security Income (SSI). SSI offered aid to the disabled and to elderly Americans not eligible for Social Security by using federal funds to provide them a standardized minimum income that could then be supplemented by state-funded programs. Debates surrounding the FAP also eventually led to the adoption of the Earned Income Tax Credit (EITC), a program that uses federal tax rebates to provide the working poor a guaranteed minimum income under certain conditions. Today, the EITC is the single largest federal program providing cash assistance to low-income Americans, reaching over 27 million families in 2014. SSI has grown to serve over 8 million Americans. In addition, in 1972 Nixon and Congress indexed Social Security benefits for inflation for the first time. The federal food stamps program also grew more centralized under Nixon, in turn fueling increased standardization across the country and higher levels of participation by local governments. When Nixon took office in 1969, federal food stamps were available in 1,489 U.S. counties. By 1974, that number had surpassed 3,000.

Federal spending on the program grew more than tenfold during Nixon's term.[8]

Federal housing policy also remained a live issue during the Nixon years, resulting most famously in the creation of the Section 8 housing program. Section 8 is most often associated with the voucher system that is currently the federal government's main way of subsidizing housing for low-income Americans. Those holding a Section 8 voucher can sign leases with owners of private properties willing to participate in the program. The federal government then pays the difference between the market rent and 30 percent of renters' income (25 percent when the program was initially implemented). When Section 8 was created as part of the Housing and Community Development Act of 1974, however, it also provided federal funds for the construction of new subsidized housing and for the rehabilitation of existing units. The voucher system was just one facet of a larger nexus of policies created under Section 8 of the 1974 act.[9]

The new construction program created through Section 8 relied on public-private partnerships to build low-income housing. Specifically, the federal government offered a variety of tax write-offs and mortgage subsidies to private developers to entice them into the low-income housing market and to offer tenants lower rents. At first this system might seem like an early instantiation of the neoliberal, market-oriented policies often associated with the United States' conservative drift in the final decades of the twentieth century. In reality, the Section 8 new construction program was a modestly revised version of Great Society housing initiatives adopted under Johnson. In short, housing policy offers an example of how approaches later redubbed neoliberal at times sat at the heart of postwar liberalism. Johnson and liberals in Congress had made private-public partnerships a centerpiece of the landmark Housing and Development Act of 1968. Section 236 of that legislation, for instance, sought to encourage a cascade of low- and moderate-income housing construction by using federal funds and the tax code to promote construction of new units by private developers. In fact, the 1968 act made the traditional public housing program (in which the federal government and local housing authorities financed and directly built new projects) secondary to Section 236's new public-private model. By the late 1960s, the nation's existing public housing program was widely considered dysfunctional. Due to a combination of white resistance to public housing proposals at the local level and disagreements over funding in Washington, the federal government had failed to meet construction goals for public housing year after year since the program's inception. As whites fled American cities in the 1950s and 1960s, new housing opportunities opened in the private market for African Americans with moderate incomes. Inhabitants of public housing projects grew increasingly poor, generating less revenue from rent for maintenance. Public housing became associated in many quarters with dilapidation, crime, and concentrated and racialized poverty. Liberals and conservatives alike found little to celebrate in the program. As uprisings flared in cities like Newark and Detroit in the late 1960s, the Johnson administration in part blamed a dearth of good housing. Seeking to address an urgent crisis, Johnson saw few reasons to double down on existing housing programs. Instead, through Section 236 of the 1968 housing act, he opted for a model in which the federal government encouraged private construction. When it came to building new subsidized housing, the renamed and modestly revamped Section 8 kept the federal government on this path through the 1970s.[10]

That said, the number of new units constructed due to federal subsidies was significantly lower after the implementation of the 1974 housing act than just a few years earlier. Johnson's 1968 act (which Nixon agreed to fund generously during his first term) unleashed an unprecedented amount of new construction, exceeding three hundred thousand units through the Section 236 program alone between 1969 and 1972. By contrast, Section 8 new construction produced about half as many new units at the program's height in 1978 and 1979. Still, the voucher program that was created under Section 8 of the 1974 act grew rapidly, so much so that the combination of Section 8's construction program and the newly created voucher system brought more federally subsidized units online in the late 1970s than ever before.[11]

At first blush, the Section 8 voucher program, too, might seem merely like an early incarnation of the market-oriented social policies of later years. There is truth to this. Leading pro-market conservatives like economist Milton Friedman championed housing vouchers. But many liberal Democrats supported them as well, and their enthusiasm was not rooted in an emerging neoliberal faith in the private market. Instead, many liberals felt deeply uncomfortable with federal public housing programs' tendency to "ghettoize" the poor and limit low-income Americans' ability to choose where to live. These complaints sprang from two strains of thought that sat at the center of Lyndon Johnson's War on Poverty:

the notion that the poor needed empowerment and the conviction that highly concentrated, intergenerational deprivation had helped produce a destructive "culture of poverty" that government programs should aim to remedy. Housing vouchers promised to empower the poor by allowing them greater choice of residence while also de-concentrating poverty by breaking up public housing projects and in turn weakening the so-called culture of poverty's supposed hold over poor individuals. Just as important, many housing advocates in the early 1970s had grown reasonably satisfied with the quality of the housing stock available in U.S. cities, at least in comparison to earlier years. They increasingly diagnosed the problem of low-income housing as an issue of affordability, not of supply. Thus, a bipartisan collection of policymakers believed that the federal government needed to shift away from focusing solely on producing more housing and toward finding ways to make renting less financially burdensome for poor Americans. Vouchers promised to serve this end. Finally, the Section 8 voucher program was hardly sui generis. The Johnson administration had created a similar albeit significantly smaller initiative, known as Section 23, as part of the 1968 housing act. Like many social policies that took shape during the Nixon years, the housing voucher program in part grew from Great Society liberalism.[12]

The brief tenure of Nixon's successor, Gerald Ford, is rarely associated with landmark social legislation, and for the most part rightly so. Yet it was Ford—prodded by a Congress well to his political left—who signed arguably the most foundational piece of legislation focused on special education in U.S. history. The Education for All Handicapped Children Act of 1975 (EAHCA) followed on the heels of Supplemental Security Income's creation and, thus, helped make the 1970s a watershed moment in the federal government's relationship to the disabled. EAHCA provided only modest funds for special education when it was originally implemented. Nonetheless, it inscribed into federal law books a number of critically important court precedents that special education advocates had won in earlier years but feared judges might overturn. EAHCA made access to a "free, appropriate public education" for children with disabilities a federal right and gave states and school districts guidance about how to provide such schooling. Along with offering a modicum of federal funds to aid state and local efforts, EAHCA and its successor—the Individuals with Disabilities Education Act (passed in 1990)—have served as the principal federal statutes allowing litigants to appeal and protest how special education is provided. In short, the EAHCA was arguably to special education what the Civil Rights Act of 1964 was to discrimination by race and sex.[13]

Indeed, amid an examination of other major educational developments in the 1970s—including the rapid expansion of bilingual education, the implementation of Title IX in 1972 prohibiting sex discrimination in various educational endeavors, and the creation of the federal Department of Education—the historian Gareth Davies contends, "It is not enough to say that Great Society liberalism collapsed in the 1960s and yielded during the 1970s to a strong rightward impulse. That impulse existed, to be sure, but it cannot be taken for granted that the political system yielded to it. On the contrary, the 1970s, every bit as much as the 1960s, need to be considered as a reform decade."[14] As the Nixon and Ford years alone suggest, Davies's observation applies to a range of social policy areas beyond education, particularly if we sharpen Davies's assertion and specify that the brand of reform that thrived in the 1960s and persisted in the 1970s was one that viewed the federal government as an indispensable tool in domestic social policy—a conviction, of course, that Ronald Reagan would later reject. Jimmy Carter expressed greater skepticism regarding government's potential than many of his predecessors—most notably his Democratic forerunner Lyndon Johnson. Still, the Carter administration embraced government-sponsored social policy in a number of ways that are better seen as extensions of earlier trends than as early instantiations of the Reaganism that would follow.

The Carter Years

When Jimmy Carter took office, liberals both inside and outside of government had high hopes that a Democratic president—blessed with Democratic majorities in both houses of Congress—would approve a slew of government programs to address the countless troubles plaguing the nation. Civil rights activists called for an "urban Marshall plan." The nation's mayors looked to Carter and Congress for desperately needed assistance. In the short term, liberal policymakers and labor activists hoped the new administration would sponsor an ambitious stimulus package—a combination of federal spending on public works, tax rebates, and a federal jobs program—to help the unemployed and the nation's flailing economy. No Marshall plan materialized for American cities, and the stimulus package that Carter proposed was smaller than many advocates had hoped. These were just two examples of the various ways that Carter disappointed American liberals. Carter believed he could make existing federal expenditures go further by purging waste from the system. He also feared that increased government spending would further fuel the inflationary spiral that riddled the U.S. economy throughout his term. Meanwhile, Carter was more skeptical than many in the Democratic Party about what government could accomplish. In his first State of the Union address, Carter famously declared, "Government cannot solve our problems, it can't set our goals, it cannot define our vision. Government cannot eliminate poverty or provide a bountiful economy or reduce inflation or save our cities or cure illiteracy or provide energy." These were disappointing—even treacherous—words for many Democrats at the time.[15]

Yet Carter's pronouncements were a far cry from Reagan's declaring, "Government is not the solution to our problem; government is the problem" in his first inaugural address. As historian Sean Wilentz has argued, Carter "was not the New Deal Democrat (let alone the left-wing populist)" that liberals once "fantasized that he was." Yet neither was he "the conservative that liberal and left-wing Democrats" sometimes accused him of being. Despite disappointing many on the liberal-left, the Carter administration promoted government-sponsored social policy on multiple fronts. Meanwhile, the activism of congressional Democrats encouraged the expansion of federal social policy in other realms.[16]

Among the most important examples of Carter's embrace of government-backed social policy is arguably the most forgotten. In addition to allocating $4 billion for public works projects, Carter's stimulus package of 1977 included doubling the size of the first program explicitly designed to provide federally funded jobs to the unemployed since the New Deal. Johnson's War on Poverty had never taken such a step. Instead, at a moment when the national unemployment rate was remarkably low, Johnson tended to view the problem of poverty as a matter of the poor lacking the skills and cultural attitudes necessary to thrive in the nation's robust economy, not as a matter of the indigent lacking access to work. Johnson famously greeted proposals to start a New Deal–style federal jobs program as part of the War on Poverty with a "blank stare," making clear to his advisors that he viewed the idea as a non-starter. As the 1960s progressed, however, a growing cadre of liberals in Congress and policy experts outside of government parted ways with Johnson, underscoring the fact that pockets of very high unemployment persisted—for instance, in urban America—despite a rosy unemployment picture for the nation as a whole. By the early 1970s, creating a federally funded "Public Service Employment" (PSE) program that would provide jobs to the unemployed in state and local government became a leading Democratic goal.[17]

Despite President Nixon's opposition to PSE, congressional Democrats made headway implementing the program in the early 1970s. The Emergency Unemployment Act of 1971 brought the creation of the first 73,000 PSE slots. By the time Gerald Ford left office, and as unemployment levels rose nationally, that number had grown to 310,000. Moreover, Democrats in Congress had succeeded in folding PSE into the nation's main piece of manpower legislation, the Comprehensive Employment and Training Act of 1973, thus making PSE more than just an "emergency" program. Upon taking office, President Carter successfully called for doubling the number of PSE slots to 725,000. Many liberals wanted Carter to go further. In fact, Carter considered doing so. Not long after taking office, Carter floated a proposal to eventually increase PSE slots to 1.4 million as part of a broader attempt to overhaul the nation's welfare system. In the short term, however, members of the Carter administration feared that state and local governments lacked the administrative capacity to execute a build-up of PSE beyond 725,000 positions.[18]

PSE quickly became mired in controversy. Detractors complained that the program tended to serve a relatively educated group of the recently unemployed rather than helping the poorest Americans. Reports of corruption made headlines in many cities, and so did accusations that state and local governments were failing to use PSE to create additional employment. Instead, state and local officials were reportedly using federally subsidized PSE workers as cheap replacements for existing employees. Yet Carter remained supportive of PSE, urging Congress to renew the program in 1978 while adjusting its design to reach more of the poor, hardcore unemployed. Members of Congress who saw PSE as a boondoggle succeeded in cutting the number of slots available by 100,000. Still, Congress adopted the Carter administration's proposal to shift the target population of the program toward those most in need. Studies of the PSE program would later establish that claims of corruption and of public officials' substituting federally funded workers for state and local employees were largely exaggerated.[19]

At a moment when there were millions of unemployed Americans,

725,000 PSE slots was a small number, including in comparison to the much larger employment programs of the New Deal. That said, any comparison between PSE and New Deal jobs programs needs to take into account that there were far more federal programs available to aid the unemployed in the 1970s—from food stamps to unemployment compensation—than there had been in the 1930s. (The first unemployment compensation check, for instance, was not issued until mid-1936.) Moreover, in assessing the Public Service Employment program, it is crucial to note that the program helped make the direct provision of jobs—rather than job training—the main focus of national manpower policy for the only time in U.S. history other than during the New Deal years. In 1978, funding for PSE accounted for nearly 60 percent of budget allocations under the Comprehensive Employment and Training Act (CETA)—again, the federal government's main piece of manpower legislation. Combined with other federal employment programs, such as youth employment initiatives, funding for federally financed jobs reached 80 percent of CETA appropriations in the late 1970s. It was an exceptional moment. Yet it was also short lived. As fighting inflation became Carter's main focus, CETA funds were put on the chopping block along with appropriations for many domestic programs. The number of PSE slots shrank significantly in 1979 and 1980 before Ronald Reagan cut the program altogether.[20]

The Carter administration endorsed government spending in other social policy areas as well. Prodded especially by Secretary of Housing and Urban Development Patricia Roberts Harris, the president and Congress passed the Housing and Community Development Act of 1977 and pledged $12.5 billion to support it. The 1977 act also revamped the original funding formulas for the Community Development Block Grant (CDBG) program to better serve especially distressed cities in the Northeast and Midwest rather than suburbs and comparatively healthy urban areas in the Sunbelt. The growing power of suburban and Sunbelt regions in Congress meant that older cities would still benefit less from federal redevelopment dollars than they had in the late 1960s and early 1970s, before the federal government's shift away from the categorical programs of the Great Society years and toward block grants. Even so, revisions to CDBG funding formulas under Carter funneled a greater proportion of CDBG dollars toward struggling urban centers than the original formulas would have done. Additionally, Title VII of the 1977 law—often referred to as the Community Reinvestment Act—placed new requirements on banks to remedy discriminatory lending practices, particularly redlining, and to make it easier for minority and low-income communities to access credit. Finally, the 1977 law created an additional federal initiative, the Urban Development Action Grant (UDAG), a revised incarnation of the federal urban redevelopment programs of the 1950s and 1960s. The UDAG sought to use federal funds to encourage private investment in urban redevelopment in ways that promised "improvements in employment and tax base" especially in the urban Rust Belt. Meanwhile, often by signing legislation that originated in Congress, Carter increased the minimum wage and oversaw the enlargement of the Earned Income Tax Credit (EITC) and the food stamps program. There were 18.5 million Americans receiving food stamps in 1976 and 21 million in 1980. In fact, a short-lived welfare reform package floated by Carter would have expanded the EITC far more than Congress proved willing to do. Carter's welfare reform proposals also included plans for a guaranteed minimum income, similar to Nixon's Family Assistance Plan. In the end, however, Carter's attempt to reform the nation's welfare system fell victim to a number of forces, including opposition in Congress, political blunders by the administration, and wavering commitment from Carter himself.[21]

To be sure, Carter exhibited deep skepticism of government action in a number of social policy realms. Perhaps the best example is his administration's well-documented attempt to fashion a national urban policy. As historians have noted, the main product of that effort, a 1978 report titled *A New Partnership to Conserve America's Communities*, reads like an early manifesto for the devolutionary and pro-market, or neoliberal, approaches to urban policy that became dominant in later years. *New Partnerships* especially called for "a working alliance of all levels of government, with the private sector of our economy and with our citizens in their communities and neighborhoods." It was a plan, according to one historian, premised on "decentralization, voluntarism, and self-help." Yet the degree to which *New Partnerships* itself actually encouraged devolution and neoliberalism's ascendance should not be overstated. Indeed, historians have done little to document *New Partnership's* long-term impact. *New Partnerships* may have gestured toward what was to come, but it is not at all clear that it actually *influenced* future trends. Just as important, the social initiatives discussed above underscore that Carter's approach to social policy is best seen as a complex and sometimes confused mixture: a combination of skepticism toward government in certain areas, support for government programs in others (many of which do not neatly fit the neoliberal mold), and a heavy dash of fiscal conservatism that grew all the more robust as inflation worsened in the final years of Carter's presidency.[22]

Carter's successor, by contrast, launched an attack on social spending that continued even in better economic times. Between 1981 and 1987, with Ronald Reagan leading the charge, funding for federal housing programs was gutted by over 60 percent, and the Section 8 new construction program was abolished. The minimum wage remained static. Federal appropriations for community development programs fell. Reagan slashed funding for UDAG, sought to trim welfare spending as much as Congress would allow, abolished the Public Service Employment program, and cut food stamps. A chasm separated Carter's combination of selective skepticism toward government and fiscal conservatism from Reagan's downright hostility to most federal social programs.[23]

This chapter's effort to underscore the extent of federal social policymaking in the 1970s is not meant to romanticize the policies produced. On the contrary, many of the programs created during the 1970s had major shortcomings. Local officials tended to use Community Development Block Grants and Urban Development Action Grants to fund downtown projects while neglecting other distressed neighborhoods. Due to its reliance on government partnerships with private developers, the Section 8 new construction program disproportionately encouraged new construction of subsidized housing for populations, like the elderly, whom investors tended to view as more reliable and responsible tenants than other potential clients of subsidized housing. In this regard, however, the 1970s were similar to other moments in U.S. history that saw bursts of social policy development, from the New Deal to the War on Poverty and Great Society years: eras that brought forth a cascade of new programs that benefited portions of the population in new and important ways while nonetheless falling short on other highly consequential fronts. Like many moments in the history of U.S. social policy, especially since World War II, "people-based" policies created in the 1970s—in other words programs that sought to give specific benefits to certain categories of Americans, such as the disabled, the elderly, and the working poor, regardless of geography—have proven far more effective than "place-based" initiatives, like CDBGs and UDAGs, that sought to resurrect flailing urban economies. Finding ways to funnel federal aid to the most distressed urban places given the highly fractured nature of American federalism was a riddle that Lyndon Johnson in the 1960s did not solve, that policymakers in the 1970s failed to crack, and that lawmakers have yet to conquer.[24]

As stated at the outset, many of the social programs created in the 1970s—from SSI and the EITC to CDBGs and Section 8 vouchers—remain part of American government today. Still, the era that produced these initiatives was different from what would follow when it came to social policy. Unlike the New Federalism of the 1970s, Reagan advocated devolution as part of a vigorously antigovernment agenda. Contrary to Carter and Nixon before him, Bill Clinton attempted to slash the nation's welfare rolls—not to implement a guaranteed minimum income for all. During the most recent economic crisis, infamously the worst since the Great Depression, Barack Obama and Congress made no attempt to create a federal employment program like PSE. Whether viewed from the 1980s, 1990s, 2000s, or today, the seventies, on important fronts, hardly seem like the dawn of our current age when it comes to prevailing attitudes toward federal social policy. Rather, they seem like the final years of a moment that produced many durable results but is no more.

Notes

1. Bruce Schulman and Julian Zelizer, eds., *Rightward Bound: Making America Conservative in the 1970s* (Cambridge, MA: Harvard University Press, 2008); Laura Kalman, *Right Star Rising: A New Politics, 1974–1980* (New York: W.W. Norton, 2010); Rick Perlstein, *The Invisible Bridge: The Fall of Nixon and the Rise of Reagan* (New York: Simon & Shuster, 2014); Dominic Sanbrook, *Mad as Hell: The Crisis of the 1970s and the Rise of the Populist Right* (New York: Knopf, 2011); Judith Stein, *Pivotal Decade: How the United States Traded Factories for Finance in the 1970s* (New Haven, CT: Yale University Press, 2010); Jefferson Cowie, *Stayin' Alive: The 1970s and the Last Days of the Working Class* (New York: New Press, 2010). See also *Panic at the Pump: The Energy Crisis and the Transformation of American Politics in the 1970s* (New York: Hill and Wang, 2016). For a similar assessment of earlier literature, see Gareth Davies, *See Government Grow: Education Politics from Johnson to Reagan* (Lawrence: University Press of Kansas, 2007), 4.

Prominent recent work examining the roots of mass incarceration through a focus on the 1960s and 1970s has similarly underplayed the development of federal social policy in the 1970s. See especially Elizabeth Kai Hinton, *From the War on Poverty to the War on Crime: The Making of Mass Incarceration in America* (Cambridge, MA: Harvard University Press, 2016).

2. Bruce Schulman, *The Seventies: The Great Shift in American Culture, Politics, and Society* (New York: Free Press, 2001).

3. Bruce Schulman discusses social policy under Nixon but makes only passing mention of Congress's role in shaping legislation (Schulman, *The Seventies*, 23–35). Roger Biles primarily focuses his attention on the activities and ideology of Nixon and members of his administration (Roger Biles, *The Fate of Cities: Urban America and the Federal Government, 1945–2000* [Lawrence: University Press of Kansas, 2011], ch. 5). Joan Hoff does as well (Joan Hoff, *Nixon Reconsidered* [New York: Basic Books, 1994], ch. 4). James Patterson's brief discussion is exceptional on this front (James Patterson, *Grand Expectations: The United States, 1945–1974* [New York: Oxford University Press, 1996], 718–24). For the work of political scientists mentioned here, see the discussion and citations to follow.

Misunderstandings about social policymaking in the 1970s are in part rooted in the tendency of scholars of social policy to write about individual or small clusters of policies in isolation. One goal of this chapter is to synthesize such work.

4. Thomas J. Sugrue, "Carter's Urban Policy Crisis," in *The Carter Presidency: Policy Choices in the Post New-Deal Era*, ed. Gary M. Fink and Hugh Davis Graham (Lawrence: University Press of Kansas, 1998); Tracy Neumann, "Privatization, Devolution, and Jimmy Carter's National Urban Policy," *Journal of Urban History* 40 (March 2014): 283–300; Biles, *Fate of Cities*, ch. 7.

5. These dynamics are described by political scientist Timothy Conlan; see Timothy Conlan, *From New Federalism to Devolution: Twenty-Five Years of Intergovernmental Reform* (Washington, DC: Brookings Institution Press, 1998). Quotations are from p. 25.

6. Conlan, *From New Federalism to Devolution*, ch. 3; Biles, *Fate of Cities*, 190. For additional insight into Community Development Block Grants, see Tracy Neumann, "The Postindustrial City," in this volume.

7. Conlan, *From New Federalism to Devolution*, ch. 5, quotation on 80; Christopher Howard, *The Hidden Welfare State: Tax Expenditures and Social Policy in the United States* (Princeton: Princeton University Press, 1997), 64–67; Brian Steensland, *The Failed Welfare Revolution: America's Struggle over Guaranteed Income Policy* (Princeton: Princeton University Press, 2007). See also Marisa Chapell, *The War on Welfare: Family, Poverty, and Politics in Modern America* (Philadelphia: University of Pennsylvania Press, 2010), ch. 2.

8. Steensland, *The Failed Welfare Revolution*, 176–79; Howard, *The Hidden Welfare State*, 67–72; Jill Quadagno, *The Color of Welfare: How Racism Undermined the War on Poverty* (New York: Oxford University Press, 1994), 159; James T. Patterson, *Restless Giant: The United States from Watergate to Bush v. Gore* (New York: Oxford University Press, 2005), 113; Conlan, *From New Federalism to Devolution*, 84–85. On figures for the EITC and SSI, see United States Internal Revenue Service, "Statistics for Tax Returns with EITC," https://www.eitc.irs.gov/EITC-Central/eitcstats, and United States Social Security Administration, "A Guide to Supplementary Security Income (SSI) for Groups and Organizations," https://www.ssa.gov/pubs/EN-05-11015.pdf, both accessed February 2016.

9. On the creation and early history of Section 8, see especially R. Allen Hays, *The Federal Government and Urban Housing*, 3rd ed. (Albany: State University Press of New

York, 2012). Here, too, political scientists have given a more robust account of the politics that drove the policymaking process than historians generally have.

10. Hays, *The Federal Government and Urban Housing*, chs. 4 and 5; Alexander von Hoffman, "Calling Upon the Genius of Private Enterprise: The Housing and Urban Development Act of 1968 and the Liberal Turn to Public-Private Partnerships," *Studies in American Political Development* 27 (October 2013): 165–94.

11. Hays, *The Federal Government and Urban Housing*, 128, 152.

12. Hays, *The Federal Government and Urban Housing*, ch. 5.

13. Davies, *Watch Government Grow*, ch. 7.

14. Davies, *Watch Government Grow*, 162–63.

15. Sugrue, "Carter's Urban Policy Crisis," 138, includes first quotation; Schulman, *The Seventies*, 130; Jimmy Carter, "State of the Union Address 1978," http://www.jimmycarterlibrary.gov/documents/speeches/su78jec.phtml. On Carter's political outlook, including its relationship to the economic troubles of the time, see especially Sean Wilentz, *The Age of Reagan: A History, 1974–2008* (New York: Harper, 2008), 75, 78–83; and Julian E. Zelizer, *Jimmy Carter* (New York: Times Books, 2010).

16. First quotation: Ronald Reagan, "First Inaugural Address," http://millercenter.org/president/reagan/speeches/speech-3407. Second quotation: Wilentz, *The Age of Reagan*, 82.

17. Gary Mucciaroni, *The Political Failure of Employment Policy, 1945–1982* (Pittsburgh: University of Pittsburgh Press, 1990), 71–77. See also Margaret Weir, *Politics and Jobs: The Boundaries of Employment Policy in the United States* (Princeton: Princeton University Press, 1992), ch. 4. For Johnson's "blank stare," see Michael B. Katz, *The Undeserving Poor: America's Enduring Confrontation with Poverty*, 2nd ed. (New York: Oxford University Press, 2013), 118.

18. W. Carl Biven, *Jimmy Carter's Economy: Policy in an Age of Limits* (Chapel Hill: University of North Carolina Press, 2002), 72–75; Mucciaroni, *The Political Failure of Employment Policy*, 83–84, 170; Howard, *The Hidden Welfare State*, 143.

19. Weir, *Politics and Jobs*, 126–28; Mucciaroni, *The Political Failure of Employment Policy*, 172–82. Mucciaroni suggests that the Carter administration proposed the 100,000 cut to PSE without providing a citation to back up this statement, which copious documents in the Jimmy Carter Presidential Library archives related to CETA contradict. See, for instance, William Spring's and Kitty Higgin's Subject Files, 1977–1981, box 18, Domestic Policy Staff Collection, Jimmy Carter Presidential Library, Atlanta, GA. On evaluations of CETA, see especially Grace A. Franklin and Randall B. Ripley, *CETA: Politics and Policy, 1973–1982* (Knoxville: University of Tennessee Press, 1984).

20. Weir, *Politics and Jobs*, 119; Mucciaroni, *The Political Failure of Unemployment Policy*, 85; United States Social Security Administration, "Chronology," https://www.ssa.gov/history/1930.html, accessed February 2016.

21. Biles, *Fate of Cities*, 232–33; Hays, *The Federal Government and Urban Housing Policy*, 202–3; Patterson, *Restless Giant*, 113; Howard, *Hidden Welfare State*, 144; Biven, *Jimmy Carter's Economy*, 215–16; Steensland, *The Failed Welfare Revolution*, ch. 6; Chapell, *The War on Welfare*, ch. 4.

22. Sugrue, "Carter's Urban Policy Crisis"; Neumann, "Privatization, Devolution, and Jimmy Carter's National Urban Policy," quotations on 283, 284; Biles, *Fate of Cities*, ch. 7.

23. Biles, *Fate of Cities*, ch. 8; Hays, *The Federal Government and Urban Housing*, ch. 7; Conlan, *From Federalism to Devolution*, chs. 7–8.

24. Biles, *Fate of Cities*, 190, 248–49; Hays, *The Federal Government and Urban Housing*, 155.

15

"The Follow-Through Is the Key"

Enron, Energy, and the Politics of Climate Change at the End of the Twentieth Century

GAVIN BENKE

When Ken Lay, chairman and chief executive officer of the Houston-based natural gas company Enron, wrote to then president of the United States George H. W. Bush, his message received attention. "Ken is a good friend," a staffer wrote as one of Lay's letters was shuffled around the White House in the early days of 1992.[1] The informalities that peppered correspondence between the two men validate this assessment. "Linda and I thoroughly enjoyed our private time with you and Bar last week," the executive added to the bottom of a letter about tax policy.[2] Perhaps this is why Lay petitioned the president (unsuccessfully, as it turned out) to choose Houston as the site for his presidential library. Enron's CEO enjoyed a close and friendly relationship with the leader of the free world. Such a personal connection between the powerful men is how the now-disgraced energy executive is popularly remembered. Lay, this story goes, used such access to gain favors for his company. The back and forth between Washington and Houston was unseemly. Indeed, the firm's collapse after being exposed for accounting fraud in 2001 was so scandalous that Lay's relationship with the executive branch was surely just as outlandish. However, a letter that Lay sent to Bush in late 1991 hints at a more complex relationship.

In November of that year, Enron's CEO mailed Bush a copy of a book he thought might be illuminating as the White House prepared to make the president's National Energy Strategy law.[3] Such a letter—amounting to expert advice for the president—was in fact more typical of the back and forth between the two men. This should hardly be surprising. Energy is a matter of private enterprise and public policy, and the relationship between energy companies and presidents is an intricate one.

In this regard, the connection between Enron and three different U.S. presidents, George H. W. Bush, Bill Clinton, and George W. Bush, was no different. Enron was created in 1985, just a few years before global warming became a pressing concern, and the politics of climate change structured the firm's relationship with these three presidents. At times, Enron's goals aligned with presidential imperatives, and at other times departed from them. Throughout, Lay advocated for certain policies that would benefit his business while offering Enron as a reliable partner in executing presidential energy objectives. This dynamic, however, has largely been forgotten. No one would argue that the Houston natural gas company is not remembered first and foremost as an elaborate accounting fraud. Still, such fraudulent behavior only began in 1997, the last four years of the firm's sixteen-year lifespan. Momentarily stepping back from the scandal, one can see that Enron's broader history provides a clear example of how corporations and the White House worked together to develop a strategy to combat global warming at the end of the twentieth century. The back and forth between Enron and the presidency also demonstrates how successive presidential administrations were connected to one another through corporate activity and decision-making.

The dividing line between government and private sector actors (such as corporations) is not straight but rather twists in ways that sometimes blur distinctions between the two.[4] The state's work is often felt indirectly, through the activities of other institutions, such as corporations. In the late twentieth century, for example, energy development and production had major implications for environmental protection, trade policy, and national security. Whether energy executives liked it or not, their companies were—at least on some level—potentially instruments of the state. Enron's response to climate change initiatives during the 1990s offers a clear example of this dynamic. Furthermore, while the company's leadership shifted strategy in response to the politics of the Bush years, the actions they took also connected the outgoing administration to Clinton's presidency.

Though he was a Texan with roots in the energy industry, George H. W. Bush assumed the presidency at a moment when Americans were becoming more concerned with the environment.[5] Indeed, Bush, a seasoned politician, did not shrink from the problem. During the 1988 presidential campaign, the Republican candidate even declared he would become "the environmental president." Adopting such a title, though, meant tackling a daunting range of issues. By the end of the eighties, for instance, there was a broad scientific consensus around global warming.[6] However, climate change was not just a matter of domestic policy but also of international diplomacy.

The concerns and issues swirling around climate change (along with other environmental perils) were not new to the president. Beginning in the early 1970s, when he was the U.S. ambassador to the United Nations, Bush had developed a friendly working relationship with environmentalists that continued through his time as Ronald Reagan's vice president.[7] Such a cordial relationship was a stark contrast to that of President Reagan, who had often antagonized American environmentalists during his tenure. Bush, on the other hand, deliberately sought a change in tone when it came to this issue. Indeed, when he assumed the presidency in 1989, his staff was aware that there was "pretty much no continuity" with Reagan when it came to environmental matters.[8] While the White House had ignored and alarmed environmentalists throughout the 1980s, the Bush administration quickly established a much more cooperative stance. Not only did Bush's arrival mean a welcome change in personnel, but the president actively sought the advice of environmentalists. Perhaps less surprisingly, the president also enjoyed a good deal of credibility with the U.S. energy industry. Before entering politics, Bush founded Zapata Petroleum.[9] Because of this history in the private sector, Bush had been a preferred candidate among business executives since the 1970s.[10] Energy executives in particular could expect at the very least a sympathetic ear. President Bush seemed to be uniquely positioned to address global warming.

This was indeed fortuitous. By the late 1980s, climate change and other environmental issues were not easily ignored. Even beyond a growing alarm in the scientific community around global warming and acid rain, spectacular environmental catastrophes like the 1989 Exxon Valdez spill in Alaska and the upcoming twentieth anniversary of Earth Day (1990) meant that care for the environment would occupy a central place in American public discourse. As personnel in the White House clearly understood, there was mounting political pressure for environmental action.[11]

From Lay's perspective, natural gas companies like Enron found themselves with a potential advantage as global warming became one of the key environmental concerns of the era. Because natural gas contributed "less than any other fossil fuel to the emissions" responsible for "the greenhouse effect," Lay reasoned that Enron might well thrive in the coming decade.[12] Additionally, he had personal ties to the Bush family, and the two men collaborated early on in Bush's presidency, when Lay was asked to co-chair the World Economic Forum host's committee in Houston. What is more, that event revealed how other matters, from an economic downturn to a rapidly disintegrating Soviet bloc, would compete with the environment for the president's attention. It was an interesting time to be in the natural gas business.

Despite the range of pressing political issues, advisors to the president proposed what would be a major innovation in environmental policy while crafting new amendments to the Clean Air Act.[13] Politically, Bush's team could not (and did not want to) return to the "social regulations" of the 1970s when it came to environmental policy. Such measures had been targeted by business lobbyists as a drag on the economy.[14] Unlike the environmental regulations of the 1970s, though, the Clean Air Act relied on market incentives and mechanisms to spur environmentally responsible behavior. The legislation was a crucial moment in environmental policy, establishing for the first time a "cap and trade" scheme for harmful emissions. Under this policy, the total amount of allowable sulfur dioxide and nitrogen oxide emissions was made fixed but tradable in the hope that a market for trading the ability to pollute would encourage firms to sell their unused pollution rights and adopt cleaner production processes.[15] Rather than regulatory oversight, market solutions now moved to the center of U.S. environmental policy.[16] This new emphasis on the market as the ideal platform for environmental stewardship was also a centerpiece in Bush's more extensive National Energy Strategy, which he announced the following year.[17]

Such a shift in environmental policy must have been welcome news for Ken Lay. To be sure, he did not let the moment pass. In 1992, Enron's CEO was one of several executives advising the Republican Party's Platform Committee ahead of the presidential election. Here, Lay argued that natural gas was critical to the president's energy strategy. Not only would natural gas production spur job growth and protect the economy from oil shocks, but it was a resource that was not at odds with the administration's environmental goals. Demonstrating his political savvy, Lay wrapped his message in terms of the Republican Party's overall approach to governing. More natural gas would not have to mean more regulatory oversight. Rather, regulators could serve as "watchdog[s] for abuse" and not a "centralized planning agency for the industry."[18] The Texas energy executive surely knew his audience. In that election year, Republican politicians singled out natural gas deregulation to draw a contrast between the Carter years as a period of regulatory overreach and the Reagan and Bush presidencies, with their business-friendly approach to energy production. Onerous regulation, Republican lawmakers regularly asserted, would undoubtedly accompany a Democrat to the White House.

However, Enron's CEO was not wary about breaking from conservative politicians. While active in the Republican Party, Ken Lay ultimately pursued policies that would benefit his business. In 1992, the same year as the presidential election, the executive put himself at odds with the GOP's political impulses when lobbying the president. Such a willingness to diverge from the party when it came to presidential politics was evident in the months before the Earth Summit, a United Nations meeting devoted to a range of environmental issues scheduled to take place that summer in Rio de Janeiro, Brazil.

The politics of the Rio meeting highlighted the tightrope presidents had to walk when it came to energy and the environment. In the period leading up to the Rio conference, the White House was flooded with letters urging the president to attend. Avoiding any early commitment to attend the Earth Summit, the official White House response was to point out the many environmental steps the administration had already taken.[19] To be sure, this was not mere political rhetoric. Climate change had become an important part of the National Energy Strategy, and actions such as creating carbon "sinks" through planting trees had become part of the official response to global warming.[20] At the same time, the president and his administration were acutely aware that attending Rio would not be without political consequences. Bush also received letters asking the United States to forgo the Rio conference. For instance, the Oregon Farmers Bureau wrote to him that "at a time when socialist and communistic ideals are being repudiated around the world," the United States should not "allow them to be revived under the guise of protecting the environment."[21] The U.N. Conference was a "radical" step, another group wrote to the president.[22] Likewise, members of his own party opposed U.S. participation.

Weighing the decision publicly, Bush told audiences that he would not "go to the Rio Conference and make a bad deal."[23] The president would have to be very careful about his approach to Rio.

The White House struggled to balance these competing interests, working through drafts of a presidential op-ed called "Going to the Earth Summit." In this piece, he argued that "global economic growth" and "global environmental quality" had to be tied to one another.[24] In the op-ed, Bush's team repeatedly argued that expanding global markets through free trade agreements in the offing, including NAFTA, would create opportunities for greater environmental protections. One only needed to look at the "fouled waters" of Eastern Europe to realize the environmental catastrophe caused by central planning.[25] "Healthy natural resources and healthy people," the message went, were, "essential for economies to prosper."[26] Fighting global warming could only come through market-based ideas. If Bush did go to Rio, he noted, he would bring a gospel of "environmental protection through market-oriented economic development and free trade."[27] In the document's conclusion, the president's speech writers tried to put the idea of global warming in a broader context. "This past year we have seen absolutely historic events of enormous impact and great promise across the globe," the text read, including, "the fall of Communism, the forward march of democracy, the staunch defense of freedom, and the blossoming of free market economies."[28] The world seemed to be at the start of a "grand new order," the speech read, but significantly, it was a new order with the market at its center. It was fitting, then, that environmental protections also develop in a market, as opposed to planning, context.[29]

Such appeals revealed how the increasingly popular idea of "sustainable development" provided the president with a path to get beyond the sense of tradeoffs between environmental protections and economic growth that had characterized earlier historical moments. Though the concept had emerged during the 1970s, by the 1980s "sustainable development" could be used to imply a fundamental harmony between economic and ecological imperatives.[30] Ultimately, though, the Bush administration was inclined to side with business interests. Whereas the president had confronted the automobile industry during talks over the Clean Air Act, memoranda back and forth indicated that the White House wanted to avoid committing to specific environmental actions when it came to Rio. Indeed, environmental groups, one aide noted, were right to be upset, having grasped the full import of the White House's intentions.[31] Enron's CEO, though, saw the Earth Summit as an opportunity and made his thoughts clear to the president.

"I apologize for writing you so often," Lay began one letter to Bush in support of the Rio Earth Summit, hinting at both the executive's access to the White House and the significance of the meeting.[32] If handled properly, the U.N. conference could produce a "public policy guide, not a policy mandate" for reducing greenhouse gas emissions.[33] In contrast to the wider business community's alarm and environmentalists' sense of urgency when it came to Rio, Lay wrote to Bush that he did not "believe the oceans will boil in a few years if we don't address greenhouse gas emissions," before adding, "but I also do not believe the U.S. will suffer from economic ruin if prudent steps are taken to reduce CO2 emissions in order to protect the global environment."[34] If the natural gas industry was unburdened by domestic regulation (and if protections for coal were removed), he argued, the market and natural gas would produce a cleaner environment, cheaper energy, and jobs in the United States. Lay's enthusiasm for the Earth Summit was not widely shared by some of his contemporaries. The larger political environment made it clear that either participating in or eschewing the meeting would have political consequences. However, with so many other heads of state attending, the White House saw few realistic options.[35] In June 1992, Bush went to Rio.

If the Earth Summit had promised to be a watershed event, though, the meeting concluded with a mixed record.[36] The administration's prevarication was on full display at the Earth Summit. For the United States, the meeting was marked by political posturing and gamesmanship (including a leaked memo meant to embarrass the head of the Environmental Protection Agency).[37] Senator Al Gore, a longtime environmentalist who would be running on the Democratic presidential ticket against Bush and Vice President Dan Quayle, also went to Rio.[38] The U.S. refrained from signing some treaties, and while conference participants agreed to reduce CO2 emissions to 1990 levels by the start of the next century, the agreements were nonbinding.[39] The president's address at the meeting was hardly a high watermark for presidential oratory.[40] Later, some of his advisors would admit that the Rio Earth Summit had compounded their political woes heading into the election.[41] However, the significance of the Earth Summit, which put the environment at the center of the global economy, was not lost on Lay.[42]

Indeed, Enron's CEO had become a deft political operator. While President Bush faced criticism for his initial reluctance to attend the Brazil meeting, and what some regarded as "obstructionism" in Rio's wake, Enron's CEO wasted little time in championing efforts to halt climate change in a way that revealed the complex interplay between industry and the state.[43] Though he self-consciously assumed a "greener" posture than his friend in the White House, Bush's political rhetoric profoundly influenced the ways in which Lay framed his positions on international energy policy.

For instance, Bush referred to the "new world order" when speaking about the coalition he had assembled for the first Gulf War. Just like the new community of nations that seemed to come together after the Cold War, Enron's executive imagined "A New Energy and Environmental Order."[44] With such a phrase, Lay argued that the private sector was a crucial partner in fighting climate change. During a follow-up meeting to the Earth Summit in Washington, DC, Lay suggested that corporations would be essential to going about "the arduous work of transforming into reality the world's commitment to reducing greenhouse gas emissions and mitigating the threat of global warming."[45] In business, Lay declared, "the follow-through" was "the key," and natural gas could become "the 'bridge' fuel" that would "deliver" the entire world from "the oil era" to "a renewable energy based economy."[46] Though he had borrowed the president's language, Lay's speech also marked a break with the White House. Bush had been criticized for the United States' obstructionism at the Rio conference. The president's rhetoric was hollow, his critics suggested. But this was typical of government, Lay's words implied (even if he would not have dared to criticize his friend). It would be up to businesses to follow through. "Sustainable growth in the developing countries means increased use of natural gas," he said before going on to highlight a power plant that the company was building in England.[47] Lay had every reason, it seemed, to encourage an approach to energy that accounted for climate change. Over the course of his presidency, Bush had established a business-friendly brand of environmental policy that companies like Enron could capitalize on.

The Bush administration's insistence on market incentives (which had been viewed with suspicion at Rio) represented a clear opportunity for natural gas companies like Enron. Removing protections that coal producers and users enjoyed in some states would help realize the Bush market-centric approach to environmentalism. "If allowed to compete in a free and fair competitive market," Lay reasoned, natural gas would become a key energy source in an era of worldwide concern over global warming.[48] What should happen next, Lay suggested in his public statement after the Rio summit, was that the energy industry should build on the 1990 amendments to the Clean Air Act and look toward fuel sources that would reduce CO2 emissions. By taking up the cause of climate change and referencing the Clean Air Act, Lay and Enron had, in very real terms, become custodians of Bush's legacy. Though the president did not win reelection that November, the Houston company's leadership had committed to a long-term business strategy that was predicated on the survival and extension of the outgoing administration's environmental policies. At the same time, the Texas energy executive had reason to hope that the political shift in Washington would not be bad for business. Indeed, Al Gore, whose presence at the Rio Earth Summit had irritated Bush officials, was now the vice president.[49] Environmentalism and climate change were only going to get more attention. At least rhetorically, Lay had positioned Enron as a more progressive force than the president, despite their friendship. Here again, Lay was a savvy political operator.

Still, in contrast to the access Lay had to President Bush (and his Department of Energy), Enron's executives were uncertain about what to expect from Bill Clinton's first energy secretary, Hazel O'Leary. Early on in the Clinton presidency, Terry Thorn, who worked in Enron's Government Affairs department, offered an invitation for the new cabinet member to meet energy executives to "clarify the Clinton administration's energy agenda."[50] Such a meeting was crucial, Thorn counseled, since the new administration was "an unknown quantity for people in the industry."[51] Despite any initial apprehension, however, the company's management soon found that there would be a great deal of continuity between the two presidents when it came to energy matters. In the days leading up to the 1992 presidential election, Bush signed the Energy Policy Act into law, which was a direct reflection of his National Energy Strategy. It would be Clinton's administration, though, that would implement the law.

Lay, for his part, might not have had the same connection (either politically or personally) that he had enjoyed with George H. W. Bush, but the Houston businessman soon found a way to work with the new Democratic administration. In 1993, Lay was named as a member of the President's Council on Sustainable Development, a group meant to demonstrate the new administration's dedication to the goals set out in Agenda

21, the Earth Summit's central document. In joining Clinton's Council on Sustainable Development, Lay was one of a few corporate executives and directors (from Dow Chemicals, BP Amoco, and General Motors) among an otherwise diverse set of participants, including members of the president's cabinet and officials from environmental nonprofits such as the Nature Conservancy, the Environmental Defense Fund, the Sierra Club, and the Natural Resources Defense Fund.[52] Through the council, Enron's chief was well positioned to expand on his self-fashioned role as a wise voice on global matters.

While serving on the president's council, Lay was a co-chair of the "International Leadership Task Force," which was supposed to help "advise the President on policies that foster U.S. leadership in sustainable development internationally."[53] One of the stated goals of the International Task Force was to "encourage foreign investment" by U.S. businesses that would be "consistent with the principles of sustainable development."[54] In many ways, Lay's service on the council was consistent with the projects that the company had prior to the 1992 election.

Even before Clinton's arrival in Washington, Lay had aligned some of Enron's operations with prevailing notions of sustainable development and had little trouble standing on the rhetorical foundation he had built during Bush's term. "If we keep junking up our environment through current means of economic growth and development," he said in the pages of *Enron Business*, the employee magazine, "eventually we will have serious problems whether it be global warming, contaminated food chains or polluted water."[55] But such "green" statements did not mean a return to regulation. Bush-era market-based sensibilities articulated in documents such as the National Energy Strategy had survived presidential and party transition. If Enron's Government Affairs team had been apprehensive about Clinton's first energy secretary, Terry Thorn now celebrated the administration's "willingness to use market-based solutions to solve environmental problems as progressive, innovative and a step in the right direction."[56] In fact, the opportunities for a company like Enron actually expanded in the early days of Clinton's presidency. Developing economies, such as India's, were beginning to open up to foreign capital, and the world energy market seemed ripe for the sort of gas-fired power plants that Enron had already built in other areas of the world.[57] Thorn himself would soon be working closely with the administration on global economic development.

In 1994, Thorn traveled (along with other business executives and environmentalists) with U.S. government officials as part of a "Presidential Mission on Sustainable Energy and Trade" to India. A pattern of cooperation between Enron executives and the Clinton administration was emerging. This partnership, especially when it came to India, would prove helpful to Enron when political developments in that country threatened plans to build a massive gas-fired plant in Dabhol, an area south of Mumbai on India's west coast.[58] Likewise, the Houston company's executives sometimes found themselves temporarily cast in political roles when called upon by administration officials.

In November of that year, for instance, Enron hosted India's power minister during a visit to the United States. Such hospitality could only help "the evolving partnership between the United States and India to promote sustainable development in energy, environment and trade," Clinton's energy secretary wrote appreciatively to Enron executives.[59] Similarly, in 1996, Ken Lay hosted a reception "in honor of the Republic of South Africa and United States delegations to the Binational Commission" in Washington, DC, and extended an invitation to Energy Department officials.[60] That same year, Secretary O'Leary requested the attendance of Enron officials at an event hosting Pakistani government officials.[61] Such invitations were typical of the correspondence between Clinton's Energy Department and company executives during these years. However, cooperation extended beyond the level of catered receptions in Washington. This pattern of working together in a way that sometimes obscured any demarcation between international diplomacy and the activities of a multinational corporation similarly informed the findings of Lay's task force as part of the President's Council on Sustainable Development.

A 1996 report from the International Leadership Task Force that Lay co-chaired further tied the concepts of a global economy and the environment together. However, much like Lay's correspondence with Bush earlier in the decade, the task force's recommendations did not include new environmental regulations. Corporations could "voluntarily" adopt "consistent goals that are protective of human health and the environment in its operations around the world."[62] A genuine partnership between the public and private sectors, the report's authors suggested, could "promote voluntary actions to build commitments and incentives for resource efficiency, stewardship, information sharing, and collaborative decision-making processes."[63] Such language reflected Lay's long-standing attempts to position Enron as a resource to be tapped by the White House. Incentivizing sustainable development, rather than issuing new, restrictive regulations, had survived the Bush presidency. In fact, such principles had become further entrenched under Clinton. Despite such policy similarities between the two presidents, though, the Clinton administration did not face the same tortured political decisions that Bush had when the U.N. convened a follow-up to the 1992 Earth Summit during Clinton's second term.

The year 1997 was turning out to be crucial for the environmental task force. Indeed, a second meeting in Brazil, Rio+5, was scheduled to take stock of what had happened since the publication of Agenda 21.[64] Similarly, a Conference of the Parties (a phrase that referred to the participants at such U.N. meetings) held in Kyoto, Japan, represented more substantial progress than did the Rio meeting five years earlier. The agreements that emerged from that meeting, the Kyoto Protocol, called for binding (instead of aspirational) commitments from developed countries to lower their levels of carbon emissions.[65] What is more, the agreements moved closer to establishing a carbon emissions trading system. The trading expertise Enron developed in response to deregulation and natural gas seemed perfectly suited to the emerging international system for sustainable energy development. By the time the President's Council had released its final report in 1999, Lay had brought his business in line with the directives of the council.

When an employee wrote to Enron's leadership about the company's official stance on global warming, Lay and Jeff Skilling (the soon-to-be-infamous company president) responded that although management was not sure about the severity of the threat, caution dictated that "companies begin looking for ways to reduce emissions now." In some ways, Enron's official position was not much different from Lay's old advice to President Bush when it came to global warming. Now, however, this middle-of-the-road stance was embedded in a larger set of specific ideas and initiatives. Enron, Lay and Skilling informed the employee, had been "involved in climate change discussions for several years" and had been in attendance at all of the Conference of Parties meetings. Officially, the company was supportive of "early crediting, carbon trading, and other flexible mechanisms." More specifically, the company was going to begin trading carbon, and was helping to "design international programs such as the Clean Development Mechanism (CDM)" that would "encourage the use of natural gas and renewable energy in developing countries."[66] As Lay and Skilling's response to the inquiry suggests, the Clinton years and developments such as the Kyoto Protocol could only help Enron's operations. However, U.S. participation in the agreement stalled.[67] While Clinton signed the agreement, he did not submit it for ratification to the Senate, where some worried about the agreement's potential impact on industry.[68] It seemed that just as Clinton had been crucial in executing Bush's National Energy Policy, the responsibility for acting on the Kyoto agreements would fall to the next president—another Bush, as it turned out. The 2000 election seemed to be a lucky break for the company.

Surely the company could expect a good relationship with the incoming president. Beyond his connection to the Bush family, Lay had successfully lobbied the younger politician on domestic matters while he was the governor of Texas.[69] When the Bush administration came to Washington in early 2001, Lay was one of many energy executives who participated in the vice president's Energy Task Force.[70] However, if Enron's leadership enjoyed a remarkable degree of agreement with the new administration on a range of issues, the forty-third president's arrival also marked a break with what had been an overall stable approach to climate change. While both his father and Bill Clinton had embraced the ideal of "sustainable development," George W. Bush's administration departed from the conciliatory and cooperative approach to environmental matters that characterized the 1990s.[71] While the Bush administration expanded some of the emissions trading plans that had developed after the Clean Air Act, it otherwise halted the implementation of recent environmental regulations.[72] Significantly, but perhaps unsurprisingly, under the younger Bush's leadership, the United States did not sign the Kyoto treaty. At least when it came to climate change, Lay had more policy disagreements with George W. Bush than he had with the more liberal Clinton White House. But such differences are not how the company is usually remembered.

Ironically, as Enron collapsed in accounting fraud at the end of 2001, the company would become connected to the second Bush White House in a very intimate way. Enron, as it turned out, had been overstating profits and hiding failing businesses for years using intricate and complicated accounting schemes. While his father's relationship with Ken Lay had been something of an asset, George W. Bush was forced to quickly distance himself from the Houston executive. In 2002, the summer after Enron collapsed, the potential political fallout for the president was notable.

Research that Republican pollster Bob Teeter conducted revealed that most Americans felt that the president cared more about corporate interests than about the public good.[73] Enron, rather than becoming a partner with the White House in crafting energy strategy, became the impetus for new financial and accounting regulations and campaign finance rules that the president signed into law.[74] Despite the potentially disastrous association with Enron, though, the political storm passed. To be sure, Bush's Democratic opponent, Senator John Kerry, repeatedly tried to connect Bush and Enron. In at least one speech, the Democratic candidate told an audience, "You don't value families by kicking kids out of after school programs and taking cops off our streets, so that Enron can get another tax break," but the line ultimately had little effect.[75] By the time he ran for reelection in 2004, Bush had overcome the association with the Houston company. Still, that presidential campaign introduced what has become the most durable link between Enron and the American presidency.

The word "Enron" now serves as a rhetorical device to conjure the specter of dirty money and political corruption. For instance, when the solar energy company Solyndra failed after receiving federal money, Republicans were quick to invoke Enron in the hopes of hurting President Barack Obama politically.[76] Given the revelations of corporate fraud, it is hardly surprising that politicians use the company in this way. Still, such shorthand obscures the much more complex relationship the company's leadership had with multiple presidential administrations, and by extension how presidents have used American businesses to help shape the post–Cold War world.

Corporations outlive presidencies and frequently commit resources to business endeavors with timelines that extend beyond four-year election cycles. Because of this, projects that a corporation undertakes in cooperation with one White House occupant might be well underway by the time a new president arrives in Washington. In this way, corporations become powerful sources of continuity between presidencies. With each presidential transition, Lay aligned his company's long-term interest with shifting political imperatives. Looking at Enron's interest in international business projects in an age of global climate change politics offers a vivid demonstration of this nuanced interplay between the American presidency and private enterprise.

Notes

1. Roger B. Porter, memorandum to George H. W. Bush, January 16, 1992, ID# 312644SS, FI0010.02, WHORM: Bush Presidential Records, George H. W. Bush Presidential Library, College Station, TX.

2. Kenneth Lay to George H. W. Bush, December 16, 1991, ID# 295446, FI010.02, WHORM: Bush Presidential Records, George H. W. Bush Presidential Library, College Station, TX.

3. Kenneth Lay to George H. W. Bush, November 4, 1991, Bush Presidential Library, College Station, TX.

4. As the historian Brian Balogh has argued, "Americans had braided public and private actions." Balogh contends that state action is often directed through intermediary institutions, such as corporations, and that the importance of such institutions means that election cycles are less important than ongoing processes; see Brian Balogh, *The Associational State: American Governance in the Twentieth Century* (Philadelphia: The University of Pennsylvania Press, 2015), 3.

5. The historian Richard Sicilia, for instance, has demonstrated how the U.S. chemical industry underwent a "greening" in the late 1980s and early 1990s. See David B. Sicilia, "The Corporation under Siege: Social Movements, Regulation, Public Relations, and Tort Law since the Second World War," in *Constructing Corporate America: History, Politics, Culture*, ed. Kenneth Lipartito and David B. Sicilia, 188–220, 206 (New York: Oxford University Press, 2004).

6. Kevin C. Armitage, "State of Denial: The United States and the Politics of Global Warming," *Globalizations* 2, no. 4 (December 2005): 417–27, 420.

7. Stephen J. Macekura, *Of Limits and Growth: The Rise of Global Sustainable Development in the Twentieth Century* (New York: Cambridge University Press, 2015), 272–73. However, Armitage argues that the Bush administration was adept at raising doubts about global warming. See Armitage, "State of Denial," 422.

8. Bobbie Greene Kilberg, interviewed by Russell Riley and Kathryn Dunn, George H. W. Bush Oral History Project, Miller Center, University of Virginia, November 20, 2009, http://millercenter.org/oralhistory/interview/bobbie-greene-kilberg.

9. "George H. W. Bush: Life before the Presidency," Miller Center of Public Affairs, University of Virginia, http://millercenter.org/president/biography/bush-life-before-the-presidency.

10. Benjamin C. Waterhouse, *Lobbying America: The Politics of Business from Nixon to NAFTA* (Princeton: Princeton University Press, 2014), 192.

11. Michael Boskin, interviewed by Russell Riley and Stephen Weatherford, George H. W. Bush Oral History Project, Miller Center, University of Virginia, July 30–31, 2009, http://millercenter.org/oralhistory/interview/michael-boskin (hereafter Boskin interview).

12. Kenneth Lay, *The Enron Story* (New York: Newcomen Society of the United States, 1991), 7.

13. As Michael Boskin notes, the basic idea for cap-and-trade had existed long before Bush took office (Boskin interview).

14. Waterhouse, *Lobbying America*, 35–37.

15. U.S. Environmental Protection Agency, "Cap and Trade: Acid Rain Program Results" (Washington, D.C., n.d. [2009?]), https://grist.files.wordpress.com/2009/06/ctresults.pdf.

16. Meg Jacobs, "The Politics of Environmental Regulation: Business-Government Relations in the 1970s and Beyond," in *What's Good For Business: Business and American Politics since World War II*, ed. Kim Phillips-Fein and Julian E. Zelizer, 212–32, 228 (Oxford: Oxford University Press, 2012).

17. There were other reasons, of course, for a greater reliance on natural gas. Indeed, the recent Gulf War was a stark reminder that much of the nation's oil supply came from a politically unstable part of the world.

18. Enron Corp., "Enron Corp. Chairman Ken Lay Promotes Natural Gas in Testimony Before Republican Platform Committee," news release, April 13, 1992.

19. D. Allan Bromley to Douglas H. Breese, April 21, 1992, ID# 321394, F0006-16, WHORM: Bush Presidential Records, George H. W. Bush Presidential Library, College Station, TX.

20. D. Allan Bromley to Douglas H. Breese, April 21, 1992. On the National Energy Strategy, see Holly Idelson, "Provisions: National Energy Strategy Provisions," *CQ Weekly*, November 28, 1992, http://library.cqpress.com.ezproxy.bu.edu/cqweekly/document.php?id=WR102409071.

21. Douglas H. Breese to George H. W. Bush, April 6, 1992, ID# S21394, FO006-16, WHORM: Bush Presidential Records, George H. W. Bush Presidential Library, College Station, TX.

22. Competitive Enterprise Institute, "Letter to the President of the United States on the United Nations Conference on the Environment and Development [open letter]," April 7, 1992, ID# 321395, WHORM: Bush Presidential Records, George H. W. Bush Presidential Library, College Station, TX.

23. George H. W. Bush, "Young Presidents Organization" (speech), April 21, 1992, ID# 32270033, F0006-16, WHORM: Bush Presidential Records, George H. W. Bush Presidential Library.

24. Draft Speech, "Going to UNCED," 1992, ID# 323678, FO006-16, WHORM: Bush Presidential Records, George H. W. Bush Presidential Library, College Station, TX.

25. Bush, Draft Speech, "Going to UNCED."

26. Bush, Draft Speech, "Going to UNCED."

27. Bush, Draft Speech, "Going to UNCED."

28. Bush, Draft Speech, "Going to UNCED."

29. Bush, Draft Speech, "Going to UNCED."

30. Stephen J. Macekura, *Of Limits and Growth: The Rise of Global Sustainable Development in the Twentieth Century* (New York: Cambridge University Press, 2015), 9.

31. Clayton Yeutter, memorandum to George H. W. Bush, May 1, 1992, ID# 325581SS, F0006.16, WHORM: Bush Presidential Records, George Bush Presidential Library, College Station, TX.

32. Ken Lay to George H. W. Bush, April 3, 1992, Department of Energy Records http://energy.gov/sites/prod/files/maprod/documents/enron1992.pdf.

33. Ken Lay to George H. W. Bush, April 3, 1992, Department of Energy Records, http://energy.gov/sites/prod/files/maprod/documents/enron1992.pdf.

34. Ken Lay to George H. W. Bush, April 3, 1992.

35. Clayton Yeutter, interviewed by James Sterling Young and Russell Riley, George H. W. Bush Oral History Project, Miller Center, University of Virginia, January 19, 2001, http://millercenter.org/oralhistory/interview/clayton-yeutter (hereafter Yeutter interview).

36. Yeutter interview, 294.

37. Yeutter interview.

38. Macekura, *Of Limits and Growth*, 289–93.

39. Macekura, *Of Limits and Growth*, 293–94.

40. Macekura, *Of Limits and Growth*, 261.

41. Yeutter interview.

42. Yda Schreuder, *The Corporate Greenhouse: Climate Change Policy in a Globalizing World* (New York: Zed Books, 2009), 38–39.

43. Early coverage of the Clinton administration's environmental efforts offered a contrast to the first Bush administration by referencing the "Bush Administration's obstructionist image" after the Earth Summit that made the United States look like a "global foot-dragger." See William K. Stevens, "Gore Promises U.S. Leadership On Sustainable Development Path," *New York Times*, June 15, 1993.

44. In fact, Lay also connected gas to national security, stating that the Gulf War has revealed the country's vulnerability to "oil shocks" and "unstable energy supplies."

45. Kenneth Lay, "Natural Gas: The Cost Effective Link between Robust Economic Growth and Aggressive Environmental Protection" (speech), Global Warming and the Earth Summit Alliance to Save Energy Conference, Washington, DC, June 23, 1992, Department of Energy Records, http://energy.gov/sites/prod/files/maprod/documents/enron1992.pdf.

46. In the prepared remarks, the statement was underlined, suggesting that he intended to place particular emphasis on it.

47. Lay, "Natural Gas."

48. Lay, "Natural Gas."

49. Yeutter interview.

50. Terry Thorn to Hazel O'Leary, May 13, 1992, Department of Energy Records, http://energy.gov/sites/prod/files/maprod/documents/enron1992.pdf.

51. Terry Thorn to Hazel O'Leary, May 13, 1992.

52. National Archives, *President's Council on Sustainable Development*, http://clinton2.nara.gov/PCSD/Members/index.html.

53. National Archives, *President's Council on Sustainable Development*.

54. National Archives, *President's Council on Sustainable Development*.

55. Kristin Rankin, "Sustainable Development Assures Americans a Rosy Future,"

Enron Business, 1993, Southwest Collection/Special Collections Library, Texas Tech University, Lubbock, TX.

56. Mary Clark, "Promoting Natural Gas Underscores Enron's Environmental Activities on Capitol Hill," *Enron Business*, May 1994, Southwest Collection/Special Collections Library, Texas Tech University, Lubbock, TX, 4.

57. Robert Shiller, *Irrational Exuberance*, 2nd ed. (Princeton: Princeton University Press, 2005), 139.

58. Hazel O'Leary to Terrence Thorn, August 2, 1994, Department of Energy Records, http://energy.gov/sites/prod/files/maprod/documents/enron1994.pdf.

59. Hazel O'Leary to Terrence Thorn, August 2, 1994.

60. Enron was developing a gas field in South Africa and had been in touch with the Department of Energy about economic development in that country; see Kenneth Lay to Hazel O'Leary, July 16, 1996, Department of Energy Records, http://energy.gov/sites/prod/files/maprod/documents/enron1996.pdf.

61. Hazel O'Leary to Terrence Thorn, June 6, 1996, Department of Energy Records, http://energy.gov/sites/prod/files/maprod/documents/enron1996.pdf.

62. President's Council on Sustainable Development, *Building on Consensus: A Progress Report on Sustainable America*, President's Council on Sustainable Development, January 10, 1997, http://clinton2.nara.gov/PCSD/Publications/Progress_Report.html#chap3.

63. I am not arguing that Lay was the sole author of this document. Indeed, he was only one of several committee members, and the document was likely authored at the staff level (President's Council on Sustainable Development, *Building on Consensus*).

64. President's Council on Sustainable Development, *Building on Consensus*.

65. Macekura, *Of Limits and Growth*, 299.

66. Kenneth Lay and Jeffrey Skilling, "Take It to the Top," *Enron Business*, 1999, Southwest Collection/Special Collections Library, Texas Tech University, 11.

67. Macekura, *Of Limits and Growth*, 300.

68. John H. Cushman, "U.S. Signs a Pact to Reduce Gases Tied to Warming," *New York Times*, November 13, 1998. Indeed, the ultimate fate of the Kyoto Protocol is part of a broader pattern of failed attempts to ratify international environmental agreements. See Guri Bang, Jon Hovi, and Detlef F. Sprinz, "U.S. Presidents and the Failure to Ratify Multilateral Environmental Agreements," *Climate Policy* 12, no. 6 (2012): 755–63.

69. For an example of Lay's relationship with George W. Bush while he was governor of Texas, see Kenneth Lay to George W. Bush, July 11, 1996, George W. Bush Papers, Texas State Archives.

70. Rosalie Genova, *Big Business, Democracy, and the American Way: Narratives of the Enron Scandal in 2000s Political Culture* (PhD diss., Department of History, University of North Carolina, Chapel Hill, 2010), 44.

71. Macekura, *Of Limits and Growth*, 301.

72. Michael Grunwald and Eric Pianin, "Bush EPA Expands Emission Trading," *Washington Post*, February 15, 2001.

73. NBC/WSJ Survey, July 2002, box 88, folder "July 2002," Robert Teeter Papers, Gerald R. Ford Library, Ann Arbor, MI.

74. Genova, *Big Business, Democracy, and the American Way*, xxxiv.

75. John Kerry, "The Hope Is There," *Vital Speeches of the Day* 70, no. 20 (2004): 610–15, http://search.proquest.com/docview/221458847?accountid=9676.

76. For one such example, see Michelle Malkin, "Obama's Big Green Boondoggles," *Human Events* 67, no. 32 (September 19, 2011): 19, http://search.proquest.com/docview/896622883?accountid=967.

16

Ecological Imperialism Revisited

Genetic Engineering and Presidential Foreign Assistance Policy, 1980–2015

BARTOW ELMORE

Introduction

In 2014, Hillary Clinton gave a speech at the Biotechnology Industry Organization (BIO) Convention in San Diego expressing support for genetically engineered (GE) crops. She explained that she had worked hard as secretary of state to "create a different vocabulary to talk about what [American GE firms were] trying to help people do," and she encouraged businesses to "really be more thoughtful" about how they sold their products in foreign markets so as not to "raise that red flag." "Genetically modified," she explained, "sounds Frankensteinish. Drought-resistant sounds [like] something you want."[1]

Anti-GE activists were incensed. They portrayed Clinton as a politician in bed with big business, and when it became clear in 2015 that the Clinton Foundation had received an estimated $500,000 to $1 million in contributions from Monsanto, the world's leading GE seed producer, the firestorm intensified. As Clinton began campaigning in earnest for the 2016 presidential election, the GE issue dogged her, some calling her the "Bride of Frankenfood."[2]

But despite all the fuss, there was really nothing new about Clinton's stance on GE foods. Every president from Ronald Reagan to Barack Obama (Republicans and Democrats alike) had been supportive of agricultural genetic engineering, pitching this technology as both an essential stimulator of the American economy and a powerful development tool for impoverished nations overseas.

This chapter seeks to explain this continuity in U.S. presidential policy regarding GE products and to expose the ways in which executive branch interventions in international negotiations facilitated the consolidation of corporate control over global biotechnological resources. When Ronald Reagan came into office in 1981, the rules concerning the international exchange of genetic resources had yet to be defined. A year earlier, the U.S. Supreme Court had decided that genetically engineered organisms could be patented by private companies, but whether such a proprietary regime would extend overseas had yet to be decided. This was all so new. At the time, some countries proposed alternative visions for the exchange of genetic resources, with the United Nations declaring in 1983 that plant genes should be treated as "the common heritage of mankind." U.S. presidents in the 1980s and 1990s fiercely fought such proposals, arguing that the best way to serve the needs of the developing world was to respect private property claims to genetic resources.[3]

In so doing, the executive branch promoted the idea that capitalism, extended to the domain of cellular DNA, was the antidote to the developing world's twin evils of poverty and famine. This was the presidential mantra, developed during the waning years of the Cold War, which echoed into the twenty-first century. Only by accepting proprietary rights to genetic resources, the pitch went, would developing nations realize the benefits of rapid innovation stimulated by the power of profit incentives.

In 2008, George W. Bush said as much. That year, the president preached that the United States should help "people in dry areas develop agriculture so they don't have to rely upon the world," adding, "we ought to look at these [GE crops] with science in mind so that agriculture, sustainable agriculture, can be developed in the places . . . where people are suffering." Four years later, the message coming from the White House was the same. Then, Barack Obama announced a partnership with Monsanto and other biotechnology businesses to help provide food relief to Africa. The president argued that the "whole purpose of development is to create the conditions where assistance is no longer needed, where people have the dignity and the pride of being self-sufficient." To accomplish this goal, Obama promised that the United States was "going to speed up the development and delivery of innovation—better seeds, better storage—that unleash huge leaps in food production." Deliverables included Monsanto's patented Bollgard cotton seeds produced from genetic engineering.[4]

Thus, both Democrats and Republicans occupying the highest office in the land made clear their view that genetic engineering would seed an economic revolution in the Global South and free developing nations from colonial-style dependency on industrialized nations' bulk food donations. This was what America could give the world.

But if presidents pitched GE technology in development policy speeches as the great liberator of famished nations, at home the White House made clear that liberalizing access to American biotechnology was actually anathema to the country's core economic objectives. After all, biotechnology became by the 1990s one of the great profit generators in the American economy, and presidents therefore worked hard to curtail international competition in this exciting new industry. In other words, exclusion, not inclusion, was the goal of presidential economic advisors who helped construct international patent protections that secured America's early lead in biotechnology innovation. International treaties, codified by organizations such as the World Trade Organization (WTO), essentially preserved U.S. dominance in the industry, ensuring that if developing nations wanted GE technology in the future, they were going to have to pay a premium price to industrialized nations for the privilege.

In sum, from Reagan to Obama, U.S. presidential policy regarding genetic engineering was a contradiction, one that preached salvation through democratization of GE technology while simultaneously promoting the adoption of international intellectual property law that hindered developing nations, such as India, from gaining access to technologies that might have helped them establish food security for years to come. New international treaties adopted in the 1990s sought to preserve a genetic commons in the Global South while simultaneously strengthening industrialized nations' control over GE technologies often mined from those commons. Rather than alleviating Global South dependencies on industrialized nations, White House development policies regarding GE technologies could more aptly be described as inaugurating a new era of ecological imperialism that strengthened rather than abated colonial relationships between rich and poor countries. By the 2010s, it was clear that the American government wanted developing nations to be the buyers of advanced agricultural technologies rather than the masters of their own biotechnological future. Colonial contracts between developing and industrialized nations had not been abrogated by the deployment of GE technologies overseas; they had merely been rewritten in the genetic codes of plant life.

A Brief History of How GE Seeds Became Patentable in the United States

There is almost nothing homegrown about the DNA of American agriculture. Many of the major U.S. commodity crops now in cultivation were indigenous to countries beyond American borders. Wheat covering the Great Plains, for example, was native to fertile soils near the Mediterranean Sea and came to North America via European colonists who had free and open access to seed back home. The great Corn Belt of the United States owes its origins to Native American transfers of germplasm from modern-day Mexico to the Mississippi Valley. And the story is much the same for many fruits, such as oranges and peaches, which came to the United States from the Eurasian landmass.[5]

The great environmental historian Alfred Crosby dubbed many of these transatlantic biological transfers "ecological imperialism," rightly noting that the suitability of Eurasian flora and fauna to North America's temperate climes proved an invaluable asset for colonists in their conquest of the New World. But the term "ecological imperialism," connoting national dominion over nature, obscures the reality that the literal seeds of the Columbian Exchange were not owned by anyone. Throughout the Age of Discovery, westerners and Native Americans alike considered germplasm part of the commons, available for free and open exchange across national and tribal boundaries. Thus, America's early commodity crop economy was rooted in the idea that plant seeds were not commodities but rather public goods to which no one could claim absolute title.[6]

In the twentieth century, however, things began to change when the widespread adoption of hybridization techniques allowed corn farmers to produce prolific crops from seeds generated by crossing two inbred lines. (An inbred line refers to a corn plant variety that farmers deliberately force to self-pollinate over a period of time, usually to preserve a desired genetic trait.) From the perspective of American corporations eyeing future investment in hybridization technology, the great thing about corn seeds generated from a cross of inbred lines (referred to as F1 hybrids) was that the seeds yielded by these plants often produced offspring (F2 plants) that were inferior to their parents (either because they were less prolific or lacked desired attributes, such as pest resistance). American corporations recognized that they could capitalize on hybrid corn's unique reproductive properties, and thus was born the country's first major seed companies, including future secretary of agriculture Henry A. Wallace's (1933–1940) Hi-Bred Corn Company founded in 1926. Firms, such as Hi-Bred, realized that the inferiority of F2 plants meant that farmers would have to repurchase company seed each year, creating the ideal capitalist relationship between company and client. The commodification of germplasm in the United States began to take off.[7]

Still, in the first two decades of the twentieth century, there were no federal laws to protect American companies' proprietary claims to hybrid seeds. In 1930, the U.S. Congress passed the Plant Patent Act, which extended patent rights to farmers that produced plants through asexual means (via grafting, for example), but the law said nothing about the patenting of sexually reproducing plants. From the 1920s through the 1970s, no U.S. statute codified the patenting of plant seeds for most major commodity crops.[8]

In 1970, Congress—led by heartland senators Jack Miller of Iowa, Bob Dole of Kansas, and Milton Young of North Dakota, as well as southern congressmen James Eastland of Mississippi and B. Everett Jordan of North Carolina—began to look for ways to provide greater protections for plant breeding innovations. That year, these senators from America's farm country helped to pass the Plant Variety Protection Act, which stated that unique plant varietals for sexually reproducing plants could attain special intellectual property protection. The 1970 act did not officially confer a patent to owners of qualified varieties but rather offered certificates that gave plant breeders exclusive rights to sell seed for twenty to twenty-five years. Still, it dramatically expanded the proprietary protections provided to American breeders by the 1930 act.[9]

The big moment in plant patenting came just a few years later. By the mid-1970s, scientists began seeking patents for new creations produced via cross-species genetic transfers, and perhaps no one was more eager for such government protection than microbiologist Ananda Mohan Chakrabarty. In 1972, Chakrabarty had genetically engineered a bacterium for General Electric that could be used to clean up oil spills. That year, he applied for a patent for his creation, but the U.S. Patent Office denied his request, arguing that "micro-organisms are 'products of nature,' and . . . that, as living things, they are not patentable." Chakrabarty sought relief in the federal courts, ultimately taking his case to the highest court in the land by the end of the decade.[10]

The 1980 Supreme Court decision in *Diamond v. Chakrabarty* paved the way for the widespread patenting of genetic resources in the United States. The court ruled that Chakrabarty should not have been denied patent protections considering there was no congressional statute specifically outlawing the patenting of living organisms—that Chakrabarty, through genetic manipulation of DNA, had indeed created a unique and patentable product deserving of federal protection. Companies invested in biotechnology could now point to this Supreme Court ruling in making property claims to genetically engineered organisms.[11]

Yet, even if the U.S. Supreme Court had given its sanction to the patenting of genetically engineered products, it was not at all clear whether the U.S. public and the international community were going to accept this new legal order. In 1980, the judicial branch had hoed fertile ground for the GE revolution; now it was up to the executive branch to make those seeds grow.

Reagan, the GE Revolution, and International Development Policy

Even as federal courts issued favorable decisions for GE businesses, the Reagan administration believed that America's biotechnology industry would thrive only if nurtured by executive policy. Led by the president's chief advisor on biotechnology, National Science Foundation assistant director and Berkeley microbiologist David Kingsbury, the White House fought proposals, introduced by the House of Representatives in 1983, that called for the Environmental Protection Agency (EPA) to assume chief regulatory oversight of GE creations. Reagan favored diluting the environmental agency's regulatory authority and wrestled control from Congress on this issue in 1984. That year, the administration created the special Cabinet Council Working Group on Biotechnology, with Berkeley scientist Kingsbury at its head, and tasked it with coming up with federal regulatory policy regarding genetically engineered products manufactured and sold in the United States. In May, the committee proposed the Coordinated Framework for Regulation of Biotechnology, which recommended dividing up GE regulatory responsibilities among three agencies: the FDA, the EPA, and the USDA. Each agency would have proscribed powers rather than broad statutory authority to impede introduction of GE products. From the White House's perspective, this segregation would result in fewer instances of regulatory enforcement, thus creating a suitable environment for commercialization of new innovations.[12]

The White House working group also proposed something that biotechnology firms' earnestly desired: a clear federal policy that GE products would not "require any additional laws or regulations." In the proposed framework, the White House made clear that any regulation of GE products "must be based on the rational and scientific evaluation of products and not on *a priori* assumptions about certain processes." In other words, just because a company produced corn seeds through genetic manipulation did not mean that those seeds should face tougher scrutiny under the law. A corn seed was a corn seed, whatever breeding process brought it into existence.[13]

In 1986, the White House officially entered the Coordinated Framework for Regulation of Biotechnology into the Federal Register, signaling to American biotechnology firms that they would face limited regulatory hindrances. Throughout the remainder of the Reagan era, industry upped their investment in biotechnology research and development with sound assurances that they had the support of the White House. U.S. chemical companies, such as Monsanto, swiftly divested much of their chemical commodity production business, sinking large amounts of capital in agricultural genetic engineering research. America's biotechnology boom had arrived.

Ronald Reagan insisted that his policies regarding biotechnology were beneficial to the world, not just American corporations. Reagan positioned biotechnology as a powerful component of his overseas development policy and argued that such private-sector innovation could serve developing nations' dire needs. In 1986, for example, Reagan declared, "Biotechnology has invented new grains that are a winning weapon in the war against hunger." Reagan spoke in hyperbole, considering major GE seed exports to developing nations were years away, but he nevertheless made clear his position that supporting American industry at home was the best way to solve global problems abroad.[14]

Vice President Bush also heralded GE crops as tools of food liberation in the developing world. In a March 1985 U.N. speech announcing U.S. plans to deliver food aid to Africa, Bush noted that bulk food donations would merely prolong famine and hardship in arid regions of the African continent if such actions were not coupled with developing nations' adoption of advanced agricultural techniques. Bush called for a "Green Revolution" in Africa that would use "research to develop new seed varieties appropriate for Africa's fragile soils and its fickle climate" and held that the United States had a "responsibility to our own citizens and to Africa alike to give both relief and forms of aid that do not perpetuate dependency."[15]

But if Bush's words hinted that the United States might be open to the idea of freely sharing its new biotechnological innovations with developing nations eager to reform their agricultural systems, internal memoranda in the Reagan White House revealed another reality. Roughly three years prior to Bush's remarks, Office of Science and Technology Policy assistant director Denis J. Prager corresponded with presidential advisor Jay Keyworth about a proposal before the United Nations Industrial Development Organization to create an International Center for Genetic Engineering and Biotechnology (ICGEB). The United Nations hoped that that ICGEB would "help developing countries reap the fruits of the new biological technologies" by creating a centralized place for exchange of biotechnological research. In his memorandum to Keyworth, Prager explained that the State Department had met to consider U.S. involvement in the organization and ultimately decided "to oppose the establishment of such a Center," a decision Prager supported. He called the ICGEB proposal "a turkey, poorly conceived and not worthy of serious consideration," concluding, "We stand to gain little, if anything, from this venture and could lose plenty." As of 2016, the United States remained unaffiliated with the international center.[16]

In addition to rejecting the ICGEB, the Reagan administration also refused to sign an international agreement that sought to create opportunities for open transfers of genetic resources across international boundaries. Proposed by the Food and Agriculture Organizations (FAO) in 1983, the International Undertaking on Plant Genetic Resources (IUPGR) offered a radical challenge to the proprietary patenting of DNA that was fast becoming codified in American law. The IUPGR proposed that plant genetic resources should be considered "the heritage of mankind," and should therefore "be available without restriction." If adopted, the IUPGR would have undermined biotechnology businesses' property claims to their genetically engineered creations. In large part because of the Reagan administration's keen interest in protecting America's biotechnology industry—especially in the midst of a Cold War battle that pitted capitalist nations against communist polities—the United States, represented by Reagan's secretary of agriculture John Block at the FAO conference, refused to sign on to the initiative.[17]

Far from embracing open exchange of genetic engineering research, throughout the 1980s, the Reagan administration expressed an arresting preoccupation about the potential for American biotechnology discoveries to make it into overseas competitors' hands. Reagan's advisors were particularly concerned about small American businesses that, unable to scale up their GE discoveries at home in the mid-1980s, had begun licensing their innovations to foreign companies, largely in Japan. In the Cold War political climate, it was critical that U.S. capitalist enterprises did not lose to overseas competitors, thereby potentially undercutting American economic strength. Reagan policy advisor Martin L. Smith likened what might happen in the biotechnology industry to the recent offshoring of America's semiconductor business and suggested that the federal government might want to "place restrictions on joint ventures with foreign companies when the basic research has been funded by the federal government."[18]

Thus, even as Reagan held out GE technologies as tools of empowerment for the Global South, it was clear that his top officials also did not want developing nations to become makers of their own tools. These fears of foreign competition would not be resolved when Reagan left office in 1989. In the 1990s, Reagan's successor would have to fight off developing nations that clamored for real control over their own agricultural future.

George Bush, a Biodiversity Treaty, and the Fight to Preserve America's GE Lead

The Reagan administration may have made it easier to sell genetically modified products in the United States, but it was left to George H. W. Bush to take U.S. GE global. Bush became president at a critical time in the history of international property law regarding genetically engineered products, and his diplomatic decisions would have far-reaching implications for the international spread of American-made biotechnological products.

George H. W. Bush's Council on Competitiveness, a cabinet group headed by Vice President Dan Quayle, largely developed the president's biotechnology policy. Formed in March of 1989, the Council on

Competitiveness's foundational mission was "to continue United States economic progress by maintaining and improving international competitiveness." Disciples of Reagan's deregulatory regime, the members of the council sought to identify and eliminate government regulations that might hinder speedy adoption of new technologies critical to American economic growth.[19]

From inception, the Council on Competitiveness viewed biotechnology as a key industry in need of the administration's support. In the fall of 1989, the council established a Biotechnology Working Group, made up of over a dozen cabinet-level officials, tasked with advising the council on how best to use federal government power to promote this industry. By February of 1990, biotechnology was at the top of the council's agenda, and by summer, Vice President Quayle wrote to President Bush to explain that the council had "decided that biotechnology—already a $1 billion industry with great potential for new drugs, pesticides, environmental, and agricultural products—should be the first target for [the council's] competitiveness review."[20]

America was clearly the world leader in the biotechnology industry by 1990. But what scared the Council on Competitiveness and the president's Council of Economic Advisers was the possibility that foreign competitors, especially in Europe and Japan, might begin to undercut American firms' early lead if regulatory impediments hindered U.S. businesses' ability to innovate. Michael Boskin, chair of Bush's Council of Economic Advisers, addressed this directly in a briefing to the Council on Competitiveness and suggested that Japan was currently "targeting pharmaceutical applications in the same way that it earlier targeted the semiconductor, automotive, and consumer electronic industries." Boskin's statement revealed that the recent offshoring of some of America's biggest manufacturing enterprises was clearly on Bush advisors' minds as they strategized the future of biotechnology policy.[21]

As the Council's Biotechnology Working Group met to come up with policy proposals in the spring of 1990, it solicited the advice of private industry, reaching out to the Monsanto Company as well as smaller businesses invested in genetic engineering. In March of 1990, Larry Lindsey, advisor to the president for domestic economic policy, revealed findings from those corporate conferences in a memorandum to the Biotechnology Working Group.[22]

Lindsey's report addressed many concerns, but one that made it to the top of the list was ensuring "adequate protection for intellectual property rights," specifically in overseas markets. Lindsey noted that biotechnology businesses wanted standardization of international patent law that would ensure their proprietary claim over genetic resources beyond U.S. borders. Private property rights to genetic codes had already been codified in U.S. law; now the goal was to ensure that such a proprietary system extended into foreign nations—a critical requirement if America's biotechnology businesses hoped to yield profits through international sales.[23]

This concern about international patent law became even more important in light of a new international treaty: the United Nations Environmental Programme's (UNEP) Convention on Biological Diversity (CBD). Beginning in 1989, UNEP began organizing what would become the 1992 Earth Summit in Rio de Janeiro. The United Nations designed the conference with the goal of bringing countries together to work out international plans for reducing greenhouses gas emissions, curbing deforestation, and protecting biodiversity.

Among the many issues UNEP proposed for negotiation in Rio, one of the more contentious was a convention ensuring international cooperation in protecting global biodiversity. Over the next three years, UNEP member nations debated the terms of this treaty, and in May of 1992, over a hundred countries, including the United States, met at UNEP's headquarters in Nairobi to flesh out the final draft of what would become known as the Convention on Biological Diversity.

The convention's primary objective was the "conservation of biological diversity," but it also included new rules governing international trade of GE technology. For example, the convention called for all signatory nations to agree to the "fair and equitable sharing of the benefits arising out of the utilization of genetic resources," though the specifics of such exchanges remained vague. It also called for the "transfer of technologies" as well as financial resources from countries rich in biotechnology to developing nations so that they could better deal with the expensive tasks associated with ecological conservation. In addition, the biodiversity treaty proposed the creation of international "programmes for scientific and technical education and training."[24]

Bush's advisors believed that the CBD represented a fundamental affront to free-market capitalism. How could the engines of the new American economy—computer firms and biotechnology businesses—expect to make profits if they had no market assurances that their intellectual property, one of the most valuable things they owned, was protected? After looking over an early draft of the CBD completed in November of 1990, Assistant Attorney General Dick Stewart wrote to Bush's counsel, C. Boyden Gray, and explained that the CBD threatened to alter "patent laws in order to make patented material available to developing countries on a 'concessional, low-profit or non-profit basis.'" He urged the president not to "agree to inclusion of regulation of biotechnology in the biodiversity convention," noting that the CBD was "likely to conflict with environmental and trade-oriented concessions of biotechnology in the OECD and GATT."[25]

As Stewart's memorandum explained, the United States had long been working to erect international legal infrastructure through the General Agreement on Tariffs and Trade (GATT) that would protect American GE patents overseas. In the Uruguay Round of GATT trade negotiations, which began in 1986, United States diplomats proposed the creation of a multilateral regulatory mechanism, later called the Trade-Related Aspects of Intellectual Property Rights (TRIPS) agreement, which would ensure the protection of intellectual property rights in international trade. This new intellectual property regime would essentially strengthen protection mechanisms established by the United Nations' World Intellectual Property Organization, which was founded in 1967 but which some U.S. policymakers believed was weak in enforcing proprietary claims to intellectual property by the time Bush came to office. In 1991, the United States was in the sixth year of the Uruguay negotiations, and it was not yet clear whether it would get the standardization of international intellectual property law it desired. As the 1992 Rio conference neared, Bush's advisors had made up their mind to oppose the CBD, a measure they believed was at odds with ongoing GATT negotiations and fundamentally undermined Americans' ability to commodify natural resources for private profit.[26]

And Bush listened. On June 11, 1992, just hours before his departure to the Earth Summit in Brazil, Bush addressed the American people and explained his intentions not to sign the CBD. He argued that his decision to reject the biodiversity treaty was not driven by a lack of concern for the environment but chiefly by an aversion to the agreement's anti-capitalist provisions regarding biotechnology. Bush insisted that the treaty turned biotechnology products into "common property though they are developed at great cost by private companies and American workers." In Bush's telling, the battle over the CBD was essentially between those who believed the free market could best solve the world's environmental problems and those that supported the elimination of the profit incentive and the collectivization of private property.[27]

Despite Bush's rhetoric, developing nations under the CBD did not seek the decommodification of genetic resources. In fact, the CBD was in many ways a rejection of common ownership rights to genetic materials, a principle first proposed in the United Nations' 1983 International Undertaking on Plant Genetic Resources. As we saw, that earlier agreement had called for "common heritage" rights to genetic information. In contrast, the CBD conceded that the rights to genetic resources could be owned by both private and public entities but pushed for a new international system that would give developing nations better brokering power when it came to gaining title to genetic resource within their borders. In other words, rather than the "common heritage" rights called for in the 1983 agreement, the CBD made clear that "the authority to determine access to genetic resources rests with the national governments and is subject to national legislation." Thus, developing nations were actually moving closer to what might be called an American-style commodification of genetic information.[28]

Nevertheless, Bush stood his ground and refused to sign the CBD, even though over 160 countries agreed to the convention by December of 1993 when the agreement became effective. As this book went to press, the United States remained the only major UN member country that had not ratified the treaty.[29]

After Rio, Bush toured the nation and pitched himself as a maverick defender of the free enterprise system in the face of developing nations' dictatorial demands. Seven days after his speech at Earth Summit, Bush told a crowd in California that he defeated a treaty that would have insisted the United States "hand . . . over to others" America's biotechnological treasures. Addressing Congress on the matter, he likewise claimed he had stood up against a treaty that "fails to protect America's property rights."[30]

Thus, when defending his position regarding the CBD, Bush skillfully deployed buzz phrases, positioning himself as a defender of "America's property rights" against anticapitalist property regimes. In so doing, Bush sought to brand his vision for international environmental policy as patently pro-capitalist, but what Bush omitted in his speeches was an acknowledgement that the American biotechnological industry was built on exploitation of common property, not competitive exchange of private property. For centuries, American firms had mined the genetic resources of the developing world and paid nothing to Global South communities for the privilege of such extraction. Thus, in rejecting the CBD, Bush was saying no to an instrument that actually sought to take the genetic raw materials of the biotechnology industry out of the commons and create a more competitive market for the use and exchange of those resources. What Bush wanted, in other words, was the preservation of a dual property regime: one that protected Americans' free and unrestricted access to a genetic commons in the developing world while simultaneously strengthening private property claims to finished biotechnological goods sold by U.S. businesses.[31]

In the final months of his presidency, Bush had much to revel about when it came to biotechnology policy. Besides defeating the CBD, the Bush administration helped ensure by 1992 that Trade-Related Aspects of Intellectual Property Rights (TRIPS) would become part of the new World Trade Organization (WTO). (The U.S. officially signed the agreement establishing the WTO and TRIPS in 1994). It became clear that the United States was going to have new international instruments to enforce intellectual property rights. In addition, by May of 1992, the Council on Competitiveness could chalk up another victory on the domestic policy front when the FDA issued a new regulatory policy reaffirming the 1986 Coordinated Framework on Biotechnology. The FDA made clear that it would regulate foods derived from GM crops "within the existing framework . . . utilizing an approach identical in principle to that applied to foods developed by traditional plant breeding." Bush's 1992 quashing of the CBD, in other words, was just one of his administration's accomplishments in the avowed fight to protect biotechnology businesses.[32]

President Bill Clinton's GE Policy and International Development Policy

When Bill Clinton replaced George H. W. Bush in 1993, it appeared U.S. policy regarding the CBD might change dramatically. In Clinton's first term, Monsanto, Genentech, and other big biotechnology corporations got behind the CBD, recognizing the valuable role the U.S. government could play in shaping negotiations over market exchanges of genetic resources. With business backing, Clinton signed the CBD on June 4, 1993, and sent the document on to the Senate for ratification. Clinton believed the CBD might help biotechnology businesses gain access to genetic resources in the Global South rather than hinder innovation in the industry.[33]

In the fall, Clinton worked to convince congressional skeptics that the treaty did not represent a radical redirection of American development policy toward gratis sharing of proprietary technology. "Economic incentives," Clinton explained in a Senate communiqué regarding the CBD, "will help all Parties achieve the environmental benefits of conservation and sustainable use of biological diversity." Clinton was clear that as a new party to the biodiversity convention, the U.S. would "strongly resist any actions taken by Parties to the Convention that lead to inadequate legal protection of intellectual property rights." In short, Clinton argued that the CBD was compatible with capitalism in that it sanctified the idea that privatization of ecological resources was the key to environmentally sound economic growth in the developing world.[34]

Clinton's statements regarding intellectual property protections calmed some politicians' fears about the CBD, evidenced by the fact that the treaty made it through the Senate Foreign Relations Committee via a 16 to 3 vote in June of 1994. But as the CBD came to the Senate chamber that summer, Republicans stymied the measure. Conservatives were convinced that the CBD fundamentally threatened American firms' private property rights. Despite the president and big business's assurances to the contrary, Republicans remained leery of granting an international body control over biotechnology transfers. As a result, the CBD, approved by a new executive, languished in the Senate chamber. It remained unratified as of 2016.[35]

Even if the Senate had approved the CBD, it is not clear whether that would have fundamentally changed U.S. policy regarding the deployment of biotechnology to protect biodiversity. As his earlier message to the Senate showed, Clinton was a firm believer that strong protections for GE patents were essential to stimulating innovation that would benefit developing nations. In this sense, he differed little from Bush and Reagan. Like them, he did not believe that development goals could be met through free exchange of technology. Developing nations, under Clinton's vision for international development, would remain buyers of technologies manufactured and patented in the United States, not pioneers of their own systems of salvation.

The failure on the part of the United States to engage in concessional exchanges of biotechnology during the Bush and Clinton years had predictable results. By the end of the 1990s, American firms along with a few competitors in Europe enjoyed oligopolistic control of the GE market, and that consolidated dominance continued into the 2000s. According to one 2008 study, U.S. biotech firms controlled roughly 42 percent of the "proprietary seed market," while European firms, based mainly in Switzerland, France, and Germany, controlled another 20 percent of the market. The St. Louis–based Monsanto Company captured roughly 23 percent of the global seed market alone in 2008. That year, no developing nation made it onto the list of top countries producing genetically engineered seeds.[36]

Countries in the developing world simply did not have the legal, political, or technological infrastructure to create biotechnology that could compete with major operations in Germany, Switzerland, France, and the United States. Without generous technology transfers coupled with major capital investment in Global South biotechnology infrastructure, developing nations had little chance of becoming empowered producers of genetically engineered products.[37]

And yet despite the fact that presidential policy appeared to widen rather than narrow the growing gap between nations with biotechnology and nations without genetic engineering infrastructure, Clinton argued that biotechnology would help eliminate global inequities. In his 2000 "White House Conference Speech on the New Economy," Clinton held that "biotechnology of the 21st century and the information technology, if we can take it to scale, can close the divide" between rich and poor countries. These comments clashed with domestic policy discussions that focused almost exclusively on how best to maintain America's lead over other countries eager to enter the biotechnology sector. Clinton's chief science advisor, John Gibbons, succinctly summarized this administration concern in the foreword to a 1995 policy pamphlet called *Biotechnology for the 21st Century*: "The United States is currently the world leader in research and commercialization of biotechnology. Given its tremendous potential, other countries are investing heavily in their own biotechnology enterprise and our lead is precarious. The Clinton administration is committed to ensuring that we don't lose our competitive edge."[38]

In sum, United States policy regarding biotechnology, as promoted by both Republican and Democratic administrations in the 1980s and 1990s, had contradictory objectives. On the one hand, presidents saw biotechnology as an engine of the American economy and therefore fought to create an international trading regime that preserved U.S. firms' exclusive control over patented technological resources. On the other hand, the executive branch held out biotechnology as a powerful development tool that could reduce global inequality. But just how the United States could simultaneously democratize the benefits of biotechnology while fiercely defending its "competitive edge" in the industry was never fully fleshed out. The country never committed to open exchange of biotechnological inventions with developing nations, ensuring Global South polities remained clients rather than collaborators in the genetic engineering revolution.

Coda: Bush II and Beyond

In 2003, President George W. Bush spoke at the same BIO conference that became the site of such controversy for Hillary Clinton a dozen years later. In his speech, Bush focused on European Union member nations' de facto moratorium on the acceptance of GE food imports, a ban that had been in place since 1998 and that Bush challenged through the WTO that year. "Because of these obstacles," Bush argued, "many African nations avoid investing in biotechnology, worried that their products will be shut out of important European markets." Europe's restrictive trade policies, in other words, explained why GE agricultural technology adoption stalled in the Global South. Bush concluded with a call to arms: "We should encourage the spread of safe, effective biotechnology to win the fight against global hunger."[39]

We had heard this all before. From Reagan to Clinton, presidents promised developing nations that GE technologies would save them from famine and argued that the United States would do everything in its power to provide the tools these countries needed to become, as Bush put it in another 2003 speech, "self-sufficient in the production of food." The key to such success was open trade.[40]

Yet Bush proved no more willing than his predecessors to encourage the international sharing of genetic research findings made by American corporations nor to invest large amounts of capital in building GE technological infrastructure in poor nations. These were the real keys to

Global South empowerment when it came to agricultural biotechnology. Throughout his tenure in office, Bush made no effort to push for ratification of the CBD, ensuring that America remained unbound to the provisions of the international agreement that called for cooperative and open exchanges of GE resources with developing nations.[41]

Bush's successor, Barack Obama, would stay the course. In 2010, CBD member nations approved the Nagoya Protocol, which specifically sought to develop mechanisms to implement the "access and benefit-sharing" (ABS) provisions of the 1993 treaty. The Obama administration did not sign the agreement, continuing the two-decades-old tradition of shunning foreign aid instruments that might diminish American GE firms' commanding control of biotechnological development.[42]

Thus, beyond Bush, presidential policies continued to shape a new era of ecological imperialism, one in which American-owned seeds remade Global South environments. In 2014, over 448 million acres of agricultural land around the world used seed with GE technology, up from approximately 4 million acres in 1996. Developing nations alone represented greater than 53 percent of that 2014 acreage. The vast majority of the seeds sown in this agricultural revolution came from the United States and a few European countries. This was ecological imperialism in perhaps its purest form, even if it was served to the developing world in the language of liberation.[43]

Notes

1. "Hillary Clinton at BIO Convention 2014," YouTube video, 53:16, posted by "Ken Stone," June 27, 2014, https://www.youtube.com/watch?v=Hypwb_SYaAc.

2. "Hillary's Agribusiness Ties Give Rise to Nickname in Iowa: 'Bride of Frankenfood,'" *Washington Times*, May 18, 2015; Judy Frankel, "Hillary v. Bernie on Frankenfood," *Huffington Post*, June 23, 2015, http://www.huffingtonpost.com/judy-frankel/hillary-vs-bernie-on-fran_b_7638846.html.

3. Susan Bragdon, Kathryn Garforth, and John E. Haapala Jr., "Safeguarding Biodiversity: The Convention on Biological Diversity," in *The Future Control of Food: A Guide to International Negotiations and Rules on Intellectual Property, Biodiversity and Food Security*, ed Geoff Tansey and Tasmin Rajotte (London: Earthscan, 2008), 83.

4. George W. Bush, "The President's News Conference with Prime Minister Silvio Berlusconi of Italy in Rome," June 12, 2008, American Presidency Project, http://www.presidency.ucsb.edu/ws/?pid=77487; "Remarks by President Barack Obama at Symposium on Global Agriculture and Food Security," May 18, 2012, White House website, https://www.whitehouse.gov/the-press-office/2012/05/18/remarks-president

-symposium-global-agriculture-and-food-security. For a list of the corporate partners in the New Alliance for Food Security and Nutrition, see the Summary of New Alliance Letters of Intent 2012–2013, https://new-alliance.org/resource/summary-new-alliance-letters-intent-2012-2013.

5. In *First the Seed: The Political Economy of Plant Biotechnology, 1492–2000* (Madison: University of Wisconsin Press, 2004), Jack R. Kloppenburg Jr. describes "advanced capitalist nations" of the twentieth century, such as the United States, as "gene-poor" lands prior to colonization, and notes that they received "much more [genetic] material than" they "provided to the periphery" (14–15, 50).

6. Alfred Crosby, *Ecological Imperialism: The Biological Expansion of Europe, 900–1900* (Cambridge, UK: Cambridge University Press, 1986). It is important to point out that, in Crosby's telling, much of this biological invasion was accidental and was not something that European colonists intentionally or knowingly set in motion. See Anthony J. Stenson and Tim S. Gray, *The Politics of Genetic Resource Control* (New York: St. Martin's, 1999), 13; Kloppenburg, *First the Seed*, 15.

7. Stenson and Gray, *The Politics of Genetic Resource Control*, 10. Journalist Michael Pollan details this process of "corn sex" in *The Omnivore's Dilemma: A Natural History of Four Meals* (New York: Penguin Books, 2006), 31.

8. Stenson and Gray, *The Politics of Genetic Resource Control*, 10–11.

9. Stenson and Gray, *The Politics of Genetic Resource Control*, 15; Senate Subcommittee on Agricultural Research and General Legislation, Committee on Agriculture and Forestry, *Plant Variety Protection Act*, 91st Cong., 2nd sess., June 11, 1970, 47; Keith Aoki, *Seed Wars: Controversies and Cases on Plant Genetic Resources and Intellectual Property* (Durham, NC: Carolina Academic Press, 2008), 36–37; Kloppenburg, *First the Seed*, 11.

10. Diamond v. Chakrabarty 447 U.S. 306 (1980); Committee on a National Strategy for Biotechnology in Agriculture, National Research Council, *Agricultural Biotechnology: Strategies for National Competitiveness* (n.p.: National Academies of Science, 1987), 57.

11. Diamond v. Chakrabarty 447 U.S. 303 (1980); Jack R. Kloppenburg Jr. made clear that immediately after the Supreme Court decided the Chakrabarty case, much debate ensued about whether the Plant Variety Protection Act or the Plant Patent Act would complicate attempts to extend patent protections to plants. According to Kloppenburg, it actually took a separate 1985 patent case, *Ex parte Hibberd*, to finally settle the legal question that plants were patentable (*First the Seed*, 261–63).

12. Mark A. Pollack and Gregory C. Shaffer, *When Cooperation Fails: The International Law and Politics of Genetically Modified Foods* (New York: Oxford University Press, 2009) 45–46; Diahanna Lynch and David Vogel, "The Regulation of GMOs in Europe and the United States: A Case-Study of Contemporary European Regulatory Politics," *Council on Foreign Relations*, April 5, 2001, http://www.cfr.org/agricultural-policy/regulation-gmos-europe-united-states-case-study-contemporary-european-regulatory-politics/p8688; Adam D. Sheingate, "Promotion versus Precaution: The Evolution of Biotechnology in the United States," *British Journal of Political Science* 36, no. 2 (April 2006): 247–250. For more on David Kingsbury and his views on biotechnology, see "Kingsbury

on NSF, Biotech Regulation," *The Scientist*, March 23, 1987; "Scientist and Rule-Maker: Dr. David T. Kingsbury," *New York Times*, July 21, 1986.

13. Fact Sheet: Proposal for a Coordinated Framework for Regulation of Biotechnology, John A. Svahn (Jack) Files, box 13531, folder Biotechnology (2), Ronald Reagan Presidential Library, Simi Valley, CA (hereinafter RRPL).

14. Ronald Reagan, "Remarks to Students and Faculty at Thomas Jefferson High School of Science and Technology in Fairfax County, Virginia," February 7, 1986, Public Papers of Ronald W. Reagan, RRPL.

15. "Bush Assures Food Aid for Africa to Continue," *Washington Post*, March 12, 1985.

16. Memorandum from Jay Keyworth to Denis J. Prager, Re: Proposed International Biotechnology Center, November 23, 1982, Keyworth, George A., III, "Jay" Files, box 012R-Keyworth, folder Office of Science and Technology Policy Interagency Working Group on Biotechnology, RRPL; Frederick H. Buttel, "Biotechnology and Agricultural Research Policy: Emergent Issues," in *New Directions for Agriculture and Agricultural Research: Neglected Dimensions and Emerging Alternatives*, ed. Kenneth A. Dahlberg (Totowa, NJ: Rowman & Allanheld, 1986), 344. A 2016 phone call to officials at ICGEB confirmed that the United States is still not a signatory country to the organization. For a list of signatory countries, see "Signatory Countries," ICGEB website, http://www.icgeb.org/signatory-countries.html.

17. Stenson and Gray, *The Politics of Genetic Resource Control* (New York: St. Martin's, 1999), 17–18; Susan Bragdon, Kathryn Garforth, and John E. Haapala Jr., "Safeguarding Biodiversity: The Convention on Biological Diversity," 83; Krishna Ravi Srinivas, "Intellectual Property Rights and the Politics of Food," in *The Oxford Handbook of Food, Politics, and Society*, ed. Ronald J. Herring (New York: Oxford University Press, 2015), 384; Aoki, *Seed Wars*, 71; Kloppenburg, *First the Seed*, 172–74, 368.

18. Memorandum from Martin Smith to Members of the Working Group on Biotechnology, Re: Biotechnology: International Trade, April 3, 1985, John A. Svahn (Jack) Files, box 16629, folder Biotechnology (1), RRPL.

19. President's Council on Competitiveness, Report on National Biotechnology Policy, June 28, 1990, NLGB Control # 40029, George H. W. Bush Library, College Station, Texas (hereinafter GHWBL), Stephen Hopgood, *American Foreign Environmental Policy and the Power of the State* (New York: Oxford University Press, 1998), 141.

20. President's Council on Competitiveness, Report on National Biotechnology Policy, June 28, 1990, NLGB Control # 40029, GHWBL; Memorandum from Vice President Dan Quayle to President George H. W. Bush, July 24, 1990, NLGB Control # 2106, GHWBL.

21. Michael Boskin, Council of Economic Advisers, Briefing for the Council on Competitiveness Fostering the Competitiveness of the U.S. Biotechnology Industry, n.d., NLGB Control # 8436, GHWBL.

22. Larry Lindsey, domestic economic policy advisor to George H. W. Bush, Memorandum for the Biotechnology Working Group of the Council of Competitiveness, March 9, 1990, NLGB Control # 2105, GHWBL.

23. Larry Lindsey, domestic economic policy advisor to George H. W. Bush, Memo-

randum for the Biotechnology Working Group of the Council of Competitiveness, March 9, 1990, NLGB Control # 2105, GHWBL.

24. United Nations, Convention on Biological Diversity, https://www.cbd.int/doc/legal/cbd-en.pdf. Though published and opened for signing in 1992, the treaty ultimately became effective in the winter of 1993.

25. Memorandum from Dick Stewart, Assistant Attorney General, to C. Boyden Gray, Counsel to the President, and Allan Hubbard, Counsel to the Vice President, RE: International Regulation of Biotechnology, February 15, 1991, NLGB Control # 2124, GHWBL.

26. Pedro Roffe, "Bringing Minimum Global Intellectual Property Standards into Agriculture: The Agreement on Trade-Related Aspects of Intellectual Property Rights (TRIPS)," in *The Future Control of Food: A Guide to International Negotiations and Rules on Intellectual Property, Biodiversity and Food Security*, ed. Geoff Tansey and Tasmin Rajotte (London: Earthscan, 2008), 48–49; Stenson and Gray, *The Politics of Genetic Resource Control*, 2; Aoki, *Seed Wars*, 91.

27. George H. W. Bush, "Remarks on Departure for the United Nations Conference on Environment and Development," June 11, 1992, American Presidency Project, http://www.presidency.ucsb.edu/ws/?pid=21070.

28. Stenson and Gray, *The Politics of Genetic Resource Control*, 22, 124; Aoki, *Seed Wars*, 78–79; United Nations, 1992 Convention on Biological Diversity, 9.

29. Convention on Biological Diversity website, "History of the Convention," https://www.cbd.int/history/; Dan L. Burk, Kenneth Barovsky, and Gladys H. Monroy, "Biodiversity and Biotechnology," *Science* 260 (June 25, 1993): 1900; Society for Conservation Biology, "Convention on Biological Diversity," http://conbio.org/policy/policy-priorities/treaties/cbd; United Nations, "South Sudan becomes 194th Party to Convention on Biological Diversity," March 7, 2014, https://www.cbd.int/doc/press/2014/pr-2014-03-07-cbd-south-sudan-en.pdf.

30. George H. W. Bush, "Remarks and a Question-and-Answer Session with Employees of Evergreen Oil in Newark, California," June 18, 1992, American Presidency Project, http://www.presidency.ucsb.edu/ws/?pid=21113; George H. W. Bush, "Remarks and a Question-and-Answer Session with the Agriculture Communicators Congress," June 30, 1992, American Presidency Project, http://www.presidency.ucsb.edu/ws/?pid=21168.

31. George H. W. Bush, "Remarks and a Question-and-Answer Session with the Agriculture Communicators Congress," June 30, 1992, American Presidency Project, http://www.presidency.ucsb.edu/ws/?pid=21168; Kloppenburg, *First the Seed*, 15.

32. Aoki, *Seed Wars*, 82; FDA Statement of Policy, Guidance to Industry for Foods Derived from New Plant Varieties, *Federal Register* 57 (May 29, 1992), http://www.fda.gov/Food/GuidanceRegulation/GuidanceDocumentsRegulatoryInformation/Biotechnology/ucm096095.htm; Marie-Monique Robin, *The World According to Monsanto: Pollution, Corruption, and the Control of the World's Food Supply* (New York: New Press, 2010), 145.

33. For a list of companies that supported the CBD by 1994, see Senator George John Mitchell, speaking on the Convention of Biological Diversity, 103rd Cong., 2nd sess., *Congressional Record* 140 (October 8, 1994): S 15066. For an example of industry lobbying

efforts on behalf of the CBD, see Lisa A. Conte, President and CEO of Shaman Pharmaceuticals, Inc., to President William Jefferson Clinton, March 8, 1993, Carol Rasco (Domestic Policy Council)—Meetings, Trips, and Events Series, "Pel-Freez/David Dubbell 2-9-91 10:00 p.m.," Clinton Digital Library, http://clinton.presidentiallibraries.us/items/show/19883.

34. William J. Clinton, "Message to the Congress Transmitting the Convention on Biological Diversity," November 19, 1993, American Presidency Project, http://www.presidency.ucsb.edu/ws/?pid=46145; Robert F. Blomquist, "Ratification Resisted: Understanding America's Response to the Convention on Biological Diversity, 1989–2002," *Golden Gate University Law Review* 32, no. 4 (2002): 534–36, 550–51; Roger Schlickeisen, "The US Won't Be Shielded in the Event of a Biocrisis," *Christian Science Monitor*, November 23, 1994, 19.

35. Robert F. Blomquist, "Ratification Resisted," 557–59.

36. Action Group on Erosion, Technology and Concentration (ETC), "Who Owns Nature? Corporate Power and the Final Frontier in the Commodification of Life," November 2008, 11, http://www.etcgroup.org/content/who-owns-nature.

37. Susan Bragdon, Kathryn Garforth, and John Haapala Jr., "Safeguarding Biodiversity: The Convention on Biological Diversity," 100.

38. William J. Clinton, "Remarks at the Second Session of the White House Conference on the New Economy," April 5, 2000, American Presidency Project, http://www.presidency.ucsb.edu/ws/?pid=58332; National Science and Technology Council, Committee on Fundamental Science, *Biotechnology for the 21st Century: New Horizons*, report from the Biotechnology Research Subcommittee (July 1995), http://babel.hathitrust.org/cgi/pt?id=purl.32754066322128;view=/up;seq=5..

39. George W. Bush, "Remarks to the Biotechnology Industry Organization Conference," June 23, 2003, American Presidency Project, http://www.presidency.ucsb.edu/ws/?pid=64580.

40. George W. Bush, "Remarks at the Corporate Council on Africa's United States-Africa Business Summit," June 26, 2003, American Presidency Project, http://www.presidency.ucsb.edu/ws/?pid=62947.

41. Russell E. Train, *Politics, Pollution, and Pandas: An Environmental Memoir* (Washington: Island, 2003), 323.

42. Christian J. Martinez, "The Convention on Biological Diversity's Nagoya Protocol: Halfway to Ratification," *Travaux: The Berkeley Journal of International Law Blog*, October 26, 2013, http://berkeleytravaux.com/convention-biological-diversitys-nagoya-protocol-halfway-ratification/.

43. Clive James, "Global Status of Commercialized/GM Crops," International Service for the Acquisition of Agri-Biotech Applications (ISAAA) Brief No. 49 (Ithaca, NY: ISAAA, 2014), http://www.isaaa.org/resources/publications/pocketk/16/. See also Jack A. Bobo (deputy chief, Bureau of Economic and Business Affairs, U.S. Department of Agriculture), "State Department Outreach Activities on Agricultural Biotechnology" (presentation at Iowa State University's Biosafety Institute for Genetically Modified Agricultural Products, Ames, IA, April 19, 2005). It is worth noting that Clive James is a

scientist who promoted the Green Revolution, working alongside Norman Borlaug and the Rockefeller Foundation to spread industrialized agriculture to the developing world. He is very much pro-biotech and preaches the benefits of GE seeds for impoverished nations. For more on Clive James's views, see International Service for the Acquisition of Agri-Biotech Applications website, "Q&A with Clive Owens," http://www.isaaa.org/resources/videos/qa_clivejames/.

Contributors

Daniel Amsterdam is assistant professor of history at Georgia Tech.

Brian Balogh is professor of history at the University of Virginia.

Gavin Benke is a lecturer in writing with a focus on the history and culture of capitalism at Boston University.

Roger Biles is professor of history emeritus at Illinois State University.

Brent Cebul is Mellon Postdoctoral Research Scholar in the Digital Humanities at the University of Richmond.

Allison Elias is visiting assistant professor in the Department of Labor Relations, Law, and History at the Cornell ILR School. Her forthcoming book examines the contested meaning of feminism for women working in U.S. corporations from the 1960s to the 1990s.

Bartow Elmore is a Carnegie Fellow at New America and assistant professor of environmental history at the Ohio State University.

Paula K. Gajewski received her PhD from Vanderbilt University.

Pamela Walker Laird is professor of history at the University of Colorado Denver.

Andrew Meade McGee is visiting assistant professor of history at Carnegie Mellon University.

Iwan Morgan is professor of United States studies at University College London.

Tracy Neumann is assistant professor of history at Wayne State University.

Margaret O'Mara is associate professor of history at the University of Washington.

Mark H. Rose is professor of history at Florida Atlantic University. He is completing a book on American bank politics since the 1960s.

Elizabeth Tandy Shermer is assistant professor of history at Loyola University of Chicago and the author of *Sunbelt Capitalism: Phoenix and the Transformation of American Politics* as well as numerous articles, literature reviews, and opinion pieces.

Sean H. Vanatta is a PhD candidate in history at Princeton University, where he is completing a dissertation on the political economy of consumer finance in the postwar United States.

Mark R. Wilson is professor of history at the University of North Carolina at Charlotte. He is the author of the books *The Business of Civil War* and *Destructive Creation: American Business and the Winning of World War II.*

Index

Page numbers in *italics* refer to illustrations.

CPSIA information can be obtained
at www.ICGtesting.com
Printed in the USA
LVOW11*0340091117
555265LV00006BA/27/P

9 780813 056524